"*Thus Spoke Zarathustra* is fascinating and beautiful, but difficult to understand. Matthew Meyer appreciates both the scientific and aesthetic dimensions of Nietzsche's philosophy, and provides a clear and helpful interpretation. He makes a convincing argument that Nietzsche structured *Zarathustra* like a three-act Greek tragedy followed by a satyr play. Meyer's interpretive insights will advance scholarly understanding of *Zarathustra*, and his accessible presentation will help ordinary readers better understand Nietzsche's masterpiece."

Neil Sinhababu, *National University of Singapore*

The Routledge Guidebook to Nietzsche's *Thus Spoke Zarathustra*

The Routledge Guidebook to Nietzsche's Thus Spoke Zarathustra is an engaging introduction to this rich and provocative philosophical text. Nietzsche is arguably one of the most influential and yet least understood philosophers of the nineteenth century. The same can be said of his self-proclaimed magnum opus, *Thus Spoke Zarathustra*. The work has influenced everything from poetry, literature, and music to philosophy, psychoanalysis, and soldiers on the battlefields of World War I. Its contents, however, are still far from being understood. On the one hand, the principal aims and even the genre of *Zarathustra* remain unclear. On the other hand, the work expresses, in poetic fashion, some of Nietzsche's most important, controversial, and enigmatic doctrines: the *Übermensch*, the eternal recurrence of the same, and the will to power.

The Routledge Guidebook to Nietzsche's Thus Spoke Zarathustra is essential reading for students of nineteenth-century philosophy, German philosophy, and intellectual history and suitable for anyone studying Nietzsche's most famous text for the first time.

Matthew Meyer is Professor of Philosophy at The University of Scranton, USA. He is the author of *Reading Nietzsche Through the Ancients: An Analysis of Becoming, Perspectivism, and the Principle of Non-Contradiction* (2014) and *Nietzsche's Free-Spirit Works: A Dialectical Reading* (2019). With Paul Loeb, he is the co-editor of *Nietzsche's Metaphilosophy: The Nature, Method and Aims of Philosophy* (2019).

THE ROUTLEDGE GUIDES TO THE GREAT BOOKS

The Routledge Guides to the Great Books provide ideal introductions to the texts which have shaped Western Civilization. The Guidebooks explore the arguments and ideas contained in the most influential works from some of the most brilliant thinkers who have ever lived, from Aristotle to Marx and Newton to Wollstonecraft. Each Guidebook opens with a short introduction to the author of the great book and the context within which they were working and concludes with an examination of the lasting significance of the book. *The Routledge Guides to the Great Books* will therefore provide students everywhere with complete introductions to the most significant books of all time.

Foucault's The History of Sexuality
Chloe Taylor

The New Testament
Patrick Gray

James's Principles of Psychology
David E Leary

Berkeley's Three Dialogues
Stefan Storrie

Smith's Wealth of Nations
Maria Pia Paganelli

Paine's Rights of Man
Frances A. Chiu

Moore's Principia Ethica
Susana Nuccetelli

Nietzsche's Thus Spoke Zarathustra
Matthew Meyer

For more information about this series, please visit:
https://www.routledge.com/The-Routledge-Guides-to-the-Great-Books/book-series/RGGB

The Routledge Guidebook to Nietzsche's *Thus Spoke Zarathustra*

Matthew Meyer

Routledge
Taylor & Francis Group

LONDON AND NEW YORK

First published 2025
by Routledge
4 Park Square, Milton Park, Abingdon, Oxon OX14 4RN

and by Routledge
605 Third Avenue, New York, NY 10158

Routledge is an imprint of the Taylor & Francis Group, an informa business

© 2025 Matthew Meyer

The right of Matthew Meyer to be identified as author of this work has been asserted by them in accordance with sections 77 and 78 of the Copyright, Designs and Patents Act 1988.

All rights reserved. No part of this book may be reprinted or reproduced or utilised in any form or by any electronic, mechanical, or other means, now known or hereafter invented, including photocopying and recording, or in any information storage or retrieval system, without permission in writing from the publishers.

Trademark notice: Product or corporate names may be trademarks or registered trademarks and are used only for identification and explanation without intent to infringe.

British Library Cataloguing-in-Publication Data
A catalogue record for this book is available from the British Library

ISBN: 978-0-415-79106-9 (hbk)
ISBN: 978-0-415-79107-6 (pbk)
ISBN: 978-1-315-20947-0 (ebk)

DOI: 10.4324/9781315209470

Typeset in Times New Roman
by codeMantra

Contents

	Acknowledgments	x
	Notes on Texts, Translations, and Abbreviations	xii
1	**Introduction to Friedrich Nietzsche's *Thus Spoke Zarathustra***	**1**
	1.1 Nietzsche's Life, Works, and the Reception of *Zarathustra*	9
	1.2 The Tragedy of *Zarathustra* and Nietzsche's Pre-*Zarathustra* Writings	17
	1.3 *Zarathustra, Revaluation,* and the Comedy of Nietzsche's Post-*Zarathustra* Works	25
	Notes	32
2	**The Tragedy and Satyr Play of *Zarathustra***	**36**
	2.1 Interpreting *Zarathustra*	37
	2.2 Evidence for Reading *Zarathustra* as a Tragedy and Satyr Play	46
	2.3 Nietzsche's Theory of Tragedy	59

	2.4	Metaphysics, Heraclitean Becoming, and the Tragic Worldview	71
	2.5	The Eternal Recurrence, the Will to Power, and the Naturalism of *Zarathustra*	77
	2.6	The Übermensch	86
	2.7	Revenge and the Eternal Recurrence (Again)	102
	2.8	The Tragedy of *Zarathustra I–III* and the Satyr Play of *Zarathustra IV*	108
	Notes		114
3	**Thus Spoke Zarathustra I**		**119**
	3.1	The Prologue and the Apollonian Übermensch	120
	3.2	Zarathustra's Speeches: Chapters 1–22	128
	Notes		162
4	**Thus Spoke Zarathustra II**		**164**
	4.1	On the Blessed Isles: Chapters 1–8	165
	4.2	Descending into the Dionysian: Chapters 9–13	177
	4.3	Zarathustra Speaks Again: Chapters 14–17	185
	4.4	The Need for Redemption: Chapters 18–22	189
	Notes		203
5	**Thus Spoke Zarathustra III**		**205**
	5.1	Zarathustra Sets Sail: Chapters 1 and 2	206
	5.2	On the Way Home: Chapters 3–8	212
	5.3	Back to the Cave and a Revaluation of Values: Chapters 9–12	218
	5.4	Zarathustra's Initiation into the Dionysian Mysteries: Chapters 13–16	236
	Notes		258
6	**Thus Spoke Zarathustra IV**		**260**
	6.1	Encounters with the Higher Humans: Chapters 1–9	263
	6.2	A Drunken Interlude at Noon: Chapter 9	279
	6.3	Zarathustra's Feast: Chapters 10–18	283
	6.4	Zarathustra's Final Farewell: Chapters 19 and 20	295
	Notes		306

7	**The Philosophical Significance of *Zarathustra***	**308**
	7.1 *Nietzsche's* Zarathustra *and Plato's* Phaedo	*309*
	7.2 *Zarathustra, Free Will, and the Metaphysics of Revenge*	*315*
	7.3 *From Tragic Fate in* Zarathustra *to Comic Self-Creation in* Ecce Homo	*322*
	Notes	*330*

Appendix: The Works of Friedrich Nietzsche:
An Interpretation   331
Bibliography   333
Index   347

Acknowledgments

This work is the result of what has become a life-long engagement with Nietzsche. In my first attempts as a graduate student to grapple with *Zarathustra*, I "discovered" that Nietzsche introduces the text under the title of "incipit tragoedia" in *The Gay Science*, and I quickly concluded that to understand Nietzsche's *magnum opus*, I needed to pay closer attention to *The Birth of Tragedy* and become better acquainted with antiquity on its own terms. This led me on an intellectual adventure in which I learned both German and ancient Greek, and I found myself studying everything from ancient Greek theater—including the wonderful world of ancient comedy—to Wagnerian opera. The journey has been a long one, and I could not possibly acknowledge everyone who has helped me along the way. However, I do want to thank all those who have facilitated the project since signing on with Routledge a few years ago. I begin by thanking The University of Scranton for awarding me two interim research grants to support projects related to my work on *Zarathustra* in 2020 and 2024. I would also like to thank the University for supporting my travel to conferences at which I presented various aspects of this manuscript. Colleagues who have provided feedback on my work have been numerous. A special thanks goes out, first and foremost, to my co-collaborators and longtime Nietzsche companions, Kaitlyn

Creasy and Paul Loeb. I have enjoyed working with both and have profited greatly from our numerous conversations about Nietzsche, especially with Paul about all things *Zarathustra*. Paul Katsafanas and Melanie Shepherd have also been valuable interlocutors and conference companions over the past few years, and I have been lucky to form such good friendships in the world of Nietzsche studies. Also deserving of my gratitude are the participants in the virtual *Zarathustra* reading group that ran during the summer of 2022. Our in-depth discussions inspired, informed, and shaped much of my understanding of *Zarathustra*. Participants included Katie Brennan, Richard Elliott, Pete Groff, Bob Guay, Larry Hatab, Scott Jenkins, James Mollison, Melanie Shepherd, Neil Sinhababu, and Gabriel Zamosc. I am very grateful for this experience and the friendships that have emerged from it. I would also like to thank Justin Remhof for organizing virtual workshops during COVID (and beyond) at which I was able to present my work. Here, I would like to thank Rebecca Bamford, Ian Dunkle, Allison Merrick, Mark Migotti, Robert Miner, Alexander Prescott-Couch, and Tom Stern—along with several others already mentioned—for taking time to engage my work and providing stimulating and helpful feedback. I am also thankful for the conversations (and subsequent email exchanges) that I have had at numerous APA, NiNE, and FNS conferences over the past few years with the likes of Lanier Anderson, Christian Benne, Jessica Berry, Daniel Blue, Maudemarie Clark, Jeremy Fortier, Paul Kirkland, Andrew Huddleston, Anthony Jensen, Thomas Lambert, Michael McNeal, Katrina Mitcheson, Bernard Reginster, John Richardson, Daniel Rodriguez-Navas, Carlotta Santini, and Joel Van Fossen. My apologies to anyone I may have overlooked. I would like to thank Katharina Grätz for sending me an advanced copy of her *Zarathustra* commentary as I was completing this manuscript. Adam Johnson and the entire editorial staff at Routledge also deserve much credit for their patience and help. It has been a long time, and we are all excited to see this in print. Finally, I could not have done any of this without the continual love and support of my wife, Renata, and son, Sebastian, and I would like to dedicate this work to my mother, Judy, and to the memory of my father, Dennis.

NOTES ON TEXTS, TRANSLATIONS, AND ABBREVIATIONS

The following abbreviations and translations of Nietzsche's works are used in this volume. In the references to Nietzsche's works, Roman numerals generally denote the volume number of a set of collected works or the standard subdivision within a single work and Arabic numerals denote the relevant section number. "Pref" is the abbreviation for the preface to a given work (except for the preface to the 1886 edition of *The Birth*). Page numbers are added when sections are long, providing more precise information about the location of the relevant text. In citing Nietzsche's notes in KGW and KSA, references provide the volume number (and part for KGW) followed by the relevant fragment number. The one exception is KSA 14, in which case the page number is provided. In citing KGB, the division (in Roman numerals) and volume (in Arabic numerals) numbers are given and the relevant letter number. Corresponding references to *The Will to Power* (WP) will be given only when deemed important to do so. In citing KSB, the volume number is followed by the number of the letter.

I have decided to base my commentary on Walter Kaufmann's translation of the text (1954). There are ways in which Kaufmann's translation of *Zarathustra* (and Nietzsche's other texts) can be improved, and subsequent translators have tried to do just that. However, I have yet to find a translation in which the gains made on certain points (such as Kaufmann's use of outdated gendered language) are outweighed by the drawbacks. I also believe that whatever gets lost in Kaufmann's translation is best remedied not by turning to another translation, but by learning some German and consulting the original text. Much of my own study of *Zarathustra* has been based on the original, and I have used Kaufmann to avoid translating the entire text myself. However, I do use my own translations—and indicate this accordingly—when needed. For a helpful, albeit somewhat dated, overview of translations of *Zarathustra*, see Martin (2008). To my knowledge, the most recent translation is by the poet Michael Hulse (2022: Notting Hill), and Loeb and Tinsley are currently working on a translation for Stanford University Press' *The Complete Works of Friedrich Nietzsche*.

ABBREVIATIONS FOR NIETZSCHE'S COLLECTED WORKS IN THE ORIGINAL GERMAN

KGB   *Friedrich Nietzsche: Briefwechsel. Kritische Gesamtausgabe*. Edition founded by G. Colli and M. Montinari, continued by N. Miller and A. Pieper. Berlin, New York: Walter de Gruyter (1975ff.).

KGW   *Friedrich Nietzsche: Werke. Kritische Gesamtausgabe*. Edition founded by G. Colli and M. Montinari, continued by V. Gerhardt, N. Miller, W. Müller-Lauter and K. Pestalozzi. Berlin, New York: Walter de Gruyter (1967ff.).

KSA   *Friedrich Nietzsche: Sämtliche Werke. Kritische Studienausgabe*, eds. G. Colli and M. Montinari, 15 vols. Berlin, New York, Munich: DTV, De Grutyer (1999).

KSB   *Friedrich Nietzsche: Sämtliche Briefe. Kritische Studienausgabe*, eds. G. Colli and M. Montinari, 8 vols. Berlin, Munich: Walter de Gruyter (1986).

ABBREVIATIONS AND TRANSLATIONS FOR TITLES OF PUBLISHED WORKS*

AOM *Vermischte Meinungen und Sprüche* ((1879); republished in 1886 in *Menschliches, Allzumenschliches* II); translated as *Assorted Opinions and Maxims*. In *Human, All Too Human*, trans. R. J. Hollingdale, 215–299. Cambridge: Cambridge University Press (1996).

BGE *Jenseits von Gut und Böse* (1886): translated as *Beyond Good and Evil*. In *Beyond Good and Evil*, trans. Walter Kaufmann. New York: Vintage (1989).

BT *Die Geburt der Tragödie* (1872/1886); translated as *The Birth of Tragedy*. In *The Birth of Tragedy and the Case of Wagner*, trans. W. Kaufmann, 15–151. New York: Vintage (1967). The "Attempt at a Self-Criticism" added to the 1886 edition is cited as "ASC" followed by the relevant section number.

CW *Der Fall Wagner* (1888); translated as *The Case of Wagner*. In *The Birth of Tragedy and the Case of Wagner*, trans. W. Kaufmann, 153–192. New York: Vintage (1967).

D *Morgenröthe* (1881/1887); translated as *Daybreak*. In *Daybreak*, ed. M. Clark and B. Leiter, trans. R. J. Hollingdale. Cambridge: Cambridge University Press (1997).

DS *David Strauss* (*Unzeitgemässe Betrachtungen* I) (1873); translated as *David Strauss* (*Untimely Meditation* I). In *Untimely Meditations*, ed. D. Breazeale, trans. R. J. Hollingdale, 1–55. Cambridge: Cambridge University Press (1997).

GM *Zur Genealogie der Moral* (1887); translated as On the Genealogy of Morals. In On the Genealogy of Morals and Ecce Homo, trans. W. Kaufmann, 13–163. New York: Random House (1989).

GS *Die fröhliche Wissenschaft* (1882/1887); translated as *The Gay Science*. In *The Gay Science*, trans. W. Kaufmann. New York: Vintage Books (1974).

NOTES ON TEXTS, TRANSLATIONS, AND ABBREVIATIONS xv

HH *Menschliches, Allzumenschliches* (1878/1886); translated as *Human, All Too Human*. In *Human, All Too Human*, trans. R. J. Hollingdale, 5–205. Cambridge: Cambridge University Press (1996). References to the two-volume 1886 edition are indicated by Roman numerals (*HH* I and *HH* II).

HL Vom Nutzen und Nachteil der Historie für das Leben (Unzeitgemässe Betrachtungen II) (1874); translated as On the Uses and Disadvantages of History for Life (Untimely Meditation II). In In Untimely Meditations, ed. D. Breazeale, trans. R. J. Hollingdale, 57–123. Cambridge: Cambridge University Press (1997).

RWB *Richard Wagner in Bayreuth* (*Unzeitgemässe Betrachtungen* IV) (1876); *Richard Wagner in Bayreuth* (*Untimely Meditation* IV). In In *Untimely Meditations*, ed. D. Breazeale, trans. R. J. Hollingdale, 195–254. Cambridge: Cambridge University Press (1997).

SE *Schopenhauer als Erzieher* (*Unzeitgemässe Betrachtungen* III) (1874); translated as *Schopenhauer as Educator* (*Untimely Meditation* IV). In In *Untimely Meditations*, ed. D. Breazeale, trans. R. J. Hollingdale, 125–194. Cambridge: Cambridge University Press (1997).

TI *Götzen-Dämmerung* (1888); translated as *Twilight of the Idols*. In *The Portable Nietzsche*, ed. and trans. W. Kaufmann, 463–564. New York: Viking Press (1954). References include an abbreviated chapter title and section number.

UM *Unzeitgemässe Betrachtungen* (1873–1876); translated as *Untimely Meditations*. In *Untimely Meditations*, ed. D. Breazeale, trans. R. J. Hollingdale. Cambridge: Cambridge University Press (1997).

WS Der Wanderer und sein Schatten (1880; republished in 1886 in Menschliches, Allzumenschliches II); translated as The Wanderer and His Shadow. In Human, All Too Human: A Book for Free Spirits, trans. R. J. Hollingdale, 301–395. Cambridge: Cambridge University Press (1996).

Z   *Also sprach Zarathustra* (1883–1885; part IV was only distributed privately during Nietzsche's lifetime); translated as *Thus Spoke Zarathustra*. In *The Portable Nietzsche*, ed. and trans. W. Kaufmann, 109–439. New York: Viking Press (1954). References include part number (I–IV), abbreviated chapter title, and section number if relevant.

*Dates are years of publication.

ABBREVIATIONS AND TRANSLATIONS FOR PRIVATE PUBLICATIONS, AUTHORIZED MANUSCRIPTS, AND UNPUBLISHED WORKS**

A   *Der Antichrist* (1888); translated as *The Antichrist*. In *The Portable Nietzsche*, ed. and trans. W. Kaufmann, 565–656. New York: Viking Press (1954).

DD   *Dionysos-Dithyramben* (1888); translated as *Dithyrambs of Dionysus*. In *Dithyrambs of Dionysus*, trans. R. J. Hollingdale. London: Anvil Press Poetry (1984).

DW   "Die dionysische Weltanschauung" (1871).

EH   *Ecce Homo* (1888); translated as *Ecce Homo*. In *On the Genealogy of Morals and Ecce Homo*, trans. Walter Kaufmann, 215–335. New York: Random House (1998). References include abbreviated chapter title and section number; in the chapter "Books," the section number is preceded by the abbreviation of the relevant book title.

PPP   "Die vorplatonischen Philosophen" (1872–1876); translated as *The Pre-Platonic Philosophers*. In *The Pre-Platonic Philosophers*, ed. and trans. G. Whitlock. Urbana, IL: University of Illinois Press (2001). References are to page numbers.

PTAG   "Die Philosophie im tragischen Zeitalter der Griechen" (1873); translated as *Philosophy in the Tragic Age of the Greeks*. In *Philosophy in the Tragic Age of the Greeks*, trans. M. Cowan. Washington, DC: Gateway (1962).

**Dates are years of composition.

ABBREVIATIONS AND TRANSLATIONS FOR NIETZSCHE'S UNPUBLISHED NOTEBOOKS

CWFN 14　Unpublished Fragments from the Period of Thus Spoke Zarathustra (Summer 1882–Winter 1883/84), trans. P. S. Loeb and D. F. Tinsley. In The Complete Works of Friedrich Nietzsche, eds. A. D. Schrift and D. Large, vol. 14. Stanford: Stanford University Press (2019).

CWFN 15　Unpublished Fragments from the Period of Thus Spoke Zarathustra (Summer 1882–Winter 1883/84), trans. P. S. Loeb and D. F. Tinsley. In The Complete Works of Friedrich Nietzsche, eds. A. D. Schrift and D. Large, vol. 15. Stanford: Stanford University Press (2022).

WP　*Der Wille zur Macht* (1883–1888); translated as *The Will to Power*. In *The Will to Power*, ed. W. Kaufmann, trans. W. Kaufmann and R. J. Hollingdale. New York: Vintage (1968).

ABBREVIATIONS FOR SCHOPENHAUER'S WORKS

PP I　*Parerga und Paralipomena, Band I* (1851); translated as *Parerga and Paralipomena: Volume I*, trans. and ed. by S. Roehr and C. Janaway. Cambridge: Cambridge University Press (2014). Citations include section number.

PP II　*Parerga und Paralipomena, Band II* (1851); translated as *Parerga and Paralipomena: Volume II*, trans. and ed. by A. Del Caro and C. Janaway. Cambridge: Cambridge University Press (2015). Citations include section number.

WWR I　*Die Welt als Wille und Vorstellung, Band I* (1819); translated as *The World as Will and Representation: Volume I*, trans. C. Janaway, J. Norman, and A. Welchman. Cambridge: Cambridge University Press (2010). Citations include chapter number.

WWR II	*Die Welt als Wille und Vorstellung, Band II* (1844); translated as *The World as Will and Representation: Volume II*, trans. C. Janaway, J. Norman, and A. Welchman. Cambridge: Cambridge University Press (2018). Citations include chapter number.

1
INTRODUCTION TO FRIEDRICH NIETZSCHE'S *THUS SPOKE ZARATHUSTRA*

Only a few months before he was deemed insane, Friedrich Nietzsche writes in *Ecce Homo*: "Among my writings my *Zarathustra* stands to my mind by itself. With that I have given mankind the greatest present that has ever been made to it so far" (EH "Pref":4). After being ignored upon publication, *Thus Spoke Zarathustra: A Book for All and None* (1883–1885) eventually gained the recognition Nietzsche thought it deserved. It was considered necessary reading for German soldiers on the front lines of World War I (Kaufmann 1974:8) and went on to influence intellectuals and artists far and wide. After World War II, *Zarathustra* fell on hard times, especially in the Anglo-American reception of Nietzsche, and its poor reputation has largely stuck until this day. The bombastic tone, the archaic language, and the overly dense field of metaphors tend to repel rather than attract contemporary readers, and other than a few commentaries over the past few decades, *Zarathustra* has been largely neglected in current scholarly debates about Nietzsche. Even as a work of poetry, it has few admirers. According to Andrew Huddleston's recent assessment, *Zarathustra* is a marked failure when judged aesthetically: Nietzsche "goes grotesquely overboard" with his use of literary devices and produces a book that is "an ill-judged, pompously-inflated, crudely-didactic, and nearly unreadable confection of outlandish mock-biblical mumbo jumbo" (2020:6).

For Anglo-American philosophers interested in Nietzsche, *Zarathustra* presents additional hurdles. They often approach Nietzsche's texts with an eye to extracting various views with which they can engage contemporary philosophers and current philosophical debates. The problem with *Zarathustra* is not only that it is hard to extract such views from the poetic text but also that the views one can extract seem to have little merit when judged by contemporary standards. The work begins with the main character, Zarathustra, exhorting us to give birth to a curious figure known as the *Übermensch* or "superhuman."[1] We then encounter what is known in Nietzsche secondary literature as the cosmological versions of the will to power and the eternal recurrence.[2] Whereas the former states that all of reality—even inorganic matter—can be understood as interrelated wills to power, the latter is the claim that everything we will do is something that has already happened an infinite number of times before and will happen an infinite number of times again in the same sequence and in the same way. Not only does the *Übermensch* seem to be the stuff of science fiction or even comic books, but also the cosmological versions of the will to power and the eternal recurrence might be characterized as forms of "crackpot metaphysics" (Leiter 2013:594).[3] In sum, there are good reasons for contemporary philosophers to ignore *Zarathustra*, perhaps wishing that Nietzsche had never written such an embarrassing text.

The primary purpose of this guidebook is to introduce *Zarathustra* to a broad audience and guide readers through its contents. At the same time, the current assessment of *Zarathustra* in contemporary Anglo-American philosophy also demands that such a guide makes a case for its significance. For if one can readily dismiss *Zarathustra* as a text unworthy of study, it makes little sense to read, let alone write, a guidebook that will help potential readers wade through its perplexities. To this end, I will try to make good on Nietzsche's claim that *Zarathustra* is perhaps his most important work, and I will argue that once we understand its nature and purpose, we will see why we cannot make sense of Nietzsche's project without understanding *Zarathustra*. Along the way and especially in the final chapter, I will also try to offer some reasons why it may even be interesting to contemporary philosophers.

Although Anglo-American philosophers over the past fifty years would often approach Nietzsche's texts through the lens of contemporary interests and concerns, there are exceptions to this trend. Most notably, Bernard Reginster's work, *The Affirmation of Life* (2006), took an important step in trying to understand Nietzsche's works through Nietzsche's own interests as well as his historical context. Rather than simply inquiring into Nietzsche's views on topics interesting to contemporary philosophers, Reginster stresses Nietzsche's engagement with the tradition of philosophical pessimism and focuses on the question of whether one can affirm life in the face of meaningless suffering. In my view, Reginster is right in this respect, and I think we can only begin to understand the significance Nietzsche attaches to *Zarathustra* by reading him through this lens and the way in which the task of affirming life animates his overall project.

Nietzsche inherits this question from his philosophical predecessor, Arthur Schopenhauer (1788–1860), and therefore some familiarity with Schopenhauer's work—most notably his two-volume *The World as Will and Representation*—is essential for understanding Nietzsche's philosophy as a whole and *Zarathustra* in particular.[4] The key proposition that Nietzsche inherits from Schopenhauer is the pessimistic thesis that all life is essentially suffering. To be sure, many of us will resist this claim and intuitively defend some version of optimism, which can be understood as the view that some version of happiness or what ancient Greek philosophers called *eudaimonia* is possible. For the optimist, the task of philosophy and even existence is to figure out what truly makes a flourishing life possible—this often involves cutting through appearances and grasping the truth about nature and ourselves—and to live accordingly. In contrast, a pessimist like Schopenhauer holds that the fundamental illusion which philosophy reveals is that such happiness will never be attained. Whereas we typically think that suffering occurs when desires are frustrated, Schopenhauer shows, first, that we suffer simply by desiring and, second, that we find ourselves bored in those rare instances when our desires are satisfied. Because life oscillates between unsatisfied desire and boredom, Schopenhauer concludes that all life is suffering.

According to Schopenhauer, accepting the insight that all life is suffering naturally leads to a further conclusion: life, so understood, is not worth living. To understand how Nietzsche relates to Schopenhauer, we need to recognize that although Nietzsche accepts Schopenhauer's description of human existence that makes suffering an ineluctable feature of it—let's call this "factual pessimism"—he nevertheless rejects Schopenhauer's conclusion that life is therefore not worth living—let's call this "evaluative pessimism" (Nietzsche will later call this nihilism).[5] That is, Nietzsche thinks that human beings can find ways to affirm life, even though suffering is an ineluctable feature of it, and therefore, evaluative pessimism does not necessarily follow from factual pessimism. Although many thinkers have assumed it does, Nietzsche points to individuals and even entire cultures, such as the ancient Greeks, who were able to affirm existence, even though they accepted the truth of factual pessimism. Herein lies the fundamental thought of Nietzsche's philosophical project and the essence of his originality as a thinker.

This original thought was the central thesis of Nietzsche's first work, *The Birth of Tragedy* (1872), and Nietzsche ascribed such significance to ancient tragedy precisely because he felt it presented the key to understanding how one could affirm life in the face of meaningless suffering. Indeed, he also argued that the operas of Richard Wagner could be understood as a rebirth of ancient tragedy, and therefore the Wagner's operas—especially *Tristan and Isolde*—provided a life-affirming alternative to the evaluative pessimism of Schopenhauer. *The Birth* is essential for understanding the significance Nietzsche attributes to *Zarathustra* because there are good reasons for thinking that *Zarathustra* is Nietzsche's own tragedy. As Reginster remarks,

> Nietzsche initially believed that the Wagnerian musical drama would overcome modern nihilism, but, once he became disenchanted with Wagner, he offered instead his own *Thus Spoke Zarathustra*, a work explicitly devoted to determining the conditions of a new 'affirmation of life,' as the beginning (or rebirth) of a form of tragedy.
>
> (2006:51–52)[6]

Nevertheless, Reginster remains relatively silent about *Zarathustra* in his own work. In contrast, I want to make the case for the importance of *Zarathustra* by providing an extended defense of the claim that the work should be read as a tragedy that dramatizes Zarathustra's own quest to affirm life in the face of meaningless suffering. Specifically, it will be argued that the first three parts of *Zarathustra* should be understood as a tragic trilogy and the fourth part should be understood as what is known as a satyr play (a satyr play typically followed a tragic trilogy in ancient Greek theater). The idea is that if Nietzsche thinks that the affirmation of life is central to his overall project and that tragedy, along with the other poetic genres associated with the Greek god Dionysus, is central to this project of life affirmation, then *Zarathustra*, as a tragedy, is going to be central to Nietzsche's overall project. In this way, we will make sense of why Nietzsche attributes such importance to the work and why he thinks of it as his *magnum opus*.

By reading *Zarathustra* I–III as a tragedy (and *Zarathustra* IV as a satyr play), we do run the risk of showing exactly why contemporary philosophers marginalize the text. Just as Sophocles' *Oedipus Rex* or even Homer's *Iliad* are not required readings in philosophy and are largely regarded as falling outside the bounds of the discipline, there seems to be little reason for philosophers to engage seriously with *Zarathustra* if it is a tragedy. Although this may very well be true for those who understand philosophy entirely in contemporary terms, for those who think of Plato as a founding figure of philosophy even as we practice it today, the genre of tragedy does show itself to be of deep philosophical interest. This is not because Plato felt that tragedy represented a necessary component of his own philosophical project. Indeed, it was just the opposite: he saw in tragedy the expression of an entire worldview and corresponding way of life that opposed his own understanding of philosophy and the philosophical life.[7] In this broad sense, tragedy was, for Plato, deeply philosophical, but tragedy also conveyed an understanding of life and the world that needed to be excluded from the city, the soul, and the philosophical life. In Plato's view, there is an ancient quarrel between philosophy and poetry, and although tragedy is a major player in this quarrel, it nevertheless stands outside of and so opposed to philosophy as Plato conceived it.[8]

Much of Nietzsche's project can be understood as an attempt to re-establish the supremacy of art or poetry over the philosophical project as Plato conceived it, and Nietzsche is consciously participating in this quarrel by writing his own tragedy in *Zarathustra*. Interesting here is that for both Plato and Nietzsche this quarrel rests on philosophical questions of fundamental ontology and a larger worldview, and although this debate is often articulated in the language of "being" and "becoming" from ancient philosophy, we can also understand this debate in terms of a contrast between transcendent metaphysics and naturalism. Whereas Plato closely associates the philosophical life with the quest to contemplate metaphysical ideas or "Forms," Nietzsche eventually aligns his call for a rebirth of tragedy with a claim that nature or the sensible world is all there is (naturalism). This is important because Brian Leiter (2002 and 2013) has argued that Nietzsche is best understood as a naturalist and therefore a thinker relevant to debates about naturalism in contemporary philosophy. Although there is a lot of variety in how both "metaphysics" and "naturalism" are defined and there is slippage in the use of these terms, I think that Leiter is right to understand Nietzsche as a naturalist in the general sense that he appeals to the results of the natural sciences to jettison any commitment to transcendent metaphysics.[9]

Nevertheless, Leiter's naturalist reading is problematic in at least two respects. First, he opposes Nietzsche's naturalism to an aestheticism that Alexander Nehamas makes central to his interpretation of Nietzsche in *Nietzsche: Life as Literature* (1985) (see

Leiter 1992). There is no doubt that Leiter's naturalist reading is incompatible with specific features of Nehamas' aestheticist reading, but the main upshot of Nietzsche's project is that he is trying to combine a thoroughly naturalistic understanding of the world, life, and the human being with an aestheticism that identifies art and poetry as the primary means by which we can accept and even affirm a world so understood. For this reason, I have argued that we should look for ways to synthesize these two aspects of Nietzsche's project. Specifically, Nietzsche is best understood as advancing what I have called a "naturalized aestheticism," and this naturalized aestheticism opposes a metaphysical-moral tradition that runs from the likes of Plato through the work of Schopenhauer (Meyer 2015).

The second problem with Leiter's reading is that it largely ignores, and perhaps even consciously excludes, *Zarathustra* as an important part of Nietzsche's naturalism. In my view, *Zarathustra* is a major contribution to Nietzsche's naturalized aestheticism for at least two reasons. First, he introduces two doctrines, the will to power and the eternal recurrence, that effectively complete the naturalist project (in the sense of eliminating transcendent metaphysics). As I explain elsewhere (Meyer 2022), they do this by making nature into a self-contained system that explains itself, thereby closing off any need for metaphysical explanations on the micro- and macro-levels. Thus, even if we follow Leiter in labeling these views as "crackpot," they should at least be understood as part of Nietzsche's "crackpot naturalism" (not his "crackpot metaphysics"). Second, *Zarathustra* provides us with a drama in which the main character, Zarathustra, must come to terms with the consequences that naturalism has for his own sense of self and agency. Specifically, Nietzsche's naturalism in general and the eternal recurrence in particular entail a form of determinism or fatalism in which there is no self or soul that can change the course of nature and so oneself in any way.[10] In contemporary terms, such a view forces us to abandon what is known as a libertarian conception of free will and the corresponding idea that how we act is ultimately up to us. There is just one world, and this world will never be anything other than it is. This is also true for the self: we are who we are and cannot be otherwise.

This, of course, can be a hard view to accept, especially when one adds to this fatalism the thought that this fate will recur again and again and again. In terms of the self, one only needs to think of a character like Oedipus who lives his life trying to resist fate only to realize his destiny. In terms of the world, one only needs to meditate on some horrific event in the past that will now repeat for eternity. Although Nietzsche acknowledges the terrifying aspects of such a thought, he ultimately stresses the liberating and life-affirming aspects of both naturalism and fatalism. By giving up the idea that we can effectively alter or change the world and who we are, we leave behind the idea that the world *ought* to be other than it is and therewith the categories of "good and evil" that we have typically used to judge the world. For Nietzsche, such categories are far from benign: once we couple the demand that the world be other than it is with the insight that the world cannot be other than it is, moral judgment leads to a condemnation of the world as such, and this puts us on a path toward nihilism. Moreover, the moral demand that we be other than who we are and act differently than we do leads to a system of sin, punishment, guilt, and the bad conscience that has plagued humanity for millennia. In contrast, the goal of the tragedy of *Zarathustra* is nothing less than the attempt to overcome the idea that we are morally responsible for who we are and thereby restore what Nietzsche calls "the innocence of becoming." By restoring this innocence and curing us of the sickness of sin, guilt, and punishment, a complete affirmation of life and the world becomes possible.

So understood, we not only see how *Zarathustra* is central to Nietzsche's overall project, but also how it deals with topics, such as naturalism, free will, agency, and morality, that have been central to philosophy from antiquity until today. This, however, presupposes that this is the right way to understand the text, and we can only make such a determination by taking the time and effort necessary to work through a text that might initially seem to be "pompous, overstuffed, and downright boring" (Huddleston 2019:351). There are undoubtedly parts of *Zarathustra* that will remain obscure and even unpalatable to contemporary readers, but I hope that the study of the text reflected in the following pages will show how Nietzsche is working through some of the most important and profound questions of philosophy.

1.1 NIETZSCHE'S LIFE, WORKS, AND THE RECEPTION OF *ZARATHUSTRA*

Nietzsche was born on October 15, 1844, in the small German town of Röcken. He was the son of a protestant minister, Carl Ludwig Nietzsche, who died when Nietzsche was only four years old. Having also lost a brother at a very young age, Nietzsche grew up with his sister, Elisabeth, and under the care of his mother, Franziska. He attended the renowned boarding school near his birthplace, Schulpforta, and went on to study theology in Bonn and then ancient philology or classics at Leipzig. He was a star student, and, upon the urging of his advisor, Friedrich Ritschl, he received a job offer from the University of Basel as a professor of classical philology in 1869 at the age of twenty-four prior to completing his doctoral dissertation.

After writing some smaller scholarly pieces, Nietzsche published his first major work, *The Birth of Tragedy out of the Spirit of Music*, in 1872. What many thought would be a scholarly investigation into the origins of tragedy turned out to be a rather speculative and even polemical work that heralded the rebirth of tragedy in the operas of Richard Wagner at the inaugural Bayreuth Festival in 1876. Indeed, Nietzsche dedicated the preface of the work to Wagner, where Nietzsche suggests that his own work amounts to a "vortex and turning point" of world history (in the text itself, Socrates is cast as the other "vortex and turning point" (BT 15)). The seriousness Nietzsche attached to the work is reflected in his letters from the time. Writing to Ritschl, Nietzsche claims that the book is something like a "manifesto" (KSB 3:194), and he explains to his mother and sister that the work expresses "what I want, what I am striving for with all of my power" (KSB 3:181). As noted above, what Nietzsche wanted was a rebirth of an art form that could both acknowledge the truth of factual pessimism and yet overturn the evaluative pessimism of Schopenhauer. In terms he uses in the 1886 preface to the work, Nietzsche was seeking to revive a "pessimism of strength" that he found in ancient Greek culture (BT "ASC":1).

Although Nietzsche pinned his hopes for a rebirth of tragedy on the work and operas of Richard Wagner, Nietzsche tried his hand at writing his own tragedy during the time he was composing

The Birth. Thus, we possess a series of fragmentary notes from 1870 to 1871 for plans for a tragedy featuring the pre-Socratic philosopher Empedocles, modeled on Friedrich Hölderlin's unfinished drama, *The Death of Empedocles* (KSA 7:5[116–117]; 8[30–37]). Important for my argument is that scholars have shown how Nietzsche's engagement with Hölderlin and Nietzsche's initial attempt at an Empedocles tragedy influenced and shaped key concepts of *Zarathustra*.[11]

Even though he never completed the Empedocles project, Nietzsche largely left behind scholarly pursuits in classical philology after the publication of *The Birth* for works written for a broader public that would advance art, culture, and philosophy. Thus, he penned a series of what he called "untimely meditations" in which he reflected on religion in *David Strauss, the Confessor and the Writer* (1873), history in *On the Uses and Disadvantages of History for Life* (1874), philosophy and education in *Schopenhauer as Educator* (1874), and finally, the significance of Wagner's upcoming Bayreuth festival in *Richard Wagner in Bayreuth* (1876). Despite his continued public support for Wagner and Wagner's festival, Nietzsche had been harboring concerns about the artist for some time, and it was at the much-anticipated festival that Nietzsche's frustrations boiled over.[12] He abruptly left the festival after only a few days and fled to the neighboring town of Klingenbrunn. There, he penned some of the first aphorisms of *Human, All Too Human* (1878), a work that would later make public his break with Wagner. In the academic year of 1876–1877, Nietzsche took a leave of absence from his professorship in Basel to work in a self-proclaimed community of "free spirits" in Sorrento, Italy, with the likes of the philosopher Paul Reé and feminist Malwida von Meysenbug. Shortly thereafter (1879), he would permanently leave his position as a philology professor to wander throughout Europe and write the works for which he is now famous.

From the perspective of his larger oeuvre, *Human* is perhaps his most puzzling work. Whereas he had, up to the Bayreuth festival in 1876, been a staunch advocate of the role art plays in the advancement of culture and the affirmation of life, Nietzsche devotes himself in the work to an unrelenting, even Socratic, quest for truth by means of a "historical philosophy" that he links to the methods and results of the natural sciences (HH 1). Even more surprising is that Nietzsche subjects art—implicitly attacking Wagner—to a scathing critique. The oddities of this text have led some to speculate that he went through a period of positivism under the influence of Reé[13] and that he wrote *Human* largely to distance himself from his early hopes for a rebirth of tragedy.

The problem with this reading of *Human* is that Nietzsche understands the work to be the first in a series of works that fall under the rubric of the free spirit. These works largely consist of the aphorisms for which Nietzsche would become famous: *Assorted Opinions and Maxims* (1879), *The Wanderer and His Shadow* (1880), *Daybreak* (1881), and *The Gay Science* (1882). The difficulty here is that in *The Gay Science*, the final work of the free spirit series, Nietzsche effectively returns to celebrating art in a way that is reminiscent of *The Birth*. Not only does he praise art's life-affirming powers and conceive of existence in aesthetic terms (GS 290 and 299), but he also adds his own poetry to the beginning of the work under the title, "Joke, Cunning, and Revenge." Moreover, the 1882 edition of *The Gay Science*—he republished the work in 1887, adding another book of aphorisms—ends with an aphorism with the title, "incipit tragoedia" or "let the tragedy begin," and the aphorism contains what would become the opening lines of the work that followed, *Zarathustra* (GS 342). The importance of this aphorism for interpreting *Zarathustra* as a tragedy should be obvious. But what should not be overlooked is that by connecting *Human* to *The Gay Science* and then by ending *The Gay Science* with "incipit tragoedia," Nietzsche is indicating to readers that the free spirit project, which begins with *Human*, culminates in the rebirth of tragedy in *Zarathustra*. So understood, *Human* cannot be a break with the project of *The Birth*, but rather the first step in the fulfillment of the goals Nietzsche articulated in his first work.[14]

Scholars often debate about how to periodize Nietzsche's works, and although most agree that *Human* marks a significant break with Nietzsche's earlier writings in both content and style, there is some question as to whether *Zarathustra* initiates a new period in Nietzsche's thinking and so a break with the free spirit project. For reasons I explain later, I think it is a bit of both. On the one hand, Nietzsche intends *Zarathustra* to be a continuation of the free spirit project which *Human* initiates and *The Gay Science* concludes. At the same time, *Zarathustra* is clearly different from Nietzsche's free spirit project, evidenced by the stylistic shift from aphorisms in the free spirit works to the poetry of *Zarathustra*. The shift is also marked by the introduction of the semi-fictitious character of Zarathustra. Nevertheless, this stylistic break is not as significant as it may initially seem. In the free spirit works, there seems to be a fictitious persona of the free spirit that inhabits the texts, and this free spirit is the subject of what is arguably a *Bildungsroman*. Similarly, a number of interpreters have claimed that *Zarathustra* is also a *Bildungsroman* in which Zarathustra undergoes a process of education,[15] and there is a clear sense in which the *Bildungsroman* of *Zarathustra* develops the insights of the free spirit writings.

There is another interesting parallel worth noting between the free spirit works and *Zarathustra*. Just as Nietzsche wrote and published the free spirit works in installments, later looking to publish them as a single unit (KSA 10:1[14]), Nietzsche also published the four books of *Zarathustra* in installments from 1883 to 1885, and he distributed the fourth and final part only to a small group of friends upon completion. In fact, when Nietzsche did publish *Zarathustra* in his lifetime as a single volume in 1887, he only included the first three parts, and it was only until after his death that readers were presented with all four books of *Zarathustra* in a single volume.

The works Nietzsche published immediately after *Zarathustra*, namely, *Beyond Good and Evil* (1886) and *On the Genealogy of Morals* (1887), generate the most scholarly interest today (*The Gay Science* is a close third). Many consider these works to be written by a "mature" Nietzsche, and they deal with themes more familiar to contemporary philosophers such as philosophy, metaphysics, epistemology, and ethics. Nietzsche would go on to write—but not necessarily publish—several other works in 1888, the final year of his sanity. These include *Twilight of the Idols*, *The Case of Wagner*, *Ecce Homo*, and *The Antichrist*, and he also compiled and composed works such as *Nietzsche contra Wagner* and his own *Dithyrambs of Dionysus*.

What Nietzsche did not write was a work for which he became infamous: *The Will to Power*. Instead, this work was posthumously compiled and published by his sister, Elisabeth Förester-Nietzsche, and longtime companion, Heinrich Köselitz (also known as Peter Gast), and it was created from his extensive unpublished notes and sketches—mostly taken from 1883 to 1888—known as his *Nachlass* or literary remains.[16] Nietzsche's fame began to spread in the final year of his productive career and then after his mental breakdown in 1889, and he soon became a figure that nearly every educated German felt compelled to engage in one way or another.[17] During the first and second world wars, Nietzsche's ideas were marshaled to support the relevant cause, and just as *Zarathustra* was carried by troops into battle in World War I, the compilation of *The Will to Power* provided fertile ground for interpreters like Alfred Baümler to link Nietzsche's ideas to National Socialism and the Third Reich.[18]

Having already been blamed in Great Britain for World War I, the substantive links between Nietzsche's philosophy and National Socialism were enough to make him a *persona non grata* in the Anglo-Saxon world following World War II. However, much of this began to change, at least in the United States, through the work of Walter Kaufmann. He set out to undermine what he felt was a false narrative or "legend" that led to the association between Nietzsche and National Socialism, and he largely succeeded through his widely read book, *Nietzsche: Philosopher, Psychologist, Antichrist* (first published in 1950), and his many translations of Nietzsche's works, including *Zarathustra*.

Although Kaufmann's work did much to make Nietzsche a more acceptable figure with the larger public, it did not mean that Nietzsche had gained acceptance in the world of professional philosophy. At the time Kaufmann was writing, there was very little respect for the history of philosophy, and there was a lot of skepticism—besides a reluctant willingness to offer obligatory classes on existentialism—about continental European philosophy. Although Nietzsche was being widely read by "continental" philosophers who took seriously the French and German traditions as well as those in literature departments interested in a movement often referred to as "postmodernism," his status as a legitimate philosopher was in serious doubt among so-called "analytic" philosophers, i.e., those who followed a philosophical tradition forged by the likes of Gottlob Frege, Bertrand Russell, and Rudolph Carnap, which was the predominant way of doing philosophy in the Anglo-American world during this time.

For Nietzsche to be taken seriously in these circles, it needed to be shown that he was indeed a philosopher in their understanding of the discipline. This mostly meant that it needed to be shown that Nietzsche (1) offers arguments for (2) specific views or positions that are (3) relevant to contemporary philosophical debates in areas such as metaphysics, epistemology, ethics, and aesthetics, and this is precisely what scholars such as Arthur Danto and Richard Schacht tried to do. In *Nietzsche as Philosopher* (1965), Danto offers a chapter-by-chapter account of Nietzsche's philosophical views, with the hope of showing that Nietzsche is indeed a philosopher. In his book, *Nietzsche* (1983), Schacht canvasses, in a chapter-by-chapter account, Nietzsche's views on philosophy, truth, knowledge, metaphysics, life, values, morality, and art, and he does his best to reconstruct Nietzsche's arguments in favor of each of the positions he attributes to Nietzsche.[19]

A common feature of both texts is their systematic neglect of *Zarathustra*. This is in part because they do not endeavor to read Nietzsche's texts as texts. Instead, the shared methodology is one of mining Nietzsche's published and unpublished notes for philosophical views or what I call "Nietzsche's theory of X." Not only does Danto begin with the claim that there is no order or structure to Nietzsche's works, either internally or in relation to each other, but also the views Nietzsche expresses in his published works are often "lumped" together with those in the *Nachlass*. The situation for *Zarathustra* is even worse because, as Kathleen Higgins explains, Schacht's book is in a series that bears the title, "The Arguments of the Philosophers." Although *Zarathustra* might present philosophical views, there are very few arguments in *Zarathustra* that defend or support the philosophical views expressed in the work (1987:xvii). Instead, a prophet-like Zarathustra just "speaks" thusly whatever views he holds. As Schacht explains, this is why a text like *Zarathustra* does not lend itself "to the sort of analysis undertaken" in his work (1983:xiii–xiv).

Another conviction that guides Schacht's reading is that Nietzsche's thought is "fundamentally coherent," such that we need not "saddle him with numerous basic inconsistencies" as commentators have been wont to do (1983:xiv). Thus, there is a way in which Schacht's reading is guided by a principle of interpretive charity that other Nietzsche scholars would go on to endorse. For Maudemarie Clark, this means that we should, to the extent that the texts allow, avoid attributing positions to Nietzsche "against which there are obvious objections" (1990:ix).[20] Although it is not an unreasonable principle to adopt in interpreting a past thinker, this principle has marginalized *Zarathustra* even further. This is because much of the text is structured around three philosophical ideas that very few, if any, contemporary philosophers would accept: the *Übermensch* and the cosmological formulations of the eternal recurrence and the will to power. Since we ought to avoid attributing philosophically suspect views to Nietzsche, it only follows that we ought to find reasons to avoid making *Zarathustra* a centerpiece of a given interpretation.

It would, of course, be wrong to think that no scholarly attention has been devoted to *Zarathustra* in the Anglo-American context. For instance, *Zarathustra* plays a central role in Harold Alderman's 1977 work, *Nietzsche's Gift*, and a little less than a decade later, Laurence Lampert (1986) published a detailed and extensive commentary on the text. Kathleen Higgins (1987) and then Gary Shapiro (1989) followed Lampert's work with interpretations that emphasize the literary aspects of the work (thus, pointing back to Alderman's efforts). In 1990, Greg Whitlock produced a commentary on the text. In 1995, Peter Berkowitz devoted central chapters of his *Nietzsche: Ethics of an Immoralist* to interpreting *Zarathustra*, and Stanley Rosen published a commentary—similar to Lampert's—on *Zarathustra* under the title, *The Mask of Enlightenment*. After the turn of the century, three of the most philosophically astute works on *Zarathustra* were published: Robert Gooding-Williams' *Zarathustra's Dionysian Modernism* (2001); T. K. Seung's *Nietzsche's Epic of the Soul: Thus Spoke Zarathustra* (2005); and Paul Loeb's *The Death of Nietzsche's Zarathustra* (2010).[21] Most recently, Richard Velkley has edited and published Leo's Strauss' lecture notes on *Thus*

Spoke Zarathustra, and in the same year (2017), Heinrich Meier released another commentary on *Zarathustra* in German: *Was ist Nietzsches Zarathustra? Eine philosophische Auseinandersetzung*. Finally, Keith Ansell-Pearson and Paul Loeb published a collection of important papers on the philosophical significance of *Zarathustra* in 2022, and, in the German world, Katharina Grätz (2024 and 2024b) has just published an extensive two-volume commentary on *Zarathustra*.[22]

The amount of literature on *Zarathustra* is therefore not insignificant. However, it remains the case that, as Higgins quipped some years ago, "the mainstream of Nietzsche scholarship still treats *Zarathustra*, if at all, as an afterthought" (1987:xviii). My hope—expressed both here and elsewhere—is to convince scholars as well as a broader readership that Nietzsche's texts have more structure and purpose, both internally and in relation to each other, than has hitherto been realized and that there can be a big payoff if we take the requisite time and effort to engage in a historical reconstruction of his texts and try to understand Nietzsche as he understood himself. In my view, a proper understanding of the nature and significance of *Zarathustra* is key to recognizing that Nietzsche's post-1877 works hang together in some significant respect. This emerges once we understand six key points about *Zarathustra* and its relationship to Nietzsche's other works: (1) *Zarathustra* is a tragedy (and a satyr play in the fourth part); (2) as a tragedy, *Zarathustra* should be understood in relation to the project of a rebirth of tragedy that Nietzsche first articulated in *The Birth*; (3) the tragedy of *Zarathustra* emerges from *The Gay Science* as well as the other free spirit works; (4) *Zarathustra* is an attempt to affirm the pessimistic (factual) worldview articulated in *Human, All Too Human*; (5) by teaching the cosmological formulations of the will to power and the eternal recurrence, *Zarathustra* completes the project of naturalism, eliminates the metaphysical world, restores the "innocence of becoming," and advances to a standpoint "beyond good and evil," thereby laying the foundations for the philosophical project Nietzsche announces in *Beyond Good and Evil*; and (6) Nietzsche's post-*Zarathustra* project culminates in a comedy and thereby completes a Dionysian festival in Nietzsche's works that includes a tragedy, a comedy, a satyr play, and dithyrambs. If the points sketched here are right, we can see how understanding Nietzsche's larger project hangs on understanding *Zarathustra* as a tragedy, and what I want to do in the next two sections is say more about the important role that *Zarathustra* plays in Nietzsche's corpus and why it might provide the key to seeing how Nietzsche's post-1877 writings form a coherent whole.[23]

1.2 THE TRAGEDY OF *ZARATHUSTRA* AND NIETZSCHE'S PRE-*ZARATHUSTRA* WRITINGS

As I noted above, one of the predominant ways of approaching Nietzsche's texts in the Anglo-American context is a quest to find and articulate Nietzsche's "theory of X."[24] What is Nietzsche's view of the self? What is Nietzsche's metaphysics of objects? What is Nietzsche's moral psychology? What is Nietzsche's political theory? I also noted above that this approach has often gone hand in hand with a view that Danto articulated at the beginning of his 1965 book, *Nietzsche as Philosopher*:

> Nietzsche's books give the appearance of having been assembled rather than composed. They are made up, in the main, of short, pointed aphorisms, and of essays seldom more than a few pages long; each volume is more like a treasury of the author's selections than like a book in its own right. Any given aphorism or essay might as easily have been placed in one volume as in another without much affecting the unity or structure of either. And the books themselves, except for their chronological ordering, do not exhibit any special structure as a corpus. No one of them presupposes an acquaintance with any other.
> (1965:19).

Very few scholars today would accept such an extreme view, as Danto's hyperbolic claim is obviously false. However, many scholars do seem to accept, at least in practice, some watered-down version of Danto's claim. That is, such scholars implicitly believe that it is not necessary to think seriously about the structure and purpose of Nietzsche's texts as well as their relation to each other to engage in quality scholarship on Nietzsche.[25] However, Nietzsche expresses the exact opposite view. For instance, he claims that the "worst readers" are "those who behave like plundering troops; they take away a few things they can use, dirty and confound the remainder, and revile the whole" (AOM 137). Regarding *Zarathustra*, Nietzsche also rejects this approach. Specifically, he argues that

> in order to have an understanding of Zarathustra (an event *without comparison* in literature and philosophy and poetry and morals [...])— *all* of my previous writings must be seriously and profoundly understood; likewise the *necessity* of the order of these writings and the development they express.

According to Nietzsche, we cannot understand *Zarathustra* if we do not, first, read all his previous works and, second, read these works in the order in which they were written. This is the reason why Nietzsche decided to republish many of his previous works with new prefaces in 1886–1887. Each of these prefaces—along with the works themselves—provides a "true *enlightenment*" about Nietzsche and is "the very best preparation for his daring son Zarathustra" (KSB 7:740).[26]

Some of this might sound like Nietzsche's own hyperbole, written in a letter to his publisher to make a case for republishing his previous works. After all, many Nietzsche scholars would be surprised to learn that Nietzsche's 1873 untimely meditation on David Friedrich Strauss is necessary to understand *Zarathustra*. However, even if there is some hyperbole, we see that Danto's approach to Nietzsche's works is entirely at odds with Nietzsche's self-understanding. Nietzsche explicitly tells us that in order to understand one work, we need to understand the whole, and in order to understand the whole, we need to pay attention to the structure and ordering of each of his published works. Indeed, I think that a good amount of sense can be made of Nietzsche's claim about his previous texts once we understand *Zarathustra* as a tragedy and recognize that the free spirit works are intimately connected to *Zarathustra*. Let me explain.

If *Zarathustra* is a tragedy, it cannot be just another work in Nietzsche's corpus. To recall, the point of Nietzsche's first book,

The Birth of Tragedy, was to argue that we need a rebirth of tragedy to confront and even affirm the ugly truths that Kant and Schopenhauer have revealed through their philosophies (BT 19), and we know from Nietzsche's letters that the rebirth of tragedy at Wagner's Bayreuth Festival was the goal of his efforts. Now it could be that Nietzsche decided to abandon this entire project in 1876, only to recommit himself to the project roughly six years later with the tragedy of *Zarathustra*. One piece of evidence against this reading is that Nietzsche republished the second edition of *The Birth of Tragedy* in 1878. If he has abandoned the project, there would be little reason for him to republish the work at this time. Moreover, this flip-flopping on such an important matter is rather odd, even schizophrenic, given that it happens so quickly. Thus, there are good reasons for thinking that the significance of 1876 is that Nietzsche became even more committed to the project by deciding to take it on himself. If this is right, then a work like *The Birth*—in addition to a work like *Richard Wagner in Bayreuth*—will be essential background reading for unlocking the structure and purpose of a work like *Zarathustra*.

To make sense of how some of Nietzsche's other works relate to *Zarathustra*, we can begin by recalling that the most important piece of evidence for reading *Zarathustra* as a tragedy comes from the final section of the 1882 edition of *The Gay Science* (in 1887, Nietzsche republished the book with an added preface and a fifth book; thus, the 1882 edition only had four books). As noted above, Nietzsche introduces the opening lines of what will become *Zarathustra* under the title of "incipit tragoedia" or "let the tragedy begin" (GS 342). The fact that Nietzsche introduces *Zarathustra* under this title suggests that the work should be read as a tragedy. The fact that Nietzsche ends the original edition of *The Gay Science* with the opening lines of *Zarathustra* suggests that Nietzsche wants to establish some significant connection between *Zarathustra* and *The Gay Science*. Moreover, we know that Nietzsche understood the eternal recurrence to be the fundamental conception of *Zarathustra* (EH "Books" Z:1), and although he first introduces the idea in GS 109 and mentions it in GS 285, it is in GS 341—and so the aphorism immediately preceding the introduction of Zarathustra in GS 342—that we encounter the most robust presentation of the doctrine. However, this is not the only evidence linking *The Gay Science* to *Zarathustra*. Not only do important references to tragedy run throughout the text (see GS 1, 107, and 153), but also Nietzsche originally planned to have Zarathustra make numerous appearances in the text. Most notably, preliminary drafts have Zarathustra, not the madman, pronouncing the death of God in the third book of *The Gay Science* (GS 125; see KSA 14:256). Taken together, we can say that Nietzsche consciously constructed much of the 1882 edition of *The Gay Science* to flow into the tragedy of *Zarathustra*.

Given these connections, we are left wondering if we can establish similar connections to Nietzsche's other pre-*Zarathustra* works. After all, Nietzsche says that we must read all his preceding works to understand *Zarathustra*. The clearest case here is *Daybreak* (1881), the work immediately preceding *The Gay Science*. Again, knowing the compositional history of these texts is crucial. This is because Nietzsche originally wrote the first three books of *The Gay Science* as books VI, VII, and VIII of *Daybreak* (KSB 6:190).[27] Based on this fact, I have argued elsewhere that the death of God and the elimination of his shadows, which is the centerpiece of the third book of *The Gay Science* (GS 125), can be understood as the culmination of the project of *Daybreak* (Meyer 2019). As the subtitle of *Daybreak* indicates, "Thoughts on the Prejudices of Morality," Nietzsche's aim is to eliminate the "prejudices of morality," and there are reasons for equating the shadows of God with the prejudices of morality. What we see is that just as *The Gay Science* is intimately linked to *Zarathustra*, *Daybreak* is intimately linked to *The Gay Science*, and therefore, by extension, we can conclude that *Daybreak* must also be linked to *Zarathustra*. This is something that Nietzsche confirms in an 1884 letter: "In reading through *Daybreak* and *Gay Science*, I found by the way that there is almost no line that cannot serve as an introduction, preparation, and commentary to the aforementioned *Zarathustra*. It is a fact that I made the commentary before the text" (KSB 6:504).

We can extend these connections back to the very beginnings of Nietzsche's free spirit project. This includes works like *Human,*

All Too Human (1878), *Assorted Opinions and Maxims* (1879), *The Wanderer and His Shadow* (1880). Here, it should be noted that the latter two works were originally conceived as appendices of the first, and Nietzsche published all three works together in 1876. Thus, the only question is whether we can connect *Human* (and its two appendices) with *Daybreak* and *The Gay Science*. There are two pieces of evidence that allow us to do this: first, Nietzsche had planned to publish all the free spirit works as a single, two-volume set in 1882 (KSA 10:1[13–14]). Second, Nietzsche informs his readers—on the back side of the title page of *The Gay Science*— that *The Gay Science* is the final installment in a series of works that date back to *Human* and have the singular intention of "erecting a new image and ideal of the free spirit."[28] Thus, the free spirit works from *Human* to *The Gay Science* should be understood as a single project published in installments. As I have argued in detail elsewhere (Meyer 2019), the almost 2,000 aphorisms found in the free spirit works are not a collection of disparate reflections on random topics, waiting to be rearranged by later commentators. Instead, they form a continuous *Gedankenkette* or thought-chain that tells the story of how Nietzsche becomes a free spirit (KSB 6:264), and this project, in turn, flows into the tragedy of *Zarathustra*.

Reading the free spirit works in this way may also find support from and have implications for how we understand the opening speech of *Zarathustra*, "On the Three Metamorphoses." In the speech, Zarathustra explains how the spirit first takes on a camel-like form in pursuing truth into the desert of knowledge, but then morphs into a lion that slays a god-like dragon that represents all hitherto created values; in the final stage, the spirit morphs into a child, one capable of creating new values. Holding that Nietzsche wants us to apply these metamorphoses to his own works, most commentators have assumed that these stages are to be found within the narrative of *Zarathustra* itself.[29] However, I think the best way to understand these metamorphoses is by mapping them onto the entire progression of texts that begins with *Human* and culminates in *Zarathustra*.[30] Specifically, Nietzsche's uncompromising quest for truth in *Human*—along with the two appendices, *Assorted Opinions and Maxims* and *The Wanderer*—can be understood as the time in which he takes the form of the camel, bears the burden of truth, and finds himself alone in the desert of knowledge. He takes on the form of the lion when he subjects the prejudices of morality to critique in *Daybreak* and ultimately slays the dragon of all values by killing God (and eliminating his shadow) in the third book of *The Gay Science*. On this view, the fourth book of *The Gay Science* marks a new phase in which the spirit eventually transforms into a child, and the transformation into the child comes to completion when Zarathustra summons the eternal recurrence at the end of the third book of *Zarathustra*.

Of course, some might be surprised to learn that *Human*—a work in which Nietzsche praises truth and science and largely rejects art and so tragedy—is now part of a larger project that crescendos into the tragedy of *Zarathustra*. Indeed, Nietzsche himself remarks in *Ecce Homo* that if he had published *Zarathustra* under another name like Richard Wagner, "the acuteness of two thousand years would not have been sufficient for anyone to guess that the author of *Human, All Too Human* is the visionary of *Zarathustra*" (EH "Clever":4). But here is where a familiarity with Nietzsche's earliest works, *The Birth* (1872) and *Philosophy in the Tragic Age of the Greeks* (1873), becomes essential. In *The Birth*, Nietzsche claims that the rebirth of tragedy would emerge from the self-overcoming of the Socratic quest for truth. Specifically, the uncompromising (and Socratic) quest for truth would reveal that Socratic optimism—the belief that humans can achieve genuine happiness by pursuing the truth—is a mere myth, and given that philosophers in the Socratic tradition like Kant and Schopenhauer have shown that suffering is an ineluctable feature of existence (factual pessimism), we now need to turn to art to justify and affirm an existence so understood (overturning evaluative pessimism) (BT 18–19). Taken together, the cultural ideal of *The Birth* is a music-playing Socrates (BT 15). As I have argued elsewhere, Nietzsche can be understood as taking on the role of this music-playing Socrates in the works from *Human* to *Zarathustra* (Meyer 2004). This is because *Human* initiates a truth-seeking project that eventually bites itself in the tail in *The Gay Science* and makes possible the rebirth of tragedy in *Zarathustra*.

There are worries, however, about using *The Birth* to interpret Nietzsche's later writings. This is because Nietzsche initially articulates his vision of tragedy in terms of Schopenhauer's metaphysics, and by the time he wrote *Zarathustra*, he will have rejected metaphysics in all its forms. Although there are some legitimate concerns here, it is important to note that Nietzsche rethinks his ontological commitments in a way that is continuous with the argument of *The Birth*. In *The Birth*, we find Nietzsche appealing to the pre-Socratic philosopher, Heraclitus, to explain how tragedy—rooted in musical dissonance—can justify existence. In particular, he points to the Heraclitean child who playfully builds and then destroys sandcastles as a figure which exemplifies the attitude that the tragic experience instills (BT 24). The idea is that tragedy helps us adopt a new and accepting attitude toward change, destruction, and death, and it is through this shift in attitude toward these disharmonic elements of existence that we become capable of laughter and play.

Heraclitus is important because only one year later (1873) in an unpublished manuscript, *Philosophy in the Tragic Age*, Nietzsche singles out Heraclitus as the philosopher of the tragic age of the Greeks, and in so doing, he presents Heraclitus as an anti-metaphysical thinker who rejected the metaphysical notion of "being." Instead, Heraclitus' vision is a world of "becoming." It is also one that corresponds to an artistic and child-like vision of existence that finds "play in necessity" (PTAG 8) and experiences coming-to-be as an amoral "game" of creation and destruction (PTAG 7). Thus, Heraclitus' philosophy of becoming not only contrasts sharply with Parmenides' philosophy of being but also the moral worldview that Nietzsche attributes to Anaximander (and associates with Kant and Schopenhauer) in which creation or coming-to-be is seen as a sin and destruction as retribution for this original sin (PTAG 4). Although Nietzsche never published *Philosophy in the Tragic Age*, he does reveal his Heraclitean commitments in print as early as 1874 in the important untimely meditation, *On the Uses and Disadvantages of History for Life* (HL 1 and 9).

With these key points in hand, we can begin to understand how a familiarity with the key ideas of *Human* is necessary for understanding *Zarathustra*. *Zarathustra* is a tragedy, and, according to *The Birth*, tragedy emerges from and responds to a "tragic worldview." On the one hand, this tragic worldview can be understood as equivalent to the aforementioned "factual pessimism," one in which suffering is said to be an essential feature of existence. So construed, *Human* lays the foundations of this tragic worldview because Nietzsche, throughout the first four books, stresses how knowledge about the suffering of existence threatens to lead to *despair* (HH 33). At the same time, we know from *Philosophy in the Tragic Age* that Nietzsche also understands the tragic worldview in Heraclitean terms, and I have argued elsewhere (Meyer 2014c) that the historical philosophy Nietzsche adopts and develops in *Human* is itself intimately bound up with Heraclitus' philosophy of becoming and his related doctrine of the unity of opposites (HH 1). So understood, *Human* lays out a tragic worldview to which the tragedy of *Zarathustra* will provide a life-affirming response.

Understanding the possible connections between *Human* and *Zarathustra* are not the only reasons for turning to early texts like *The Birth* and *Philosophy in the Tragic Age*. In the next chapter, I argue that *The Birth* is essential for understanding *Zarathustra* as a tragedy and that *Zarathustra* itself can be understood through the dialectical interplay of Apollonian and Dionysian motifs that Nietzsche identifies in ancient Greek tragedy. In my view, this is why Nietzsche claims that *Zarathustra* is the work in which his concept of the "Dionysian"—first articulated in *The Birth*— becomes a supreme deed (EH "Books" Z:6). Similarly, the tragedy of *Zarathustra* I–III seems to culminate in a child-like attitude toward existence, and Nietzsche's description of Heraclitus' philosophy in *Philosophy in the Tragic Age* provides important insight into the nature of this attitude and how it relates to the affirmation of existence. Finally, Nietzsche claims, in *Ecce Homo*, that the "idea of Bayreuth," developed in both *The Birth* and *Richard Wagner*, is translated into the "great noon" of *Zarathustra* (EH "Books" BT:4). For this reason, we can effectively replace the name "Wagner" in *Richard Wagner* with "Zarathustra," as "the entire picture of the dithyrambic artist is a picture of the pre-existent poet of *Zarathustra*" (EH "Books" BT:4).

At the same time, we need to be cognizant of an important difference between Nietzsche's earliest writings and his post-1876 works. Based on Nietzsche's comments in *Ecce Homo* about the relationship between *The Birth* and *Zarathustra*, we can say that the difference between the early works and Nietzsche's post-1876 writings is a difference between thought and deed, theory and practice. Specifically, the works prior to Nietzsche's break with Wagner (from 1872 to 1876) are initially written as theoretical tracts about the importance of tragedy and topics such as philosophy, art, education, and culture. However, when Nietzsche breaks with Wagner at the Bayreuth festival in 1876, he decides to undertake himself the cultural and philosophical projects he mapped out in theory in earliest works. In this way, the early works come to function as rough blueprints for his later works. Whereas he writes about philosophy in *Philosophy in the Tragic Age*, Nietzsche becomes a philosopher in works like *Human* and *The Gay Science*.[31] Whereas he outlines a program of education in *Schopenhauer as Educator*, he undertakes his own educational program of "becoming who he is" in the free spirit works and beyond. Whereas he talks about the genre of tragedy in *The Birth* and *Richard Wagner*, he writes his own tragedy in *Zarathustra*. Whereas he presents a music-playing Socrates as his new ideal in *The Birth*, he becomes a music-playing Socrates in works that stretch from *Human* to *Zarathustra*.

1.3 ZARATHUSTRA, REVALUATION, AND THE COMEDY OF NIETZSCHE'S POST-ZARATHUSTRA WORKS

On the interpretation of Nietzsche's corpus that has been presented thus far, *Zarathustra* functions as the fulfillment of Nietzsche's initial hopes for a rebirth of tragedy that he published in *The Birth* in 1872. It is the moment in which Nietzsche, through his fictional character Zarathustra, provides a life-affirming response to the pessimistic worldview he inherits from Schopenhauer and the larger scientific and philosophical climate of his day. But if this is the case, then how are we to understand Nietzsche's post-*Zarathustra* writings? If he has achieved what he had hoped to achieve and thereby given humanity "the greatest present that has ever been made to it so far," then why does he continue to write and publish after *Zarathustra*? This question is even more pressing given that Nietzsche publishes some of his most famous works, such as *Beyond Good and Evil* and *On the Genealogy of Morals*, after *Zarathustra*.

The significance of this question has not been lost on other interpreters who stress the importance of *Zarathustra* and read the work as a tragedy and a satyr play. Indeed, Loeb is one such interpreter, and he devotes the final chapter of *The Death of Zarathustra* (2010) to providing a framework for understanding Nietzsche's post-*Zarathustra* publications.[32] Based on Nietzsche's remarks in *Ecce Homo*, Loeb claims that all of Nietzsche's post-*Zarathustra* works should be understood as "'fishhooks [*Angelhaken*]' meant to attract and prepare readers for the superior insights of *Zarathustra*."[33] So understood, everything published after *Zarathustra* points back to the tragedy of *Zarathustra*, and therefore everything Nietzsche writes can be said to culminate with the tragic conclusion of *Zarathustra* III. For Loeb, this is a tragic conclusion because it ends with "the self-sacrificial death of humankind itself" (2010:241), which, in turn, is supposed to prepare the way for the birth of a new species of *Übermenschen*.

Loeb believes that the true end of *Zarathustra* and therefore the true culmination of Nietzsche's philosophy is *Zarathustra* III. He can hold this position because he believes that *Zarathustra* IV is what he calls an "analeptic" satyr play. By analeptic, Loeb means that the narrative events of *Zarathustra* IV occur chronologically prior to the events of the end of *Zarathustra* III, even though Nietzsche wrote *Zarathustra* IV after writing *Zarathustra* III. In this sense, *Zarathustra* IV is an extended flashback (2010:94) that Nietzsche designs to "supplement, clarify, and expand certain dramatic and philosophical events that had already taken place in the published Parts I-III" (2010:90). So understood, *Zarathustra* III marks the proper ending of *Zarathustra*, and therefore *Zarathustra* culminates in the "death of Zarathustra" in *Zarathustra* III.

I will say more about Loeb's reading of *Zarathustra* IV in the next chapter. Here, I will simply say that we both agree that *Zarathustra* IV should be understood as a satyr play. However, we disagree about whether Nietzsche intended the work to be "analeptic." In my view, we should read *Zarathustra* IV in a way that best makes sense of Nietzsche's claim that it is an interlude ("*Zwischenspiel*" or "*Zwischenakt*") between "*Zarathustra*" and "that which follows" (KSB 8:1075). Because "that which follows" is *not* part of *Zarathustra*, it is difficult to see how this could mean, *pace* Loeb, an interlude between events that occur within *Zarathustra* I–III, which is what it would have to be if *Zarathustra* IV were an analeptic satyr play. Instead, *Zarathustra* IV stands between *Zarathustra*, which presumably means *Zarathustra* III, and "that which follows," and this presumably means the works that Nietzsche writes after the interlude of *Zarathustra* IV starting with *Beyond Good and Evil*.[34]

For these reasons, I think Thomas Brobjer (2023) provides a better way of understanding the relationship between *Zarathustra* and Nietzsche's later writings. Although Nietzsche stresses the importance of *Zarathustra* in a work like *Ecce Homo*, *Zarathustra* is nevertheless a *Vorhalle* or "entrance hall" into his later philosophy (KSB 6:498). According to Brobjer, the philosophy to which Nietzsche is referring is his project of the revaluation of values. Brobjer argues that Nietzsche's interest in a revaluation of values can be traced back to his notes from 1881, around the time he formulated the eternal recurrence, and that this interest intensifies in the period just after he completed *Zarathustra* III (and before writing *Zarathustra* IV). Indeed, Brobjer points out that many scholars have overlooked the fact that Nietzsche spent much of his time immediately after the publication of *Zarathustra* III working on material for a planned *Hauptwerk* or *magnum opus* that would come to have the title, "The Revaluation of Values." It was only toward the end of 1884 that Nietzsche set to work on *Zarathustra* IV.

One of the upshots of Brobjer's argument is that there is a close association between *Zarathustra* and Nietzsche's project of a revaluation of values, so much so that he understands *Zarathustra* IV as a bridge between *Zarathustra* I–III and the revaluation of values in Nietzsche's later works (2023:136–137). Thus, when Nietzsche has Zarathustra claim that he is concerned with his work at the end of *Zarathustra* IV, we should understand this as a reference to the revaluation of values that Nietzsche himself was already planning to undertake in his later works. According to Brobjer (2023:3–4), both projects, Zarathustra and the revaluation of values, were already conceived in 1881 when Nietzsche mentioned Zarathustra in his notes under the title "noon and eternity [*Mittag und Ewigkeit*]" (KSA 9:11[195]), and we know that the first mention of "an attempt at a revaluation of all values" in Nietzsche's *Nachlass* occurs as a subtitle under the main heading, "Philosophy of the Eternal Recurrence" (KSA 11:26[259]), written just after Nietzsche had completed *Zarathustra* III.

Indeed, *The Gay Science*, the book in which Nietzsche first mentions the eternal recurrence (GS 109, 285, 341), contains what seem to be proleptic references to both *Zarathustra* and the revaluation of values. Whereas GS 342 clearly foreshadows *Zarathustra*, Nietzsche announces at the end of the third chapter of *The Gay Science* that "the weights of all things must be determined anew" (GS 269). This statement is then followed by the claim that conscience now tells us that we must become the persons we are (GS 270). This coupling of a revaluation of values with the task of becoming who one is points back to *Schopenhauer as Educator*, in which both projects are first adumbrated (SE 3), and it points forward to two of Nietzsche's final works: *Ecce Homo*, the work in which Nietzsche explains how he became what he is, and *The Antichrist*, the work in which Nietzsche sets out to revalue values.

The prolepticism of *The Gay Science* is also important for my own reading of *Zarathustra* IV and how *Zarathustra* relates to Nietzsche's subsequent works. I agree with Brobjer that the function of *Zarathustra* IV is to transition from *Zarathustra* I–III to Nietzsche's subsequent works and a project of revaluation of values. However, I also argue that the satyr play of *Zarathustra* IV is an interlude between the tragedy of *Zarathustra* and what I think is the Dionysian comedy of Nietzsche's 1888 works. Whereas *Twilight of the Idols*, *The Case of Wagner*, *The Antichrist*, and *Nietzsche contra Wagner* constitute a comic *agon*, *Ecce Homo* functions as a *parabasis* and so the centerpiece of this comedy. I have presented evidence for this reading elsewhere and explained the notions of an *agon* and a *parabasis* in more detail (see Meyer 2012; 2018), but I will point out here that Nietzsche often mentions comedy in tandem with tragedy as a response to the death of God (GS 153) and as a means of making life at least bearable (GS 107). Indeed, he begins *The Gay Science* by claiming that waves of uncountable laughter will overwhelm even the greatest of tragedians (GS 1). Applied to Nietzsche's works, it means that Nietzsche is already promising that a comedy will follow upon the tragedy of *Zarathustra*. If this is right, Nietzsche's works exhibit all four poetic genres associated with the Greek god Dionysus: tragedy (*Zarathustra* I–III), satyr play (*Zarathustra* IV), comedy (his 1888 works), and dithyramb (*Dithyrambs of Dionysus*).

Although such a reading explains the status of *Zarathustra* IV as an "interlude," it says little about the works that Nietzsche wrote between *Zarathustra* IV and the comedy of his 1888 writings. The first of these is *Beyond Good and Evil* (1886). We know from an 1886 letter to Jacob Burkhardt that Nietzsche understands *Beyond Good and Evil* to be closely related to *Zarathustra*, presenting it as saying much the same thing but in a much different style (KSB 7:756). However, we can establish an even deeper connection. We also know from Nietzsche's notes that he closely linked the eternal recurrence, which is the fundamental conception of *Zarathustra*, with the concept of "beyond good and evil" (KSA 11:26[325]). As I argue in the next chapter, the eternal recurrence plays a central role in Nietzsche's larger aim of completing a system of naturalism that puts an end to morality, and one of the upshots of this naturalization process is the restoration of what Nietzsche calls the "innocence of becoming." So construed, the standpoint that Nietzsche occupies in *Beyond Good and Evil* is a direct result of the teachings and the drama of *Zarathustra*.[35]

Immediately after writing *Beyond Good and Evil*, Nietzsche set out to republish some of his previous works, adding prefaces to *The Birth* and the free spirit works. Although these prefaces largely focus on his philosophical development, there are two important moments I want to highlight for understanding Nietzsche's post-*Zarathustra* works as a comedy. First, Nietzsche ends the preface of the 1886 edition of *The Birth* by quoting extensively from *Zarathustra* IV. Specifically, he claims that in place of the comfort provided by the otherworldly metaphysics of his first work, he now recommends the this-worldly comfort of Dionysian laughter that Zarathustra extolls to the higher humans in *Zarathustra* IV (BT "ASC":7). Second, the developmental story Nietzsche tells in these prefaces culminates in the preface of the 1887 edition of *The Gay Science*, and that preface concludes with a critique of the will to truth. Specifically, Nietzsche associates the desire to know the truth with the desire to see everything naked, and he argues that there is something indecent about this drive. In the end, Nietzsche claims that the truth just might be Baubo, an obscene figure from Greek mythology known for inciting laughter (GS "Pref":4).

This is not the only reference to laughter and comedy in the 1887 preface to *The Gay Science*. The first section couples a reference to "incipit tragoedia" with the phrase, "incipit parodia" (GS "Pref":1). Although many have followed Walter Kaufmann in thinking that both "incipit tragoedia" and "incipit parodia" refer to *Zarathustra* and therefore try to understand *Zarathustra* as both a tragedy and a parody,[36] I think it is a proleptic reference to the comedy that Nietzsche will write in his 1888 works. By supplementing "incipit tragoedia" with "incipit parodia" in the 1887 edition, Nietzsche is drawing upon the themes of laughter and comedy already present in the 1882 edition, and he thereby creates a double ending to the work[37]: whereas the 1882 edition transitions to the tragedy of *Zarathustra* I–III, the 1887 edition points forward to the comedy of the 1888 works.

If this is right, it still raises the question regarding the role that the *Genealogy* (1887) might play in relation to Nietzsche's own comedy. Here, it should be noted that the *Genealogy* is meant to complete and clarify the views expressed in *Beyond Good and Evil* (KSA 14:377). Moreover, it is interesting to note the parallels between *Human* and *Daybreak*, on the one hand, and *Beyond Good and Evil* and the *Genealogy*. Whereas both *Human* and *Beyond Good and Evil* focus on a range of fundamental questions in the areas of philosophy, ontology, aesthetics, and ethics, *Daybreak* and the *Genealogy* focus primarily on morality. The suggestion here is that just as *Human* and *Daybreak* can be understood as first parts of a series of works that eventually unfold into the tragedy and satyr play of *Zarathustra*, *Beyond Good and Evil* and the *Genealogy* can be understood as foundational works that flow into a Dionysian comedy.[38] Indeed, both the preface and the final sections of the *Genealogy* suggest just this. Whereas Nietzsche claims in the preface that "our old morality too is part *of the comedy*" and subtly refers to himself as "the grand old eternal comic poet of our existence" (GM "Pref":7), the *Genealogy* concludes with the claim that comedians are the only ones capable of harming the ascetic ideal (GM III:27).

Indeed, when we look at the works Nietzsche wrote after *Zarathustra* III and before 1888, we find that they *all* conclude with some significant reference to laughter or comedy. For instance, *Beyond Good and Evil* ends with the idea that philosophers should be ranked according to their ability to laugh (BGE 294). My view is that these references are designed to point readers toward the comedy that Nietzsche enacts in his 1888 works. As I have argued elsewhere, this comedy is grounded in two structural elements common to what is known as "Old" or "Dionysian" comedy: the *agon* and the *parabasis*.[39] Whereas Nietzsche's *agon* with the likes of Socrates, Wagner, and Paul has been well documented,[40] my claim is that this *agon*, enacted in works such as *Twilight of the Idols*, *The Case of Wagner*, and *The Antichrist*, should be understood as part of Nietzsche's comedy. This *agon*, in turn, revolves around what is known as a *parabasis*, which functions as the centerpiece of comedy. In terms of Nietzsche's works, I locate the comic *parabasis* in *Ecce Homo*, the work in which Nietzsche, like Aristophanes in the *Clouds*, proclaims his special relationship with Dionysus.

Although casting Nietzsche's 1888 works as a comedy explains why he repeatedly emphasizes his discipleship to Dionysus, some might worry that such a reading undercuts the seriousness of his 1888 works and undermines his quest to become who he is and revalue values. However, I think comedy is compatible with both projects. Because comedy provides a space in which the poet is liberated from convention and social norms, the comic poet can freely create who she is and transfigure her persona into an aesthetic phenomenon. At the same time, Old Comedy often imagines a world in which reigning conventions are overturned and a new world emerges, and a life-affirming atmosphere of celebration and revelry ensues. Indeed, comedy comes from the Greek word *komos*, and a *komos* was a procession or drunken revel that celebrated all the life-affirming forces (sexuality, drunkenness) that Christianity would later condemn.[41] Thus, interpreting Nietzsche's 1888 works as a comedy goes hand in hand with the idea that he is celebrating a victory over the Christian-moral understanding of the world that dominated Europe for almost two millennia and culminated in Schopenhauer's nihilism.

If this reading of Nietzsche's late works is right, then *Zarathustra* is not the only highpoint in Nietzsche's overall project: just as the free spirit works that precede *Zarathustra* crescendo into Nietzsche's own tragedy, the works that come after *Zarathustra*, including the double ending of the 1887 edition of *The Gay Science*, crescendo into Nietzsche's own comedy. Nevertheless, it can be argued that *Zarathustra* is the lynchpin around which much, if not all, of Nietzsche's corpus revolves. As a tragedy, it points back to his first work, *The Birth of Tragedy*. As a tragedy and a satyr play, it transitions the reader forward to the Dionysian comedy contained in Nietzsche's 1888 works. So understood, we can begin to see why Nietzsche attributed such importance to *Zarathustra* and why wrestling with *Zarathustra* is necessary for anyone attempting to understand Nietzsche as he understood himself.

NOTES

1 The translation of *Übermensch* is difficult and controversial. I think the best translation is "superhuman." This is close to and inspired by the translation offered by Loeb and Tinsley (2019:748–757). However, I resist their attempt to translate *Übermensch* with the plural, "superhumans," in all cases. Because of the perplexities here, I will use the untranslated German throughout this text. I also quote from the Kaufmann translation which uses "overman."
2 As Loeb (2010:1n1) explains, Nietzsche uses two German terms for the same concept, "*Wiederkehr*" and "*Wiederkunft*," which are often translated as "return" and "recurrence," respectively. Like Loeb, I do not believe there is an important philosophical distinction between the two, and I will default to using "eternal recurrence" when speaking more generally about the concept.
3 Leiter explicitly applies this to the will to power, but he would likely extend the concept to include the cosmological version of eternal recurrence.
4 There is an entire tradition of pessimists that follow Schopenhauer. See Beiser for an overview of this tradition, even though Beiser's definition of pessimism corresponds to what I am calling evaluative pessimism and therefore implicitly denies that Nietzsche is a part of this tradition (2016:4).
5 See Soll (1988:113–114) for a similar distinction. See Creasy (2020: Chs.2–3) for a developed account of nihilism that largely corresponds to my own view. In Meyer (2019b), I briefly present nihilism as the judgment that the world

INTRODUCTION TO *THUS SPOKE ZARATHUSTRA* 33

ought not be (and therefore a judgment linked to the evaluative pessimism of Silenus) (KSA 12:9[60]).

6   Bleeckere (1995) also discusses the close connection between *Zarathustra* and *The Birth*.
7   See Halliwell (1996) on this ancient quarrel between Plato and his poetic predecessors and the idea that the "tragic," for Plato, represented an entire way of life and larger worldview. On this point, Plato and Nietzsche agree.
8   See Meyer (2014) for more on this quarrel.
9   Remhof (2022) has argued that Nietzsche is a metaphysician and has criticized me for claiming he is not. The argument, however, trades on the definition of "metaphysics." Here, I will use the term as Aristotle, Schopenhauer, and Nietzsche used it, a use which entails a commitment to the existence of entities such as "beings" or "things-in-themselves" that transcend what is directly perceived by the senses. Like Remhof, I think Nietzsche is clearly a metaphysician in the contemporary sense of the term and can be understood as trying to naturalize metaphysics. Indeed, I have argued that Nietzsche's views can be associated with a contemporary theory—known as ontic structural realism—that "naturalizes metaphysics" (2018b). To help avoid confusion, I will often refer to the metaphysical tradition Nietzsche critiques as "transcendent metaphysics."
10 Leiter also attributes to Nietzsche a form of fatalism, but he says relatively little about *Zarathustra* in this context. He also defines Nietzsche's fatalism differently. For Leiter, Nietzsche's fatalism is the view that "the basic character of each individual's life is fixed in advance in virtue of an individual's nature, that is, the largely immutable physiological and psychological facts that make the person who she is" (2001:283). For Leiter, these facts "significantly circumscribe the possible trajectories" of one's life. They do not (along with environmental factors), however, determine "*all the details* of one's life" in advance (288). I think this view is too weak, and it is not wholly supported by Nietzsche's texts. In contrast, I use fatalism and determinism largely synonymously, with the common idea that natural necessity governs the world and fixes all the facts such that things or events cannot be other than they are.
11 See Vivarelli (1989), Söring (1990), and Haase (1994) for more on this point.
12 Nietzsche was also frustrated with himself for relying on Wagner rather than having the courage to take on the project himself.
13 See, for instance, Huddleston (2019:346).
14 See Meyer (2019) for a detailed defense of this point.
15 See Young (2010:366) and Higgins (1987:100).
16 However, *The Will to Power* should not be equated with the *Nachlass*. The *Nachlass* consists of all of Nietzsche's literary remains that extends well beyond the period of *The Will to Power*. *The Will to Power* was compiled from selected portions of the later *Nachlass*.
17 See Brinton (1948: Ch.7).
18 See Brinton (1948: Ch.8).
19 Schacht's most recent book (2023) is another attempt to explain and defend Nietzsche's way of doing philosophy. However, in contrast to his 1983 book,

he does so by paying attention to the order and structure of Nietzsche's published works, including *Zarathustra*.

20 Leiter also argues that we ought to avoid attributing to Nietzsche substantive views that may seem weak or silly by contemporary standards (2013:594). Here it should be noted that this is not an idiosyncratic way of approaching texts in the history of philosophy. Leiter, Clark, and Schacht can be understood as offering what is known as a "rational reconstruction" of Nietzsche's views—one that primarily aims to present an interpretation that is philosophically attractive for contemporary readers—rather than a "historical" or "contextual" reconstruction that primarily aims at historical accuracy.

21 Burnham and Jesinghausen also published a commentary in 2010, but I find it less insightful than the three works mentioned above. Other works include Santaniello (2005) and Luchte's (2008) collection of essays.

22 Although published just as I was completing this manuscript, Grätz's work has been immensely helpful. Other important works in German scholarship include Bennholdt-Thomsen (1974), Zittel (2000), and Flucher (2022).

23 See the appendix for an overview and my interpretation of Nietzsche's published (and some unpublished) works that is the basis for the next two sections of this chapter. See Löwith (1997:23) for an alternative but overlapping periodization of Nietzsche's works.

24 To be clear, I am not opposed to these efforts. Indeed, I am currently co-editing a Cambridge Elements project with Kaitlyn Creasy in which we hope to publish more than 30 short volumes based on this approach ("What is Nietzsche's Theory of X?"). What I do oppose is the extent to which this is the dominant, perhaps even exclusive, way of approaching Nietzsche's texts in contemporary scholarship.

25 Mark Alfano's (2019) recent use of digital humanities techniques to make Nietzsche's scholarship more rigorous and systematic continues in the tradition of Danto, as his method consists in gathering Nietzsche's various statements on a given topic with little concern for the text or context in which they occur.

26 Also see KSB 7:730.

27 For this reason, it is puzzling why commentators like Huddleston (2019) separate *Daybreak* from *The Gay Science*. If there is a possible break in Nietzsche's free spirit period, it is between the second appendix of *Human* (i.e., *The Wanderer and His Shadow*) and *Daybreak*.

28 Taken from the Kaufmann translation of *The Gay Science* (1974:30) and KSB 6:256.

29 Gooding-Williams (2001) and Loeb (2010) locate these transformations in *Zarathustra*. Clayton (1985:183) suggests that "the whole of Zarathustra's message is contained" in the passage and that "the structure of the first book's first three parts" is "laid bare." Lampert (1986:35) sees them as a preview of the speeches of the first part. In contrast, Heller (1973) applies the transformations to Nietzsche's own life and development.

30 See Meyer (2019) for a detailed defense of this claim. Brobjer (2008:36) also argues that Nietzsche understood the three metamorphoses as something that

applied to his own development. See KSA 11:26[47] for evidence in support of this reading.
31 See KSB 5:734 as evidence of this distinction and Nietzsche's transformation in relation to philosophy.
32 Loeb's interpretation of Nietzsche's post-*Zarathustra* works can also be found in (2006) and (2021a).
33 In *Ecce Homo*, Nietzsche does not explicitly say that these books are fishhooks for "the superior insights of *Zarathustra*."
34 Also see Röllin (2012:105) on this point.
35 Gooding-Williams (2001:26–27) also stresses the continuity between *Zarathustra* and *Beyond Good and Evil*.
36 See Zavatta (2022) for a recent example of this. Also see Zittel (2000:132ff.) and Tevenar (2013).
37 I borrow the idea of a "double ending" from Groddeck (1997).
38 Nietzsche also characterizes the *Genealogy* as "three decisive preliminary studies by a psychologist for a revaluation of all values" (EH "Books" GM). Thus, it is clearly a transitional work that points forward to Nietzsche's later works.
39 See Biles (2011) for an understanding of the *parabasis* within the overall agonistic atmosphere of Old Comedy.
40 See Acampora (2013).
41 For more on the *komos*, see Pütz (2003). As she writes, "the symposium and komos are mainly employed in comedy in order to create an atmosphere of exuberance (fitting the nature of the genre), usually in a celebration of a victory or an improvement within the community" (2003:8).

2

THE TRAGEDY AND SATYR PLAY OF *ZARATHUSTRA*

In the first chapter, I talked generally about Nietzsche's life and works and made a case for why reading *Zarathustra* is important both on its own terms and for understanding Nietzsche's larger project. The case I presented depended on understanding *Zarathustra* I–III as a tragedy and *Zarathustra* IV as a satyr play. In this chapter, I want to develop a framework for interpreting the work in this way. A tradition of reading *Zarathustra* as a tragedy and a satyr play is starting to develop in Anglo-American scholarship, and I want to contribute to this tradition with my own reading of the text. In so doing, I stress the way in which the work roughly follows the theory of tragedy Nietzsche developed in *The Birth of Tragedy*, responds to the tragic worldview that Nietzsche unpacks in *Human*, completes a system of naturalism with the doctrines of the will to power and the eternal recurrence, and points forward to the comedy of Nietzsche's 1888 works.

2.1 INTERPRETING *ZARATHUSTRA*

Anyone approaching *Zarathustra* for the first time will find it a bewildering text. This is even more so if *Zarathustra* is the first text by Nietzsche that one encounters. This was how I first came to Nietzsche, and it was nearly impossible to make sense of almost anything in *Zarathustra*. The purpose of my efforts here is, borrowing language from Gudrun von Tevenar, to "tame" the text by making it more intelligible to the reader than it would otherwise be without such a commentary (2013:272). This runs the risk of sacrificing the complexity, nuance, and metaphoricity of the text for the sake of intelligibility and understanding. *Zarathustra* is undoubtedly a poetic text that must be approached anew with each reading, and the poetic language, symbols, and imagery can always be subject to fresh interpretations. At the same time, one cannot begin to appreciate the text without having some provisional sense of its nature, purpose, and structure.

This, of course, presupposes that such a structure exists. Some scholars, however, have doubted this. For instance, Nehamas has claimed that the most serious problem with *Zarathustra* is that it "resists a unified reading, concealing its general structure and strategy, its overall point" (2012:124). Arthur Danto has claimed that *Zarathustra*, like *The Birth*, lacks any sort of ordered development, and so the text can be entered at any point (1965:19–20). Similarly, Julian Young asserts that *"Zarathustra* is little more than a collection of its hero's 'speeches'" (2010:367).

According to Robert Pippin, *Zarathustra* is so inaccessible because it is not clear what kind of work it is supposed to be. The book either resists categorization or seems to fall into a wide range of genres. Pippin lists different possibilities: an epic poem, a novel, a dithyramb, a tragedy, or music (1988:46). As Jörg Salaquarda points out (2012:51), Nietzsche himself referred to the first book of *Zarathustra* in a variety of ways in his letters. In one letter, he calls it a sort of "moral preaching" (KSB 6:321). In another to his publisher, he writes: "it is a 'poem,' or a fifth 'Gospel' or something for which there is no name" (KSB 6:327). Elsewhere, Nietzsche claims that the work is a "symphony" (KSB 6:321), an idea that Graham Parkes has developed in some detail (2008).

Some earlier treatments of *Zarathustra* argued that the work is fundamentally about language and communication. In the German secondary literature, Anke Bennholdt-Thomsen places the text in a long philosophical tradition that considers the literary form of philosophy just as important as the content of its philosophical claims; in this way, it opens the age-old question of the relationship between philosophy and poetry (1974:2; see also Loeb 2013). In Anglo-American literature, Harold Alderman has argued that *Zarathustra* explores the way in which philosophical doctrines cannot be separated from the style in which they are communicated. For these reasons, he claims that *Zarathustra* is "a revolution in the art of philosophical communication" (1977:38).

Kathleen Higgins also understands Nietzsche to be dealing with questions of communication and the limits of discourse in *Zarathustra*. In particular, she argues that Nietzsche writes a work of fiction to engage in indirect communication, which allows Nietzsche to communicate philosophical ideas with a temporal dimension (1987:115–116). At the same time, Higgins looks at the question of genre, and she identifies three possibilities: parody, tragedy, and *Bildungsroman*. It is a parody because Zarathustra functions as "a parodic counterpart" to Socrates and Jesus. It is a tragedy, first, because it expresses a tragic worldview and, second, because Zarathustra fails to come to terms with the meaning of life. According to Higgins, it is the recurrent failure of Zarathustra that links the tragic work to the notion of a *Bildungsroman* (or a narrative of education). On this view, Zarathustra's failures are occasions for self-development and maturity (1987:104).

In a similar vein, Tevenar has argued that *Zarathustra* can be read as a parody, a tragedy, and a counter-ideal to the ascetic ideal. According to Tevenar, Nietzsche's mention of "incipit parodia" in the 1887 preface to *The Gay Science* counts as evidence for reading *Zarathustra* as a parody, and she points not only to the slapdash nature of *Zarathustra* IV but also to the more refined parody and irony that runs throughout the first three books. However, Tevenar also notes that Nietzsche attaches far too much significance to the work for it simply to be a parody (2013:274). Thus, she also understands it as a tragedy. Although she acknowledges that its tragic nature is not immediately obvious, she ultimately references the framework of *The Birth*, arguing that the tragedy of *Zarathustra* consists in Zarathustra taking on the heroic task of affirming all of life's joys and pains (2013:275).[1]

The idea that *Zarathustra* is a tragedy has been considered by several interpreters, and I want to focus my attention on three books on *Zarathustra* that both entertain this idea and come to different conclusions on the matter: Laurence Lampert's *Nietzsche's Teaching* (1986); T. K. Seung's *Nietzsche's Epic of the Soul* (2005); and Paul Loeb's *The Death of Zarathustra* (2010). Although they come to different conclusions about the tragic nature of *Zarathustra*, the attempts of these authors to wrestle with the narrative structure and genre of *Zarathustra* inevitably raise the important question regarding the status of *Zarathustra* IV, and the status of *Zarathustra* IV, in turn, raises questions about the meaning of both "incipit tragoedia" and "incipit parodia."

To be sure, Lampert does not make the question of genre the guiding principle of his interpretation. For him, *Zarathustra* is a "fable that chronicles the evolution of a philosopher who grows into the task that has befallen him as a result of what he has learned about mankind and its history" (1986:2). However, he does claim, toward the end of his text, that *Zarathustra* is the tragedy in which "Nietzsche undertakes for himself 'the supreme task' that he had earlier ascribed to Richard Wagner in Bayreuth" (1986:232). As Lampert develops his interpretation, key elements of Nietzsche's understanding of tragedy take centerstage. In particular, the figure of Dionysus plays an important role in Lampert's interpretation of *Zarathustra* III. As Lampert notes, both Dionysus and the Greek mythical figure of Ariadne go unmentioned in the text, but Zarathustra's calling upon the eternal recurrence at the end of *Zarathustra* is intimately connected with the Dionysian mysteries surrounding the union of the two figures (1986:234).

The union of Dionysus and Ariadne, however, occurs at the end of *Zarathustra* III, and perhaps the most notable—and most controversial—feature of Lampert's reading is that he argues that *Zarathustra* IV is a mere fragment of a larger whole that does not exist (accordingly, Lampert places his treatment of *Zarathustra* IV in an "appendix"). This will certainly come as a surprise to a reader approaching *Zarathustra* for the first time, especially since *Zarathustra* is now commonly published as if the four parts formed a single, unified text. However, the publication details of the text indicate that Nietzsche thought of *Zarathustra* IV as somewhat separate from the first three parts. As noted in the first chapter, Nietzsche considers *Zarathustra* IV to be a "*Zwischenspiel*" or "interlude," and Lampert argues that it is an interlude between *Zarathustra* I–III and a series of additional parts of *Zarathustra*—up to two more, which would have given us *Zarathustra* V and VI—that Nietzsche ultimately decided not to write. As Loeb explains, one problem with Lampert's reading is that Nietzsche continues to refer to *Zarathustra* IV as an "interlude" in 1888, long after he had abandoned any plans for further parts (2010:88–89). It is for this reason that I think, following Brobjer and in contrast to Loeb's own interpretation, that *Zarathustra* IV must be an interlude between *Zarathustra* I–III and Nietzsche's post-*Zarathustra* writings.

More so than Lampert, Seung places the question of genre at the center of his interpretation, and, in addressing this question, Seung confronts the problem of how *Zarathustra* IV relates to *Zarathustra* I–III. He begins by resisting the idea that *Zarathustra* is a collection of speeches. Instead, he presents Zarathustra as a hero, but not a hero of Greek tragedy. Greek tragedy results in the destruction of the tragic hero, and Seung claims that Zarathustra never suffers such a fate (even though Nietzsche had sketched plans for Zarathustra's death). Instead, *Zarathustra* is tragic only in the sense that it is a serious work (rather than a lighthearted comedy), and therefore Seung claims it is better to think of *Zarathustra*, like Goethe's *Faust*, as an equally serious work of epic poetry (2005:xi). This is the basis for the title of Seung's book: *Nietzsche's Epic of the Soul*.

One of the reasons Seung must resist reading the work as a tragedy—especially if one associates the genre with the destruction of the tragic hero—is because he thinks that *Zarathustra* IV is the proper conclusion of the work. Since *Zarathustra* IV does not end with the destruction of Zarathustra, *Zarathustra* cannot be a tragedy in this sense. Moreover, by making *Zarathustra* IV an essential part of Nietzsche's epic poem, Seung must reject interpretations of *Zarathustra* IV that read it as a form of parody, low comedy, or satyr play (2005:xxi). According to Seung, the four parts of *Zarathustra* stage a drama in which the glorification of an autonomous human will, symbolized by the figure of the *Übermensch* in *Zarathustra* I, comes into conflict with "the crushing weight of human necessity," symbolized by the eternal recurrence in *Zarathustra* II. In *Zarathustra* III, there is a great battle between these two elements, and it is not until *Zarathustra* IV in "The Drunken Song" that the individual will is finally "fused with the cosmic necessity of the whole universe" (2005:xxi–xxii).

There is much to recommend in Seung's interpretation. I, too, will highlight the initial tension between the ideal of the *Übermensch* and the necessity implied by the eternal recurrence and argue that *Zarathustra* exhibits what Seung calls a dialectical structure (2005:xxii). However, the attempt to see *Zarathustra* IV as extending the narrative of *Zarathustra* I–III conflicts with much of the philological evidence which supports Lampert's claim that *Zarathustra* IV is significantly distinct from the first three parts. Moreover, even if we grant that the "Drunken Song" marks the point at which the individual will is fused with cosmic necessity—and so downplay the significance of the ending of *Zarathustra* III—we are still left wondering why *Zarathustra* IV lacks a proper ending. Seung attempts to explain this "baffling feature" of the text by arguing that the dialectical motor that animates the text is interminable and eternal. Thus, there is no final closure to this process, and the epic may turn into an endless repetition of cycles (2005:359). I find this answer unsatisfying, and it points back to reasons for following Brobjer in reading *Zarathustra* IV as an interlude between *Zarathustra* I–III and Nietzsche's subsequent writings.

In my view, Loeb offers a better account of the relationship between the four parts. He has argued that *Zarathustra* I–III should be understood as a tragic trilogy and *Zarathustra* IV a satyr play.[2] As Loeb explains, this parallels the structure of ancient Greek theater, in which tragedians were asked to submit three—often related—tragedies along with a satyr play, and I agree with Loeb that this structure can be used to understand the four parts of *Zarathustra*. However, as I noted in the first chapter, Loeb argues that *Zarathustra* IV is an analeptic satyr play, such that the events of *Zarathustra* IV are nestled within the narrative of *Zarathustra* III. It is on this point that we part ways.

Loeb situates his reading between Lampert's claim that *Zarathustra* IV should be understood as an "unfortunate afterthought" and "ironic readings" of the text developed by Higgins (1987), Pippin (1988), and Shapiro (1989) (Loeb 2010:85).[3] Important here is that some of these ironic readers have followed Fink (2003) in interpreting *Zarathustra* IV as a satyr play. Whereas Higgins places *Zarathustra* IV within a tradition of Menippean satire, finding parallels with Lucian's *Story of the Ass* and Apelius' *Golden Ass* (1987: Ch.7), Shapiro argues that *Zarathustra* IV is a commentary on BGE 223 in which Zarathustra becomes a comic *Hanswurst* or clown in producing a carnival in grand style (1989:99).[4] According to Loeb's rendering of the ironic reading, *Zarathustra* IV is essential to *Zarathustra* as a whole, but it is essential because it undermines the natural culmination of *Zarathustra* III as well as the "doctrines" that Zarathustra is said to teach in the first three parts. As Higgins writes, Nietzsche presents Zarathustra as a kind of an ass in *Zarathustra* IV, and this forces us to "question whether Nietzsche intended to stand behind the previous 'doctrinal' parts of the book at all" (1988:149). Like Loeb, I find this reading unpersuasive, especially because of the important role that the eternal recurrence plays in Nietzsche's 1884 notebooks, writings that occur just prior to composing *Zarathustra* IV, and his continued commitment to a revaluation of values is based on the doctrine of the eternal recurrence (see Brobjer 2023).

The advantage of Loeb's reading is that it makes *Zarathustra* IV an integral part of *Zarathustra* and yet finds in *Zarathustra* III a natural ending to the narrative of the whole. For Loeb, *Zarathustra* III must mark the end of the narrative because it culminates in Zarathustra dying "by his own hand" (2010:199). There are, however, problems with Loeb's reading. First, there is no explicit support in the text itself or even in Nietzsche's notes and letters for the claim that *Zarathustra* is an analeptic satyr play. This does not render Loeb's thesis false, but it does say that his reading rests on inferences made to resolve the interpretive riddles that he and other readers have found in the text. Indeed, if this was Nietzsche's intention in writing *Zarathustra* IV, he left very few clues for the ordinary reader to decipher the analeptic structure of the text. This is especially true once one tries to identify exactly where *Zarathustra* IV is supposed to fit into the narrative of *Zarathustra* I–III.

To his credit, Loeb tackles this question head on, arguing that the events of *Zarathustra* IV can be inserted into the opening sections of "On Old and New Tablets" of *Zarathustra* III (2010:98). And Loeb provides some evidence to support this reading. For instance, he notes that the first section of "Tablets" refers to Zarathustra waiting for his signs to come, namely, the laughing lion with the flock of doves; only then will he go under and "go among men once more" (ZIII "Tablets":1). According to Loeb, this sign must come *before* Zarathustra summons the eternal recurrence at the end of *Zarathustra* III (whereby he goes under), and since this sign only comes at the end of *Zarathustra* IV in "The Sign," we must conclude that the events of *Zarathustra* IV come before Zarathustra summons the eternal recurrence and "goes under" at the end of *Zarathustra* III.

Although Loeb is right to get us to wonder about the possible link between the two sections, there are concerns here too. First, we are told at the beginning of *Zarathustra* IV that months and years have passed such that Zarathustra's hair is now white. For Loeb's reading to hold, it must mean that this time also elapses within the narrative of *Zarathustra* III. But such a chronological gap is nearly impossible to detect. Loeb claims that it implicitly occurs somewhere within sections three through six of "Tablets" in *Zarathustra* III, and it is evidenced by Zarathustra shifting his audience from himself in the opening of "Tablets" to his "brothers" in section six (2010:125). The shift from Zarathustra speaking to himself to addressing his brothers is puzzling, but it hardly seems to warrant the idea that years have passed in the middle of the "Tablets" chapter. Indeed, such a reading conflicts with the opening of "The Convalescent" in which we are told that Zarathustra awakens "not long after his return to the cave," which is something that occurred before Zarathustra addressed himself at the beginning of "Tablets."[5] Second, it is not clear that Zarathustra's reference to going under in the first section of "Tablets" refers to his teaching of the eternal recurrence (as Loeb holds). Although Zarathustra does associate going under with this teaching, "going under" is also a process by which Zarathustra leaves the solitude of his cave to associate with human beings.[6] The latter meaning of the phrase is explicit in section one of "Tablets," and this is what Zarathustra seems to be doing at the end of *Zarathustra* IV. So understood, the passage in "Tablets" does not require the coming of Zarathustra's sign before he summons the eternal recurrence; instead, it only requires that the sign comes before Zarathustra again leaves his solitude and goes down from his cave to be among people, which is what likely occurs at the end of *Zarathustra* IV with the coming of his sign.[7]

Loeb bases his interpretation of *Zarathustra* IV on an understanding of the ancient Greek festival in which these plays were performed in honor of Dionysus. In so doing, he appeals to the work of both Dana Sutton (1980) and P.E. Easterling (1997). From Sutton, he gleans the idea that the events of a satyr play *can* happen within or even simultaneously to the events of the tragic trilogy. What this means is that *Zarathustra* IV, as satyr play, can narrate events that take place during the events of the tragedy in *Zarathustra* I–III and therefore it can be read as an analeptic satyr play. However, Easterling's account of tragedy implicitly speaks against Loeb's interpretation in one important respect. Specifically, she emphasizes that it is the same performers who are a tragic chorus of ordinary citizens during the tragic trilogy and then transformed into a chorus of satyrs in the satyr play (1997:38). This means that the chorus undergoes a transformation from having ordinary, everyday identities in tragedy to being mystical creatures and servants of Dionysus (satyrs) in the satyr play. The implication is that the drama of the tragic trilogy effects this transformation, and therefore one must first experience the events of the tragedy in order to be transformed into a child-like satyr. If this is right, a satyr play cannot simply be placed within the events of a tragedy. Even if the satyr play narrates events that chronologically occur within the narrative of the tragic trilogy, these events are nevertheless experienced by a chorus that is fundamentally different from the tragic chorus. Initiated into the mysteries of Dionysus, the satyr chorus now experiences the suffering and death characteristic of tragedy with a playful lack of seriousness and concern, and this attitude is a result of having experienced the tragedy that precedes the satyr play.

Applying this framework to *Zarathustra*, the relatively lighthearted humor of *Zarathustra* IV is a *result of* Zarathustra having successfully vanquished the spirit of gravity that pervades the tragedy of *Zarathustra* I–III. Thus, even if the events of *Zarathustra* IV occur within the narrative structure of *Zarathustra* I–III (and I am not convinced they do), it would be wrong to think that the function of *Zarathustra* IV (as a satyr play) is to fill in a narrative gap in *Zarathustra* I–III. On Loeb's reading, the spirit of gravity would still pervade the whole of *Zarathustra* IV, and this is clearly not the case. Instead, the purpose of a satyr play like *Zarathustra* IV is to show how events, regardless of when they occur chronologically, that typically evoke tragic seriousness can now be experienced from a perspective of play, frivolity, and laughter, and the key difference between the two experiences is whether one has been initiated into the mysteries of Dionysus by means of confronting the tragic elements of existence like nature, necessity, suffering, fate, and death.

Perhaps what ultimately motivates Loeb's analeptic reading is his view that Zarathustra dies at the end of *Zarathustra* III. If this is the case, then he must hold that any events narrated in *Zarathustra* IV, in which Zarathustra is still alive, chronologically precede the conclusion of *Zarathustra* III. However, there are reasons to reject Loeb's view that Zarathustra dies at the end of *Zarathustra* III (and this, in turn, undermines his "performative reading" of the text which relies on Zarathustra's death at the end of *Zarathustra* III (2010:6–7)). Specifically, Nietzsche sketched plans, after publishing *Zarathustra* III, to have Zarathustra die in subsequent parts of *Zarathustra* (See KSA 11:29[15]; 11:34[144]; 11:35[73]; 12:2[129]).[8] The simple idea is that Nietzsche would not have sketched plans for Zarathustra's eventual death after *Zarathustra* III if he had already sent him to his death at the end of *Zarathustra* III. Because Nietzsche never followed through on these plans, we can infer that Nietzsche never presents Zarathustra as dying in the biological sense over the course of the extant parts of *Zarathustra*.

Nevertheless, it is my view that Zarathustra experiences a kind of death at the end of *Zarathustra* III by accepting his role as the teacher of the eternal recurrence. Specifically, Zarathustra dies in the same way that the "old self" of a baptized Christian is said to die, such that the Christian believer is "reborn" as a "new self" in accepting Christ as her savior.[9] In *Zarathustra*, the form of this conversion is roughly the same, but the content is radically different. Rather than being initiated into a metaphysical beyond, the self that dies in *Zarathustra* is a non-natural conception of the self that stands above nature and fate, and the self that is reborn is wholly naturalized and united with fate, necessity, and eternity. In both cases, however, the biological entity lives on. Applied to *Zarathustra*, this means that Zarathustra lives on even after his old self "dies," but he lives on, in *Zarathustra* IV, as a transformed and transfigured self free from guilt and moral responsibility, now capable of child-like play. What this also means is that the events of *Zarathustra* IV can be seen as occurring after the events of *Zarathustra* III, even if we hold that Zarathustra experiences a ritual death in *Zarathustra* III, and this means that we can read *Zarathustra* I–III as a tragic trilogy that produces a transformation in Zarathustra such that it is followed by a satyr play of *Zarathustra* IV. At the end of *Zarathustra* IV, we find Zarathustra ready to leave his cave and pursue his work, and there are reasons for thinking that this work refers to Nietzsche's project of a revaluation of values that he undertakes in his subsequent writings.

2.2 EVIDENCE FOR READING *ZARATHUSTRA* AS A TRAGEDY AND SATYR PLAY

The purpose of the previous section was to give an overview of the secondary literature in the Anglo-American context with an eye to highlighting an increasing tendency to view *Zarathustra* I–III as a tragedy that includes some sort of satyr play in *Zarathustra* IV. In this section, I want to unpack some basic information about the text that includes both its genesis and Nietzsche's retrospective interpretation of it, and I again want to do so with an eye to providing justification for reading the text as a tragedy and a satyr play.[10]

Perhaps the best place to start in trying to understand *Zarathustra* is the commentary Nietzsche provides in *Ecce Homo*. To be sure, one needs to be aware that Nietzsche is not offering a straightforward commentary that aims at maximal accuracy, and so one cannot blindly rely on everything he says. However, it does offer a good starting point, especially when we can corroborate Nietzsche's claims with other evidence. Nietzsche begins by pointing to what he calls the "fundamental idea" of the text, the eternal recurrence, and he explains that this idea came to him in almost mystical fashion in August 1881. He also refers to an event that took place a few months earlier; it was a rendezvous in northern Italy with Peter Gast (Heinrich Köselitz) in which he (re-)discovered the power of music. It was there that he became "pregnant" with the idea of *Zarathustra*, an idea which came to fruition some eighteen months later in February of 1883 (EH "Books" Z:1).

I say "rediscovered" music because Nietzsche was wholly immersed in Wagnerian opera and convinced of its cultural significance in the early years of his adult life, and when Nietzsche broke with Wagner in 1876, he underwent a period in which he largely abstained from music as he began to compose the first of his free spirit works, *Human, All Too Human*. Thus, the rendezvous with Gast marks what Nietzsche calls a "profoundly decisive change in [...] taste," and this change is reflected not only in his renewed interested in discussing art in a work like *The Gay Science* but also in the production of his own poetry and music at this time. Whereas he writes *Idylls from Messina* in the spring of 1882 and adds a prelude to *The Gay Science* of poems, "Joke, Cunning, Revenge," he claims that "perhaps the whole of *Zarathustra* may be reckoned as music." Moreover, he points to the fact that he composed his own music in the interval between the spring of 1881 and the publication of *Zarathustra* I in 1883. This is his *Hymn to Life*, which he calls "a scarcely trivial symptom of my condition during that year when the Yes-saying pathos *par excellence*, which I call the tragic pathos, was alive in me to the highest degree" (EH "Books" Z:1).

The significance of the *Hymn to Life* can also be grasped by recalling the full title of Nietzsche's first work, *The Birth of Tragedy out of the Spirit of Music*. As he explains in *Ecce Homo*,

Nietzsche understands *Zarathustra* as the work in which his concept of the Dionysian (from *The Birth*) becomes a supreme deed (EH "Books" Z:6). Of course, if *Zarathustra* is Nietzsche's own tragedy, then the fact that Nietzsche wrote the *Hymn to Life* just prior to *Zarathustra* suggests that he wants to present his own tragedy as emerging out of the spirit of music. Indeed, there is another important connection Nietzsche establishes between the *Hymn to Life* and the theory of tragedy he offers in *The Birth*. In the last words of the *Hymn*, he writes that "pain is *not* considered an objection to life: 'If you have no more happiness to give me, well then! *You still have suffering*'" (EH "Books" Z:1). Based on his theory of tragedy, we know that although the Apollonian element of tragedy is supposed to affirm life through beautiful illusions, the Dionysian element of tragedy is nevertheless able to affirm pain and suffering itself (BT 24). So understood, the *Hymn to Life* is an important precursor to the tragedy of *Zarathustra*.

The *Hymn to Life* also points to other biographical facts about Nietzsche that are potentially relevant for understanding *Zarathustra*. Specifically, the text for the hymn was based on the 1881 poem, "Prayer for Life," by Lou Salomé, a young Russian aristocrat whom Nietzsche met in Rome in April 1882. Nietzsche had been in Messina, Italy, where he composed his *Idylls from Messina*, and his longtime intellectual companion Paul Reé set up Nietzsche's meeting with Salomé after Reé had met her at the home of feminist Malwida von Meysenbug in March.[11] Nietzsche found himself intensely attracted to her, but so did Reé, and any attraction Salomé had for Nietzsche was purely intellectual. This resulted in plans for an intellectual *ménage à trois*, but also marriage proposals from Nietzsche which Salomé ultimately rejected. Nietzsche met with Salomé in Tautenburg, Germany, in August 1882, just as *The Gay Science* was being released and only a few months before he would write the first book of *Zarathustra*. Despite their intense intellectual conversations and frequent contact, the meeting proved to be the beginning of the end of any hopes for a romantic relationship.

The fact that all this occurred as Nietzsche was putting the finishing touches on his previous book, *The Gay Science*, in the spring and summer of 1882 and just before he would write the first part of *Zarathustra* in January 1883 has lent itself to speculations about Nietzsche's motivations for composing *Zarathustra*. Did the Salomé "affair"—as biographers like Julian Young (2010) refer to it—influence Nietzsche to write the text? Did it, in turn, shape its contents? In short, is *Zarathustra* Nietzsche's attempt to work through the trauma of his romantic failures? These are all valid questions, and Nietzsche's sister, Elisabeth, speculates in her introduction to the text that her brother created Zarathustra as a "perfect friend" to compensate for the loneliness he felt in response to his failing relationship with both Salomé and Reé (1929:14–15). Similarly, Mazzino Montinari suggests that Nietzsche's experience with Salomé caused him to write a much different text from the one he sketched in his notes in 1881, such that he now endeavored to "make gold from the mire of his life" (2003:77).

Unfortunately, I cannot get into the details of Nietzsche's biography here, and I will leave it to others to speculate about their significance. What I will say is that I tend to think that if there is a connection between Nietzsche's personal life and his philosophical ambitions, the causality most often runs from the latter to the former. For instance, I do not think he happens to write what he does because of where he travels; instead, his decision to travel to certain places is likely based on what he plans to write. This might be the same with his interest in and engagement with Salomé, in the sense that Nietzsche may have been, at the time, looking for someone to take on the role of his Ariadne as he composes his own Dionysian tragedy. In short, I think that his personal life after 1876 is largely the product of his philosophical and artistic ambitions rather than the other way around.

To be sure, we know that Nietzsche had plans for some sort of work involving the figure of Zarathustra as well as the eternal recurrence well before meeting Salomé. Indeed, Nietzsche's sister mentions the sketches we find in his notebooks from the summer of 1881, even as she notes that his plans for the work ultimately changed. There are undoubtedly differences between these plans and the work itself, but it is nevertheless instructive to look at these notes. The first mention of Zarathustra in the *Nachlass* occurs in a short note under the title, "noon and eternity [*Mittag und Ewigkeit*]," and the subtitle, "**pointers** to a new life." It also includes a version of the opening words of *Zarathustra*, which are also found in GS 342 (KSA 9:1[195]). This is followed by what seems to be a preliminary plan for a four-part work that is linked to the previous reference to Zarathustra by the title, "Sketch of a New Way to Live" (KSA 9:11[197]).

Although it is minimal, the sketch provides some evidence for interpreting *Zarathustra* as a tragedy. Nietzsche compares the first book to the opening of Beethoven's *Ninth Symphony*, modifies Spinoza's "*Deus sive natura*" to read "*Chaos sive natura*," and refers to Prometheus bound in the Caucasus mountains, the subject of Aeschylus' *Prometheus Bound* and the source of the image on the front cover of Nietzsche's *The Birth of Tragedy*. In the second book, Nietzsche refers to Mephistopheles and the notion of incorporating experience, even "error," for the sake of knowledge. In the sketch for the third book, we find parallels to the third book of *Zarathustra*. Most notably, Nietzsche speaks of "the *last happiness of the solitary one*" who has become "his own self" and a "completed ego." As Paul Bishop points out, declaring selfishness (*Selbstsucht*) healthy and even holy is a central theme of *Zarathustra* III, and it is a point I will emphasize in my interpretation of the text (2005:71–75). For the final book, we have a sketch for what looks to be an affirmation of the eternal recurrence and a related refence to the Dionysian dithyramb: "Dithyrambic—all-embracing. 'Ring of eternity.' Desire to experience everything once more an infinite number of times."[12] This is expressed most explicitly in "The Drunken Song" near the end of *Zarathustra* IV. In sum, this note provides evidence for a work that is connected to the Dionysian genres of music, dithyramb, and tragedy with themes that all play a central role in the published version of *Zarathustra*.

The notes from this time also reveal Nietzsche's extensive reflections on—and justifications for—the idea of the eternal recurrence. The idea first appears as a title to a note, "The return of the same [*Die Wiederkunft des Gleichen*]," that contains a sketch with five parts. In the first three parts, the key notion of "*Einverleibung*" or "incorporation" is mentioned, and in the fifth section, we find the full locution, "the eternal return of the same," in combination with the notion of a "*Schwergewicht*" or "weight" that appears in the title of GS 341, "the greatest weight [*das grösste Schwergewicht*]" Finally, the note indicates that the best way for one to incorporate this idea is to teach it, and as we will see, the drama of *Zarathustra* revolves around Zarathustra's coming to terms with this task of teaching the eternal recurrence (KSA 9:11[141]). To do this, Zarathustra will have to defeat "the spirit of gravity [*der Geist der Schwere*]" such that he no longer experiences the eternal return as a "great weight."

Nietzsche penned these notes prior to writing *The Gay Science*, and we therefore have some reason for thinking that Nietzsche structures *The Gay Science* with *Zarathustra* in view. Here, much attention has rightly been given to the final three aphorisms of what was the fourth and final book of the 1882 edition of *The Gay Science* (see Loeb 2010: Ch.2). In the antepenultimate aphorism, "The dying Socrates," Nietzsche returns to key themes of *The Birth*. Not only does Nietzsche discuss a central figure of that work, Socrates, but he also appeals to its leitmotif: the affirmation and denial of life. As Loeb has rightly argued, the life-denying Socrates in GS 340 is implicitly presented as the antipode to the life-affirming Zarathustra in GS 342 (2010:45). Unlike Zarathustra, who eventually affirms life by teaching and "incorporating" the eternal recurrence, Socrates is presented as someone who suffers from life and secretly wishes for death. Thus, he feels indebted to Asclepius, the Greek god of medicine, for curing him of the disease of "life" (GS 340). For Socrates, the eternal repetition of his own existence would be the ultimate horror. As a result, we find Socrates happily drinking hemlock to end his life in what I think is Plato's own tragedy of the *Phaedo*.[13]

Although GS 340 ends with Nietzsche exhorting his readers to overcome even the Greeks, he seems to mean that we need to overcome only the Greeks starting with Socrates and those that follow him. One reason for reading the statement in this way is that Nietzsche explicitly associates the eternal recurrence, presented in the very next aphorism, with the "mystery teachings" of the Greek god Dionysus (KSA 10:8[15]; TI "What I Owe":5). In *The Birth*, Nietzsche closely associated tragedy with the mysteries of Dionysus (BT 10). In *The Gay Science*, there is no mention of Dionysus, but the eternal recurrence is clearly associated with the theme of affirming or denying life. Under the title of "The greatest weight," Nietzsche asks whether we would, upon being confronted with the idea that the world and so our lives were repeated an infinite number of times, embrace such a teaching with joy and delight or whether we would gnash our teeth and "curse the demon who spoke thus." In short, the primary function of the eternal recurrence is to determine whether we would affirm or deny existence, and this in turn depends on how well we are disposed to ourselves and to life (GS 341).

The question "The greatest weight" poses is left unanswered, and it will remain so until the conclusion of *Zarathustra* III. Important for my purposes is the fact that Nietzsche introduces the opening lines of *Zarathustra*—the text here is virtually identical to the text of *Zarathustra*[14]—under the title of "incipit tragoedia" or "let the tragedy begin" (GS 342). It is also important because it suggests that Nietzsche has little interest in abandoning the ancient Greeks *tout court*; the genre of tragedy is a Greek invention and, for Nietzsche, characteristic of an entire period of ancient Greece. Indeed, the reference to tragedy points back to Nietzsche's first work, *The Birth*, and it is in that work that Nietzsche casts tragedy as the art form most capable of affirming existence in the face of uncomfortable or even "deadly" truths. This idea can be mapped directly onto the final aphorisms of the 1882 edition of *The Gay Science*: the eternal recurrence poses the question, "to be or not to be," by confronting us with a potentially bleak understanding of existence (see KSA 12:5[71]), and this sets the stage for the tragedy of *Zarathustra* in which the question will be answered affirmatively.

Thus, we have reasons to think that Nietzsche consciously constructs the final aphorisms of the 1882 edition of *The Gay Science* to flow directly into the tragedy of *Zarathustra* in a way that harkens back to *The Birth*. There are reasons to think that this is also true of the entire fourth and final book of the 1882 edition of *The Gay Science*, which, unlike the other books of *The Gay Science*, bears its own title, "Sanctus Januarius." Much can be said here, and aphorisms such as "One thing is needful" (GS 290), "What one should learn from artists" (GS 299), and "Long live physics!" (GS 335) seem to project even beyond *Zarathustra* by foreshadowing the central task of a late work like *Ecce Homo*. However, the first aphorism—much like the last—implicitly refers to tragedy and speaks directly to the theme of life affirmation. At stake in the aphorism is nothing less than the task of becoming a "Yes-sayer." The connection to tragedy is less explicit, but Nietzsche links the task of becoming a "Yes-sayer" to the idea of "*amor fati*" or "love of fate" (GS 276).

With the introduction of *amor fati*, we begin to see that the essence of the tragedy of *Zarathustra* is the affirmation of a world characterized by fate and necessity. We know from *The Birth* that fate is essential to Nietzsche's understanding of the genre: not only does he emphasize the importance of *Oedipus Rex* in *The Birth*, but he also speaks of "the Aeschylean view of the world which envisages Moira enthroned above gods and men as eternal justice" (BT 9). We also know that the eternal recurrence is the fundamental concept of *Zarathustra*, and Nietzsche associates the eternal recurrence with both fate and necessity in his *Nachlass*. In an 1885 note, we learn that the eternal recurrence completes "fatalism" through the elimination of the "will" (he presumably has a notion of "free will" in mind that underwrites moral responsibility) (KSA 11:25[214]). In one note from 1881, Nietzsche associates the eternal recurrence with both "necessity" and "innocence," and this is followed by a reference to "the game of life." In both GS 109 and a note that forms the basis for GS 109, Nietzsche speaks of "the absolute necessity in everything" (KSA 9:11[201]) and claims that "there are only necessities" (GS 109). Because the eternal recurrence entails a form of necessity, we can readily see its close connection to *amor fati*. In both GS 276 and *Nachlass* notes, Nietzsche presents *amor fati* as the love of what is necessary (KSA 9:15[20], 16[22]). Finally, Nietzsche links *amor fati* to the god of tragedy, Dionysus: *Amor fati* means to "stand in a Dionysian relationship to existence" where one wants the world "as it is, without subtraction, exception, or selection—it wants the eternal circulation [*Kreislauf*]" (KSA 13:16[32]).[15]

What we see from this is that there is a clear connection between the idea announced at the beginning of Book IV of *The Gay Science* (*amor fati*) and the notions of the eternal recurrence (GS 341) and tragedy (GS 342) found at the end of the book.

Although Book IV is a special book in *The Gay Science* because it is the only book in the 1882 edition to have its own title, "Sanctus Januarius," and because it was composed separately from the first three books, there are reasons for thinking that Nietzsche also designed the first three books of *The Gay Science* to crescendo into the tragedy of *Zarathustra*. Most notably, *Zarathustra* begins with the presupposition that God is "dead." Although Nietzsche had announced the death of God as early as *The Wanderer* (WS 84), the reference to the death of God in *Zarathustra* is most certainly a reference to the famous "madman" passage in the third book of *The Gay Science* (GS 125). The death of God symbolizes the elimination of a metaphysical world, and the elimination of his shadow (GS 108) means overcoming the moral prejudices that were rooted in a belief in a transcendent God. Perhaps the most important of these moral prejudices is the belief that we have an obligation to pursue truth at all costs. According to Nietzsche, this imperative is rooted in a belief in a transcendent God (GS 344). Once God "dies," there is no longer any justification for this belief, and therefore one is no longer obligated to pursue truth at all costs. For this reason, the death of God and the elimination of his shadow in *The Gay Science* can be understood as the (self-)overcoming or *Selbstaufhebung* of the morality of truth (see GM III:27).

As I have argued elsewhere (Meyer 2019), the self-overcoming of the morality of truth—and so the overcoming of the idea that we are morally obligated to pursue truth at all costs—results in an important turn in the free spirit project that eventually makes a work like *Zarathustra* possible. This is because the morality of truth, which lies at the heart of what Nietzsche calls "asceticism," places significant restraints on what Nietzsche calls the "aesthetic justification" of existence through poetry and art. Although art and poetry can represent what Nietzsche sometimes calls the "terrible truth," they also traffic in what Nietzsche provocatively calls deceptions and even lies. Thus, Nietzsche explains in the *Genealogy* that art, rather than science, is most opposed to the ascetic ideal because art is the realm in which "the *lie* is sanctified and the *will to deception* has a good conscience" (GM III:25). The idea, then, is that *Zarathustra*, as a work of art that traffics in fictions and even "lies," both presupposes and is even made possible by the death of God and the elimination of his shadow.

The connection between the death of God and the liberation of art is most evinced in an aphorism that follows upon the "madman" passage in which God's death is announced. The title of the aphorism is "*Homo poeta*," and Nietzsche speaks of a tragedy of all tragedies, having slain all gods in the fourth act for the sake of morality. Nietzsche is referring here to the *Selbstaufhebung* of morality; it is out of the morality of truth that we kill God, and God's death, in turn, undermines the basis for the morality of truth. For my purposes, the conclusion of the aphorism is equally important. There, Nietzsche refers to both a tragic and comic solution to the death of God (GS 153). On my reading, the mention of tragedy and comedy are meant to proleptically refer to *Zarathustra* (tragedy) and the comedy that Nietzsche would come to write in 1888.

The idea, then, is that the death of God in *The Gay Science* creates an existential crisis to which a work of art like *Zarathustra* responds. *Zarathustra* is implicated here because Nietzsche refers to a "tragic solution," and GS 342 indicates that *Zarathustra* is a tragedy. These, however, are not the only references to tragedy in *The Gay Science*. Indeed, Nietzsche begins the work by pointing out that "we are in the age of tragedy" (GS 1) and he ends the second book by alluding to—albeit in modified form—the leitmotif of *The Birth*: it is as an aesthetic phenomenon that life is bearable (*erträglich*) (GS 107).[16] Again, both seem to foreshadow a coming tragedy and thereby provide evidence for reading *Zarathustra* as a tragedy.

There is one more important feature of *The Gay Science* that further solidifies the connection between *The Gay Science* and the tragedy of *Zarathustra*. Specifically, we know from initial drafts of the work that Nietzsche had originally planned to have Zarathustra appear in numerous aphorisms. The most notable of these is that Zarathustra, not the "madman," was supposed to announce the death of God in GS 125 (KSA 14:256–267). Nietzsche also planned to have Zarathustra appear as early as the second book in GS 68 (KSA 14:246) and GS 106 (KSA 14:253), and he was again going to be mentioned in GS 268, which was originally intended to be the end of the third book (Brusotti 2016:213). Nietzsche also had plans to call the fourth and final book of the 1882 edition "Zarathustra's Leisure" (KSA 9:12[225]), and Zarathustra was supposed to make appearances in GS 291 (KSA 14:265) and GS 332 (KSA 14:270).

Thus, there is significant evidence for thinking that Nietzsche consciously constructed *The Gay Science* to culminate in the tragedy of *Zarathustra*. What this means is that, at the time he composed *The Gay Science*, he had plans to write a tragedy in *Zarathustra* that would teach and affirm the eternal recurrence. Although the evidence for connecting *The Gay Science* to *Zarathustra* is substantive, some have questioned just how much Nietzsche planned *Zarathustra* as a three-part tragedy with a satyr play in the fourth part. On the one hand, some have argued that when Nietzsche published the first part of *Zarathustra*, he had no intention of publishing further parts (Brusotti 1997:549). In other words, the first book of *Zarathustra* was originally intended to be the whole of *Zarathustra*. On the other hand, Nietzsche seems to have toyed with the idea of making *Zarathustra* into a six-part work. If this is right, there is reason to question the overly neat idea that Nietzsche constructed *Zarathustra* as a tragic trilogy with a satyr play to parallel the structure of ancient Greek theater.

To understand the debates here, it is important to recall that Nietzsche published *Zarathustra* in installments. That is, he did not publish the book we now have before us as a single unit. Instead, he wrote the first part in January of 1883, sent it to the publisher in February, and it appeared in March of that year. He then began working on the second part in the late spring and summer of 1883. He sent it to the publisher in July, and the second part was published in September of 1883. He then devoted the final months of 1883 to working on the third part, and Nietzsche tells his publisher in January 1884 that he has finished it. It then appears in March of that year. With a significant break in between, Nietzsche begins working on *Zarathustra* IV toward the end of 1884, and he finishes the manuscript toward the end of January/beginning of February of 1885. In April, a limited number of copies of *Zarathustra* IV are distributed privately among friends.

One of the challenges to reading *Zarathustra* I–III as a consciously constructed tragic trilogy is that there is no indication, within *Zarathustra* I itself, that *Zarathustra* I is part of a larger whole. That is, if we scour the contents of the work as it was originally published, there is nothing that points to some further part. For instance, the original title of what is now *Zarathustra* I was simply *Thus Spoke Zarathustra*; there is no mention that it is the first part of a larger project. Moreover, there are no plans or letters from the time Nietzsche was composing *Zarathustra* I which indicate that he was thinking of further parts, and Nietzsche's description of the creative process in *Ecce Homo* emphasizes the inspired and sudden nature of how *Zarathustra* came into being. Specifically, he claims that each of the first three parts were written, like a flash, in only about ten days each (EH "Books" Z:1,4). Taken together, there are reasons for thinking that Nietzsche had little premonition about how *Zarathustra* would end once he began working on *Zarathustra* I, and he may have considered, for a time, *Zarathustra* I to be the whole of *Zarathustra* upon its completion.

If one thing is certain, it is that we simply do not know how much Nietzsche had planned at any given point in the creative process (it is highly unlikely that he wrote down everything he planned and equally unlikely that we still have everything he wrote down). That said, I do find the claim that Nietzsche considered *Zarathustra* I to be the whole of *Zarathustra* upon the completion of *Zarathustra* I to be implausible. One reason is that the support for such a claim largely comes from the lack of clear evidence for greater intentions. Lack of clear evidence, however, does not prove anything. Moreover, we do have some evidence, from the 1881 notes written prior to the composition of *Zarathustra*, that Nietzsche had plans for an extended work with multiple books involving the eternal recurrence (KSA 9:11[197]). We also know from Nietzsche's retrospective account that teaching the eternal recurrence is central to the drama of *Zarathustra*. If *Zarathustra* I were initially planned to be the entirety of *Zarathustra*, there would be no mention of the eternal recurrence in the work. Finally, Nietzsche introduces *Zarathustra* as a tragedy in GS 342, but there is nothing tragic about *Zarathustra* I on its own.

If Nietzsche remains true to his expressed intention in GS 342 to write his own tragedy in *Zarathustra*, then he must have been committed to writing more than *Zarathustra* I.

Nevertheless, the relative lack of evidence for Nietzsche's intentions regarding the first three parts of *Zarathustra* makes it difficult to say with any certainty that Nietzsche intended the work, from the start, to be a tragic trilogy. The situation is even more complex when we turn to *Zarathustra* IV. Here, the evidence suggests we cannot claim that Nietzsche planned, from the start, to write a tetralogy that follows the model of ancient Greek theater. On the one hand, Nietzsche does write, in an 1883 letter to Franz Overbeck, that the recently published second part will be the second of four (KSB 6:473). However, he also writes in some letters that he has finished the whole of *Zarathustra* with the completion of *Zarathustra* III in 1884 (see KSB 6:479, 480, 490, 492). More problematic, however, is that Nietzsche considered creating as many as three more books upon the completion of *Zarathustra* III (thus running the total number to six). Not only does Nietzsche mention an "unavoidable" fifth and sixth part in a letter to his sister (KSB 6:556), but he also writes in letters to Köselitz and Overbeck stating that with *Zarathustra* IV he has completed the first part of a new work. The name of this new work is "Noon and Eternity," and the title of the first part of this new work is "Zarathustra's Temptation" (KSB 7:573, 576).[17]

This puts pressure on reading *Zarathustra* as a tetralogy with a satyr play in the fourth part that completes the tragic trilogy of the first three parts. In defense of this reading, Loeb has followed others in arguing that "Nietzsche's plans for two further parts were probably a ploy intended to attract a publisher for Part IV" (2010:89).[18] Although some have criticized Loeb on this score,[19] there is some truth to this claim. We know that Nietzsche's relationship with the publisher of the first three parts had badly deteriorated by the end of 1884 (Schaberg 1995:101), and he was actively looking for a new publisher for *Zarathustra* IV. Moreover, in the various letters in which he either mentions additional parts or presents *Zarathustra* IV as the first part of "Noon and Eternity," he also mentions the need to find a publisher. Nevertheless, there are letters to his sister and his friends about additional parts (Köselitz and Overbeck), and one wonders to what extent Nietzsche is engaged, even here, in a "ploy." Indeed, there are some notes in which Nietzsche refers to "Zarathustra 6" (KSA 11:31[19], 31[27]), and so there is evidence that Nietzsche was sketching (for himself) ideas for these six parts.

Given the evidence, my considered view is that Nietzsche did plan, from the start, to write enough parts of *Zarathustra* so that it would result in a tragedy that includes the teaching of the eternal recurrence and Zarathustra's reconciliation with fate. I also think that GS 1 and GS 153 provide important evidence for thinking that Nietzsche had plans for a comedy to follow upon the tragedy of *Zarathustra* at the time he published *The Gay Science*. However, it is not clear that Nietzsche planned, from the start, to write a tragic trilogy—although it is notable that the final product comes in three parts—and then to follow this up with a satyr play—although there are good reasons to understand *Zarathustra* IV as a satyr play. Plans for a fifth and sixth part of *Zarathustra* do put pressure on the overly neat reading of *Zarathustra* I–III as a tragedy followed by a satyr play in *Zarathustra* IV, but there is nothing that would require Nietzsche to write a satyr play in a single installment (although far less elegant, the satyr play could be extended to include parts five and six). What does seem clear is that Nietzsche understood what is now *Zarathustra* IV to be a part of a larger project that would come to be Nietzsche's own revaluation of values, and it is for this reason that the work ends inconclusively with Zarathustra leaving his cave. What also seems clear is that *Zarathustra* IV is written in the "mood of a Mr. Sausage [*Hanswurst*]" (KSB 7:573) and that a sense of frivolity and references to laughter run throughout the text. Although this might be evidence for reading *Zarathustra* IV as the comedy mentioned in GS 1, I think it is evidence for reading it as a satyr play and so a transitional genre between Nietzsche's own tragedy in *Zarathustra* I–III and his own comedy in his 1888 works, when Nietzsche presents himself as a *Hanswurst* (EH "Destiny":1).

2.3 NIETZSCHE'S THEORY OF TRAGEDY

In the previous section, I presented details of the genesis of *Zarathustra* with an eye to providing evidence that Nietzsche thought of *Zarathustra* I–III as a tragedy in some sense (and a satyr play in *Zarathustra* IV). Again, the key piece of evidence for this view comes from the title of GS 342, "incipit tragoedia," and, in my mind, this evidence shifts the burden of proof to anyone who rejects the idea that *Zarathustra* is a tragedy. Nevertheless, reading *Zarathustra* I–III as a tragedy has its challenges. Most notably, Nietzsche did not write *Zarathustra* for the dramatic stage to be performed by a dancing and singing chorus accompanied by characters engaged in dialogue. Moreover, if we adopt an Aristotelian understanding of tragedy, it becomes difficult to see how the drama of *Zarathustra* might produce in us a response of "pity and fear," something Aristotle thought essential to the genre. Thus, even if we agree that Nietzsche introduces *Zarathustra* as a tragedy, we still might wonder how we can make sense of this claim.

If we are going to understand *Zarathustra* as a tragedy, we need to do so on Nietzsche's own terms. Just as Aristotle might have us think of tragedy in terms of producing a catharsis of pity and fear, we have already encountered scholars working on *Zarathustra* who understand tragedy as implying some kind of failure. There are also those who think that the genre is essentially about death and destruction. These are common understandings and highlight important aspects of tragedy, but Nietzsche clearly does not understand tragedy in these ways. After all, it is supposed to provide a life-affirming response to the wisdom of Silenus. To avoid these pitfalls, we need to generate a Nietzschean understanding of the genre of tragedy, and although it is far from ideal, the best source we have for this is *The Birth of Tragedy*.

The Birth is not ideal because Nietzsche embraces the metaphysical framework of Schopenhauer in the work, and one might argue that these metaphysical formulas infect the entire project in a way that makes all of it unsuitable to apply to Nietzsche's later thinking. However, there are at least four reasons to resist such a view. First, Nietzsche decides to republish versions of the work in both 1878 and 1886. Although the 1886 version includes "An Attempt at a Self-Criticism," in which Nietzsche excoriates, among other things, the metaphysics of his first work, the decision to republish the work indicates that Nietzsche still values its contents. Second, Nietzsche summarizes central points from *The Birth* in his notes as he is composing *Zarathustra* II and III. Whereas he begins one note by writing that "I have always made an effort to prove to myself the *innocence* of becoming" (KSA 10:7[7]),[20] he claims in another note that his life has been the consequence of *The Birth of Tragedy*'s fundamental insight, namely, that art is capable of rescuing life (KSA 10:16[111]). Third, in *Twilight of the Idols* (1888), Nietzsche presents *The Birth* as his "first revaluation of values" and the "soil out of which [his] intention, [his] *ability* grows" (TI "What I Owe":5). Finally, Nietzsche tells us in *Ecce Homo* that *Zarathustra* is the work in which his concept of the Dionysian, originally articulated in *The Birth*, becomes a "supreme deed" (EH "Books" Z:4).

The Birth can be broken down into three parts, and it follows a quasi-Hegelian structure of thesis, antithesis, and synthesis. In the first nine to ten sections, we are presented with Nietzsche's understanding of the birth of tragedy in ancient Greece. In sections ten through fifteen, Nietzsche explains the death of tragedy at the hands of Socratic philosophy. Thus, the first fifteen sections set up an opposition between tragic art, on the one hand, and the emergence of Socratic philosophy, on the other hand. This, in turn, paves the way for the synthesis in the final ten sections of the text. Specifically, Nietzsche argues that the truth-seeking project of Socrates has culminated in the philosophies of Kant and Schopenhauer, and the pessimistic philosophies of Kant and Schopenhauer—in contradistinction to the optimistic philosophy of Socrates—provide the foundation for the rebirth of tragedy in the operas of Richard Wagner.

To understand why the philosophies of Socrates, Kant, and Schopenhauer are relevant to the death and then rebirth of tragedy, we need to recognize that Nietzsche thinks of tragedy as being embedded within and expressive of an entire worldview. Not only does Nietzsche have an early essay entitled, "The Dionysian Worldview," but he later speaks of "tragic philosophy" and "tragic wisdom" and presents himself as a "tragic philosopher" who promises a "tragic age" (EH "Books" BT:3–4). In *The Birth*, it is not a philosopher, but the mythical figure Silenus, who first presents key features of this worldview in ancient Greece: humans are miserable and transitory creatures subject to arbitrary forces beyond their control (factual pessimism); and based on this understanding of existence, Silenus recommends that it is either best for humans not to be born or to die soon (evaluative pessimism) (BT 3). According to Nietzsche, art in general and tragedy in particular flourished as a life-affirming response to the wisdom of Silenus; thus, tragedy accepted factual pessimism while rejecting evaluative pessimism.

However, Socrates eventually introduced to the Greeks a new way of thinking about the cosmos. According to Nietzsche, Socrates was an optimist who believed that the world was rational and naturally ordered for our own good, and the purpose of life was to obtain happiness by cutting through illusions and living according to nature. Nietzsche argues that this optimistic worldview rejected Silenus' factual pessimism and eventually led to the death of tragedy. Since the world is ordered for our own benefit, we do not need the life-affirming powers of art to respond to the ugly truths of reality. Indeed, on this view, art diverts us from discovering a true cosmos ordered for our own good. What we need to do instead is pursue truth at all costs. By cutting through appearances and seeing reality for what it is, we can discover the truth about how best to live and order our social and political relations accordingly. For the Socratic optimist, philosophical truth, not art, is the ultimate panacea.

Nevertheless, Nietzsche thinks that the truth-seeking element of the Socratic project is incompatible with Socrates' optimistic worldview. Therefore, when truth is pursued in an uncompromising fashion, one eventually discovers that Silenus' factual pessimism was right all along. According to Nietzsche, this self-undermining of the Socratic project is precisely what has occurred in the philosophies of Kant and Schopenhauer. In their own way, their "tragic philosophies" have put an end to the optimistic idea that truth-seeking will lead to human flourishing and have revealed that suffering is essential to life. This, according to Nietzsche, is why we need a rebirth of tragedy in the modern world, and Nietzsche believes that Wagner is the artist capable of accomplishing this feat.

That Nietzsche roots his conception of tragedy in a "tragic worldview" that stands opposed to Socratic optimism can be used to explain why his conception of tragedy differs markedly from the understanding Aristotle presents in his *Poetics*. Specifically, Aristotle's *Poetics* is an attempt to show that certain forms of poetry can properly fit within the optimist's project of attaining *eudaimonia*. Aristotle had to provide this defense because Plato notoriously expelled poetry from his ideal city in the *Republic* on the grounds that it traffics in mere appearance and encourages emotional excess, both of which are detrimental to the philosophical life.[21] This means, for Aristotle, that a proper tragedy cannot reveal a world that is fundamentally flawed or even fallen, such that characters are fated to engage in morally reprehensible acts or that good people are destined to suffer. Instead, it should display characters who suffer through mistaken judgments or excess emotion. Indeed, it is through tragedy, on Aristotle's view, that the audience can improve their practical reasoning and experience a catharsis of pity and fear, both of which contribute to living a happy and virtuous life.

Nietzsche's understanding of poetry and so tragedy also differs significantly from Schopenhauer's. Unlike Aristotle, Schopenhauer believes that tragedy represents a world that is fundamentally fallen or broken. Thus, he claims that tragedy provides us with a "portrayal of the terrible aspect of life, that the unspeakable pain, the misery of humanity, the triumph of wickedness, the scornful domination of chance, and the hopeless fall of the righteous and the innocent." However, Schopenhauer follows Aristotle in thinking that tragedy can nevertheless be ethically beneficial. By this, Schopenhauer does not mean that tragedy improves our characters or helps us attain *eudaimonia*. Instead, by teaching us the truth of the world, tragedy acts as a "quieter" of the will and ultimately teaches "resignation" (WWR II:37). In short, Schopenhauer sees tragedy as a gateway into his larger philosophical-ethical program of having us recognize the absurdity of existence and, in response, engage in ascetic practices that deny the will, life, and the world. Thus, tragedy teaches us the lesson of Silenus: the world is fundamentally fallen (factual pessimism), and it is better not to be than to be (evaluative pessimism).

There is, however, one interesting feature of Schopenhauer's theory that is especially important for understanding Nietzsche. When Schopenhauer turns to ancient Greek tragedy—and so the origins of the genre—he rarely finds instances in which the portrayal of the terrible side of life (factual pessimism) results in characters on stage exhibiting a sense of resignation (evaluative pessimism). Like Aristotle, who also argues that the early tragedies of Aeschylus represent an immature form of a genre that only later comes to maturation, Schopenhauer argues that the Greeks had yet to reach "the pinnacle and aim of tragedy, or indeed of a view of life in general." Despite their presentation of the harsh realities of the world, they "rarely portrayed the spirit of resignation, the turning away from the will to life." It was only until the advent of "Christian tragedy," which "demonstrates the abandonment of the entire will to life, a joyful forsaking of the world, conscious of its worthlessness and nothingness," that the genre achieves its true nature (WWR II:37). In short, it was only through Christianity that tragedy would finally promote evaluative pessimism.

As we read in his 1886 "Attempt at a Self-Criticism," Nietzsche's theory of tragedy could not be more different. In section six, Nietzsche explicitly refers to Schopenhauer's claim that tragedy "leads to *resignation*," and he exclaims: "How differently Dionysus spoke to me! How far removed I was from all this resignationism!" (BT "ASC":6). In agreement with Schopenhauer, Nietzsche thinks that tragedy exhibits the suffering-laden character of our existence. However, Nietzsche believes that tragedy, in its truest form, shows how life can be affirmed even in the face of meaningless suffering, and this is precisely why we need to look back to the Greeks and their tragedies as we confront the harsh truths that Schopenhauer teaches us about existence. Indeed, Nietzsche's emphasis on the birth of tragedy—and his corresponding claim that tragedy died at the hands of Euripides—inverts both Aristotle's and Schopenhauer's assessments of tragedy and its historical development. The ideal form of tragedy is not found in its later manifestations and certainly not, as Schopenhauer claims, in the Christian tragedies of Calderón (WWR I:51). Instead, true tragedy died as early as Euripides, and if we want to discover the significance and meaning of the genre, we must look to its origins and the oldest playwright from whom we have extant tragedies, Aeschylus.

According to Nietzsche, tragedy—especially those of Aeschylus—is the highest of all art forms because it is the most life-affirming, and it is the most life-affirming because it combines the two types of art that Nietzsche identifies at the beginning of the book, the Apollonian and the Dionysian. The Apollonian arts are fundamentally rooted in the imagination and have to do with the artistic representation of the dreamworlds the imagination creates (BT 2). These dreamworlds can be described in poetic verse, as they are with Homer, or directly represented through painting, sculpture, and architecture, and these dream worlds are populated with "superhuman beings [*übermenschlicher Wesen*]" such as the Greek heroes and gods. The Dionysian, in contrast, reflects what Nietzsche calls "the will," and it finds its most immediate expression in music and dance. The primary experience here is one of intoxication (*Rausch*), where the individual transcends the boundaries of the self and leaves behind her everyday identity. For Nietzsche, both Apollonian and Dionysian art have the capacity to respond to human suffering and affirm life, and Nietzsche gives such a privileged place to tragedy precisely because it combines both Apollonian and Dionysian elements.

Unfortunately, there is often some confusion about Nietzsche's argument in *The Birth* regarding the relationship between the Apollonian and the Dionysian and their respective powers to affirm existence. It is often thought that the Apollonian represents life-affirming illusions that cover over what Nietzsche sometimes calls the "Dionysian wisdom" or the ugly truth of Silenus. Although this is the relationship that Nietzsche assigns to Homeric art in sections three and four, Nietzsche identifies, in section five, Archilochus as the Dionysian poet who initiates a tradition that eventually blossoms into tragedy (BT 5). Within this tradition, the Dionysian is not *merely* the communication of "Dionysian wisdom" and so the ugly truth (although it is that, too). Instead, it also includes the Dionysian art forms of music and dance that can directly transfigure and affirm the truths of Dionysian wisdom. In perhaps the most important passage of the book, Nietzsche points to the significance of musical dissonance—the famed "Tristan chord" of Wagner's *Tristan and Isolde* is certainly on his mind—to explain how Dionysian music can transfigure even suffering and pain (BT 24). The idea is that musical dissonance shows that humans can and even do want suffering as a part of existence. Just as a purely consonant musical composition would be extremely boring, we would find a life without suffering to be utterly intolerable. Thus, musical dissonance shows that we can indeed affirm and even find joy in the disharmonic elements of existence.

To understand how tragedy reconciles and combines the life-affirming forces of these two types of art, we can turn to the account Nietzsche provides of the genesis of tragedy that runs from chapter five to nine in *The Birth*. Contrary to how we now think of the genre as something performed in a theater with no essential connection to music, Nietzsche claims that all Dionysian art, and therefore tragedy, begins with a *musical mood*. In contrast to the dream world created by Homer, the musical mood allows the Dionysian artist to merge his own identity with the forces of nature or what Nietzsche calls "the primal unity, its pain and contradiction" (BT 5). This musical mood makes possible an ecstatic experience in which the poet experiences herself as having "entered into another body, another character" (BT 8). On Nietzsche's view, this experience of ecstasy is the origin of all drama and can be used to explain the mask characteristic of Dionysian theater. Indeed, Nietzsche's creation of Zarathustra can be understood in terms of his own ecstatic experience, born of the music he rediscovered in the years of 1881–1882.

In ancient Greece, this transfigured self took the form of a satyr, which is a half human, half horse-like figure and servant of Dionysus, and Nietzsche argues that a proto-form of tragedy emerged when multiple satyrs combined to form a dancing and singing chorus. The chorus, then, is the Dionysian foundation for tragedy. Tragedy, however, is a combination of the Dionysian and the Apollonian, and the Apollonian element emerges when the Dionysian energies of the satyr chorus discharge themselves in dream images, which is the realm of Apollo. As an art form, tragedy was born when this mental imagery was represented by a performer—the tragic hero—placed in the center of the dancing chorus who acted out the contents of these dreams. According to Nietzsche, the content of the earliest tragedies was the life and sufferings of Dionysus himself (BT 10). In this way, tragedy is the successful combination of both the Apollonian—in the form of the hero—and the Dionysian—in the form of the dancing and singing chorus—art worlds.

We are now positioned to understand how the Apollonian and Dionysian elements provide a dual affirmation of existence. On the one hand, the Apollonian hero on the tragic stage represents the "apotheosis of individuation [*Vergöttlichung der Individuation*]" (BT 4), and the artistic transfiguration of the human being into a god-like figure full of power and beauty is itself a stimulant to life. In terms of *Zarathustra*, the Apollonian moment of the tragedy is the creation and presentation of the *Übermensch*. Tragedy, however, teaches that no matter how high the human being might be elevated, she will nevertheless have to confront the natural forces of fate and even death. Thus, tragedy must also portray the destruction of the individual at the hands of these forces. Although one might think that the destruction of the tragic hero is something worthy of pity and fear, Nietzsche sees in this destructive moment a symbolic overcoming of individuation and a (re-)union of the individual with other individuals and nature herself. This overcoming of individuation, which is transfigured through music, is the essence of the Dionysian element of tragedy, and there is reason to think that this corresponds to Zarathustra's "going under" at the end of *Zarathustra* III. According to Nietzsche, the musical element of tragedy allows the audience to "understand the joy involved in the annihilation of the individual" (BT 16) and to experience the cycle of creation and destruction of the individual world. To explain this point, Nietzsche refers to Heraclitus' image of a child building sandcastles only to gleefully knock them over (BT 24), a figure which appears at the end of Zarathustra's first speech in *Zarathustra* I, "On the Three Metamorphoses."

As much as *The Birth* seems to be about the genesis—and eventual death—of tragedy in ancient Greece, the primary purpose of the text is to issue a call for the rebirth of tragedy in the operas of Wagner, and Nietzsche thinks of *The Birth* as a guide for Wagner's future efforts. For the purposes of understanding *Zarathustra*, this has two important upshots. First, by reading *Zarathustra* as a tragedy, we can see how Nietzsche is effectively taking on the role he originally assigned to Wagner: in his later works, it is Nietzsche, rather than Wagner, who is responsible for the rebirth of tragedy, and *Zarathustra* is Nietzsche's attempt to fulfill his youthful hopes (here, however, we should not overlook Nietzsche's early attempts to write his own Empedocles tragedy in 1870–1871). Indeed, Nietzsche's reflections in *Ecce Homo* on *Richard Wagner in Bayreuth*—a text written in anticipation of the rebirth of tragedy at the first Bayreuth festival in 1876—suggest just such a relationship. There, Nietzsche claims that when he is speaking about Wagner, the reader should put down his name or "Zarathustra" instead (EH "Books" BT:4). Second, we can turn to both *Wagner in Bayreuth* and even some of Wagner's operas for more clues on how to understand better the structure and content of *Zarathustra*. In writing *Zarathustra*, Nietzsche's efforts are shaped by and respond to an entire literary and artistic tradition that preceded him, and Wagner's operas are important resources for the wide range of tropes and symbols found in the work.

One thing *Wagner in Bayreuth* makes clear is that Nietzsche is still, at least publicly, committed to the "hope" of "a Dionysian future of music" in 1876 (EH "Books" BT:4). And, like *The Birth*, Nietzsche continues to link both German philosophy and the music of Wagner to ancient Greek thinkers and poets. Thus, he compares Kant and Schopenhauer to the Eleactics and Empedocles, respectively, and he associates Wagner's operas with Aeschylus (RWB 4). Nietzsche also presents Wagner as the ultimate "counter-Alexander" or the figure who will fight against the "Alexandrian culture" of contemporary Germany which, according to Nietzsche, is based on Enlightenment optimism and takes great pride in cataloging and systematizing the cultural achievements of the past for the sake of knowledge (BT 18). In contrast, Wagner is the leader of a renewed tragic culture, and the festival at Bayreuth represents the hope for retaining a "sense for the tragic" (RWB 4). This is roughly the same hope that Nietzsche expresses as late as *Ecce Homo*: "I promise a tragic age: the highest art in saying Yes to life, tragedy" (EH "Books" BT:4).

In *Ecce Homo*, Nietzsche also speaks of a "great noon" in *Zarathustra* to which the elect must consecrate themselves for "the greatest of all tasks," and Nietzsche connects this notion to the "idea of Bayreuth" (EH "Books" BT:4). The idea of Bayreuth refers to language of "purification and consecration" in section six of *Wagner in Bayreuth*, and Nietzsche describes a two-step process for this purification: the artist must first liberate himself from the forces of modernity and only then can "he discover the innocence of art" (RWB 6). Nothing is explicit here, but this process can be mapped onto Nietzsche's free spirit works. There, he liberates himself from the modern prejudices of metaphysics and morality, and this makes possible his own rediscovery of the innocence of art in *Zarathustra*. Nietzsche also points to section nine of *Wagner in Bayreuth*, in which the style of *Zarathustra* is supposedly described. Specifically, we are told that art consists in the ability to communicate to others what an artist has personally experienced through mythical, rather than conceptual, "thinking." According to Nietzsche, mythical thinking means thinking in "visible and palpable events" and the communication of ideas by "a succession of events, actions, and sufferings" (RWB 9). Applied to *Zarathustra*, this means, first, that the work is Nietzsche's attempt to communicate what he himself is experiencing and, second, that he will communicate these experiences through metaphors, symbols, myth, and drama. Of course, it is this "mythical thinking" that drives analytic philosophers away from *Zarathustra* and leads to the kind of condemnations of the text by the likes of Huddleston.

In *Ecce Homo*, Nietzsche also highlights his description of the dithyrambic poet in *Wagner in Bayreuth*, and, in section seven of that work, we are told that the miracle of the dithyrambic artist consists in "the longing at once to take all that is weak, human and lost and, like a god come to earth, 'raise it to Heaven in fiery arms,' so as at last to find love and no longer only to worship, and in love to relinquish himself utterly." Similar to *The Birth*, Nietzsche claims that in this intoxicated state the dithyrambic artist produces words and melodies that follow the rhythm of the dithyrambic dance, and the melody then projects itself into the realm of images and concepts. This is further expanded into "a wholly exuberant will, of an ecstatic going-under and cessation of will," and it is here that tragedy comes into being (RWB 7). Finally, we gain some insight from *Wagner in Bayreuth* into what

Nietzsche means by the "tragic" and the "tragic sense," which is that "the individual must be consecrated to something higher than himself." According to Nietzsche, it is through this consecration that the individual is freed from "the terrible anxiety which death and time evoke" (RWB 4). In terms of *Zarathustra*, Nietzsche's claim here is that tragedy frees us from the problem of the past in the sense of transience or *Vergänglichkeit*, which is one of the central problems presented in the pivotal chapter, "On Redemption," from *Zarathustra* II.

Here again, it is worth pausing to reflect on the "tragic nature" of *Zarathustra*. From *Wagner in Bayreuth*, we see that the essence of the tragic is the overcoming of individuation and some sort of reconciliation or merging with natural forces larger than the individual. It was noted above that both the eternal recurrence and the notion of *amor fati* demand that the individual affirms both fate and necessity. Indeed, the "joyous and trusting fatalism" that Nietzsche later espouses is one in which "only the particular is loathsome, and that all is redeemed and affirmed in the whole" (TI "Skirmishes":49). Applied to *Zarathustra*, we find this very idea in Zarathustra's eventual *Untergang* or "going under." Specifically, we can say that when Zarathustra goes under by summoning the eternal recurrence, he is consecrating himself to something higher than his own individuality and merging with the cosmic forces of nature, necessity, and fate. In this way, "going under" is also "going over" and a rebirth into a new life.[22]

Roger Hollinrake has also detailed a number of illuminating connections between *Zarathustra* and Wagner's operas,[23] and he argues that "*Zarathustra* was planned as a whole and from the outset as a reply to Wagner" (1982:ix). Not only are there deep connections between Wagner's *Siegfried* from the *Ring Cycle* and the final sections of *Zarathustra* III, but Hollinrake also claims that *Zarathustra* IV is a direct response to and an inversion of key motifs in *Parsifal*. One obvious connection between *Zarathustra* and the *Ring* is that both involve a quest for a ring. In Wagner's opera, it is a ring of the Rhinegold that gives its possessor ultimate power. In Nietzsche's *Zarathustra*, it is the ring of the eternal recurrence that ultimately weds Zarathustra to eternity. Both works also exhibit a going down or under, and it is through this process that a new world order emerges. However, Hollinrake also notes that the two works could not end more differently in this respect: whereas Wotan condemns Siegfried to timeless oblivion, the eternal recurrence stands directly opposed to any sort of redemption from rebirth and this world (1982:119). *Zarathustra* IV effects this same sort of inversion of Wagner's *Parsifal*. Whereas *Parsifal* centers around the need to learn pity, *Zarathustra* IV presents pity as Zarathustra's last temptation, and whereas *Parsifal*'s Kundry is condemned to eternal rebirth for laughing at Christ, Zarathustra points to the rose-wreath crown of laughter—the opposite of pity—as a form of this worldly redemption (ZIV "On the Higher Man"; also see BT "ASC":7).

Here, one might conclude that Nietzsche effects this inversion in *Zarathustra* largely to parody Wagnerian opera. Although such a reading is not wrong, casting these inversions as mere parody would be a mistake. Instead, the life-affirming ethos of *Zarathustra*, one that includes a rejection of life-denying pity, can be understood as Nietzsche's attempt to realize the ideas he originally articulated in *The Birth* and as something that grounds his larger project of revaluing values. Rather than relying on an otherwise life-denying Wagner to produce a life-affirming tragedy, Nietzsche is now writing his own tragedy to exemplify the core idea of his Dionysian pessimism: although life is suffering, it is nevertheless something we can affirm and even love. This is the central idea of his philosophical project from beginning to end and the central motif of *Zarathustra*.

2.4 METAPHYSICS, HERACLITEAN BECOMING, AND THE TRAGIC WORLDVIEW

Nietzsche's early works are important for understanding *Zarathustra* as a tragedy. Nevertheless, there are clear differences between the ideas of *The Birth of Tragedy* and the tragedy of *Zarathustra*, and some might argue that these differences are so significant that *The Birth* cannot be used to interpret *Zarathustra*. As we have noted above, *The Birth* attaches a life-affirming theory of tragedy to a thinker (Schopenhauer) who openly espouses a theory of life denial and an artist (Wagner) whose operas often present death and renunciation as a form of redemption from an unsavory reality. Even more troubling is that Nietzsche articulates his theory of tragedy in his first work by linking it to Schopenhauer's transcendent metaphysics, and Nietzsche clearly rejects such metaphysics by the time he writes *Zarathustra*. Thus, it seems that *The Birth* will provide few, if any, resources for understanding a work like *Zarathustra*. In this section, I want to respond to these concerns by saying more about Nietzsche's persistent commitment to a tragic worldview even as he abandons Schopenhauer's metaphysics and Wagnerian opera in his later works.

Nietzsche's eventual rejection of transcendent metaphysics is not a rejection of the central thesis of *The Birth*, namely, that art can provide a life-affirming response to factual pessimism, but rather its refinement. It is a refinement because Nietzsche quickly comes to see that transcendent metaphysics is inherently hostile to the affirmation of life and the world. Metaphysics does this by establishing a second world by which the natural world is assessed and often condemned for failing to live up to the metaphysical world. Nietzsche's 1873 unpublished text, *Philosophy in the Tragic Age*, reveals how he reformulates the tragic worldview of *The Birth* in anti-metaphysical and therefore naturalistic terms.[24] There, Nietzsche embeds his critique of metaphysics in his account of the philosophies that populated the intellectual landscape during what he calls "the tragic age of the Greeks." In so doing, he identifies Heraclitus as the tragic philosopher *par excellence* and associates his anti-metaphysical philosophy of "becoming" with art, artists, and an aesthetic conception of existence. In short, Nietzsche makes Heraclitean becoming—rather than Schopenhauer's metaphysics—the fundamental principle of his tragic worldview.

It is worth pausing to reflect on what Nietzsche means by "becoming." On a standard reading, "becoming" is opposed to the notion of "being." Whereas being represents stability and permanence, becoming is supposed to represent motion or change as well as coming-to-be and passing-away. This rendering is not incorrect *per se*, but it is incomplete and therefore lends itself to misunderstanding. When we simply equate becoming with change or impermanence, we can fall into the trap of thinking that "becoming" is a claim about *things* changing (stressing the frequency and ubiquity of these changes). This, however, is not the primary meaning of becoming for Nietzsche. To see why, we need to understand that the "thing" or "substance" that is said to undergo change on this model is itself an instance of "being," and therefore this understanding of becoming includes, rather than precludes, "being." Nietzsche, however, understands Heraclitus' theory as one that does away with the notion of being and so individual entities altogether.

But if there are not any individuated entities, what can there possibly be? The answer is that, according to the theory of becoming, there are only "dynamic relations." The idea is that, for Nietzsche's Heraclitus, everything only has relative existence (PTAG 5), such that everything exists and is what it is only in relation to something else. In this way, relations are said to go all the way down, and if we try to detach any "thing" from all its relations, then there is nothing left of that "thing." Although nothing is explicit, the idea that everything has only relative or relational existence is best expressed by Heraclitus' doctrine of the unity of opposites. The idea is that fundamental reality consists of qualities (or forces) that stand in relation to opposite or opposing qualities (or forces), e.g., hot and cold, wet and dry, yin and yang. Moreover, the relations between these relata are such that each relatum is always affecting (e.g., exerting some influence upon) the other relatum in the relationship. Thus, "dynamic relations" constitute the fundamental nature of reality, and it is because there is a continual push and pull between these necessarily relational constituents that change—and so "becoming"—is an essential feature of reality.

With this understanding of Heraclitean becoming in hand, we can now look at the ways in which Nietzsche wants to link his philosophy to a tragic worldview and the poetic genre of tragedy. Although it does not explain why there is such a connection, the fact that Heraclitus' philosophy takes centerstage in Nietzsche's analysis of the philosophies that animate what he calls the "tragic age" of ancient Greece attests to such a connection. In *Ecce Homo*, Nietzsche claims that he is the first "tragic philosopher," but then remarks that he retained some doubt about Heraclitus and that he feels "better and warmer" in his proximity than anywhere else. Specifically, he points to Heraclitus' "affirmation of passing away and *destroying*," his notion of "*becoming*, along with a radical repudiation of the very concept of *being*," and the doctrine of "eternal recurrence" as all having some connection to his own "Dionysian philosophy" (EH "Books" BT:3).

One reason Nietzsche associates Heraclitus' philosophy with tragedy is that he thinks the teaching of "sovereign becoming" is "true but deadly" (HL 9) and a "terrible, paralyzing thought" (PTAG 5). We can see the "tragic" or "deadly" consequences of this doctrine once we apply it to the self. Just as there is no "thing" that stands over and above the forces that constitute it, there is no self or "doer" behind its actions or deeds (see GM I:13). As Nietzsche explains at the beginning of *History for Life*, it is only through an act of "forgetting"—which seems to be equivalent to "falsifying" a natural world of becoming—that we come to have a conception of an "I" or self at all. In reality, there is nothing more than an eternal flux of forces. This is something to keep in mind when we think about Zarathustra's "going under" at the end of *Zarathustra* III.

The idea that there is no fundamental "I" or self goes hand in hand with the idea that there is no "I" that can control or shape nature according to what it thinks best. Thus, Nietzsche also connects Heraclitean becoming to a doctrine of necessity, which, in turn, underwrites the tragic notion of fate. Nietzsche writes, "man is necessity down to his last fiber, and totally 'unfree'" (PTAG 6), and for this reason, there is no room for a moral, "thou shalt." In other words, the necessity built into Heraclitus' ontology undermines the moral vision of the world that Nietzsche attributes to Anaximander. In contrast, Nietzsche compares Heraclitus' vision of the world to the play of children and artists, and Nietzsche places this "aesthetic" affirmation of the world beyond the moral categories of "good and evil": "In this world only play, play as artists and children engage in it, exhibits coming-to-be and passing away, structuring and destroying, without any moral additive, in forever equal innocence." As Nietzsche writes, the cycle of creation and destruction "is a game. Don't take it so pathetically and—above all—don't make a morality of it" (PTAG 7).

As we can see, Nietzsche's portrayal of Heraclitus' philosophy foreshadows both *amor fati* (as the love of what is necessary (KSA 9:15[20])) and the "innocence of becoming" that Nietzsche associates with *Zarathustra* and repeats throughout his later works.[25]

As I have argued elsewhere (Meyer 2014c: Ch.3), *Human* is the work in which Nietzsche makes the philosophy of Heraclitus his own and thereby establishes the foundations for his tragic worldview. He begins the work by aligning himself with Heraclitus' denial of opposites and the related doctrine of becoming (HH 1 and 2; see also KSA 14:119), and he appeals to the natural sciences, under the moniker of a "historical philosophy," to justify his commitment to a relational ontology of force (HH 19). He then systematically attacks both metaphysics and the need for metaphysics in the first four chapters, and at the end of the first chapter, he is already raising the question of the value of existence. Although he stresses the potential "despair" that results from the loss of metaphysics (HH 31, 33, 34), he leaves the question of the value of existence unanswered. However, he gives a subtle hint that only poets can successfully respond to these tragic insights (HH 34). In my view, this subtle hint is a proleptic foreshadowing of the tragedy that Nietzsche eventually pens in *Zarathustra*.

This, however, is a controversial claim, and many scholars think a vast gulf divides *Human* from *Zarathustra*. However, if there is any doubt that Nietzsche remains committed to the Heraclitean principles he articulates in *Human*, we only need to turn to the third book of *The Gay Science* (1882). There, Nietzsche makes claims similar to those he put forward in the first chapter of *Human*. For instance, we are told that "the total character of the world, however, is in all eternity chaos," that there are no laws in nature but only "necessities" (GS 109), and that it is erroneous to believe that there are "enduring things" or "equal things" or that "there are things, substances, bodies" (GS 110). We also read that "matter is as much of an error as the God of the Eleactics" (GS 109), that it is necessary, for the purposes of survival, not to see everything "in flux" (GS 111), and that "in truth we are confronted by a continuum" (GS 112).

In the *Nachlass* from 1881, we find more evidence of Nietzsche's continued commitment to Heraclitean principles. In one detailed note, Nietzsche explains that the false belief in persistent individuals emerges with consciousness. This belief is false because persistent individuals are imaginary constructs that stand in contradiction to the "absolute flux" of reality and what Nietzsche calls the "final truth of the flux of things" (KSA 9:11[162]). These notes also show that Nietzsche is thinking of Heraclitean becoming in terms of scientific forces, and the idea that the world is composed of a finite number of forces forms a central premise in his arguments for the eternal recurrence. In one note, we find repeated references to "the world of forces" (KSA 9:11[148]). In another note that contains the title of the aphorism in which the eternal recurrence is first introduced, "Let us beware" (GS 109), Nietzsche speaks of forces that are finite, eternally active, and eternally the same (KSA 9:11[202]).

By tracing the lineage of Heraclitean "becoming" and the related notion of force back to *Philosophy in the Tragic Age* and even *The Birth*, we can recognize the ideas that Nietzsche articulates in 1881 and 1882 as giving expression to his own tragic worldview, and this tragic worldview forms the basis for Nietzsche's tragedy in *Zarathustra*. Such a connection is substantiated by the 1885 *Nachlass* note that formed the basis for the final section of *The Will to Power*. There, Nietzsche describes his "*Dionysian* world" as a continual play of forces:

> A monster of energy, without beginning, without end; a firm, iron magnitude of force that does not grow bigger or smaller, that does not expand itself but only transforms itself; [...] as force throughout, as a play of forces and waves of forces.
>
> (WP 1067; KSA 11:38[12])

Given that Dionysus is the god of tragedy and Nietzsche speaks of "tragic philosophy" and "Dionysian philosophy" interchangeably (EH "Books" BT:3), we can understand this Dionysian world of forces to be a centerpiece of his tragic worldview.

In the above *Nachlass* note, Nietzsche also mentions two doctrines that first appear in *Zarathustra*, the eternal recurrence and the will to power. Nietzsche speaks of "a sea of forces flowing and rushing together, eternally changing, eternally flooding back, with tremendous years of recurrence, with an ebb and a flood of its forces." Nietzsche ends the note by claiming that *"this world is the will to power—and nothing besides!* And you yourselves are also the will to power—and nothing besides!" In the next section, I want to show how these doctrines relate to another feature of Nietzsche's tragic worldview, namely, his naturalism, and therefore show how *Zarathustra*, the work in which Nietzsche presents these doctrines for the first time, gives expression to Nietzsche's naturalism, puts an end to the metaphysical tradition, goes "beyond good and evil" (WP 1067; KSA 11:38[12]), and restores "the innocence of becoming" (KSA 10:7[7], [21], [268]).

2.5 THE ETERNAL RECURRENCE, THE WILL TO POWER, AND THE NATURALISM OF *ZARATHUSTRA*

The eternal recurrence and the will to power are some of the most discussed, yet most maligned, features of Nietzsche's philosophy. In older interpretations, most notably Martin Heidegger's, these doctrines were presented as the foundation of Nietzsche's philosophical project. More recent interpretations still give these views significant attention, but they have challenged the idea that these views commit Nietzsche to making cosmological claims about the nature of the world. Whereas many scholars now hold that the eternal recurrence is a practical thought experiment that tests our ability to affirm life, the cosmological version of the will to power has been dismissed by scholars such as Brian Leiter as a form of "crackpot metaphysics." If the will to power has any role in Nietzsche's philosophy, it is limited to a psychological claim in which persons are said to be motivated by power in some important sense.[26]

In my reading of *Zarathustra*, I treat these views as cosmological claims, and I want to make sense of these views by linking them to another feature of my reading that connects *Zarathustra* to contemporary debates in Nietzsche interpretation. Specifically, I want to give reasons for thinking that *Zarathustra* is the work in which Nietzsche completes the very naturalism that Schopenhauer claimed could not be completed.[27] Naturalism is an important movement in contemporary philosophy, and Leiter (2002 and

2013) has argued that Nietzsche is a naturalist. Although there has been much debate about the sort of naturalist Nietzsche is supposed to be, there is an agreement that his naturalism at least entails the rejection of metaphysical or transcendent entities. Indeed, it is by turning to Schopenhauer that we will see how the cosmological formulations of the will to power and the eternal recurrence can be understood as key elements of Nietzsche's naturalism in this sense and how his naturalism takes us to a standpoint "beyond good and evil."

We know from *Ecce Homo* that the eternal recurrence is the "fundamental conception" of *Zarathustra* (EH "Books" Z:1), and we also know that Nietzsche articulates the view just prior to introducing Zarathustra in *The Gay Science*. The title of the aphorism is "the greatest weight," and in the aphorism Nietzsche has us imagine a demon—perhaps foreshadowing the spirit of gravity in *Zarathustra*—say to us, "this life as you now live it and have lived it, you will have to live once more and innumerable times more" such that "there will be nothing new in it, but every pain and every joy and every thought and sigh and everything unutterably small or great in your life will return to you" (GS 341). In a way that clearly parallels the responses to the wisdom of Silenus in *The Birth*, Nietzsche then asks whether we would either curse the demon who uttered such a thing or whether there would be a "tremendous moment [*ungeheure Augenblick*]" in which we would rejoice in such a message. As the aphorism ends, we are asked whether we could become so well disposed to ourselves and to life so as "*to crave nothing more fervently* than this ultimate eternal confirmation and seal" (GS 341).

Based on what we know from *Zarathustra*, we can see how this aphorism structures the drama of the text: Zarathustra's task is to become so well disposed to himself and to life that he desires nothing more than its eternal recurrence, and this is something he accomplishes only at the end of *Zarathustra* III. However, this aphorism has also suggested to readers that the eternal recurrence is merely a thought experiment designed to test how well disposed we are to life (Anderson 2022). It is not, so the argument goes, something that makes a truth-evaluable claim about the larger cosmos. Such a theory is obviously false, so it is argued, and Nietzsche would have understood it as such. Indeed, the hypothetical presentation of the doctrine in the aphorism provides evidence for this reading: we are asked how we *would* respond *if* some mythical creature uttered the idea to us in a moment of absolute solitude.

There is no doubt that the doctrine has the effect of testing whether we affirm or deny life, just as Silenus' wisdom posed the question to the ancient Greeks. However, there are good reasons for thinking that Nietzsche also intended the doctrine to make a claim about the world or the cosmos. For one, we have no published or unpublished statement, note, or letter which indicates that he thinks the doctrine is a counterfactual thought experiment. In contrast, we have significant evidence indicating that he considers this to be a viable hypothesis for addressing large-scale cosmological questions. In *Ecce Homo*, Nietzsche presents the doctrine as an essential part of his own "tragic philosophy," and he compares it to the cosmological theories of Heraclitus and the Stoics (EH "Books" BT:3). That the eternal recurrence has some connection to Heraclitus' philosophy—and so Nietzsche's tragic worldview—is further evidenced by Nietzsche's subtle reference to "the eternal recurrence of war and peace" in GS 285.[28]

However, this is not the first mention of the eternal recurrence in *The Gay Science*. In GS 109, Nietzsche speaks of a "musical box" eternally repeating its tune. Although it is only a brief mention, we can, by way of the aphorism's title, "Let Us Beware," connect Nietzsche's thinking about the eternal recurrence to the cosmological debates of his day. First, we can trace the title of GS 109 to at least three notes from this time in which this phrase is used, and, in these notes, Nietzsche formulates the eternal recurrence in cosmological terms (KSA 9:11[157], [201], [202]). Second, Paulo D'Iorio has shown that Nietzsche first encountered this phrase, "let us beware," in Eugen Dühring's *Cursus der Philosophie* (1875), and Dühring uses the phrase in the context of discussing cosmological questions (2014:74).[29] Taken together, the first two mentions of the eternal recurrence in *The Gay Science* are meant to be cosmological, and from this it follows that we should read GS 341 in cosmological terms.

In my view, *Zarathustra* provides substantive evidence for interpreting the eternal recurrence cosmologically.[30] There are two relevant passages from *Zarathustra* III. In "On the Vision and the Riddle":2, Zarathustra not only asks whether "all things are knotted together so firmly that this moment draws together all that is to come," thereby implying a commitment to a form of determinism, but also uses the same language Nietzsche employs in GS 341. Thus, he refers to the eternal recurrence of even "this slow spider, which crawls in the moonlight, and this moonlight itself." In "The Convalescent":2, Nietzsche repeats the language of GS 341. The animals claim that Zarathustra teaches that "there is a great year of becoming, a monster of a great year, which must, like an hourglass turn over again and again." The imagery of an "hourglass" turning over again not only occurs in GS 341 but also in the aforementioned *Nachlass* note that begins with the Heraclitean "world of forces" (KSA 9:11[148]). When we combine this with the fact that the reference to a "great year" has a Heraclitean lineage, we find further reasons for interpreting the eternal recurrence cosmologically.

The will to power plays a lesser role in *Zarathustra*. The view appears in three passages (ZI "Goals"; ZII "Self-Overcoming"; ZII "Redemption"), and it is first introduced to explain the origin of diverse cultural values and ethical norms: each tablet of good that hangs over a people is a product of their overcoming and the voice of their will to power (ZI "Goals"). Here, the view is largely limited to the psychological realm. However, the view seems to be expanded to the biological realm—such that all "life" is said to be "will to power"—in *Zarathustra* II. Specifically, Nietzsche has Zarathustra claim that "only where there is life is there also will" and that the "will to life" is the "will to power" (ZII "Self-Overcoming"). The question, then, is whether Nietzsche wants to limit the concept to the psychological and biological realms only (again, many readers think it is absurd to expand it to include all of reality). However, I think that once we interpret the concept in context, we can see that Nietzsche always thought of the will to power as a cosmological concept.

Important here is the fact that Nietzsche presents the will to power, both in the *Nachlass* and in *Zarathustra*, as a modification of Schopenhauer's concept of the will to life. In one of the first mentions of the concept in the *Nachlass*, Nietzsche writes: "Will to live? I have always found only will to power in its place"

(KSA 10:5[1]). Here again, this would seem to indicate that the will to power is clearly a biological concept. However, we can see why it is not by looking more closely at Schopenhauer's understanding of the will to life. For Schopenhauer, the will to life is synonymous with the "will," which he believes is a metaphysical thing in itself.[31] The metaphysical will is what produces, through its objectification and appearance, the natural world. Indeed, for Schopenhauer, the will is synonymous with the will to life because "life is nothing but the presentation of that willing for representation" and therefore life is equivalent to the "visible world" (WWR I:54). It is true that "everything strains and strives toward *existence*," but "*organic* existence" is only one mode of existence (WWR II:28). Thus, Schopenhauer does not limit "life" to the organic or biological realm; instead, it is a cosmological term that applies to anything that manifests itself as representation and therefore to both organic and inorganic phenomena. Transferred to Nietzsche's remarks in *Zarathustra* II, it follows that if the will to power is a modification of the will to life, the will to power is also a cosmological principle that applies to both organic and inorganic phenomena.

But if the will to power is a modification of the will to life and the will to life is equivalent to the metaphysical notion of the thing in itself, it might seem that Nietzsche has reverted to metaphysical speculation with his cosmological formulation of the will to power. That is, it seems that the will to power is now a metaphysical thing in itself. However, I think the exact opposite is the case. The speculative doctrines of the eternal recurrence and the will to power are not forms of transcendent metaphysics but rather designed to complete a project of naturalism that Schopenhauer thought could never be completed.

I have already explained that Nietzsche took aim at metaphysics and the "metaphysical need" in *Human*, and the metaphysical need is something Schopenhauer discusses at length in "On Humanity's Metaphysical Need" in the second volume of *The World as Will and Representation*. There, Schopenhauer opposes transcendent metaphysics and the metaphysical need to a naturalism that rejects metaphysical principles. According to Schopenhauer, metaphysics is

> any cognition that claims to go beyond the possibility of experience, which is to say beyond nature or the given appearance of things, in order to disclose something about that which [...] conditions appearance; or [...] about what is hidden behind nature and makes it possible.

In contrast, "genuine *naturalism*" is "a physics" which asserts "that its explanations of things [...] were really adequate and hence accounted exhaustively for the essence of the world." For Schopenhauer, physics is "concerned with the explanation of phenomena in the world," and since the naturalist tries to explain the phenomena of the world without metaphysics, naturalism is a physics without a metaphysics and "a theory that makes appearance into the thing in itself" (WWR II:17).

Schopenhauer's discussion of naturalism is relevant for my purposes both because of the significant scholarly interest in casting Nietzsche as a naturalist and because it provides a way of understanding the role the will to power and the eternal recurrence play in Nietzsche's philosophy and even *Zarathustra* itself. According to Schopenhauer, the natural sciences (and so physics) reduce everything to "forces of nature" that are governed by "laws of nature." In other words, Schopenhauer thinks that physics provides us with an understanding of nature that corresponds to what we have identified as the core constituent (forces) of Nietzsche's "tragic worldview." However, Schopenhauer also thinks that physics itself cannot provide a complete explanation of natural phenomena and instead must be supplemented by metaphysics. Specifically, he identifies two explanatory gaps that naturalism cannot fill. First, even if science can establish a system of causes and effects, this chain recedes back through time "*in infinitum*," and this infinite regress leaves the entire chain unexplained. The second problem is that causation itself "rests on something completely inexplicable." Although qualities such as weight, hardness, and elasticity are manifestations of natural forces, the forces themselves are occult and inexplicable qualities.[32] Thus, Schopenhauer writes, "there is not a single shard of broken clay, however worthless it may be, that is not composed of quite inexplicable qualities" (WWR II:17). For these reasons, Schopenhauer thinks that the naturalist will never be able to overcome our need for metaphysics.

Applied to Nietzsche, Schopenhauer's criticism means that the tragic worldview of interrelated forces remains incomplete as a system of naturalism, and if we are going to extinguish the "metaphysical need" by completing such a system, these two explanatory gaps must be filled. Interestingly, the will to power and the eternal recurrence provide a direct response to Schopenhauer's twofold challenge to naturalism. Whereas Schopenhauer uses the alleged inadequacy of naturalism to introduce his metaphysical concept of the will, Nietzsche responds to the challenge by introducing a naturalized notion of the will to power. Unlike the will to life, the will to power is not a unitary entity behind or beyond appearances. Instead, there are multiple, interrelated wills to power that constitute the natural world. Nietzsche does this by taking the "victorious concept of 'force'" from the scientific discourse of his day and ascribing an inner quality to it that he calls will to power (KSA 11:36[31] and 11:36[34]). Here, forces are reimagined as wills to power (they are numerically identical), and the key difference between the two notions is that this inner quality endows otherwise inexplicable forces with an explanatory principle. The will to power now provides us with a principle to help us understand *why* something happens without reference to a metaphysical thing in itself, and because the notions of both "will" and "power" are known to us through inner experience, we can comprehend the external world in terms that are intelligible to us (KSA 11:36[31] and BGE 36).

The second of Schopenhauer's objections is that, even if we had an explanatory basis for any given causal relation, we would nevertheless find ourselves in need of explaining the entire chain of causes and effects. This is something, according to Schopenhauer, that naturalism cannot do. However, if we think of the course of events as a chain that circles around and connects with itself, the need for a beginning is no longer necessary. Any given moment is both a beginning and an end of the chain, and the chain of events can be understood as a self-enclosed system that explains itself. Given that the cosmos is a continual cycle of creation and destruction, Nietzsche claims that "we need not worry for a moment about the hypothesis of a *created* world" because the world is something that "becomes" and then "passes away" but "it has never begun to become and never ceased from passing away" (KSA 13:14[188]). In short, the eternal recurrence eliminates the need for God, an "unmoved mover," or even a metaphysical "will" to initiate the chain of events and therefore responds to the second of Schopenhauer's objections to naturalism.

Although the cosmological versions of the will to power and the eternal recurrence address the explanatory gaps left by the natural sciences, one might wonder if Nietzsche understands these views to be justified by science itself. To be sure, he thinks that the basis for these views, namely, the idea that nature consists of a finite number of attractive and repulsive forces, is justified by scientific observation. However, both the eternal recurrence and the will to power go beyond what can be observed. In the *Nachlass*, Nietzsche tries to develop a proof for the eternal recurrence based on claims about the nature of time (that it is infinite) and force (that they are finite), but he never publishes these proofs and commentators have found them wanting (Simmel 1991:170–178). Moreover, in both *The Gay Science* and *Zarathustra*, as well as Nietzsche's retrospective comments in *Ecce Homo*, the view is presented in almost mystical fashion, and it therefore seems to recall Nietzsche's description of Thales' mystical intuition that "everything is water" (PTAG 3). Regarding the will to power, the evidence for reading it as something that goes beyond scientific discovery is even stronger. Nietzsche openly embraces the idea that the will to power is a self-conscious interpretation (BGE 22) of natural forces, and even in places where he seems to be most dogmatic in the *Nachlass*, he presents the will to power as how the world looks to *him* in *his* mirror (WP 1067; KSA 11:38[12]). For these reasons, I hold that Nietzsche considers the cosmological versions of the will to power and the eternal recurrence as views that are neither verified by the results of the natural sciences nor in conflict with those results. In this sense, they can be understood as either unverified hypotheses or unverifiable postulates that we should accept because they most promote life and the affirmation of life (BGE 4).[33]

Although it might seem odd for Nietzsche to associate cosmological versions of the will to power and the eternal recurrence with the affirmation of life, we need to recall the way in which Schopenhauer closely links metaphysics to an ethical project that culminates in the denial of life. Indeed, Schopenhauer vehemently attacks naturalism, claiming that "the necessary credo of everyone just and good" is "I believe in a metaphysics" (WWR II:17). Metaphysics is a necessary condition for morality because Schopenhauer thinks that metaphysics is a necessary condition for freedom of the will. For Schopenhauer, free will does not consist in our ability to choose this or that course of action. Like Nietzsche, he insists that our empirical characters are fated to be what they are. Instead, free will consists in our ability to transcend the principle of sufficient reason and deny the very will that expresses itself in the empirical world. In this way, metaphysics makes free will possible, and free will, in turn, makes possible the denial of the will and life itself (WWR I:70).

Schopenhauer is so concerned about naturalism that he refers to it as a "perversity of mind" and calls the naturalist the "antichrist" (PP II:109). Thus, there are good reasons for thinking that Nietzsche's appropriation of the latter epithet can be linked to his embrace of naturalism. In his 1886 preface to *The Birth*, Nietzsche refers to Schopenhauer's phrase, "perversity of mind," and Nietzsche characterizes his first book as one that "betrays a spirit who will one day fight […] the *moral interpretation* of existence" with a "pessimism 'beyond good and evil'" (BT "Attempt":5). Moreover, we can see how Nietzsche employs the eternal recurrence and the will to power to foreclose on the possibility of the sort of redemption Schopenhauer's philosophy offers. On the one hand, if everything—including ourselves—is will to power, then any attempt to negate or abolish the will is itself a manifestation—albeit a sick and self-destructive one—of the will to power (GM III:28). On the other hand, what makes the eternal recurrence so terrifying is that it precludes the possibility of any escape from the cycle of nature. Indeed, it even forecloses the possibility of returning to a better life. In this way, these two teachings entail that things cannot be otherwise: there is just this world and nothing besides.

There is significant textual evidence showing that this framework can be applied to *Zarathustra*. We know from *Twilight of the Idols* that Nietzsche considered *Zarathustra* to mark the end of the metaphysical or "true" world in that it abolishes the distinction between the true and apparent world. Indeed, Nietzsche associates the notion of "noon" in *Zarathustra* with precisely this event, a moment in which the distinction between the "true" and "apparent" worlds is eliminated (TI "Fable"). This indicates that *Zarathustra* is a work that repudiates transcendent metaphysics and so a work of naturalism, and just as Schopenhauer associates naturalism with the destruction of morality, Nietzsche associates *Zarathustra* with an immoralism that goes beyond good and evil. In *Ecce Homo*, Nietzsche explains that he picked Zarathustra so that he could reverse what the Persian prophet Zoroaster had done: whereas Zoroaster had transposed the morality of good and evil into the metaphysical machinery of things, Zarathustra is the "annihilator of morality" (EH "Books":1) who brings forth a self-overcoming of morality out of truthfulness (EH "Destiny":3).

For Nietzsche, the liberation from a morality of good and evil means the restoration of the "innocence of becoming,"[34] and this is why Nietzsche associates the destruction of morality with the affirmation of life. Simply stated, morality is a way of insisting that the world *ought* to be other than it is and therefore it is rooted in revenge, and since the world cannot be other than it is, morality results in a condemnation of this world. In contrast, Nietzsche associates the innocence of becoming with the play of the Heraclitean child, and the task of *Zarathustra* I–III is to achieve this child-like standpoint by summoning the eternal recurrence. However, in order to summon the eternal recurrence and thereby affirm existence, Zarathustra must first learn to love both himself and fate, and this only occurs toward the end of *Zarathustra* III. In contrast, the book begins with Zarathustra proclaiming his love for another controversial concept in the text, the *Übermensch*.

2.6 THE *ÜBERMENSCH*

The most puzzling feature of *Zarathustra* is that even though its main character is introduced in *The Gay Science* immediately after the presentation of the eternal recurrence, the drama of *Zarathustra* begins with no mention of the doctrine. Instead,

Zarathustra initially presents himself as the teacher of the *Übermensch*. We learn from Zarathustra that the *Übermensch* is the meaning of the earth and the goal for all human striving. We also learn that the *Übermensch* is the opposite of the "last human [*der letzte Mensch*]," a type who seems undisturbed by existence and has little interest in pursuing much of anything. What we do not learn, however, is who or what the *Übermensch* is supposed to be. That is, *Zarathustra* offers no substantive explanation of what distinguishes such a figure from an ordinary human being. Finally, we are left wondering just how this future- and goal-directed project of creating the *Übermensch* squares with the eternal recurrence, a thought which seems to eliminate any hope for a permanent improvement to our existential situation.[35]

From the 1882 *Nachlass*, we know there is some relationship between the *Übermensch* and the eternal recurrence. In some of the first mentions of the term, we encounter statements that include an "I" who has difficulty affirming life and wanting to live again. In the first case, this "I"—likely either Zarathustra or Nietzsche himself—states that he does not want life again. The only way he can "bear [*ertragen*]" and "endure [*aushalten*]" life is to create a vision of the *Übermensch* (KSA 10:4[81]).[36] In another note, Zarathustra says that he went into solitude because he wanted to love humans, but always had to hate them. In the end, he loved only the *Übermensch*, which now allows him to "bear [*ertragen*]" the human (KSA 10:4[110]). Taken together, we see Zarathustra (and possibly Nietzsche) confronting the task posed by the eternal recurrence of affirming existence, and this is linked to whether one can love humanity and wish the repetition of one's life. Just as the "I" of the first note cannot wish his own life to return without a vision of the *Übermensch*, Zarathustra cannot love humanity as such, and the only way both can "bear" existence is to create the *Übermensch*, a figure that affirms, rather than merely bears, existence.

Based on these notes, the *Übermensch* is a figure created by humans for humans. That is, the *Übermensch* is an ideal that allows a human like Zarathustra to bear humanity and existence itself. But other notes—as well as passages from the prologue of *Zarathustra*—suggest that the point of the *Übermensch* is to leave humanity behind, such that humanity has an instrumental value in relation to the *Übermensch*. Here Zarathustra's love of the *Übermensch* is combined with "contempt [*Verachtung*]." In one note, this contempt is directed toward the "last human," which is created as the opposite concept of the *Übermensch* (KSA 10:4[171]). Last humans are similar to those in the marketplace who respond indifferently to the madman's pronouncement that God is dead (GS 125). Like the folks in the marketplace, last humans remain obedient to convention (simply because it is convention), seek out a cow-like contentment (small pleasures and relaxation), and correspondingly lack any love or longing (*eros*) for anything greater than their current existence: "What is love? What is creation? What is longing? What is a star? Thus asks the last man, and he blinks" (ZI "Prologue":5).

In other *Nachlass* notes, this "great contempt" is directed at the human as such.[37] Here, we learn that contempt for the human condition drove us to look beyond the stars to religion and metaphysics. Now, however, this same drive, rooted in the same contempt for the human being, is supposed to propel us toward the *Übermensch* (KSA 10:4[214], 5[13], 27[74]). The idea here is that human beings have historically projected their yearnings (*eros*) for something greater into a metaphysical sphere beyond the natural world. The great danger we face with the elimination of God and his shadow is that we no longer yearn for something greater. Thus, we need to maintain this yearning to transcend the human condition, but now direct it toward a this-worldly goal. Although the "madman" passage from *The Gay Science* indicates that humans must try to become gods themselves, the message of *Zarathustra* I—one that differs from *The Gay Science*—is that we must look to create the *Übermensch*.

It seems that the best way to understand the human here is an unstable potentiality that can either progress toward something beyond itself or regress toward something like the last human. Whereas last humans are simply objects of contempt, ordinary humans are objects of both love and contempt. They are objects of love because they have the potential to create the *Übermensch*. They are objects of contempt because they can potentially devolve into the last human. Thus, there are two movements: one is the leveling of human beings through a doctrine of equality and the other "is conversely the intensification of all oppositions and divisions, elimination of equality, the creation of the superpowerful." As Nietzsche writes, "the *former* generates last humans. *My* movement superhumans [*Übermenschen*]" (KSA 10:7[21]).[38]

Loeb has pointed to notes like these to argue that an important outcome of *Zarathustra* is the creation of a new species of *Übermenschen* and the eventual elimination of the human. On Loeb's reading, the tragedy of *Zarathustra* consists in the fact that advanced or higher humans like Zarathustra must sacrifice themselves—in the sense of committing suicide (2010:171)—for the sake of the *Übermensch* (2010:199). This act of collective self-sacrifice is also an act of self-overcoming, and this self-overcoming is a model for the overcoming of humanity through "the suicide of humankind" (2010:171) (see KSA 10:16[65])). As Loeb writes,

> the climax of Nietzsche's book depicts the precise moment when Zarathustra acts to compel humankind to follow the tragic law of life and initiate its own self-overcoming. Just as the greatest sacrifices life for the sake of power, so too humankind must sacrifice itself for the sake of the superhuman.
>
> (2010:10)

To be sure, there is textual evidence that supports important parts of Loeb's reading. Nietzsche does speak of human beings sacrificing themselves for a greater sense of power, and Nietzsche refers to the "eternal recurrence" as a "hammer" that functions as a principle of selection which may eliminate weaker natures (KSA 11:26[376] and 12:2[131]). However, this reading conflicts with central ideas of the fourth book of *The Gay Science* as well as the initial reasons Zarathustra created the *Übermensch*. In *The Gay Science*, there is a clear emphasis on the human being and whether the human being can affirm the eternal recurrence. Thus, we hear the repeated refrain that we humans should become who we are (GS 270, 335), become the poets of our lives (GS 299), attain satisfaction with ourselves by giving style to our characters (GS 290), learn to love fate such that looking away will be our only negation (GS 276), and achieve a feeling of god-like humaneness by redeeming all of history (GS 337). In the *Nachlass* notes from the time where the *Übermensch* is first mentioned, we encounter a figure like Zarathustra finding it difficult to live up to this task, and, out of this inadequacy, he creates the *Übermensch* to help him withstand the eternal recurrence. Thus, the *Übermensch* is designed to preserve humanity, not destroy it, and the ultimate goal is for the human to overcome this sense of inadequacy.

Here, we might inquire more closely into the role that the eternal recurrence plays in this vision. Whereas the eternal recurrence is introduced in *The Gay Science* to test whether the human being can affirm such a thought, Loeb presents the idea as a tool or instrument that the *Übermensch* uses to gain control over time. For Loeb, the eternal recurrence is a teaching that enables the *Übermensch* to "backward-will [*zurückwollen*]" (ordinary humans are not able to do this).[39] Because backward willing, for Loeb, means having the ability to influence the past through present and future willing (2010:186–187), the eternal recurrence effectively endows the *Übermensch* with "power over time" (2010:9, 175, 177, 187), and it is by having power over time that the *Übermensch* is able to affirm existence. Because the capacity for backward willing distinguishes the *Übermensch* from ordinary humans, there is a perfect compatibility between the eternal recurrence and the *Übermensch* (2010:200–201)

Although Loeb's reading has the advantage of showing how these two important concepts in *Zarathustra* relate, it does raise a series of concerns. First, it makes the *Übermensch* more fundamental than the eternal recurrence, as the eternal recurrence is now an instrument that empowers and facilitates the creation of the *Übermensch* by way of backward willing. The *Übermensch* is not, in contrast, something that helps humans bear or even affirm the eternal recurrence. Second, rather than forcing us to confront and even love fate (*amor fati*), Loeb understands the eternal recurrence as something that gives us power over time and presumably fate. Although such a power is won through the capacity for backward willing, how exactly this is supposed to work is not entirely clear. Even if it does work, it is hard to square the idea of having power over time and presumably fate with the view, which Loeb endorses, that *Zarathustra* is a tragedy. Tragedy requires us to reconcile with these forces; it does not grant us power over them.[40] Third, the textual evidence we have regarding backward willing is sparse: the concept only appears in "On Redemption" from *Zarathustra* II and in one *Nachlass* note (KSA 10:18[45]). Neither passage connects backward willing to the *Übermensch*, and only "On Redemption" implies a possible connection with an unmentioned doctrine of the eternal recurrence. Moreover, commentators like Brusotti (1997:574) think the relationship between backward willing and eternal recurrence is the opposite of what Loeb argues: it is through backward willing that one can will the eternal recurrence; it is not, as Loeb claims, that the eternal recurrence enables backward willing.

Loeb's interpretation can be understood as responding to and rejecting a tradition of readings that places the *Übermensch* and the eternal recurrence in conflict and ultimately resolves the conflict in favor of the eternal recurrence. Lampert provides an early and important statement of this view in the Anglo-American secondary literature:

> It seems to me that one of the greatest single causes of the misinterpretation of Nietzsche's teaching is the failure to see that the clearly provisional teaching on the superman [*Übermensch*] is rendered obsolete by the clearly definitive teaching on eternal return.
>
> (1986:258)

In my first publication, I presented a version of such a reading. Specifically, I argued that Zarathustra must sacrifice the *Übermensch*—just as the Apollonian hero was sacrificed in Nietzsche's early understanding of tragedy—to teach and affirm the eternal recurrence (Meyer 2002). Since then, both T. K. Seung (2005) and Tom Stern (2008) have pointed to the tension between the eternal recurrence and the *Übermensch* of *Zarathustra* I.

For those who find a tension or conflict between the *Übermensch* and the eternal recurrence, the conflict is resolved in various ways but almost always in favor of the eternal recurrence. Whereas Lampert provides us with what might be called a replacement theory, Stern presents what might be called a fictionalist reading. Stern points to evidence from the chapter, "On Poets," in which

Zarathustra refers to himself as a poet who lies too much, and Zarathustra includes "gods and overmen" among the lies he tells.[41] For this and other reasons, Stern concludes that the *Übermensch* "is revealed as yet another vain fiction" (2008:314). Seung offers what can be called a revisionist account. Similar to Lampert and Stern, Seung argues that *Zarathustra* II problematizes the simplistic solution of the *Übermensch* offered in *Zarathustra* I, but rather than abandoning or rejecting the idea wholesale, the *Übermensch* undergoes revision. Whereas the *Übermensch* of *Zarathustra* I is a Faustian *Übermensch* who "asserts his autonomous will against the whole world," Zarathustra eventually embraces a Spinozan *Übermensch* who "accepts cosmic necessity as his own will" (2005:xviii). This transformation occurs, according to Seung, in the chapter, "The Convalescent," when Zarathustra accepts his role as the teacher of the eternal recurrence (2005:xiii).

In my first attempt to understand *Zarathustra* (Meyer 2002), I too emphasized the conflict between the *Übermensch* and the eternal recurrence and, like the commentators above, argued that the eternal recurrence took precedent over the *Übermensch*. Like these and other commentators, I also used notions of the Apollonian and the Dionysian from *The Birth* to interpret *Zarathustra* as a tragedy. In particular, I argued that the *Übermensch* represented the Apollonian apotheosis of individuation, and although this heroic vision constitutes a type of life-affirming response to the Silenus-like wisdom of the eternal recurrence, the Dionysian aspect of tragedy ultimately teaches that the hero is symbolically sacrificed so as to bring an end to individuation and effect a joyous reunion with nature. I found evidence for this reading not only in *The Birth* but also in the *Twilight of the Idols*:

> the will to life rejoicing over its own inexhaustibility even in the very sacrifice of its highest types—that is what I called Dionysian, *that* is what I guessed to be the bridge to the psychology of the tragic poet.
> (TI "What I Owe":5)

The idea is that the *Übermensch* represents this highest type, and it is with the sacrifice of this highest type that Zarathustra, too, overcomes individuation, "goes under," and unites with nature and so cosmic necessity. In so doing, Zarathustra experiences a ritualistic death, and he is reborn as a Dionysian child, thereby completing the three metamorphoses sketched in his opening speech.

One of the problems with my initial reading of *Zarathustra*—a nuanced version of the replacement theory—is that there is evidence that Nietzsche wants to hold onto the concept of the *Übermensch* in *Zarathustra* III–IV and even into his later writings. To be sure, references in *Zarathustra* III–IV to the *Übermensch* are relatively few and some passages can even be interpreted as retrospective accounts of Zarathustra's previous activity (see ZIII "Tablets":3 and ZIV "On the Higher Man":3). However, there are notable mentions of the *Übermensch* in the *Nachlass* as Nietzsche is composing *Zarathustra* II–IV and in his subsequent writings. In my considered view, these passages support Seung's claim that Nietzsche revises his concept of the *Übermensch* over the course of *Zarathustra*. Whereas the emphasis in the notes for *Zarathustra* I is the way in which the *Übermensch* helps Zarathustra bear humanity and endure the repetition of existence, one note that forms the basis for "On the Tarantulas" in *Zarathustra* II indicates that humanity's redemption from revenge is a rainbow and a bridge to the *Übermensch* (KSA 10:12[43]). Although the note provides little explanation of how this works, the *Übermensch* now seems to *result from* humans overcoming their dissatisfaction with existence and their revenge against time. Thus, this version of the *Übermensch* is no longer a *means* to helping someone like Zarathustra bear or even affirm an otherwise intolerable existence. Instead, the *Übermensch* is something that emerges once a human like Zarathustra comes to terms with the disharmonic aspects of existence and the negative responses (revenge) they produce.

If we accept this view of the *Übermensch*, one of the questions it raises is whether the overcoming of revenge produces an *Übermensch* that is distinct from the human who overcomes revenge or whether the human being who overcomes revenge becomes an *Übermensch*. The former reading might be suggested by a *Nachlass* note in which we are told that "the humans who were overcome were themselves the fathers of the superhumans [*Übermenschen*]" (KSA 10:18[56]).[42] So understood, we have three groups: (1) humans who have not overcome themselves; (2)

humans who have overcome themselves; and (3) *Übermenschen*. There are, however, a series of problems that confront us in trying to make sense of this reading. If humans can overcome revenge and so themselves, then what distinguishes the humans in (2) from the *Übermenschen* in (3)? Moreover, why do humans need to overcome revenge to "father superhumans"? What is it about revenge that prevents ordinary humans in (1) from fathering *Übermenschen*? Also, if a human can overcome revenge without the *Übermensch*, why do the humans in (2) need to father an *Übermensch* (as they have already achieved redemption)? Finally, how exactly does a human in (2) "father" an *Übermensch*? Is this through mating with another human who has also overcome revenge (2)? Or is it, as Loeb argues, through some act of self-sacrifice or suicide (by those in just (2) or both (1) and (2))? And if the latter, how does the sacrifice of human beings contribute (causally) to the production of *Übermenschen*?

I ask these questions because I do not think there are good answers to them. Of course, if the textual evidence on this matter were unambiguous, these would be questions for Nietzsche, not the interpreter. However, the evidence is not unambiguous, and therefore these difficulties suggest that we might want to pursue an alternative interpretive path. Take for instance Nietzsche's claim that the third part of *Zarathustra* is "the self-overcoming of Zarathustra as a model for the self-overcoming of humanity," which is done "on behalf of the superhumans" (KSA 10:16[65]). Here, it is not clear whether humans who overcome themselves become *Übermenschen* or whether *Übermenschen* are distinct beings that benefit from humanity's self-overcoming. Moreover, there is another strand of textual evidence which suggests that Nietzsche thinks that humans who overcome guilt and revenge simply become *Übermenschen*. In one note, Nietzsche writes that humans must either form themselves back into animals or form themselves into *Übermenschen* (KSA 10:15[4]). The implication of the latter alternative is that human beings can become *Übermenschen*, and they can do this by overcoming guilt and revenge. On this reading, if Zarathustra overcomes guilt and revenge by the end of *Zarathustra* III, Zarathustra himself would become an *Übermensch*.

There is evidence that supports such a reading. In a note that explains Zarathustra's convalescence at the end of *Zarathustra* III, Zarathustra is presented as a happy type who lives like an Epicurean god and an *Übermensch* (KSA 10:16[85]). Because Zarathustra achieves this happiness by turning away from humans and returning to himself, Nietzsche's portrayal recalls his earliest sketch for the third book of his proto-*Zarathustra* project, in which he speaks of "the last happiness of the solitary one," of an ego that is complete, belongs to itself, and has love (KSA 9:11[197]). In the 1883 notes, Nietzsche refers to this self-loving soul as "the *highest soul* [*der* höchsten Seele]." Such a soul is also "the most comprehensive" and "the most necessary"; it is one that, having being, falls in love with becoming, and for whom "everything is a game" (KSA 10:20[10]; see also 17[40]). In another note, Nietzsche then juxtaposes a reference to "the highest soul [*die höchste Seele*]" with a "depiction of the *Übermensch*" (KSA 10:17[41]). This suggests that Nietzsche now understands the *Übermensch* as a self-loving soul that dives into becoming and for whom everything is a game.

Is there support for the idea that Zarathustra himself becomes this "highest soul" and therefore the *Übermensch*? Perhaps the clearest piece of evidence comes from Nietzsche's reflections on *Zarathustra* in *Ecce Homo*. There, Nietzsche quotes from section 19 of "Tablets" in *Zarathustra* III (EH "Books" Z:6), and this passage employs much of the same language that Nietzsche uses to describe the highest soul in the aforementioned *Nachlass* notes:

> The most comprehensive soul, which can run and stray and roam farthest within itself; the most necessary soul, which out of sheer joy plunges itself into chance; that which, having being, dives into becoming, [...] the soul which loves itself most, in which all things have their sweep and countersweep and ebb and flood.
>
> (ZIII "Tablets":19)

Just prior to quoting this passage, Nietzsche claims that in *Zarathustra* "man has been overcome at every moment: the concept of the *Übermensch* has here become the greatest reality," and Nietzsche ascribes this overcoming to the "type of Zarathustra." He then claims that "Zarathustra experiences himself as the *supreme type of all beings* [die höchste Art alles Seienden]." Immediately after the quote, Nietzsche exclaims that this description of Zarathustra's soul "*is the concept of Dionysus himself*": he can bear the heaviest fate and nevertheless be "the eternal yes to all things" (EH "Books" Z:6).

Elsewhere in *Ecce Homo*, Nietzsche provides a much-needed definition of the *Übermensch* as "a type of the highest well-turned-outness [*eines Typus höchster Wohlgerathenheit*]" (EH "Books":1).[43] Unfortunately, *Wohlgerathenheit* or "well-turned-outness" is difficult to translate and often gets lost in translation (Walter Kaufmann seems to be unaware of its significance), but it plays an important role in Nietzsche's later works. According to Mathias Risse, a well-turned-out individual is one who is free from emotions such as guilt, revenge, and *ressentiment* (2003:147). Important here is that Nietzsche associates *Wohlgerathenheit* with *Selbstsucht* (TI "Skirmishes":33)[44] or the self-love that Zarathustra identifies as the gift-giving virtue.[45] From *The Gay Science*, we know that self-satisfaction—attained by giving "style to one's character"—is the means by which revenge is overcome (GS 290). Because the overcoming of revenge is the path to *amor fati*, Risse also argues that a well-turned-out *Übermensch* is an individual who exhibits a "joyous and trusting fatalism" in which "all is redeemed and affirmed in the whole." In *Twilight of the Idols*, Nietzsche ascribes such an attitude to Goethe and again "baptizes" it "with the name Dionysus" (TI "Skirmishes":49). So understood, Nietzsche presents the *Übermensch* in his late works as the "formula for greatness in a human being" (EH "Clever":10) and "the Dionysian affirmation of the world" (KSA 13:16[32]).

As we can see, Nietzsche's later understanding of the *Übermensch* represents a type of superior or great human being who has overcome the guilt and revenge that typically characterizes human existence. Such a reading corresponds to Nietzsche's insistence in *The Antichrist* that he is not occupied with the question as to what will "succeed mankind in the sequence of living beings" (A 4).[46] Instead, the human being is "an *end*," and the question therefore is "what type of man [*Mensch*] shall be *bred*, shall be *willed*" (A 3). Nietzsche expresses a similar idea in an 1887 *Nachlass* note entitled *"Der Übermensch"*: although a kind of *Übermensch* can be found in previous cultures, the question now is "what kind of human being [*welche Art Mensch*]" will we consciously choose to breed (there is no mention of breeding a superior species) (KSA 13:11[413]). Although there have been individuals such as Goethe or even Cesare Borgia who have approximated the ideal of the *Übermensch* in the past, these have all been fortunate accidents and do not fully live up to this ideal. Now we need to produce such human beings as a conscious goal (A 4).[47]

Based on such evidence, we might think that Nietzsche changed his mind about the matter, first presenting the *Übermensch* in *Zarathustra* as a new sort of superior species, only to revise the concept after *Zarathustra* to refer to a superior human being—perhaps in response to the "scholarly oxen" who accused him of Darwinism (EH "Books":1). The problem with such a reading is that Nietzsche casts Zarathustra as just such an *Übermensch*, and he refers to a specific passage from *Zarathustra* III to associate the *Übermensch* with the "highest" and "most comprehensive soul." As *Nachlass* notes from the time indicate, such a connection is not something that Nietzsche retrospectively invents and projects back onto *Zarathustra*; it is there all along.

Indeed, Nietzsche's later reflections on the *Übermensch* as a well-turned-out human being exhibit a deep affinity with the ideals he expresses in the closing sections of *The Gay Science*. Again, Nietzsche calls upon humans to create themselves (GS 299), love fate (GS 276), overcome revenge (GS 290), affirm life (GS 341), bless human history (GS 337), and become gods themselves (GS 125). Nothing is said about creating a new species of *Übermenschen*, and there is nothing to suggest that humanity needs to be sacrificed for the sake of this new species. Indeed, the contempt that Zarathustra initially expresses for the human in *Zarathustra* I seems to conflict with the humanism of *The Gay Science*. Taken together, the idea of creating a new species—rather than educating a certain type of human being—is largely limited to the opening stages of *Zarathustra*, and it is sandwiched between the humanism of *The Gay Science* and Nietzsche's eventual hope for a superior type of human being—a new nobility—in the closing stages of *Zarathustra* as well as his later works.

If this is right, we are left wondering how we might understand those passages in which Nietzsche seems to call for a new species of *Übermenschen* to replace the otherwise contemptible lot of humanity. Here I think that Seung's claim that there are two versions of the *Übermensch* at work even in *Zarathustra* provides a possible solution. For Seung, *Zarathustra* begins with a Faustian *Übermensch*, which represents a conception of agency that attempts to assert its autonomy *against* the world, but then shifts to a Spinozan *Übermensch*, which represents a conception of agency in which one "accepts cosmic necessity" as one's own will. In my view, this is generally right, and one can also understand this shift in terms of the Apollonian (Faustian) and the Dionysian (Spinozan). Whereas the text begins with the celebration of an Apollonian *Übermensch* that represents the "apotheosis of individuation," the text ends with Zarathustra himself either becoming or making progress toward becoming a Dionysian *Übermensch* by reconciling himself with nature and identifying with cosmic necessity. In terms of the problem at hand, Nietzsche's talk about the *Übermensch* as a species distinct from the human being corresponds to the initial Apollonian or even Faustian version in *Zarathustra* I. As *Zarathustra* unfolds, this ideal is revised such that Zarathustra, as a superior individual, either becomes or takes a step toward becoming a Dionysian *Übermensch* by overcoming revenge, "going under," loving fate, and teaching the eternal recurrence.

Of course, if there is a shift in the conception of the *Übermensch* at work in *Zarathustra*, one needs to be able to say where this occurs. For those who read the text in this way, the general idea is that it begins about halfway through *Zarathustra* II with the three songs that occupy the middle of the text—Nietzsche characterizes the "Night Song" as Dionysian in *Ecce Homo* (EH "Books" Z:7)—and the development of "the will to power" in "On Self-Overcoming." For the discussion here, the most important chapter is "On Poets." This is where Nietzsche has Zarathustra cast gods and *Übermenschen* as poetic inventions. Zarathustra acknowledges that he himself is such a poet, and he claims that he is now weary of such poets and their inventions. Whereas Stern has pointed to this passage to dismiss the *Übermensch* as a vain fiction, Loeb and Tinsley have argued that Nietzsche is criticizing a previous "supernatural" use of the term found in the German literary tradition. To make their case, they link the passage to Nietzsche's first use of the term "*Übermensch*" in his published works in GS 143, "The Greatest Advantage of Polytheism." There, Nietzsche speaks of *Übermenschen* alongside mythological creatures such as dwarves, fairies, satyrs, and gods. The point of "On Poets," according to Loeb and Tinsley, is to criticize the mythological understanding of the *Übermensch* and "to highlight the uniqueness and originality" of the new, species-based concept introduced in *Zarathustra* (2022:761).

Although Loeb and Tinsley are right to link "On Poets" to Nietzsche's remarks in GS 143, I think we should draw a different conclusion. Because Zarathustra includes himself among the poets that lie too much, Zarathustra must have told a poetic lie, and I think this lie is the Apollonian *Übermensch* found in *Zarathustra* I. If we ask why Nietzsche would have Zarathustra create such a fiction, we get two answers. First, we know from the *Nachlass* that Zarathustra (or Nietzsche) invents the *Übermensch* to compensate for his own inability to affirm existence. Just as Homer created the realm of gods and heroes in response to the terrible truths of Silenus (BT 3–4), Zarathustra creates a vision of the *Übermensch* to shield himself from the harsh consequences of the eternal recurrence, and he needs such a shield precisely because he is not yet up to the task of affirming the eternal recurrence. Second, GS 143 indicates that the invention of *Übermenschen* serves as a preliminary exercise "for the justification of the egoism [*Selbstsucht*] and sovereignty of the individual" (GS 143). Applied to *Zarathustra*, the Apollonian *Übermensch* of *Zarathustra* I is a preliminary exercise for the emergence of a self-loving and sovereign individual. In my view, Nietzsche describes such an individual in section 19 of "Tablets" in *Zarathustra* III and he later casts such an individual as a Dionysian *Übermensch*. Because Nietzsche also tells us that Zarathustra is or becomes this Dionysian *Übermensch*, we can say that the Apollonian *Übermensch* of *Zarathustra* I is a preliminary exercise for Zarathustra eventually becoming a sovereign individual and so a Dionysian *Übermensch*.[48]

It is with this distinction in hand that we can also explain how the *Übermensch* relates to the eternal recurrence. Whereas the language of evolution and progress that Nietzsche attributes to the Apollonian *Übermensch* in *Zarathustra* I ostensibly conflicts with the eternal recurrence and has led commentators to identify a tension between the two concepts, the Dionysian conception of the *Übermensch* is perfectly compatible with the acceptance and affirmation of the eternal recurrence. Indeed, the idea is that Zarathustra becomes or will eventually become a Dionysian *Übermensch* by teaching the eternal recurrence, exhibiting the "joyous and trusting fatalism" that Nietzsche equates with an affirmation of the world as it is. To do this, however, he must cast off his reliance on the Apollonian *Übermensch*, learn to love himself, and ultimately overcome his own revenge against time. On this reading, this happens when Zarathustra returns to his solitude in the last half of *Zarathustra* III.

Such a reading also resolves one of the tensions of the opening part of *Zarathustra*. In the prologue of *Zarathustra* I, Zarathustra articulates the need for human beings to create the *Übermensch*. At the same time, Zarathustra presents the Heraclitean-Dionysian child as the capstone of the three metamorphoses and therewith a second ideal. Thus, we are left wondering exactly how the *Übermensch* and the child are supposed to relate, if at all. On this reading, the child and the Apollonian *Übermensch* of *Zarathustra* I are distinct concepts, potentially in tension with each other. However, we can see a close kinship between the child and the Dionysian *Übermensch*. To see the relationship, one needs to recall that Nietzsche associates the Dionysian *Übermensch* with the highest or most comprehensive soul in section 19 of "Tablets" in *Zarathustra* III. Although the exact phrasing does not occur in *Zarathustra* III, we know from the *Nachlass* that this soul experiences everything as play or a game (KSA 10:17[40], 20[10], 22[1]). Because Nietzsche also associates the Heraclitean child with play, there is a clear link between the child and the most comprehensive soul and so the Dionysian *Übermensch*.

We can also use this understanding of the Dionysian *Übermensch* to make sense of the language of sacrifice and death that Nietzsche often associates with Zarathustra's going under. In my initial reading of the text, I held that Nietzsche had Zarathustra sacrifice his Apollonian vision of the *Übermensch* to teach the eternal recurrence, and it was through this sacrifice that Zarathustra also experienced a "ritual death" that Nietzsche associates with ancient Greek tragedy and the mysteries of Dionysus. Although such a reading allows us to map *The Birth* rather neatly onto *Zarathustra*, the lack of explicit evidence suggests that such a reading might be too neat. Nevertheless, there is textual evidence indicating that Zarathustra himself "plunges itself into chance" out of "sheer joy" and "dives into becoming." The idea is that this process of diving into becoming is equivalent to Zarathustra's "going under," and Zarathustra's going under amounts to the death of himself as an individual agent distinct from nature and necessity. Similar to Seung's Spinozan *Übermensch*, this soul then identifies itself with nature, necessity, and the cosmic will such that the "I" becomes a "*fatum*" (KSA 10:16[83], 20[3], 21[1], 21[6] and KSA 11:27[67], 29[13]). Initiated into the mysteries of Dionysus, Zarathustra's soul is then "reborn" as a child that embodies "innocence and forgetting, a new beginning, a game, a self-propelled wheel, a first movement, a sacred 'Yes'" (ZI "Metamorphoses").

For these reasons, I think there is a clear association between the Dionysian *Übermensch* and the Heraclitean child. However, they may not be necessarily identical. Instead, the child might be the precondition for the emergence of the Dionysian *Übermensch*, and the Dionysian *Übermensch*—a grown-up Heraclitean child— can instead be equated with what Nietzsche eventually calls the noble soul in the final chapter of *Beyond Good and Evil*. Of course, *Beyond Good and Evil* is not the first place Nietzsche talks about a new nobility. He mentions such a nobility in GS 337, describing the noble as "a god full of power and love" who continually "bestows its riches" like the sun over the sea, and he has Zarathustra call for a new nobility throughout "On Old and New Tablets" in *Zarathustra* III. In *Beyond Good and Evil*, Nietzsche clearly connects the noble soul to Dionysus, as the chapter concludes with Nietzsche revealing himself to be "the last disciple and initiate of the god Dionysus." This, of course, suggests that Nietzsche sees himself as such a noble soul, and this is precisely how he presents himself in *Ecce Homo*. There, he claims to embody the self-love of the noble soul and, like Zarathustra, the *Wohlgerathenheit* of the Dionysian *Übermensch*. So understood, the *Übermensch* does not disappear in Nietzsche's later writings. Instead, it appears under a different name, the noble soul, and Nietzsche not only discusses this ideal, but also he seems to present himself as having achieved this ideal in *Ecce Homo*. That is, Nietzsche presents himself as a disciple of Dionysus and an individual who, free from *ressentiment*, exhibits a "joyous and trusting fatalism."

2.7 REVENGE AND THE ETERNAL RECURRENCE (AGAIN)

In the previous section, I argued that the understanding of the *Übermensch* shifts in *Zarathustra* with the introduction of the problem of revenge in *Zarathustra* II. Rather than holding on to a vision of an Apollonian *Übermensch* that enables Zarathustra to endure the eternal recurrence, Zarathustra must himself become a Dionysian *Übermensch* who, by definition, overcomes revenge and learns to love the fatalism that the eternal recurrence entails. In the text itself, the need to overcome revenge takes centerstage in "On Redemption" in *Zarathustra* II. There, we learn that Zarathustra's previous claim that the creative will is a great liberator and joy-bringer is insufficient. The will does not stand outside or above nature such that it can exercise control over it. Instead, the will itself is still a prisoner to the past and even nature itself, and this makes the will vengeful. Although the problem of revenge is initially introduced as a response to human inequality in "On the Tarantulas" in *Zarathustra* II, Zarathustra eventually makes the claim that all revenge is revenge against time. In my view, revenge against time takes two forms. First, we are vengeful against time because it devours the present and so makes everything transient. In German, this is the problem of *Vergänglichkeit* (transience). Second, we are vengeful against a past that cannot be changed. In contrast to how we typically think about the future (as an open book), the past is sealed forever, and this is a problem when the past includes events we wish had not happened. Using another German term, we can say that this is the problem of *Vergangenheit* (the past).[49]

The text of *Zarathustra* also makes it clear that overcoming revenge is related in some significant way to the eternal recurrence. Exactly how they relate is far from clear. Is the eternal recurrence the key to overcoming revenge? Or does overcoming revenge make possible the teaching of the eternal recurrence? On my reading, the eternal recurrence only helps us address the problem of *Vergänglichkeit*, but in so doing, it makes the problem of *Vergangenheit* worse. The problem of *Vergänglichkeit* comes to consciousness most when we experience some moment of great bliss or happiness. Here, thoughts of how wonderful life is can often be accompanied by a corresponding sadness or melancholy about how such experiences will eventually come to an end. In Greek literature, Herodotus gives a moving description of this when he relates how Xerxes, upon blissfully watching his armies march from Asia into Europe, broke down in tears, subsequently explaining to his uncle that he wept because he reflected on the brevity of human life.[50] In terms of *Zarathustra*, the problem is that the more Zarathustra comes to love life, the more he is pained by its inevitable passing.

If we follow the more dominant interpretation of the eternal recurrence as a "practical *thought experiment* designed to test whether one's life has been good" (Anderson 2022), the eternal recurrence does nothing to solve the problem of *Vergänglichkeit* and so this aspect of our revenge against time.[51] Thus, those who defend such a reading—usually it is done with little reference to the actual drama of *Zarathustra*—must either deny that, for Nietzsche, *Vergänglichkeit* causes feelings of revenge or provide an account of how Nietzsche resolves the problem by some other means.[52] In contrast, if we understand the doctrine cosmologically, the eternal recurrence addresses the problem of *Vergänglichkeit* head on. Although all things are subject to cycles of creation and destruction and so nothing lasts forever, no destruction is permanent. Everything, including one's own life, is part of an ever-recurring cycle and therefore immortalized, and this, Nietzsche thinks, should overcome our revenge against *Vergänglichkeit*.[53] Thus, Nietzsche writes that we should not be afraid of the flux of all things because the flux flows back upon itself and all "it was" will again be an "it is" (KSA 10:4[85]).

There are, however, two potentially terrifying aspects of this doctrine, and the first has to do with the problem of *Vergangenheit*. By immortalizing our most cherished experiences, we also immortalize the less appealing, even appalling, moments of the past on both personal and collective levels. Just as a moment of romantic bliss or the founding of a republic might be immortalized forever, so too will everything from a painful break up to slave trade and the Holocaust.[54] Matters become particularly painful when we feel ourselves to have, through our own actions, contributed to the terribleness of the world; here, the thought of the recurrence of these events might overwhelm us with feelings of regret, shame, and guilt (think of the pale criminal in *Zarathustra* I or even Sophocles' Oedipus). Through the eternal recurrence, these fixed moments of the past become inevitable destinations of the future. That is, even if the immediate future seems open, nothing will stop the fact that the succession of future events will inevitably lead to these horrors repeating themselves not just once but an infinite number of times. Thus, we are confronted with the problem that is almost the exclusive focus of the practical readings of the eternal recurrence: are we so well disposed to our lives and the world that we would want to relive the past again and again? Or would such a thought magnify feelings of guilt and regret so much that we would be crushed by this possibility?

As we can see, the eternal recurrence, either as a thought experiment or a cosmological truth, not only fails to solve the problem of *Vergangenheit* it exacerbates it. That is, rather than providing us with a way to redeem the past, it intensifies the need for redemption. It is one thing to be frustrated by a past event that can never be changed; it is another to be confronted with the idea that this past event will recur again and again into infinity. At least in the first case, the fact that such an event is transient, that we will "never have to do that again," provides some comfort. But if the eternal recurrence only makes things worse by eliminating this comfort, what addresses the problem of *Vergangenheit*? One solution seems to be the kind of forgetting that Nietzsche ascribes to the child, and the capacity for forgetting is perhaps what allows someone like Zarathustra to experience a tremendous moment [*ungeheure Augenblick*] of bliss. But we cannot always be wholly immersed in the present like a child or even a cow (HL 1). We need to grow up and become fully human, even superhuman, and this means incorporating a sense of the past into our identities.

The answer Nietzsche proposes to the problem of *Vergangenheit* has to do with backward willing (*Zurückwollen*). In contrast to Loeb, who argues that the eternal recurrence enables backward willing by granting us power over time, I understand backward willing to be a power to reinterpret the meaning and significance of past events in ways that change the value and emotional valence we associate with them.[55] According to Brusotti (1997:572–573), Nietzsche explains this concept in the following note (even though it is not explicitly mentioned): "Whatever *I did not want before, this is what* **I must want** *afterward* (putting things right, fitting thing in—digesting—but checking to see *if* I can do it!" (KSA 10:17[38]).[56]

Like Jenkins (2020:32), I think we can also gain some insight into backward willing by looking at Nietzsche's reflections on the "it was" and the suffering it creates in *History for Life*. There, Nietzsche locates in humans a *"plastic power"* to "transform and incorporate into oneself what is past and foreign, to heal wounds, […], to recreate broken moulds." A people can perish if they lack this power. However, stronger individuals can "appropriate the things of the past" and "the most powerful and tremendous nature would be characterized by the fact that it would know no boundary at all at which the historical sense began to overwhelm it." Here, all of the past would be incorporated and transformed "into blood" (HL 1).

The connections between what Nietzsche says in *History for Life* and the drama of *Zarathustra* are both obvious and significant. In *Zarathustra*, the goal of backward willing is to interpret past events in a way that one can will, affirm, and even love the "it was" (*amor fati*) such that one can say, "thus I will it." So understood, everyone has the capacity to backward will, and we engage in a version of it, albeit most often subconsciously and not always with an eye to affirmation, whenever we construct a present narrative about the past. However, very few individuals have the psychic and spiritual power to incorporate a significant number of past events into a unifying narrative such that they could say "da capo" to everything. As Nietzsche explains in *The Gay Science*, a person who could experience his own history as human history and bless both would be like a "god full of power and love" and the ultimate expression of humaneness (GS 337).

But here we might wonder why some possess the capacity to engage in this sort of transformation and why others might be so weak that they "perish from a single experience, from a single painful event" (HL 1). In my view, psychological health and strength determines the extent to which one has this power. Here, I associate psychological health with both *Wohlgerathenheit* or well-turned-outness and *Selbstsucht* or self-love. As such, a psychologically healthy person is one who generally takes pleasure in her own existence, and the project of backward willing must begin from a present sense of self-satisfaction. I associate psychological strength with Nietzsche's teaching of the will to power. In terms of backward willing, the idea is that we can gain power over the past by reinterpreting it, and therefore interpretation itself is an expression of the will to power (GM II:12; KSA 11:2[148]). As Nietzsche explains in the *Genealogy*, guilt, sin, and "psychological pain" are mere interpretations of past events, and a strong and well-constituted (*wohlgerathenen*) person can digest these past experiences (GM III:16). Thus, the healthier and more powerful we are, the more of the past we can "digest" or incorporate into a given interpretation. At the height of this process, one is not only reconciled with the past but also longs for something higher, namely, its immortalization through eternal repetition. So understood, the ultimate object of the will to power, which I understand to be a form of love or *eros*, is the eternal recurrence (or "eternity"), a teaching which addresses the problem of transience by imposing "upon becoming the character of being" (KSA 12:7[54]).[57]

The problem, of course, is that very few people have the psychological strength to achieve this Herculean task, and the difficulty of affirming the eternal recurrence is likely one reason why Nietzsche often associates the doctrine with a "hammer" and thinks of it as a selective principle for breeding (see KSA 11:26[376] and KSA 12:2[131]). The idea seems to be that those who are too psychologically sick and weak to incorporate the past in this way will therefore be too sick and weak to endure the thought of the eternal recurrence (in GS 359, Nietzsche identifies these individuals as the *missrathen* or ill-constituted ready for revenge). Instead, they will consider the thought of the eternal recurrence to be horrifying, so much so that they, like Socrates (GS 340), might turn to suicide as an ultimate refuge. That said, I do not think, *pace* Loeb, that Nietzsche is exhorting humanity to seek out suicide, either as a refuge or for the sake of creating an *Übermensch*. As I see it, *Zarathustra* IV is about the pity that Zarathustra naturally feels for those ill-constituted "higher men" who find it difficult, if not impossible, to come to terms with the eternal recurrence, and Zarathustra seems to prescribe laughter as a temporary remedy for their illness. What this means is that Zarathustra's natural inclination is to be concerned about the fate of these individuals, even if Zarathustra is ultimately supposed to overcome this temptation and focus on his work. It is not, in contrast, an active wish for their elimination or extirpation, as such an attitude conflicts with *amor fati* and Dionysian affirmation of the whole.[58]

There is one more unsettling implication of the eternal recurrence as a cosmological theory that needs to be considered. Although some have argued that the eternal recurrence "intensifies the dynamics of choice" by infinitely repeating every choice we make (Magnus 1978:157), I think it does the exact opposite, as the view implies a form of fatalism or determinism that undermines our commonsense conception of agency as freely choosing subjects who determine our future actions (see KSA 11:25[214]).[59] It does this for two reasons. First, the eternal recurrence entails that everything we will ever do has already been done, and since there is no first cycle in which we choose how nature unfolds, we can be certain that we are not, currently, authoring otherwise undetermined lives that we will then repeat eternally hence forth. Any sense that we might have such a power to shape the course of nature is simply based on our ignorance of what has already happened. Second, Nietzsche associates the idea of the eternal recurrence with the claim that all things are knotted together, such that a change in any one event results in a change in everything else. Recall, Nietzsche's tragic worldview denies that there are individuals in any robust sense that would make them distinct from nature. Here, the "fatality" of one's "essence" cannot be "disentangled from the fatality of all that has been and will be." Taken together, individual agents are wholly natural beings who lack any independent or distinct existence and have no control over what we do or who we are: "no one gives man his qualities," not God, not society, not even ourselves (TI "Errors":8).

Although this might be terrifying for some, Nietzsche believes that fate is ultimately a liberating thought. In *The Birth*, this is precisely the lesson Nietzsche draws from the Oedipus myth: although he tears his eyes out in agony and grief in *Oedipus Rex*, Oedipus is then blessed by the gods for accepting his fate in *Oedipus at Colonus* (BT 9). In other words, the true catharsis of tragedy does not involve pity and fear, as Aristotle claimed, but rather the elimination of any sense of moral responsibility and therefore the purification of feelings of guilt, shame, and regret (this is why Plato was so opposed to the genre). In *Twilight of the Idols*, Nietzsche claims that the rejection of "intelligible freedom" means that "no one is responsible for man's being such-and-such," and because we are not responsible for our being, we are liberated from the guilt and bad conscience that has hitherto plagued humanity. Because "one is necessary, one is a piece of fatefulness, one belongs to the whole, one is the whole," "there is nothing which could judge, measure, compare or sentence our being." Thus, by adopting a "joyous and trusting fatalism" and affirming the eternal recurrence, Zarathustra restores "the innocence of becoming" and effectively "redeem[s] the world" (TI "Errors":8). Indeed, it is here that we see why Nietzsche wants us to think of *Zarathustra* as a tragedy and why this tragedy has such significance for the history of philosophy: by completing naturalism and affirming fatalism, he is liberating humanity from a morality that unfolded into the nihilism of Schopenhauer's philosophy.

2.8 THE TRAGEDY OF *ZARATHUSTRA* I–III AND THE SATYR PLAY OF *ZARATHUSTRA* IV

The point of this chapter has been to develop evidence and resources for reading *Zarathustra* as a tragedy and a satyr play. To conclude, I now want to bring these resources together to give an overview of how *Zarathustra* can be read in this way. This will then set the stage for a more detailed interpretation of the text in the following chapters.

The tragedy of *Zarathustra* is rooted in and responds to a tragic worldview. Nietzsche inherits this tragic worldview from Schopenhauer and other pessimists of his day. Essential to this worldview is the idea that suffering is an ineluctable feature of human existence (factual pessimism), and it raises the evaluative question as to whether existence should be affirmed or denied. In his early writings, Nietzsche modifies and expands this worldview into a cosmological naturalism based on the thinking of Heraclitus and supported by the natural sciences. He expresses the foundations of this tragic worldview in works like *Human* and *The Gay Science*, and he completes this tragic worldview in a way that puts an end to the metaphysical tradition with the teachings of the will to power and the eternal recurrence in *Zarathustra*.

As a text, *Zarathustra* emerges directly from Nietzsche's free spirit works in general and *The Gay Science* in particular. Nietzsche's presentation of the death of God and the elimination of his shadow in *The Gay Science* has a twofold significance. First, the death of God symbolizes the downfall of a metaphysical tradition that gave humans meaning, purpose, and a center of gravity. Now that God is dead, humans need a new way to orient themselves. Second, the elimination of God's shadow amounts to the self-overcoming of the ascetic will to truth, and the overcoming of the will to truth makes possible Nietzsche's return to music and art starting with "Sanctus Januarius" or the fourth book of *The Gay Science*. Both points are crucial for understanding the background and genesis of *Zarathustra* in relation to Nietzsche's larger oeuvre.

In line with the full title of *The Birth of Tragedy out of the Spirit of Music*, *Zarathustra* emerges from a spirit of music that took hold of Nietzsche in 1881. In this musical mood, he begins to write his own poetry, some of which appears in the 1882 edition of *The Gay Science* as well as his *Idylls from Messina*. In one of the sketches for what later becomes the poem, "Sils Maria" (published in the 1887 edition of *The Gay Science*), Nietzsche presents Zarathustra as emerging from his own "noon day" in which suddenly "one became two" such that "Zarathustra came into view" (KSA 10:4[145]). Thus, Nietzsche is presenting Zarathustra as the product of his own Dionysian ecstasy, such that Nietzsche is standing outside of himself now in a transfigured state (BT 5). So understood, Nietzsche is like the Dionysian artist Archilochus described in *The Birth of Tragedy*, and Zarathustra is Nietzsche's second self or, as Nietzsche often refers to him, his "son" (KSB 6:407, 421, 431, 438).

It is in this transfigured state that Nietzsche *qua* Zarathustra creates the image or ideal of the *Übermensch*, and this vision emerges as a direct response to the Dionysian wisdom expressed in the form of the eternal recurrence. The idea is that Zarathustra cannot bear such a reality, much like the Homeric Greeks, and so he needs to imagine an ideal being that will help him "bear" this wisdom and even his own existence. In terms of the tragedy of *Zarathustra*, the *Übermensch* begins as the Apollonian hero, whereas Zarathustra can be construed as the leader of a Dionysian chorus, which was, according to Nietzsche, the main protagonist in the earliest tragedies.

The Apollonian *Übermensch* is the central figure of the prologue and *Zarathustra* I, and the drama here consists in Zarathustra's attempt to communicate this vision to others. This attempt largely fails, even though Zarathustra does gather some disciples along the way. The drama of *Zarathustra* intensifies when this lofty Apollonian vision confronts the chthonic and Dionysian elements of existence in *Zarathustra* II. These elements come to the fore in the three songs that constitute the center of *Zarathustra* II. Immediately thereafter, we are presented with the idea that the will to power animates all living things in "On Self-Overcoming," and then we are introduced to an "overhero" who approaches the soul (Ariadne) once "the hero has abandoned her" (ZII "On the Sublime"). From the *Nachlass*, we know that Nietzsche associates the hero with Theseus, and the "overhero" with the coming of Dionysus (KSA 10:13[1]). Since Theseus can be understood as an Apollonian hero, I read this passage as signaling a shift away from the Apollonian *Übermensch* of *Zarathustra* I toward the arrival of Dionysus and a Dionysian *Übermensch* in *Zarathustra* III.

In *Zarathustra* II, there are additional indicators that Zarathustra must revise his initial strategy of relying on the *Übermensch* as a response to the unannounced doctrine of the eternal recurrence. In "On Poets," Zarathustra acknowledges his status as a poet, admitting that he lies too much, and the *Übermensch* is included among the fictions that such poets create. In "The Soothsayer," we are presented with the thought that "all is empty, all is the same, all has been," and this turns the mood dark and dreary, filling the air with melancholy. Thus, it seems that Zarathustra must abandon any hope that the (Apollonian) *Übermensch* offers a permanent solution to the problem of existence. These reflections lead directly into what most commentators believe is the key turning point in *Zarathustra*, "On Redemption." Here, we learn that Zarathustra's previous redemption strategy of creative willing is insufficient. The will itself is fettered by the past and embedded within nature. Thus, the will must learn to transform the "it was" into "thus I willed it" by reconciling itself with and ultimately affirming nature and time. In short, Zarathustra must now learn to love fate (*amor fati*).

Zarathustra III eventually ushers in the arrival of Dionysus. For Dionysus to come, Zarathustra must confront and defeat his archenemy, the spirit of gravity. The spirit of gravity personifies feelings of melancholy and revenge, and Zarathustra's eventual confrontation with the spirit of gravity is initially portrayed in "On the Vision and the Riddle." The chapter also dramatizes the nausea Zarathustra feels about affirming the eternal recurrence. This is symbolized by the shepherd choking on a snake that has crawled into his mouth. As we later learn in "The Convalescent," Zarathustra's disgust at the thought of the eternal recurrence has to do with the disgust he feels about the eternal recurrence of the "small human." As Seung has argued, Zarathustra's disgust with the small human is actually a disgust with humanity as such (2005:xvii–xviii), and Zarathustra eventually recognizes that his disgust with humanity is rooted in the disgust he feels about himself. For Zarathustra to overcome this disgust, he must start with himself, and it is for this reason that Nietzsche has Zarathustra return to his cave and his solitude in the latter half of *Zarathustra* III.

The process of overcoming the disgust Zarathustra feels with himself occurs in the chapters "The Return Home," "On the Three Evils," and "On the Spirit of Gravity." In these passages, Zarathustra pronounces *Selbstsucht* or self-love blessed and speaks of a "self-enjoying soul." This "self-enjoying soul" is not projected onto some future hope for an Apollonian *Übermensch*. Instead, Zarathustra must learn to take pleasure in his own existence by learning to love himself.[60] By learning to love himself, Zarathustra overcomes his disgust with himself, the small man, and humanity as such, thereby biting off the head of the snake in "On the Vision and the Riddle." In this state of self-enjoyment, Zarathustra vanquishes the spirit of gravity and finally learns not only how to walk and run but also how to dance and fly. As a god-like self-enjoying soul, Zarathustra is now ready to summon the eternal recurrence.

It is interesting to note that the final chapters of *Zarathustra* III roughly follow Nietzsche's 1881 sketches to depict "the last happiness of the solitary one" in the third book. According to these sketches, the fourth book is then supposed to be "dithyrambic" as there is now a desire "to experience everything again and an infinite number of times" (KSA 9:11[197]; see also GS 370). The dithyramb is a poetic genre performed in honor of Dionysus, and Dionysus makes his appearance toward the end of *Zarathustra* III. Indeed, Nietzsche had originally planned to have "Dionysus" as the title of the third section of "The Seven Seals," and subtle references to Dionysus run through the final chapters of the text.[61] Most notably, in "On the Great Longing," which was originally titled, "Ariadne," Zarathustra calls upon a "nameless one," a "vintager who is waiting with his diamond knife." The name of this "vintager" and "nameless one" is none other than Dionysus.

The presence of Dionysus at the end of *Zarathustra* III provides substantive evidence that Nietzsche wrote *Zarathustra* I–III as a tragedy, given that Nietzsche emphasized, in *The Birth*, the Dionysian origins and essence of the genre. The problem, of course, is making sense of exactly how the ending of *Zarathustra* III unfolds in a "tragic" fashion, and it should be noted here that any account requires speculation and interpretation of passages in which nothing is explicit. In my view, Zarathustra's teaching of the eternal recurrence effects his "going under," and his "going under" amounts to a "tragic death." Here, Zarathustra becomes the "most comprehensive soul" sketched in section 19 of "Tablets" and the Heraclitean child of "On the Three Metamorphoses" by diving into becoming. His union with nature amounts to the death of an "old self" that tried to remain distinct from nature and necessity. However, this ritual death results in Zarathustra being reconstituted as a wholly natural being now in love with and wedded to nature, necessity, and eternity. In this way, the tragedy of *Zarathustra* I–III dramatizes a process in which Zarathustra himself is naturalized (GS 109; see also BGE 230),[62] achieves the ideal of *amor fati* set forth in GS 276, and follows the teaching Nietzsche attributes to tragedy in his first book: "We believe in eternal life" (BT 16).

As a "new" self, Zarathustra has a child-like attitude toward the world, one that has restored "the innocence of becoming" and takes a playful delight in the eternal game of creation and destruction (BT 24). This new perspective, won through the confrontation with nature and necessity in *Zarathustra* III, sets the stage for the satyr play of *Zarathustra* IV. There is a seriousness about Zarathustra at the beginning of *Zarathustra* IV, but the spirit of laughter and play eventually come to dominate, most notably in the "Ass Festival." The satyr play results from the incongruity between Zarathustra, who, much like a Papa Silenus figure, has come to terms with both himself and the eternal recurrence, and the "higher men," much like a chorus of buffoonish satyrs, who eventually gather around Zarathustra. These higher men are like Zarathustra in that they stand above or beyond conventional norms and recognize, even feel, the problem of existence. However, unlike Zarathustra, they have not yet learned to love themselves and therefore cannot bear the thought of the eternal recurrence on their own. Thus, they cry out for something to worship, some redeeming figure who will give their lives meaning and comfort. These yearnings seem to be initially directed at a Jesus-like Zarathustra, but the worry is that these higher men will revert to believing in the old God and other metaphysical comforts. To avoid this disastrous result, their desire to worship is eventually directed at an ass, and the laughter and mockery typical of a satyr play ensues.

The satyr play of *Zarathustra* IV ends on three points that indicate its status as a *Zwischenspiel* or "interlude" between *Zarathustra* I–III and what I think is the Dionysian comedy that Nietzsche writes in his subsequent works. The first is that Zarathustra exhorts his higher men to laugh. As we learn from the 1886 preface to *The Birth*, the exhortation to laugh is a "this-worldly" comfort designed to eliminate any temptation to return to metaphysical comforts (BT "ASC":7). As we are told in section one of "The Ass Festival," laughter kills most thoroughly, and therefore making a comedy of Christianity would most thoroughly kill the Christian God. Second, Zarathustra prophesizes in "The Welcome" that a *"fröhlicher Hanswurst"* or "joyous Mr. Sausage" will come one day. Although this could signal Zarathustra's own coming as a *Hanswurst*, it is significant that Nietzsche repeatedly presents himself as a *Hanswurst* in his final letters and writings (EH "Destiny":1; KSB 8:1240). Finally, the lions that appear at the end of *Zarathustra* IV are *laughing* lions, and their laughter foreshadows the laughter that characterizes Nietzsche's philosophers of the future and his new nobility (see BGE 223 and 294). For these reasons, I read these features of *Zarathustra* IV as proleptic references to the comedy of Nietzsche's 1888 writings, and therefore when Zarathustra refers to his "work" at the end of *Zarathustra* IV, he is referring to the work that Nietzsche himself will undertake in his post-*Zarathustra* writings: a dual project of becoming who he is (*Ecce Homo*) and a revaluation of values (*The Antichrist*) that takes the form of a Dionysian comedy.

NOTES

1. Gadamer (1988) also emphasizes the tragic nature of the drama of *Zarathustra*.
2. One of the first mentions of the satyr play in relation to *Zarathustra* IV can be found in Knortz (1906:43). Nehamas (2012:135) mentions reading *Zarathustra* in this way but does not develop the idea in much detail. Hatab (2005: Epilogue) claims that *Zarathustra* IV is a satyr play that follows upon a tragic trilogy. See also Burnham and Jesinghausen (2010:169–170). However, I resist the idea that the satyr play of *Zarathustra* IV somehow undermines the significance or seriousness of the first three parts, just as the Aeschylus' *Proteus* would not undermine the serious and significance of the *Oresteia* trilogy.
3. More recently, Schacht (2023:125) has presented a version of the ironic reading in which the parody of *Zarathustra* IV is supposed to undercut a dogmatic understanding of the teachings of *Zarathustra* I–III. Zittel (2000) can also

be understood as offering an ironic reading of *Zarathustra* and the doctrines presented therein. See Cauchi (1998) for a reading of *Zarathustra* IV that emphasizes self-parody and presents Zarathustra as the tragic buffoon.
4 In contrast, I interpret BGE 223 as important evidence for reading Nietzsche's 1888 works as a Dionysian comedy (see Meyer 2012 and 2018).
5 For a more developed version of this concern, see Gooding-Williams (2011). See Loeb (2010:101n36) for his response.
6 See both Stern (2008:313) and Tevenar (2013:277) for the different meanings of this term.
7 We know that Nietzsche at least had plans for Zarathustra to leave his cave (KSA 11:29[24], 29[26], 31[9]). In the published version, one can only infer that Zarathustra leaves.
8 Another issue for Loeb's reading is that Nietzsche was also sketching plans for Zarathustra's "final farewell" from the cave at the end of *Zarathustra* IV (KSA 11:29[24], 29[26], 31[9]). If this is the case, Nietzsche cannot be trying to connect *Zarathustra* IV to the action of section six of "Tablets" in *Zarathustra* III in which, on Loeb's reading, Zarathustra remains in the cave only to die in the presence of his children at the end of *Zarathustra* III.
9 In *The World as Will and Representation*, Schopenhauer also employs this language to describe how someone who renounces the world is liberated from the kingdom of nature and necessity and enters the kingdom of grace (WWR I:70). Also see Löwith (1997:122) for a similar reading.
10 In the German literature, see Grätz (2024:3–69) for a comprehensive and detailed account of these matters.
11 In 1876, Nietzsche was living with Reé and Meysenbug in Sorrento, Italy as he began work on the first of his free spirit works. See D'Iorio (2016) for an account of this time in Nietzsche's life.
12 This and the other translations of this passage can all be found in Bishop and Stephenson (2005:71–75).
13 All references to Plato's works are based on the translations found in *Plato's Complete Works* (1997).
14 There is a bit more variation between GS 342 and KSA 9:11[195].
15 For alternative understandings of *amor fati*, see Han-Pile (2011) and Stern (2013).
16 I explain the discrepancy between the positions of *The Gay Science* and *The Birth* in Meyer (2019:201–203).
17 Brobjer (2023: Ch.6) for a helpful discussion of the philological details surrounding *Zarathustra* IV.
18 Also see Pippin (1988) and Nehamas (2012).
19 See Del Caro (2011:88).
20 Translation from CWFN 14. This note appears exactly in the interlude between the completion of *Zarathustra* I and the composition of *Zarathustra* II.
21 See Halliwell (1996 and 1998).
22 See Hollinrake (1982:78–79) for a similar understanding of *Untergang*.
23 Also see Vivarelli (2017 and 2018).

24 For more on this point, see Meyer (2014c: Ch.1).
25 See Wohlfart (1997) for more on the close connection between Heraclitus and Zarathustra.
26 For instance, see Riccardi (2021: Ch.2.6).
27 I have developed this argument in greater detail in Meyer (2022).
28 For more on this aphorism, see Loeb (2021b).
29 This phrase also occurs at the end of Dühring's *Der Werth des Lebens* (1865), where Dühring is attacking what he calls the "metaphysics of revenge" (1865:234). I discuss the connection between metaphysics and revenge in more detail in the final chapter. Jenkins (2019) provides a helpful discussion of the topic but says little about Dühring's relevance.
30 See Sinhababu (forthcoming) for detailed evidence of this point.
31 See Janaway (2022:89).
32 For more on forces as occult qualities, see Poellner (1995:46–57), who traces this objection back to Berkeley.
33 Lampert (1986:260) also casts the eternal recurrence as a postulate or a regulative idea.
34 Nietzsche first mentions this phrase in KSA 10:7[7] within the context of summarizing *The Birth of Tragedy*. This is written just as he is starting work on *Zarathustra* II.
35 See Kaufmann (1974: Ch.11) for a good introduction to the topic as well as the claim that Nietzsche takes the term from Lucian's *hyperanthropos* (see also Babich 2012). Haase (1984) is also helpful on the topic. For more recent discussions, see Havas (2013) and Loeb and Tinsley (2019:757ff.).
36 Loeb (2010:212–213) claims that this note explains why Nietzsche did not write *Zarathustra* in his own voice. But the note does not explain why Nietzsche created the fictional character of Zarathustra. Instead, it explains why a certain "I"—not necessarily Nietzsche—created the *Übermensch*.
37 See Jenkins (2022) for more on contempt.
38 Translation from CWFN 14.
39 Loeb also grants this power to Zarathustra but denies that Zarathustra is an *Übermensch*. Thus, Zarathustra seems to occupy a speciesless middle ground: he is no longer human, but he is not yet an *Übermensch* (2010:199).
40 Loeb's main work on *Zarathustra* says very little about fate and necessity (2010). However, see (2021a), for Loeb's reflections on *amor fati*.
41 See Loeb and Tinsley (2019) for a response to this point.
42 Translation from CWFN 14.
43 Because Nietzsche presents himself as someone who is well-turned-out in *Ecce Homo* (EH "Wise" 2), this definition would also mean that Nietzsche wants to present himself as an *Übermensch*. For an alternative reading of the *Übermensch*, see Richardson (2020: Ch.12.1).
44 In his helpful feedback, Tom Stern has noted the weakness of the connection between *Wohlgerathenheit* and *Selbstsucht* in this passage. However, we can clearly see the way that Nietzsche links *Missrathenheit* to forms of self-contempt and self-hatred in passages such as GS 359 and GM III:14, and

we can therefore infer that self-love, self-satisfaction, and self-enjoyment are essential to *Wohlgerathenheit*.
45 The emphasis on self-love or egoism also links the *Übermensch* to the noble soul in *Beyond Good and Evil* (see BGE 265).
46 Contrast this with KSA 11:26[232], where we are told that the *Übermensch*, not humanity, is the goal.
47 Franco (2022:189) concurs with this reading.
48 It is worth noting in this context that Nietzsche describes, at some length, a "sovereign individual" at the beginning of the second essay of the *Genealogy*, and this has been a subject of significant discussion in the secondary literature. For instance, see Loeb's (2006) account. There may be a significant connection between what I am calling the Dionysian *Übermensch* and the sovereign individual.
49 I adopt this distinction from Brusotti (1997:557ff.).
50 See Book VII of Herodotus' *Histories*. The uncle responds by noting that most prefer death to life.
51 Heidegger (1967) identifies transience as central to revenge against time.
52 Jenkins (2020) emphasizes the problem of transience and sketches an alternative solution.
53 Richardson (2020:510–511) is right to deny that a numerically identical "I" would return via the eternal recurrence (this could only be the case if we rely on a soul that persists through multiple cycles, which Nietzsche clearly rejects). Instead, the best we can have is the recurrence of qualitatively identical, but numerically distinct, replicas of ourselves. But if this is right, should we be worried about the ability of the eternal recurrence to address the problem of transience (*Vergänglichkeit*)? Perhaps. But I think Nietzsche would respond by noting that immortality comes in degrees and that the eternal recurrence, in which exact replicas of ourselves are repeatedly produced through infinite time, maximizes the degree to which the world and ourselves can be immortalized and therefore the degree to which we can overcome the problem of transience. That immortality admits of degrees is evidenced by Diotima's speech in Plato's *Symposium*. There, various degrees of immortality were thought to be attained through anything from having children to achievements worthy of fame or *kleos* (immortal glory), and these forms of (partial) immortality provided ways of responding to and even overcoming our eventual death. If having children or being enshrined in a walk or hall of fame can ease the pain caused by our awareness of our finitude, then it seems that the belief that exact replicas of ourselves will recur in infinite time can overcome our revenge against time in the sense of transience. See Shepherd (2018) for further reflections on the relationship between the eternal recurrence and Plato's *Symposium*.
54 See Sinhababu and Teng (2019) for more on emotional responses to the eternal recurrence.
55 See Schutte (1999) for more reflections on the notion of backward willing.
56 Translation from CWFN 14.

57 Heidegger (1967:426–427) also emphasizes this point but concludes that Nietzsche ultimately fails to overcome revenge against time as transience.
58 Although see A 2, where Nietzsche points to the harmfulness of pity and encourages the weak and ill-constituted (*missrathen*) to perish (even offering help).
59 I use the terms of determinism and fatalism interchangeably, even though philosophers typically distinguish them.
60 In this sense, I agree with Ioan's (2021) claim that learning self-love is essential to confronting the eternal recurrence.
61 See Vivarelli (1992).
62 I argued this in Meyer (2022). See Creasy (2022) for a similar claim.

3
THUS SPOKE ZARATHUSTRA I

Nietzsche began writing the first book of *Zarathustra* toward the end of 1882 and completed the manuscript in February of 1883. It was published in March 1883 separately from the other three books with no indication that further parts were to follow. The main theme of the text is clearly the *Übermensch*, and Zarathustra's attempt to convince others of the need to create the *Übermensch*. Read as a standalone text, *Zarathustra* itself would be about the *Übermensch* and only the *Übermensch*. In other words, it would have little to do with what Nietzsche later calls the fundamental conception of the book, the eternal recurrence. This would be an odd result, especially given the immediate proximity between the presentation of the eternal recurrence (GS 341) and the introduction of Zarathustra in *The Gay Science* (GS 342). Indeed, the question in *The Gay Science* is whether humans could affirm—or would be crushed by—the eternal recurrence. It is not whether humans can give birth to an *Übermensch*. Thus, one of the issues going forward will be how to reconcile Zarathustra's teaching of the *Übermensch* in *Zarathustra* I with his eventual acceptance of his role as the teacher of the eternal recurrence in *Zarathustra* III.

The text of *Zarathustra* I is broken into two parts, "Zarathustra's Prologue," and the main text or "Zarathustra's Speeches." The prologue both introduces Zarathustra and the teaching of the *Übermensch* that he brings to the people of an unnamed town. Zarathustra's teaching is, however, rejected by the townspeople in the prologue, and so he proceeds to another town called the Motley Cow, limiting his teaching to a few chosen disciples who understand the need to create a *Übermensch*. *Zarathustra* I ends with Zarathustra exhorting his disciples not to believe in him but rather to find him by first finding themselves. Along the way we are introduced to Zarathustra's archenemy, the spirit of gravity, who will take on a more prominent role in subsequent parts, as well as the will to power and a healthy form of *Selbstsucht* or self-love that also play important roles later in the text. At the same time, Zarathustra's primary role here is one of teacher, preacher, and prophet. Although his audience dwindles significantly to a select audience of disciples as *Zarathustra* I unfolds, there is little sense that Zarathustra himself will engage in the project that he outlines for his pupils. As we will see, this is something that will change dramatically in *Zarathustra* II and III.

3.1 THE PROLOGUE AND THE APOLLONIAN *ÜBERMENSCH*

The "**Prologue**"[1] of *Zarathustra* and therefore *Zarathustra* itself begins with an almost word-for-word repetition of the lines that conclude the 1882 edition of *The Gay Science*, which, in turn, are based on an 1881 note (KSA 9:11[195]). The most notable difference is that the title of the aphorism, "incipit tragoedia," is absent, and thus, an apparent claim about the genre of the text is left outside the text itself. Thus, unlike *The Birth*, in which Nietzsche talks about tragedy and its significance, Nietzsche's own tragedy—like most tragedies—lacks any explicit discussion of the genre and its importance.

We know that the character Zarathustra is modeled on Zoroaster and that Nietzsche borrowed much of the opening of *Zarathustra* from Friedrich von Hellwald's description of the Persian prophet in his *Culturgeschichte in ihrer natürlichen Entstehung bis zur Gegenwart* (1874).[2] At the beginning of the text, Zarathustra is forty years old. We are told that he left his home on the lake, which in *The Gay Science* is lake Urmi (this detail is absent in *Zarathustra*), located in the northern part of modern-day Iran, at the age of thirty. We are also told that he has lived in solitude for ten years. Although separated from humans, he has his animals, an eagle and a serpent, and these will be present when he finally teaches the eternal recurrence at the end of *Zarathustra* III. We learn at the end of the prologue that the eagle, which can soar above the earth, represents his pride, and the serpent, which is bound to the earth, represents his wisdom (ZI "Prologue":10). In one 1882 note, Nietzsche associates the serpent with eternity, and this suggests a possible connection between the serpent and the eternal recurrence (KSA 10:2[9]).

Zarathustra's age has suggested to some a parallel to the life of Jesus, and there is no doubt that Nietzsche presents Zarathustra as an alternative to historical-literary figures like Jesus and Socrates. There are also reasons for thinking that Zarathustra's time in solitude is meant to represent Nietzsche's own flight from Bayreuth in the summer of 1876 and eventually his career as a professor at the University of Basel in 1879. At that time, Nietzsche was in his early thirties. Although he began writing *Zarathustra* roughly six—not ten—years later (although there is a ten-year gap between *Zarathustra* and *The Birth of Tragedy*), he lived a life of relative solitude as he wrote the free spirit works and thus can be said to have lived in his own "cave." Moreover, Nietzsche spent the summer of 1881 in the Swiss village of Sils Maria, and it was there, alongside Lake Silvaplana, that he claims to have discovered the eternal recurrence.

The drama begins with Zarathustra no longer satisfied with his solitary condition. Just as the sun would not be happy without those for whom it shines, Zarathustra realizes that his ideas—symbolized by the sun—must be shared with others. This necessity, however, is not logical; instead, it is one of desire. Zarathustra is "suffering" from a satiety and overfullness that needs to give to others: "bless the cup that wants to overflow" and "behold, this cup that wants to become empty again." In this way, Zarathustra embodies, at the beginning of the text, the gift-giving virtue of self-love (*Selbstsucht*) that he extolls to his disciples at the end of *Zarathustra* I.

The locution of *untergehen* (as a noun: *Untergang*) or "going under" is admittedly an odd one, and it does not translate well into English. It occurs on several occasions in the text and seems to have multiple meanings.[3] The prologue both begins and ends with a reference to Zarathustra's going under. On the one hand, it seems to have the literal meaning of moving from a higher to a lower location. In terms of the prologue, Zarathustra's wish to go under refers, in the first instance, to his desire to leave his cave and descend to the town below. On the other hand, going under can also mean a descent into the earth and so a form of death and destruction. In this way, "going under" can be associated with the genre of tragedy, and so the claim that "Zarathustra began to go under" at the end of the final section of the prologue (ZI "Prologue":10) can be directly linked to "incipit tragoedia" of GS 342. So understood, the phrase both points to his immediate plans to go down to the town below as well as a kind of death or destruction that he experiences toward the end of *Zarathustra* III, where we read: "Thus *ends* Zarathustra's going under" (ZIII "The Convalescent":2).

In the next section of the prologue, Zarathustra makes his way down the mountain. In so doing, he comes upon an old saint living in the forest. Nietzsche first characterizes the saint as a "wanderer," a term that appears in all four books of *Zarathustra*. It also has a rich history in Nietzsche's own thinking and beyond. For instance, Wotan appears in *Siegfried* of the *Ring* as a wanderer, and Nietzsche presents himself as a free-spirited wanderer in his book, *The Wanderer and His Shadow*. In GS 380, "'The Wanderer' Speaks," we learn that the wanderer is a figure who takes a standpoint outside of the customs of the city—symbolized by leaving town—to assess morality from a distance. Applied to Nietzsche's writings, *The Wanderer* is the work in which Nietzsche establishes a position outside of society so that he can then, in *Daybreak* (with the subtitle, "thoughts on the prejudices of morality"), assess morality from this standpoint. Applied to *Zarathustra*, we can infer that both Zarathustra and the old saint occupy a standpoint beyond the conventions of the town and therefore are to be differentiated from "the good and the just" that Zarathustra often criticizes.

The old saint is the first to provide us with a description of how Zarathustra appears to others. Specifically, he claims that Zarathustra's eyes are pure, that he hides no disgust, that he walks like a dancer, that he is an awakened one, and that he has become a child. The claim that Zarathustra is a child poses a potential problem for my interpretation of the text. As I explained in the previous chapter, it is my view that Zarathustra achieves a child-like state of innocence at the end of *Zarathustra* III by teaching the eternal recurrence. But if Zarathustra is already a child (and even a dancer) in *Zarathustra* I, then Zarathustra has already achieved this standpoint at the beginning of the text. This would seem to speak against my interpretation. However, there is another piece of textual evidence that complicates this picture. At the end of *Zarathustra* II, Zarathustra is told that he must "become as a child and without shame" (ZII "Stillest Hour"). This implies that Zarathustra is not yet a child and that Zarathustra's eventual goal is to become such a child. Indeed, we also learn in *Zarathustra* II—in contrast to the description here—that Zarathustra is reluctant to dance, and this is because the spirit of gravity is weighing him down. In short, the saint's description is one that implicitly denies the presence of the spirit of gravity, a figure that will soon haunt much of the text.

How we might reconcile this tension is not clear. Loeb has argued that this remark, in combination with the claim that "Zarathustra wants to become human again," should be read as anticipating Zarathustra's later achievements. In this case, it anticipates his own vision of becoming a child that is first articulated in "On the Three Metamorphoses" and then actually becoming a child at the end of *Zarathustra* III (2010:202). Then again, this is the saint's perception of Zarathustra and not necessarily Zarathustra himself. What seems clear is that Zarathustra's state is not a result of his confrontation with the eternal recurrence and his corresponding defeat of the spirit of gravity. Instead, we learn in the next section that Zarathustra excitement is rooted in his new-found love for humans. That is, he loves them enough to want to give them a gift, and what he loves about humans is their potential to become or somehow create the *Übermensch*. That is, he loves humanity not as an end but rather as a means to something greater. It is this teaching that fills Zarathustra with hope and life.

The old saint, however, counsels Zarathustra to stay away from humans, to remain in the forest. If we are to do anything for humans, it is to bear, in Christ-like fashion, their suffering. If one wants any consolation for oneself, one can, like the saint, compose and sing songs in praise of God. For Zarathustra, the problem is that God is dead, and the saint seems to be ignorant of this fact. Of course, a reader lacking the context of Nietzsche's other works will be taken aback by this proclamation: where, when, and how did God "die"? For those, however, who see that Nietzsche's free spirit works provide the necessary backdrop for understanding the drama of *Zarathustra*—a fact which suggests a continuity between Nietzsche and Zarathustra—this is a clear reference to the madman's proclamation of God's death in *The Gay Science* (GS 125).

In the passage from *The Gay Science*, the message of God's death is presented to an unsuspecting and unconcerned marketplace of people, and the madman—madness itself is a symbol of the unconventional nature of the message and the messenger—is mocked for the strangeness of his ideas. That said, in *The Gay Science*, many in the marketplace already agree that God no longer exists, even though they fail to see the earth-shaking implications of this event. In contrast, the solitary saint is one of the last persons to get the message. In *The Gay Science*, we also learn from the madman that "we"—likely "we free spirits"—are the ones who have killed God, and the madman asks whether we ourselves must not become gods to atone for this deed (GS 125). Nietzsche's own answer seems to be clearly affirmative, and this seems to parallel Zarathustra's call to create the *Übermensch*.

The teaching of the *Übermensch* is initially presented in quasi-Darwinian or evolutionary terms. I say "quasi" because in Darwin's theory species do not evolve toward higher levels of being; instead, the point of the theory is to explain how diversity arises due to selective pressures.[4] In contrast, Zarathustra's language is clearly one of development and progress, in which human beings emerged from species that are now painful embarrassments to the human, namely, the worm and the ape. However, Zarathustra's message is not one of celebration and achievement, but rather the claim that just as we have overcome the worm and the ape, we must now overcome our own condition of being human. Thus, the *Übermensch* is that name for the eventual self-overcoming [*Selbst Überwindung*] of the human condition.[5]

As both the prologue and the final lines of the final chapter of *Zarathustra* I make clear, the *Übermensch* is a response to and, arguably, a replacement for the dead God. It is a replacement for God because the *Übermensch* is now "the meaning of the earth." This goal gives our lives meaning and orientation, a meaning and orientation that was lost with the death of God. It is important to notice that there is common structure to both: It is implied that human existence has no intrinsic or inherent meaning and value; instead, all meaning comes from a goal or point of orientation that goes beyond the human. At the same time, there is an important difference between the two. Whereas the believer in God shoots his arrow of longing toward a transcendent being—thereby creating a desire to leave our earthly existence behind—the *Übermensch* has a this-worldly orientation. It is part of Zarathustra's larger program of remaining "*faithful to the earth*" (ZI "Prologue":3), a program that can be directly linked to what I have called the naturalism of *Zarathustra*.

One striking feature of Zarathustra's teaching of the *Übermensch* is the contempt he reveals for the human. For instance, we hear that the human "is a polluted stream" and that human happiness is disgusting, a mark of "poverty and filth and wretched contentment." According to Zarathustra, humanity only has a value insofar as it is a means to the *Übermensch*: "What is great in man is that he is a bridge and not an end: what can be loved in man is that he is an *overture* and a *going under*" (ZI "Prologue":3). Thus, the teaching of the *Übermensch* is also a moment of "great contempt." As a *Nachlass* note makes clear, the teaching of the *Übermensch* goes hand in hand with Zarathustra's teaching of the "last man" or last human (KSA 10:4[171]), and whereas the *Übermensch* is the ultimate object of longing, the last human is the ultimate object of contempt (KSA 10:4[167]).

It is difficult to generate exact definitions of both the *Übermensch* and the related last human. Indeed, the *Übermensch* is a concept that lacks any significant content in *Zarathustra* beyond the idea that it somehow transcends or goes above or beyond the human. In contrast, Zarathustra provides more description of the last human. One marker of the last human is a lack of love, longing, or *eros*: "What is love? What is creation? What is longing? What is a star? Thus asks the last man, and he blinks" (ZI "Prologue":5). This longing creates a chaos in the soul that makes possible the birth of a dancing star (a likely reference to Dionysus). This is what the last human lacks. However, it is also not entirely clear who or what the last human is supposed to be. One possible candidate is the Epicurean. Here, one finds happiness in pleasure and the avoidance of pain, but the pleasures are small, and the goal of the Epicurean is to calm the soul and eliminate any overriding fear or passion. The existence or non-existence of God should be of little concern: "One has one's little pleasure for the day and one's little pleasure for the night." Another possible candidate is the person who adheres to convention for the sake of conformity and a comforting fellow-feeling with one's neighbors. In *Daybreak*, Nietzsche expresses the worry that the conventional morality of sympathy and the promotion of the common good will eventually turn humanity into "sand" (D 174). Zarathustra articulates a similar worry: "No shepherd and one herd! Everybody wants the same, everybody is the same: whoever feels different goes voluntarily into a madhouse" (ZI "Prologue":5). Finally, there is a sense in which the last human represents humanity's descent into nihilism, where the difficulties of life outweigh its fleeting satisfactions and thereby generate a preference for non-existence. Whatever the last human is supposed to be—and it could be all these things combined—we know that the townspeople welcome the coming of this human, all the while mocking and ridiculing Zarathustra— much like the madman in GS 125—for teaching the *Übermensch*.

Nietzsche draws a parallel between Zarathustra's teaching of the *Übermensch* and the events going on in the marketplace. There is a tightrope walker performing that day, and Zarathustra claims that the human being is a rope that hangs over an abyss stretched between animal and *Übermensch*. The tightrope walker, therefore, seems to represent humanity's gradual progression toward the *Übermensch*. However, the slow-going tightrope walker is soon pursued on the rope by a jester or *Possenreisser* who commands him to move out of the way. Here again, we are confronted by a rather curious figure for which there is little explanation. The jester exhibits a mocking laughter and a spirit of playfulness that knows no fear, and this sort of individual clearly opposes the "spirit of gravity" who is later identified as Zarathustra's archenemy. Indeed, there are reasons for thinking that Zarathustra may even eventually take on the role of the jester such that the jester is a future representation of what Zarathustra will become. In one *Nachlass* note composed after *Zarathustra* I, Nietzsche says just this: "Zarathustra himself the jester who jumps over the poor tightrope walker" (KSA 10:16[88]).[6] In this way, the *Possenreisser* may be a foreshadowing of the attitude that Zarathustra will come to embody, and therefore it may also foreshadow Zarathustra's eventual transformation into a *Hanswurst* or even an *Übermensch* (or some combination thereof).

The jester knocks the tightrope walker off the rope and sends him falling into the abyss and to his eventual death. As Grätz (2024:317) notes, gravity causes his fall, and it subtly foreshadows the appearance of the spirit of gravity in subsequent chapters of *Zarathustra*. As he falls, the crowd splits like the sea, but Zarathustra nevertheless goes to his aid. Zarathustra picks him up and begins to carry him on his back. At this point, the jester sneaks up behind Zarathustra and instructs him to leave the town with his message. The problem is that "the good and the just"—those who seek to preserve conventional morality—hate him, and they see him as a danger to the herd-like multitude. Here, Zarathustra realizes that if he is going to be successful in communicating his teaching of the *Übermensch*, he must lure potential disciples away from the "herd." Zarathustra understands that his desire to create new tables of value implies that he will necessarily break the tables of conventional morality that the good and the just defend. Thus, Zarathustra ends his speech to himself by noting that he, like the jester, will go his own way and leap "over those who hesitate and lag behind." In this way, his going on will be their going under. At the same time, Zarathustra's going on is also his going under, and the final section of the prologue ends the same way the first section of the prologue ends: "Thus Zarathustra began to go under." The question it leaves to the reader is whether Zarathustra's "going under" now has a different meaning than it had at the beginning of the prologue when Zarathustra went down from his cave to the townspeople. It now seems to mean that Zarathustra's going under is the beginning of a narrative that leads to some sort of death through his teaching of the eternal recurrence. If this is right, then the end of the prologue is foreshadowing events that will occur beyond the scope of *Zarathustra* I.

3.2 ZARATHUSTRA'S SPEECHES: CHAPTERS 1–22

Zarathustra's speeches begin with "**On the Three Metamorphoses**." Although I have already discussed this speech in previous chapters and how it can be applied to Nietzsche's free spirit works, it is worth saying more about its contents in relation to the narrative of *Zarathustra*. Zarathustra explains three stages and two metamorphoses of the spirit that begins with the camel, moves to the lion, and then culminates in the child (the first metamorphosis into the camel is left unexplained). Here, we notice that Zarathustra gives the first speech now in the town of The Motley Cow. However, the addressee of the speech is unspecified. In the beginning, it is spoken to an ambiguous "you," but then moves on to address "my brothers" (this resembles the transition in "On Old and New Tablets" in *Zarathustra* III), even though there is no indication of any "brothers" in Zarathustra's presence. It is also not clear what is supposed to initiate the first transformation into a camel. That is, it is not clear what moves the spirit from a herd-like acceptance of conventional morality to taking on a heroic task that separates oneself from the larger community. Perhaps it is the *eros* that the last humans lack? In any case, the task is especially difficult because the camel's quest leads the individual into a lonely desert of truths that are anything but comforting. This, of course, is exactly how Nietzsche portrays his own quest for truth at the end of *Human*, and the desert-like imagery associated with the realm of truth recalls the factual pessimism or tragic philosophy that Nietzsche embraces throughout his writings.

What the truth-seeking camel also does not find in the desert is any natural support for the ethical norms and values of the city. Instead, all such values are creations of the people in the city, and this includes the creation of the gods they worship. In the passage, God is represented by the great dragon, and it functions as the guarantor of the "thou shalt" or moral obligation. The "thou shalt," however, stands opposed to "I will," and although the camel may have liberated the spirit from the city, the values of the city persist in the "thou shalt" or what Nietzsche calls the "shadows of God" (GS 108). The task of the lion is to confront this dragon and eliminate the shadows of the "thou shalt."

One of the more significant questions confronting the interpretation of this passage is whether the lion stage can be applied to *Zarathustra* itself. In my view, the fact that it includes a confrontation with God strongly suggests that the lion stage occurs prior to *Zarathustra* in works like *Daybreak* and *The Gay Science* (and thereby suggests a continuity between Nietzsche's own work and Zarathustra's task). This is because *Zarathustra* presupposes the death of God. However, a case can be made that chapters in *Zarathustra* III, such as "On the Three Evils" and "On Old and New Tablets," present Zarathustra's own confrontation with and destruction of the values of the past. Indeed, "On Old and New Tablets" begins with a reference to a "laughing lion," and this laughing lion appears at the end of *Zarathustra* IV as Zarathustra's sign to go under. As I noted in the introductory chapters, Loeb (2010) uses this passage to read *Zarathustra* IV as an analeptic satyr play, thereby placing Zarathustra at the stage of the lion within the "On Old and New Tablets" chapter, just before Zarathustra becomes a child in the concluding chapters of *Zarathustra* III.

In my view, the work that Zarathustra is doing in *Zarathustra* III can be understood as transitioning from the lion to the child. In one sense, this work is largely a final reckoning with the values that persist after the lion-like spirit killed God in *The Gay Science*, and it thereby prepares the way for Zarathustra's rebirth as a child at the end of *Zarathustra* III. However, we need to distinguish between the lion of the three metamorphoses and the "laughing lion" that finally appears at the end of *Zarathustra* IV.[7] What is common to both is that the lion represents the ability to command and say, "I will." The difference is that in the three metamorphoses, the lion represents the ability to take control of one's own freedom and one's own desert in a moment of solitude. In contrast, the "laughing lion" of *Zarathustra* III and IV represents a ripeness that is ready to rule others and usher in the "rulers of the earth" (KSA 11:32[15]). In short, the lion of the final part of *Zarathustra* represents the transition from a free spirit and hermit who has already conquered his own desert to one who is "ripe" enough to rule others in society (KSA 10:16[51]).[8]

So understood, *Zarathustra* seems to be located within or just prior to the third metamorphosis and before Zarathustra-cum-Nietzsche becomes ripe and turns toward the political project of revaluating values.[9] That is, it begins with the need for the spirit to be able to create new values now that the old God is dead. The lion itself cannot create new values, and therefore the spirit needs to transition to the child. The child represents "a sacred 'Yes,'" and it seems to correspond to the "yes-saying" project outlined in GS 276 and the notion of *amor fati*. As noted above, the child's innocence gestures to a standpoint beyond moral evaluations of good and evil, and the notion of a "game" points toward the playful attitude that Nietzsche associates with tragedy in *The Birth* (BT 24). In short, the child stands opposed to the spirit of gravity that will soon be identified as Zarathustra's archenemy.

Even here, however, there is some question as to whether the child itself is capable of creating new values or whether it is a mere precondition for the creation of such values. Given my twofold understanding of the symbol of the lion, it requires that the child-like standpoint that Zarathustra occupies at the end of *Zarathustra* III is merely a precondition for a larger ethical-political project of revaluing values that has the eternal recurrence as its foundation. Thus, the child marks a new beginning and "a first movement," but it is still only a beginning. This leads to a second question: how is the child supposed to relate to Zarathustra's call for the *Übermensch*? They both function as a *telos* for Zarathustra's project, but at this juncture they seem to represent distinct ends with little, if anything, in common. As I argued in the previous chapter, the concept of the *Übermensch* will become more Dionysian as *Zarathustra* unfolds, and as it does, it will move closer to Zarathustra's vision of the child. But even then, it is still not clear whether the Dionysian *Übermensch* just is the Heraclitean child or whether, again, the Heraclitean child represents a new beginning that makes the Dionysian *Übermensch* possible. Language such as "a first movement" suggests that the child is already something like a god capable of being a self-moved mover who creates new values.[10]

In the next speech, **"On the Teachers of Virtue,"** Zarathustra finds himself in the town of The Motley Cow, and rather than presenting his own speech, he decides to sit at the feet of another sage. The speech that he hears opposes much of what we have already encountered in the opening portions of the text, and it is modeled on and even parodies teachings of past philosophers that Nietzsche rejects. The term "virtue [*Tugend*]" in the title harkens back to a tradition of virtue ethics now most closely associated with Aristotle but includes Socratic and much of post-Socratic philosophy. In this tradition, virtue or *arete* is understood as an excellence, and there is a particular focus on excellences of the soul, which include both rational and non-rational elements. The guiding idea of virtue ethics is that acquiring the virtues leads to happiness or human flourishing (*eudaimonia*). According to Aristotle, this means developing virtues of the mind that lead to a theoretical understanding of oneself and the larger cosmos and the ability to make practical judgments about the best course of action for a well-lived life. It also means training the non-rational emotions and desires so that they harmonize with the judgments of reason. In later philosophical movements, the quest for happiness or the good life becomes increasingly associated with the notion of *ataraxia* or a peaceful state in which the soul remains undisturbed by the passions or desires. Both the Epicureans and the Stoics upheld *ataraxia* as an ethical ideal, and, on some accounts, this paved the way for the Christian longing for everlasting peace in an other-worldly heaven.

This is relevant to the speech at hand because the sage to whom Zarathustra is listening promotes virtue primarily as a means to "sleep." The purpose of the virtues and even waking life is to sleep well, and sleeping well means sleeping without disturbance.

We can begin to see the connection between the virtue tradition discussed above and the Christian tradition once we associate sleep with the cessation of desire and ultimately life itself. If the purpose of waking life is sleeping well, then the purpose of life is attaining a peaceful calm, and this peaceful calm can either come in this life, the next, or even through death itself. So understood, the reason we live is to learn how to die—indeed, this is the purpose of philosophy according to Plato's *Phaedo*—and we learn how to die by calming the passions and disturbances characteristic of this life. So understood, the sage's teaching is directly opposed to Zarathustra's message in the prologue and the task of affirming life. It is not calm, but a chaos in one's soul, that creates the conditions for the birth of a "dancing star" (ZI "Prologue":5), and it is the birth of this dancing star that makes this life—not some afterlife or even death—the ultimate object of one's affection and affirmation.

These themes are further developed in "**On the Afterworldly**." The chapter begins with what seems to be Nietzsche's own *mea culpa* (this again suggests a continuity between Nietzsche and Zarathustra). Zarathustra explains that he himself once "cast his delusion beyond man" and that, to him, the world seemed to him to be the work of a tortured god. In *The Birth*, we know that Nietzsche had done just this: he had conceived of the world of appearances as the product of a primordial unity (*Ur-Eine*) that itself was riddled with suffering and contradictions. In this passage, Nietzsche also gestures toward the Dionysian joy and loss of self that he attributes to tragedy in the work: "Drunken joy it is for the sufferer to look away from his suffering and to lose himself"; "Drunken joy and loss of self the world once seemed to me."

Assuming the self-reference here, Nietzsche-cum-Zarathustra now acknowledges his regret in having held these metaphysical commitments: "This god whom I created was man-made and madness, like all gods!" Again, the passage assumes what has already been announced: God is dead. However, Nietzsche does not just mean the Christian God, but all gods (including his own "Ur-Eine"), and it is not just all gods, but any metaphysical afterworld whatsoever. The elimination of metaphysics was precisely the task that Nietzsche undertook in *Human*, a work that breaks with the metaphysics of *The Birth* by rejecting any sort of metaphysical philosophy. According to the account here, Zarathustra overcame his belief in gods by inventing "a brighter flame" for himself (the *Übermensch*). Now his condition is the opposite: rather than suffering from not believing in a god, he would suffer if he had to believe in a god.

Zarathustra's self-diagnosis is important because it leads to a broader claim about the psychological basis for metaphysical beliefs: "it was suffering and incapacity that created all afterworlds" and "a poor ignorant weariness" that created "all gods and afterworlds" (later this suffering will be understood in terms of "revenge"). The implied lesson here is that one does not overcome the belief in the afterworldly through rational argumentation alone, but rather through changes in one's psychology and even physiology. The latter comes out in Zarathustra's claim that "it was the body that despaired of the earth and heard the belly of being speak to it," and this led to a "dehumanized human world which is a heavenly nothing." In short, it is a sickness of both the body and then the "mind" that invents and maintains a belief in an afterworld. In contrast, Zarathustra's ego, which "speaks of the body and still wants the body," has taught him something that he now teaches to others: not "to bury one's head in the sand of heavenly things, but to bear it freely, an earthly head, which creates a meaning for the earth." The implication here is that Zarathustra has—at least in part—overcome the sickness that creates the longing for the afterworld. Whether he has overcome this sickness entirely is, however, something that remains to be seen and even drives the drama of the text, as this issue takes center stage in "The Convalescent." As noted above, Zarathustra has yet to confront and affirm a doctrine that would put an end to all "afterworldly" beliefs, namely, the eternal recurrence.

If there is a chapter in *Zarathustra* in which Zarathustra confronts god in a lion-like fashion, "On the Afterworldly" might be it. However, the death of God seems to be presupposed, and what we get here is an analysis of why people nevertheless persist in believing in such an entity even after the rational basis for such a belief has been undermined. In short, the passage seems to presuppose the work that Nietzsche undertook in the free spirit project in general and *The Gay Science* in particular. Indeed, "On the Afterworldly" gestures back to the free spirit works. Specifically, Zarathustra speaks of the "lover of knowledge" and "that youngest among the virtues, which is called 'honesty.'" We know that Nietzsche identifies honesty as the youngest virtue in *Daybreak* (D 456) and that honesty, along with the passion for knowledge [*die Leidenschaft der Erkenntnis*], plays a central role in the free spirit works (see also GS 110 and GS 335). In fact, honesty is one of the core virtues that drives Nietzsche's critique of metaphysics in *Human* and ultimately leads to the death of God in *The Gay Science*.

At the end of the passage, Zarathustra calls on his audience to listen to the healthy body, one that speaks with a "more honest and purer voice," and this transitions to the next chapter, "**On the Despisers of the Body**." There, Zarathustra attacks a standard dualism which claims that "I" am both body *and* soul. This is a child-like attitude that needs to be replaced by an enlightened perspective in which one says, "body am I entirely, and nothing else; and soul is only a work for something about the body." Indeed, the body is what Nietzsche calls our "great reason." In addition to this, we have a "little reason," which is a mere toy or instrument of our "great reason" and so the body. This distinction, in turn, seems to map onto a subsequent distinction between the "I" or "ego" ("little reason") and the "self" ("great reason" and so the body).[11] Whereas much of the philosophical tradition—one can think of figures such as Plato and Descartes—has held what Nietzsche calls our little reason or ego to be the essence of who we are and the commander of a ship that is the body, Nietzsche, like Schopenhauer before him, reverses this relationship, holding that unconscious forces associated with the self are the "mighty ruler" of the conscious "ego." Thus, the self says, "feel pain here" or "feel pleasure here," and the ego suffers or is pleased accordingly. Indeed, it is the self, not the ego or even some transcendent deity, that creates respect and contempt and even notions of value. This, however, is the healthy self. Those who despise the self have a self that "wants to die and turns away from life." It cannot engage in this creative activity, and for this reason the despisers of the body are angry with life and therefore cannot serve as a bridge to the *Übermensch*.[12]

It is worth pausing to note that Nietzsche's naturalist commitments are playing a central role in the opening portions of the text. First, Zarathustra criticizes an understanding of virtue that seeks to quiet all longing and overcome even life itself. Second, Zarathustra rejects the notion of other- or after-worldly gods and metaphysical concepts, thereby leaving us with only the natural world. Finally, he attacks the idea that we might have a soul that stands above, transcends, and governs the body, and it is this idea that made possible a robust or non-compatibilist conception of free will. According to Zarathustra, the conscious self or the rational soul is itself a byproduct of and controlled by a self that is reducible to the body and so nature. In short, the opening chapters of *Zarathustra* have already taken aim at the two errors of Platonic philosophy that Nietzsche identifies in the preface of *Beyond Good and Evil*: The notion of the pure good and spirit as such (BGE "Pref"). That said, we have yet to inquire into the nature of the body, which, at this juncture, seems to be a marker of the real or the "thing in itself." What we find out, rather obliquely and only later in *Zarathustra* but much more explicitly in *Beyond Good and Evil*, is that the body is itself a constellation of equally natural drives, affects, and even wills to power (BGE 12 and 36).

In "**On Enjoying and Suffering the Passions**," Zarathustra provides an understanding of virtue that contrasts sharply with the notion of virtue in "On the Teachers of Virtue." Rather than understanding virtue as a means to a peaceful sleep, Zarathustra grounds virtue in the passions (something that is certainly related to the drives and affects that constitute the self). Here, virtue is tied to the good, but for Zarathustra each good is only a "my good" and so something that distinguishes oneself from others. The idea that the good derives from a passion that makes one unique points back to Zarathustra's previous assertion that "this creating, willing valuing ego" is "the measure and value of things."[13] It also recalls Nietzsche's criticism of Kant's categorical imperative in the fourth book of *The Gay Science*, in which Nietzsche exhorts his readers to create their own tables of good, tables that make us "new, unique, incomparable" (GS 335). The passions and virtues that Nietzsche commends are this-worldly, not signposts "to overearths and paradises."

According to Zarathustra, passions were once called evil, but now virtues grow out of the passions, and goals, in turn, grow from these virtues. In this way, the passions that make us suffer—as "wild dogs" in a "cellar" and "poisons"—turn into balsam and lovely singing birds. This points back to Zarathustra's claim that we must have chaos in our souls to give birth to a dancing star (ZI "Prologue":5), and it points forward to Zarathustra's attempt to revalue the negative value that philosophical and religious traditions have attributed to the passions. As Nietzsche repeatedly emphasizes, the tallest tree will also have the deepest roots (ZI "Tree on the Mountainside"), and therefore the greatest events come from the deepest passions. Indeed, a central argument of *The Birth* is that the ancient Greeks' capacity for suffering provided the springboard for the beautiful art world that justified their existence (BT 3). In *Zarathustra*, the passions are presented as a path to creation and value, but also a source of suffering and even the cause of one's destruction. Thus, the passage concludes: "Man is something that must be overcome; and therefore you shall love your virtues, for you will perish of them" (ZI "Passions").

"On the Pale Criminal" is one of the most difficult chapters in *Zarathustra* I to interpret. As the title indicates, it is about a "pale criminal," and it begins with a pale criminal nodding like a sacrificial animal which is then interpreted as consent for its own death. The nod of the pale criminal symbolizes his own judgment that he deserves to die, and therefore the killing of the judges is done out of pity, not revenge. The criminal is pale because the criminal has interpreted his past crime as something he ought not have done: "He was equal to his deed when he did it; but he could not bear its image after it was done." Even worse is the fact that he wholly defines himself in terms of this one deed: "Now he always saw himself as the doer of one deed." In this sense, he suffers from what I have called, in the second chapter, the problem of the past or *Vergangenheit*. Thus, he feels guilty for his past deeds, and he only wishes he could shake his head—a public acknowledgement that he deserves punishment—to relieve himself of the burden of his guilt. The root of his guilt, however, lies in his acceptance of the norms established by the "good people" who stand in judgment over him. These good people—and here we should think of the "good and the just"—nauseate Zarathustra, and he wishes they suffered from a madness that might make them perish, just like the pale criminal.

Zarathustra's speech is undoubtedly obscure, but Brusotti has argued that the discussion of the pale criminal points forward to the problem of revenge against time and the "madness" it creates in "On Redemption" from *Zarathustra* II (1997:557). It may also recall the free spirit works. In an aphorism from the third book of *Daybreak*, one that endorses "*little deviant acts*" that run contrary to social norms and customs (D 149), Nietzsche speaks of a "criminal of a possible future." This criminal, according to Nietzsche, would openly accept punishment for his misdeeds. However, this criminal would only do so on the condition that she was the author of the law to which she then willfully submits. The dictum here is: "I submit only to the law which I myself have given, in great things and in small" (D 187). The idea of submitting only to a law that one gives to oneself is directly correlated to the transition from the lion to the child in "On the Three Metamorphoses." The lion-will is one that attacks the reigning conventions, ultimately symbolized by God, and it is this destructive task that makes way for the creation of new norms that govern oneself (also see GS 335). What we also learn in GS 125 is that the murderers of God must find a way to justify this great deed. If they do not, they will ultimately become like the pale criminal or even the "ugliest man" in *Zarathustra* IV, as feelings of guilt and remorse will emerge as a form of "madness *after* the deed."

"On Reading and Writing" is important for myriad reasons. First, it gives us some insight into the aphoristic form that characterizes Nietzsche's free spirit works: "Whoever writes in blood and aphorisms does not want to be read but to be learned by heart." We can only speculate on the meaning but writing in "blood" seems to be writing that reflects an inner experience that one has "incorporated" into one's psychology and even physiology (one's blood). "Learning by heart" also suggests a similar experience by the reader, i.e., that one will "incorporate" the aphorism into one's very being. Moreover, aphorisms are only peaks that make leaps from peak to peak, leaving the reader to figure out how to connect the peaks. This suggests that the aphorism is an esoteric form, written in thin air and at a height, designed to be accessible only to the "courageous" few, and this sort of elitism points back to one of Nietzsche's favorite philosophers who also wrote in aphorisms: Heraclitus.

The speech also contains two passages that Nietzsche quotes at later junctures in his writings. Perhaps the most famous of these appears as the epigram affixed to the beginning of the third essay of the *Genealogy*: "Unconcerned, mocking, violent—thus wisdom wants us: she is a woman and always loves only a warrior." The other appears at the beginning of *Zarathustra* III:

> You look up when you feel the need for elevation. And I look down because I am elevated. Who among you can laugh and be elevated at the same time? Whoever climbs the highest mountains laughs at all the tragic plays and tragic seriousness.

In both passages, there are references to a brave and mocking laughter, and the latter passage directly connects mockery to overcoming tragic seriousness. This is significant for the reading of the text I have proposed. Laughter signifies and is perhaps even the result of overcoming tragic seriousness, and although the placement of the quotation at the beginning of *Zarathustra* III might suggest that *Zarathustra* III is the place for such laughter, I think it is the result of what occurs in *Zarathustra* III and therefore meant to foreshadow the laughter that takes centerstage in *Zarathustra* IV as well as in Nietzsche's subsequent works. So understood, the conclusion of *Zarathustra* III represents the end of the tragedy, the moment in which tragic seriousness is overcome, thereby transitioning to the lighthearted satyr play in *Zarathustra* IV and even the comedy of the post-*Zarathustra* works.

"On Reading and Writing" is also important because it introduces us to Zarathustra's archenemy, the spirit of gravity, which comes to personify melancholy and revenge.[14] The spirit of gravity opposes all laughter, and Zarathustra will eventually do battle with him. Here, Zarathustra gives an account of how the spirit can develop in a way that opposes the spirit of gravity: one must first learn to walk and then run and finally fly. Again, we encounter the motif of elevation and flight, and this symbolizes the unleashing of *eros* and an erotic love of life. Such a progression from slowly walking to fast paced leaping and even flying recalls the difference between the tightrope walker and the jester in the prologue. The chapter also reveals how the spirit of gravity can be vanquished: "Not by wrath does one kill but by laughter." In the "Ass Festival," this line is repeated—with an explicit reference to Zarathustra's previous speech—and then applied to Zarathustra himself. That is, Zarathustra is, in *Zarathustra* IV, "the annihilator without wrath" (ZIV "Ass Festival") and the one who teaches the higher men the this-worldly comfort of laughter.

In "On Reading and Writing," Zarathustra also refers to the ass, calling us all "fair beasts of burden, male and female asses," and Zarathustra provides an oblique reference to Dionysus: "I would believe only in a god who could dance." This points back to the idea of giving "birth to a dancing star" (ZI "Prologue":5), and it hints at the connection between dance, laughter, and Dionysus. Dancing becomes more prominent in *Zarathustra* II and even more so toward the end of *Zarathustra* III, and laughter is central to *Zarathustra* IV. Taken together, the chapter "On Reading and Writing" contains myriad ideas that foreshadow further developments in *Zarathustra*. If this is right—and we cannot be sure that it is—there is reason for thinking that Nietzsche had intentions (at this time) to write further parts of *Zarathustra* in contrast to those who think that he conceived, at this time, of what is now *Zarathustra* I as the entirety of *Zarathustra*.

Given the relative lack of dramatic action in *Zarathustra* I, the reader can easily get lost among its speeches. Thus far, Zarathustra has been searching for disciples in the town of the Motley Cow. In "**On the Tree on the Mountainside**," Zarathustra seems to have found a potential candidate, and he engages a youth leaning on a tree just outside the city. In the passage, we encounter several familiar themes. Just as invisible forces like the wind can influence a tree much more than the visible hand, so too are we moved by unconscious forces much more than we are directed, if at all, by conscious thought or our "little reason." Similarly, we learn that for a tree to reach great heights, its roots must descend into the depths of what is often called evil. As we know from the larger context, pushing downward into the depth of "evil" often means animating those passions that Nietzsche understands as a springboard to greatness. In the passage itself, Nietzsche connects the dual movement of going down and going up to the increase of both longing—presumably for the *Übermensch*—and contempt—presumably for the human as the last human. We also know that this longing and contempt pushes the individual to climb higher on the mountain, and it is at these heights that the climber finds herself in a state of solitude with few who can hear or even understand. At these heights, the climber now longs for the "first lightning," and we know from the prologue that this lightning is the *Übermensch* (ZI "Prologue":4).

The youth admits that he is filled with envy toward Zarathustra, claiming that Zarathustra himself is this lightning (in contrast to his own inability to live up to Zarathustra's ideals). Zarathustra, however, points out that the youth is still striving for freedom. He has "wild dogs"—a metaphor for the passions—that bark in the cellar and want freedom. In this way, the youth is noble, and Zarathustra contrasts the nobility of the youth with the good (presumably referring to the "good and the just"). Whereas the "good" want to preserve the old, the noble want to create something new and a new virtue (this foreshadows Zarathustra's later exhortations to the new nobility in "On Old and New Tablets" from *Zarathustra* III). However, the nobility of the youth requires that he maintains these high hopes. Without such hopes, he can devolve into a voluptuary who only lives for the day (a possible reference to the last humans or maybe even the old saint). Thus, the passage ends with Zarathustra beseeching the youth to maintain his highest hope, which is likely a hope for the *Übermensch*.

"**On the Preachers of Death**" touches on the leitmotif of Nietzsche's writings, the affirmation and denial of life, and just as it points back to the argument of *The Birth*, it foreshadows ideas he develops in the *Genealogy*. The preachers of death are those who preach the "renunciation of life." As we have seen, Schopenhauer is one of the main proponents of such renunciation, and Zarathustra presents the presumably Christian longing for "eternal life" as another form of life renunciation. Common to both is that they want to flee this life—the exact opposite of willing the eternal recurrence—and the preachers of death speak to an underlying psychological longing to escape this world. In this way, "On the Preachers of Death" continues the line of argumentation found in "On the Teachers of Virtue" and "On the Afterworldly."

Zarathustra then points to the multifarious causes and manifestations of such renunciation. For instance, we learn that certain "beasts of prey" are filled with a "lust" that discharges itself internally through self-laceration. In the second essay of the *Genealogy*, Nietzsche explains how this self-laceration is a result of placing these "beasts of prey" within the walls of society. Others simply suffer from a general weariness and are therefore already open to embracing these teachings. Others point to sickness and death, and still others say that "life is suffering." Important here is that Nietzsche has Zarathustra agree with the claim that life is suffering, which is central to his factual pessimism. However, preachers of death, like Schopenhauer, conclude that life itself should therefore cease (a form of evaluative pessimism). The preachers of death also cast sexual lust as sinful and childbearing as a misfortune because it only increases the suffering of the world. Finally, these preachers claim that "pity is needed." Here again, we know that Schopenhauer directly links pity to Christian *agape* (or neighbor love) and sees it as a steppingstone toward the renunciation of existence (WWR I:67).

In "**On War and Warriors**," Zarathustra implicitly contrasts his own teaching with the preachers of death. The warriors here are Zarathustra's warriors, and they share Zarathustra's highest hope for the *Übermensch* and follow his command that the human needs to be overcome. In contrast to Schopenhauer's ethics of pity, Zarathustra praises both courage and war: "War and courage have accomplished more great things than love of the neighbor. Not your pity but your courage has so far saved the unfortunate." We also know that Schopenhauer contrasts pity with mockery and laughter, and Nietzsche again associates the warrior with prankishness and sarcasm. Nietzsche's praise of war can be linked to his early celebration of contest or *agon* in ancient Greek culture and his own agonistic practice in his later works.[15] As Grätz points out, this chapter recalls the Heraclitean claim that war is the father of all things and a "war of opposing qualities" in Heraclitus' philosophy (2024:336–337). These ideas can also be linked to the will to power: the will to power is a relational concept, and the experience of overcoming resistance is built into our awareness of any increase of power. Contest and war are arenas in which resistance is experienced and, in cases of victory, overcome. This also seems to be the reason why Zarathustra insists that we should be proud of our enemy. We can hate them, but we cannot despise them. This is because enemies who are our equals provide us with the resistance we desperately crave.

In "**On the New Idol**," Zarathustra attacks the notion of the modern state in a way that is reminiscent of Nietzsche's own attacks in chapter eight of *Human*. Here, Zarathustra contrasts the state with the notion of a people. Peoples are created by creators who create the loves and values of a people; in so doing, such creators serve life (we hear more about this in "On the Way of the Creator"). The presumably liberal state, however, is a mere conglomeration of peoples—it is pluralistic—and thereby creates a "confusion of tongues of good and evil" and gives a home to the "superfluous," i.e., those who read newspapers and live to accumulate money. Moreover, the state has made itself into a replacement for the dead God and thus a "new idol": "On earth there is nothing greater than I: the ordering finger of God am I." Such a state seeks heroes, those who wish to sacrifice themselves for the benefit of the state, and the individual loses herself in this entity. Thus, the state is "where the slow suicide of all that is called 'life,'" and this is why Zarathustra ends his speech by counseling his audience to "escape from the idolatry of the superfluous!" "Only where the state ends, there begins the human being who is not superfluous." Only where the state ends can one find "the rainbow and the bridges" of the *Übermensch*.

"**On the Flies of the Market Place**" continues the idea that a disciple—he addresses him as a "friend"—of Zarathustra needs to flee the confines and norms of society. Solitude, not the state or the marketplace, is where one needs to be. The marketplace is presented here as the opposite of quiet and solitude. The noise in the marketplace is generated by two types that Zarathustra discusses in the chapter: the "great actors" and the "poisonous flies." As Zarathustra explains, our lived worlds and respective cultures revolve around the inventors of values: "Around the inventors of new values the world revolves," and "invisibly it revolves." In contrast, "around the actors revolve the people and fame." For instance, the political and socio-economic landscape of the United States revolves around the values of freedom and equality articulated by Enlightenment philosophers and then established by the founders. Similarly, Mormonism revolves around the values invented by Joseph Smith. Within these cultural caves or "the marketplace," the great actors and "the people of fame" make their mark. That is, they accept the "way of the world" established by the founders, and they look to act out a script that has been written for them. For all his greatness, even someone like Martin Luther King Jr. can be understood as an actor in this sense: he is someone who carries forward the values of Christian neighbor love and advances the political principle of equality. Thus, Zarathustra would say that he has "spirit but little conscience of the spirit." That is, although he was critical of the practices and institutions of his time, the values Martin Luther King Jr. used to criticize these institutions were themselves not subject to critical examination and overcoming.

One reason for fleeing the marketplace is that new values can only be created in solitude, and the actors who enact and enforce previously created values stand in the way of such creation. The other reason is the poisonous flies. In contrast to the great actors, the flies are "the small and the miserable," and their poison is their "invisible revenge." Rather than trying to shoo or swat these numberless flies, Zarathustra insists that one must flee them. They want to suck the blood of the great, and their numerous bites can make one weary. They do this out of revenge—a key motif of *Zarathustra* II and beyond—and they are vengeful because they suffer from self-dissatisfaction and a bad conscience. However, those who have potential for the type of greatness Zarathustra describes are the source of this bad conscience. They feel unworthy in comparison to such greatness, and their lack of self-worth results in hatred and a desire for revenge. This, then, is the source of their poison.

In the next two chapters, Zarathustra considers more intimate relationships. If one wants to leave behind the city for the blessings of solitude, we learn in "**On Chastity**" that one must also be prepared for a chaste life, at least for a time. Chastity, however, is certainly not a command or even a spiritual ideal, and Zarathustra counsels against it for most people: "Chastity is a virtue in some, but almost a vice in many." This is a significant break with Schopenhauer, who sees in chastity an important step in the ascetic's quest to deny the will. For Nietzsche, the problem is that for most people sensuality is not extirpated through chastity. Instead, it "leers enviously out of everything" one does, and this "beast" remains within them. Thus, in trying to drive out the devil, they themselves are turned into swine. As Grätz (2024:371) has pointed out, Nietzsche's antagonism toward chastity reaches its highpoint in *Ecce Homo*: "The preaching of chastity amounts to a public incitement to antinature. Every kind of contempt for sex, every impurification of it by means of the concept 'impure,' is the crime *par excellence* against life" (EH "Books":5).[16] In *Zarathustra* III, we will also encounter Zarathustra placing a positive value on sex and sexuality (ZIII "On the Three Evils").

In "**On the Friend**," Zarathustra again reflects on friendship in relation to his solitude. In solitude, one is not alone: "always one times one—eventually that makes two." There is a conversation that the hermit is having with himself, and thus "for the hermit the friend is always the third person." However, the friend is also someone who prevents the conversation from "sinking into the depths." At the same time, the friend must also be capable of being an enemy. The implication here is that friends must be on equal footing with each other such that they not only offer companionship but also resistance. Moreover, one must also be "an arrow and a longing" for the friend. The idea is that relationships, such as friendship, must be directed toward the ultimate goal that Zarathustra has set for humankind: the creation of the *Übermensch*. The chapter ends with some disparaging remarks about women's capacity for friendship, remarks that are certainly regrettable from a contemporary point of view but are symptomatic of the way in which Nietzsche rejects modern equality and its implications.

"**On the Thousand and One Goals**" is one of the most important chapters in *Zarathustra* I. In it, we are presented with an account of the origin of moral values and the introduction of the notion of the will to power (the first mention of the concept in Nietzsche's published works). In the introductory chapters, I argued that *Zarathustra* should be understood as a work of naturalism that puts an end to the metaphysical tradition and takes us beyond good and evil. Here, we find Zarathustra taking an important step in this direction. Just as he assumed the death of God in the prologue, we learn that good and evil are human creations that vary with and are relative to the society that created them. In the language of *The Gay Science*,

> whatever has *value* in our world now does not have value in itself, according to its nature—nature is always value-less, but has been *given* value at some time, as a present—and it was *we* who gave and bestowed it.
>
> (GS 301)

In this passage from *Zarathustra*, we are told that good and evil emerge from what Zarathustra calls esteeming [*Schätzen*], and these valuations can often be reversed for different peoples: "much that was good to one people was scorn an infamy to another."

Indeed, Zarathustra implies that the creation of good and evil is a necessary condition for a people to be a people, as it defines and distinguishes them from others: "A tablet of the good hangs over every people. Behold it is the tablet of their overcomings." The notion of "overcoming" is vague, but it seems to mean the process by which a people increased or expanded its power, especially if this involves the conquering of some difficulty or resistance. So understood, "overcoming" and "will to power" are closely linked. Here we overcome our current condition and progress to a new state of being with an expanded range of ability and control. "Good" is the valuation that is attached to such an overcoming and the feeling of increased power it generates. For instance, if a certain warm-up ritual is causally connected to a team's victory, then that warm-up ritual becomes something that is "good" for that team (even a tradition or "the way"), as it is understood as a means to success and a corresponding increase in power. Thus, Zarathustra claims that "praiseworthy is whatever seems difficult to a people" and that "high" is "whatever makes them rule and triumph and shine." In this way, pronouncing something "good" is "the voice of the will to power." Here, there is a clear connection between this account of how "good" is created and the noble mode of evaluation that Nietzsche describes in the first essay of the *Genealogy* (GM I:2).

In "On the Afterworldly," Zarathustra introduced the Protagorean claim that the creative ego is the "measure and value of things," and Nietzsche has Zarathustra return to it here. Human beings did not find good and evil in nature, and it was not given to them "as a voice from heaven." Instead, human beings have given "themselves all their good and evil" and thereby projected values into things for the purpose of preservation and power. Indeed, this is what makes us human: we are "esteemers" who give value to things. Such esteeming is a form of value creation; without this act of esteeming and so creation, there would be no value as "the nut of existence would be hollow." In the language of *The Gay Science*, we can say that we are effectively poets who create—albeit most often unconsciously—the world that concerns us, and without this poetry, existence would have no meaning (GS 301).

It is worth pausing to reflect on the significance of these claims. First, we have an assertion of what has been called Nietzsche's value anti-realism in the secondary literature.[17] The significance of this claim for the philosophical project as Plato once conceived of it cannot be underestimated. For Plato, the philosopher is supposed to break the chains of social norms and flee the cave of convention to find the ultimate source of value in the Form of the Good—a basic template for an objective notion of value and a monotheistic deity. On the view Zarathustra espouses, there is no objective source of value outside the cave of culture. At the same time and for precisely this reason, Zarathustra praises our ability to create. In terms of the Platonic allegory, we are the ones who have created the caves of cultures and religions, and the highest task is therefore not to discover the Form of the Good outside the cave but rather to create a lifeworld or cultural cave most conducive to the flourishing of an individual or an entire culture. As Nietzsche explains in *The Gay Science*, the world or culture we create is much like a poem, and it is from this poem that the aforementioned actors or "so-called practical human beings" learn their roles and "translate everything into flesh" (GS 301). In this way, Nietzsche's call to create new values goes hand in hand with his insistence—one that dates back to *The Birth*—that poetic creation has a greater significance for human life than philosophical discovery.

There is, however, more in "On the Thousand and One Goals" that needs to be discussed. The closing sections of the speech begin when Zarathustra notes that initially peoples or collectives created these values, and it was only later that the individual could engage in this project. In the language of contemporary discourse in ethics, Nietzsche is having Zarathustra shift from a form of "conventionalism" to a form of "subjectivism" (both forms of ethical relativism). For the individual to emerge, the bad conscience created by herd conformity (conventionalism) needed to be overcome. Of course, it is precisely this herd conformity and customary morality that Nietzsche set out to overcome in *Daybreak*. In *The Gay Science*, Nietzsche hints at this idea in "The Greatest Advantage of Polytheism." There, Nietzsche explains how the luxury of being an individual was first permitted in a polytheistic culture. Although there must be conformity among humans, "a plurality of norms" in the divine sphere is nevertheless permitted. Thus, the invention of "gods, heroes, and overmen [*Übermenschen*] of all kinds, as well as near-men and undermen, dwarfs, fairies, centaurs, satyrs, demons, and devils" was a "preliminary exercise for the justification of the egoism and sovereignty of the individual" (GS 143). Nothing is explicit, but the mention in the aphorism of invented *Übermenschen* certainly has relevance for *Zarathustra* I, and it raises the question as to whether the invention of the *Übermensch* in *Zarathustra* I is itself a preliminary stage for the emergence of a self-loving and sovereign individual at later stages in *Zarathustra* and beyond.

Another important theme that emerges from these passages is what falls under the word "love" in the English language. This is implicit in Zarathustra's discussions of chastity and friendship but becomes even more important with the introduction of the will to power. The connection between love and the will to power may sound strange, but it is not if we understand the English word "love" to refer, in part, to the Greek notion of *eros* (the etymological root of "erotic"). For the Greeks, *eros* is often understood as a cosmological force that refers to the most fundamental longings of human beings and even nature herself. We know from the *Symposium* that Plato understood this force as something that compels all human beings to want to know the ultimate realities of the Forms. However, we also know that there is an understanding of *eros* that predates Plato in poets like Hesiod (see his *Theogony*) and even Aristophanes (see *The Birds*), and Plato's *Symposium* can be understood as an attempt to replace this poetic understanding of *eros* with his own philosophical understanding of *eros*. Indeed, if we look at both the speech of Aristophanes in the *Symposium* as well as the role that *eros* plays in his comedy, *The Birds*, we begin to see the way in which poetic *eros* is closely connected with notions of power, earthly immortality, self-love, and even self-deification.[18] In short, there are ways in which this sort of poetic *eros* can be linked to central ideas in *Zarathustra*, most notably self-love (*Selbstsucht*) and the will to power, and the ultimate object of this sort of *eros* may be the immortalization of life through the eternal recurrence.

Such associations are more than mere associations. As we noted in the previous chapter, Nietzsche understands the will to power to be a modification of Schopenhauer's cosmological principle of the will to life, and Schopenhauer explicitly thinks of the will to life as a form of Greek *eros* (WWR I:60). Moreover, Schopenhauer translates the notion of *eros* as *Selbstsucht* or self-love (WWR I:67), and this provides a clear connection between *eros* and what Zarathustra praises as the gift-giving virtue at the end of *Zarathustra* I. Indeed, Schopenhauer explicitly connects the affirmation of the will to life to ancient Greek fertility cults, symbolized by the worship of the phallus (WWR I:60). There is no mention of Dionysus, but we know that Nietzsche associated Dionysus with such fertility cults as well as the affirmation of the will to life (TI "What I Owe":4). Taken together, we see a close connection between Dionysus and a certain kind of *eros* and so the will to power.

"On the Thousand and One Goals" ends with remarks by Zarathustra that seem to explain the title. Although there have been a thousand different ways in which a people has become a people by creating a shared value system and a common goal, there now needs to be one goal that brings all of these people together. Thus, Zarathustra remarks: "The one goal is lacking. Humanity still has no goal." In the speech itself, Zarathustra never states what this one goal is supposed to be. However, the context suggests that this one goal is his teaching of the *Übermensch*. Here, the goal would no longer be to create a people or a herd that follows a collective goal, but rather an individual or individuals who stand above herd-like conventionality.

Whereas "On the Thousand and One Goals" contains allusions to the Greek notion of love or *eros*, "**On Love of Neighbor**" can be understood as a chapter about a form of Christian love or *agape* that Nietzsche contrasts with Greek *eros*. In terms of Nietzsche's response to Schopenhauer, such a contrast is significant because Schopenhauer also contrasts these two types of love, but he then advocates for a life-denying ethics that is an outgrowth of *agape* (WWR I:67). In the opening lines of the chapter, we are told that the love of neighbor (*agape*) is rooted in a bad love for the self and so a form of self-dissatisfaction or self-hatred. As the speech continues, Zarathustra claims that we flee to the neighbor because we cannot stand being with ourselves, and therefore neighbor love or *agape* isn't really about the neighbor but rather ourselves. Moreover—and the argument here clearly anticipates Nietzsche's argument in the first essay of the *Genealogy*—these self-haters try to make a virtue of their neighbor love. Nietzsche has Zarathustra claim that he can see through this "selflessness," which is another term closely associated with and expressive of Schopenhauer's ethics of life-denial.

In contrast to Christian love of neighbor or *agape*, Zarathustra recommends a "flight from the neighbor and love of the farthest." This contrast sets up a distinction between *eros* and *agape* (one which I think is central to Nietzsche's later revaluation of values).[19] Whereas the *eros* motif is a type of love that moves the human upward toward human excellence, distinction, and even divinity— thus it is often associated with wings and flight—the *agape* motif typically moves downward, first, from the divine to the human (God becomes flesh) and then from well-situated humans to less fortunate humans in acts of charity and kindness (the story of the good Samaritan is paradigmatic).

Here, Zarathustra also presents his teaching on the friend (and so another type of love, *philia*). The key difference between friendship and neighbor love is that the former is preferential and often based on merit or distinction, whereas the latter is an indiscriminate love of another without preference or distinction. In Plato's *Phaedrus*, we learn that friendship can be based on a shared love or *eros* for knowledge of the Forms; in short, friendship goes hand in hand with a shared philosophical project. This sort of structure can also be found in *Zarathustra*. The sort of friendship Zarathustra recommends is bound together by a shared anticipation of the *Übermensch*. That is, the *Übermensch* is the proper object of one's love or *eros* that is "the farthest and the future," and friendship or *philia* is generated when two or more individuals commit themselves to this common project.

"**On the Way of the Creator**" develops some of the themes we encountered in "On the Three Metamorphoses." To recall, the latter concludes with the description of a child who is a necessary condition for "the game of creation." Here, Zarathustra speaks of one who is willing to leave the "herd" behind to become a "first movement" and a "self-propelled wheel." To do this, solitude is necessary, and therefore one must, like a camel, speed into the desert. However, the herd says that such solitude is loneliness and guilt. To overcome these feelings of guilt, one must overcome the conscience that produces such guilt. In other words, one must become a lion-like destroyer of the values that produce the bad conscience in the creator. Thus, Zarathustra asks in this chapter, "are you capable of this—to be a murderer?" That is, is one capable of murdering the very feelings that would kill those who flee into solitude?

This liberation from the values of the herd or even all values created hitherto is, however, only a first step in a larger project. Zarathustra suggests as much when he distinguishes between being free "*from* what" and being free "*for* what." At the risk of anachronism, we can say that the distinction Zarathustra is drawing here largely parallels the distinction that Isaiah Berlin makes between "negative" and "positive" freedom. Whereas a negative freedom means freeing oneself from impediments that stand in the way of one's desires and goals, positive freedom can be closely aligned with notions of autonomy or self-rule in which individuals or collectives obey laws that they themselves have prescribed. In terms of Nietzsche's project, we can understand the free spirit works as a quest to attain negative freedom or a freedom "from." Now, however, we find Zarathustra sketching out a form of freedom as autonomy, one that will require the creation of new measures and values. In my view, *Zarathustra* plays an important role in transitioning from a free spirit project focused on negative freedom to a "philosophy of the future" in Nietzsche's later works that seeks to legislate new, life-affirming values (BGE 211).

In the philosophical tradition, Kant coupled this latter sort of freedom with the self-legislation of a universal moral law. We know from Nietzsche's remarks in the free spirit works that he both follows Kant's emphasis on autonomy but also diverges from it significantly (GS 335). Rather than associating autonomy with morality and universality, Nietzsche associates such autonomy with individuality and artistic creation. In "On the Way of the Creator," Zarathustra asks whether the creator is able to do just this: "Can you give yourself your own evil and your own good and hang your own will over yourself as a law?" So understood, we see the way in which Nietzsche now links value creation to the emergence of the individual rather than the formation of a people as described in "On the Thousand and One Goals."

Drawing from other scholars, Grätz has also pointed to the possible influence of Max Stirner here. In *The Ego and His Own* (1844), Stirner distinguishes between being free "from what" and being free "for what." There is no evidence that Nietzsche read Stirner, but there is reason to think that he was familiar with Stirner's philosophy through the work of Eduard von Hartmann (Grätz 2024:413). For my purposes, the possible connection to Stirner's philosophy is an important one. Insofar as this depiction of the creator is also meant to describe the *Übermensch* in *Zarathustra* I, such a conception is very similar to Stirner's conception of a self-creating ego or an absolute-I that is meant to replace a supernatural God. Although versions of this idea continue through Nietzsche's own work—and Brusotti (2019) has argued that Nietzsche's sovereign individual in the second essay of the *Genealogy* is meant, in part, as a response to Stirner—what is lacking in both Stirner's philosophy and Zarathustra's presentation of the (Apollonian) *Übermensch* in *Zarathustra* I is any connection to nature and history. In Seung's language, this version of the *Übermensch* is a Faustian attempt to assert one's autonomy *against* the world (2005:xviii). As we shall see, Nietzsche's creator and eventual *Übermensch* will first have to be reconciled to the world, ultimately merging with nature and necessity.

Nevertheless, the way for the creator is undoubtedly a dangerous one. Zarathustra again stresses that the "good and the just" or those who uphold the reigning customs and moralities will oppose the solitary creator. But Zarathustra also points to an even greater enemy, one's own self, and this is where Zarathustra's ethics of creation gets coupled with a form of destruction. Such a creator will be a lover of self, but this self-love will mean that the creator despises himself. The enflamed love, however, will also result in a self-conflagration. The idea is that one can only become new unless one first becomes ashes. Thus, Zarathustra ends the chapter by connecting the idea of overcoming oneself to the idea of perishing and, presumably, going under (and thus a possible reconciliation with nature). It is passages like these that lend support to Loeb's view that Nietzsche's hopes for the birth of a new species of *Übermenschen* is bound up with the self-sacrifice of the human. That said, the idea that something new can arise from the ashes of what has perished suggests that Zarathustra is not speaking here of a biological death, but rather of a process of spiritual or psychological death and rebirth like the mythological Phoenix. Indeed, the implicit reference to the child of "On the Three Metamorphoses" at the beginning of the speech—"a first movement" and "a self-propelled wheel"—suggests just this: The going under is a necessary step in a rebirth that makes possible the kind of creation Zarathustra describes here. However, this conception of creation resembles descriptions of a divine entity capable of self-motion, and as I will explain later, it is this conception of creation—one that totally divorces the subject from any connection to the causal network of nature and history—that Zarathustra will reveal as deficient in "On Redemption" in *Zarathustra* II.[20]

"**On Little Old and Young Women**" is undoubtedly offensive to contemporary readers, and in this respect parallels Nietzsche's remarks on women in the final aphorisms of chapter seven in *Beyond Good and Evil*. It assigns clearly defined gender roles to men and women and largely subordinates women to men: "The happiness of man is: I will. The happiness of woman is: he wills." For a woman to love a man is for that woman to obey the man. Women are riddles, and pregnancy is the solution to the riddle. In contrast, "real men" or "warriors" love "danger and play," and this is why such men want women to be "the most dangerous plaything." Whereas men should be educated for war, women should be educated "for the recreation of the warrior." If this isn't bad enough, the chapter ends with the notorious and much-discussed claim: "You are going to women? Do not forget the whip!"

There are, of course, interpretive strategies one can take to soften the edge of some of Nietzsche's remarks. For instance, Nietzsche repeatedly refers to life, truth, and wisdom as women, and so perhaps Nietzsche should be understood as referring to these rather than actual women. But it is perhaps better to acknowledge that what Nietzsche says challenges the way we now think and that one of the reasons for reading him is that he challenges this way of thinking. The challenge that Nietzsche issues is not just about gender equality but rather about the modern commitment to equality as such. Thus, Nietzsche is not only attacking a particular application of the principle of equality but also the principle itself, and it is this attack that underwrites his hostility to democracy, his occasional remarks about the necessity of slavery, and his offensive comments about women.

Indeed, Zarathustra's attempt to teach the *Übermensch* represents a clear rejection of modern equality, and it is important to note the way in which both men and women are subordinated to and instrumentalized in this overall project. In the previous chapter, Zarathustra speaks of individuals—presumably men—ready to perish for this goal. In "On the Friend," he presents the friend as "an arrow and a longing" for the *Übermensch*. In this chapter, we hear that the hope of women is to "give birth" to the *Übermensch*. In short, when Zarathustra is not praising solitude as a means to value creation, he is reconceiving human relationships so that they serve the ultimate goal of producing the *Übermensch*. This is something we will hear more about in "On Child and Marriage."

Between Nietzsche's reflections on women and marriage is an odd chapter, "**On the Adder's Bite**." We encounter Zarathustra sleeping under a fig tree. As he is sleeping, an adder bites him on the neck. The bite of the adder parallels Zarathustra's description of the tarantula's bite in *Zarathustra* II. Both bites are filled with poison. The tarantula's poison represents the desire for revenge, and it is the foundation for the morality of equality. The poison of the adder seems to be the feeling of guilt. So understood, the adder is trying to poison Zarathustra with the feeling of guilt for breaking the conventional rules of justice. Zarathustra suggests as much when he explains the meaning of the parable to his disciples: "The annihilator of morals, the good and just call me: my story is immoral."

The adder's poison, however, does not affect Zarathustra. Zarathustra compares himself to a dragon, and the poison of an adder is not enough to kill the dragon. Indeed, Zarathustra shows no signs of anger toward the adder. Instead, he simply brushes off the attack, much like the nobles of the *Genealogy* who either quickly avenge or simply ignore the attacks of their enemies. Most of the remainder of Zarathustra's speech in "On the Adder's Bite" is devoted to lessons on how to respond to one's enemies. Implicitly rejecting Christianity's teaching to love one's enemies, Zarathustra counsels that "a little revenge is more human than no revenge." However, whatever revenge one takes, the thought of revenge must not blacken one's soul. In terms of the *Genealogy*, it must not turn into *ressentiment*. Thus, Zarathustra claims: "And if you have been done a great wrong, then quickly add five little ones: a gruesome sight is a person single-mindedly obsessed by a wrong."

In "**Child and Marriage**," the topic shifts back to desire and human relationships. The chapter begins with Zarathustra questioning the motives that drive one to procreate. The distinction he draws between those self-conquerors who are entitled to procreate and those who procreate out of need or a sense of loneliness parallels a later distinction he makes between Dionysian artists who create from an overfullness of life and romantic artists who create out of impoverishment (GS 370). Here, Zarathustra says, "let your victory and your freedom long for a child," as this child will be a monument to one's victory and liberation. However, the precondition for such a child is that one first builds oneself "perpendicular in body and soul." This will allow one not simply to reproduce but produce "something higher." This seems to be a reference to the *Übermensch*. At the same time, Zarathustra's next words recall the description of the child in "On the Three Metamorphoses": "You shall create a higher body, a first movement, a self-propelled wheel—you shall create a creator." Such words also recall the language from "On the Way of the Creator."

This goal supposedly gives marriage meaning; it is "the will of two to create one that is more than those who created it." Zarathustra contrasts a marriage dedicated to producing an *Übermensch* with the marriage of the so-called superfluous. These latter marriages—possibly marriages of Christians or even the last humans—aim at "wretched contentment" and are made for heaven and blessed by God. The individuals in these marriages have not learned the right sort of love. There is a bitterness in this sort of love, but it is a bitterness that creates a longing for the *Übermensch*, and it is this arrow of longing and love for the *Übermensch* that sanctifies the marriage. For readers, the problem here is that we still have not been presented with a clear conception of what the *Übermensch* is supposed to be or even how individuals committed to the project of giving birth to such an *Übermensch* might go about doing this. Is it a mere interest in this project that is determinative, such that if I want to create an *Übermensch* I can create an *Übermensch*? Or are there genetic or physiological or even psychological markers by which individuals can identify each other as suitable partners for reproductive success? If there are such markers or traits, what are they? Unfortunately, we are provided little guidance here.[21]

Whereas "Child and Marriage" is about birth, "**On Free Death**" is about death. Common to both passages is that life and death, creation and destruction, are understood in relation to the creation of the *Übermensch*. In the *Nachlass*, Nietzsche writes that he wants to make a festival out of both procreation and death (KSA 10:4[77]). In this passage, Zarathustra counsels a death at the right time. Dying at the right time is connected to consummating one's life to some higher goal.[22] A "free death" is therefore a death that comes when one wants death, and one will want death when it is the right time to die for this goal. To express the idea of the right time, Zarathustra compares life to a ripening fruit, and it is a comparison that Nietzsche makes elsewhere in *Zarathustra*. Indeed, Nietzsche describes his own life in these terms at the beginning of *Ecce Homo*, and he connects the idea of a ripe fruit to the notion of having turned out well (*wohlgerathen*). Here, in contrast, the talk is about fruit that does not turn out so well. The German word is *missrathen* or ill-constituted, and this is the exact opposite of *wohlgerathen*, which is what Nietzsche later ascribes to the *Übermensch* (EH "Books":1). In "On Free Death," these ill-constituted individuals have poisonous worms eating their way into their hearts (the worm is a symbol for revenge (GM III:14)), and Zarathustra wishes that a storm would shake these worm-eaten apples from the tree. In other words, Zarathustra wishes for them to experience a "*quick* death."[23]

In contrast to Zarathustra, there are those who preach a slow death. These preachers honor the Hebrew Jesus, and Jesus is someone who died too early. Jesus had only known tears and melancholy and the hatred of "the good and the just." Thus, he developed a desire for death, and although he had, much like the "camel" of the three metamorphoses, fled the good and the just by going into the desert, he nevertheless returned to the city for an all-too-early death. It is a striking passage because Nietzsche attributes a certain nobility to Jesus. His nobility is linked to his willingness to separate from the herd, but his teaching—presumably of neighbor love—was still a product of immaturity. There is, according to Zarathustra, more melancholy in youth, and there is a greater ability in maturity to be like a child. The idea is that the mature person knows how to die and therefore knows how to live, and in knowing how to live, one presumably knows how to play like a child. Indeed, Nietzsche suggests that if Jesus had lived to maturity, he would have learned to live and love the earth, and he may have even learned the laughter that will be practiced and preached in *Zarathustra* IV.

The chapter ends with another reference to the "badly constituted [*schlecht gerathen*]" and how their deaths compare with the deaths of those who are presumably well constituted. The latter die with "honey" in their souls, and their deaths will spread a glow "like a sunset around the earth." Of course, we know that Zarathustra will later be described as having honey in his veins (ZIV "The Honey Sacrifice"), and Zarathustra later compares himself to a sun that, when setting, gives golden oars to even the poorest fishermen (ZIII "Tablets":3; see also GS 337). Here, Zarathustra claims that it is by dying in this way that one encourages others to love the earth even more.

However, the ending of the passage is rather odd. Zarathustra acknowledges that he wants to die so that his friends (disciples) "may love the earth more for [his] sake." One might interpret this as Zarathustra expressing his wish to die now. He has his goal, and he will now die for the sake of this goal. How he might die is unclear: Drowning? Starvation? Hanging? Hemlock? Jumping into a volcano like Empedocles? It is also unclear what practical effect his death will have in relation to his goal. Here, one might think that his continued presence would better serve his goal than his free death. In the passage, Zarathustra seems to agree. Thus, he passes his ball—a symbol for the goal of creating the *Übermensch*—to his heirs (disciples), and he wants to see them throwing this ball to each other. Thus, he wants to linger a little longer on earth to watch them spread his word and realize his teaching. For this, he asks for forgiveness.

Loeb has appealed to this passage to argue that "Nietzsche must show Zarathustra freely choosing to die at a later point in the narrative when it is actually the right time to die" (2010:135). According to Loeb, this occurs at the end of *Zarathustra* III. However, we know that Nietzsche sketched plans for staging Zarathustra's biological death in subsequent parts after the publication of *Zarathustra* III (KSA 11:34[144]; 11:35[73]; 12:2[129]), and therefore, we have good reason to think that Zarathustra does not die at the end of *Zarathustra* III. Given this, there seems to be four other ways of interpreting "On Free Death": (1) the passage is not intended to foreshadow anything that will happen in subsequent parts of *Zarathustra*; (2) the passage is intended to foreshadow subsequent events, but the promise or plan goes unfulfilled in later parts of *Zarathustra*; (3) the passage refers to a free death of Zarathustra's non-biological "self" or psyche at the end of *Zarathustra* III; and (4) the passage foreshadows Nietzsche's own life and his descent into madness at the end of 1888 and his eventual death in 1900.

Option (1) is always a possibility, but I tend to agree with Loeb that Nietzsche is doing some foreshadowing here. Given that we have sketches for Zarathustra's eventual death—written after *Zarathustra* III—that Nietzsche never included in *Zarathustra* itself, option (2) might be the best or even the default reading of the passage. However, one could make a case for reading (3). After all, the language at the end of *Zarathustra* III that Loeb uses to support the idea that Zarathustra dies in a biological sense—most notably section 30 of "Tablets"—is language that I will use to support my reading of Zarathustra's psychic or spiritual death. The primary worry is that the language of "On Free Death" suggests a biological death. However, as I explain below, I do think the language of "going under" in the next chapter ("Gift-Giving Virtue":3) implies a psychological death of the self and therefore a transformation to a new sort of life.

Option (4) has been proposed by Claudia Crawford (1995), and there is some textual evidence to support this. In *Ecce Homo*, Nietzsche compares his own life to a ripening fruit that has achieved a certain sort of perfection (he also presents himself as exemplifying *Wohlgerathenheit*). Given his state of perfection, it seems that it is the right time for him to die, and Crawford points to evidence from a dithyramb like "Last Will" (in *Dithyrambs of Dionysus*) to make this argument. Interestingly, Crawford explains that the first version of "Last Will" was written in 1883, and it forms the basis for section 30 of "Tablets" in *Zarathustra* III (1995:245). Although Loeb appeals to this passage to argue that it refers to Zarathustra's death, it is important to note that Nietzsche had planned to use this passage as a second epilogue to *Ecce Homo*, following the chapter "Why I am a Destiny" (see Brobjer 2023:45). Thus, this gives us a further reason for thinking that "On Free Death" is foreshadowing Nietzsche's own fate. But here again, Crawford's argument focuses on Nietzsche's descent into madness in 1888-1889, not his biological death in 1900. So construed, Nietzsche's own "death," i.e., his madness, is really a death of the self or psyche and its dissolution into nature. Thus, we are again thrown back on the idea that "On

Free Death" might be referring to a psychic death of the self, and the problem with this is that the passage seems to be focused on a biological death.[24] In the end, option (2) might therefore be the best reading of the passage. However, even if it is, it still does not preclude the psychological death of Zarathustra in *Zarathustra* or some sort of psychic death associated with Nietzsche's collapse in 1888-1889.

In the final chapter of *Zarathustra* I, "**On the Gift-Giving Virtue**," Zarathustra bids farewell to the town of the Motley Cow, now followed by "many who called themselves his disciples." To honor Zarathustra, these disciples present him with a staff that has a golden handle and a serpent coiled around the sun. As Grätz (2024:471) notes, the serpent was often associated with Asclepius, the Greek god of medicine, and it can be understood as a symbol for healing. If this is right, there is an interesting contrast here between Zarathustra's staff of life-affirming wisdom and Socrates' own need to thank Asclepius for prescribing death as the ultimate cure for life (see GS 340).

The gold on the handle initiates Zarathustra's reflection on the value of gold as he speaks to his disciples (the ball he threw to his disciples was also gold). Gold has the highest value because it is "uncommon and useless and gleaming," and it is therefore the symbol of the highest virtue. Like gold, this virtue is a gift-giving virtue. In a move that stands in opposition to much of Nietzsche's religious and philosophical heritage, Zarathustra names selfishness or *Selbstsucht* as the gift-giving virtue.[25] The move here is an obvious rebuke and reversal of the traditional idea, articulated most recently by Schopenhauer, that *selflessness* is the essence of a Christian love that gives itself away in the form of charity. In contrast, Zarathustra identifies a healthy and a sick form of self-love (*Selbstsucht*). Whereas the healthy form of self-love (*Selbstsucht*) forces "all things to and into" the self so that "they may flow back out" as gifts of love (the language here parallels GS 337), the sick form of self-love (*Selbstsucht*) takes from others and keeps for oneself. Thus, the latter says, "everything for me" and gives nothing in return. The former, in contrast, flies upward and goes "from genus to overgenus [*von der Art hinüber zur Über-Art*]."[26] It is, as Zarathustra claims, "a parable of elevation," and it subtly connects the gift-giving virtue to the *Übermensch* (ZI "On the Gift-Giving Virtue":1).

We have already stressed the important role that *eros* plays in *Zarathustra* I, and we have noted the connections between *eros* and self-love (*Selbstsucht*) as well as the will to power. The language of upward flight and elevation can be tied to a tradition that symbolizes *eros* with wings, and Zarathustra refers to an elevated body that turns "creator and esteemer and lover and benefactor of all things." Here again, we are told that the "heart flows broad and full like a river." Moreover, we learn that a lover's will, which is above praise and blame, wants to command all things and that virtue originates when we will with a single will and "call this cessation of all need 'necessity'" (ZI "On the Gift-Giving Virtue":1). The proleptic foreshadowing of Zarathustra's own fate is clear, as this latter line is repeated almost verbatim at the end of section 30 of "Tablets" in *Zarathustra* III. The difference is that in *Zarathustra* III, Zarathustra has achieved this standpoint, whereas at the end of *Zarathustra* I, Zarathustra is merely describing it.

Despite his talk of upward elevation, Zarathustra nevertheless exhorts his disciples to remain "faithful to the earth." The worry is that the flight of *eros* will result in the longing for an other-worldly heaven, like the ladder of love that Plato describes in the *Symposium*. The virtues of self-love and power need to serve the earth, and the love of knowledge needs to be used to make experiments for health. By making such experiments, all the instincts become holy, and the elevated soul becomes "gay" or *fröhlich* (this is a possible reference to *The Gay Science* [*Die fröhliche Wissenschaft*]). These healthy individuals will then, in turn, prepare the way for the coming of the *Übermensch*, thereby bringing healing, hope, and salvation.

Indeed, Zarathustra maps out a very extensive plan for the creation of the *Übermensch*. Specifically, he tells his disciples that they will form a people who have chosen themselves. From these self-chosen people, a "chosen people" will grow. Finally, it is from the chosen people (not the self-chosen disciples) that the *Übermensch* will be born. Only then will the earth become a sight of recovery or convalescence (*Genesung*). How this is supposed to work or even how many generations this will take is not clear (we can reckon at least two). In any case, Zarathustra's hope for the *Übermensch* is a distant one, and there is no mention of the role that Zarathustra will play in any of this (nothing is said about the possibility of Zarathustra's own convalescence, which occurs at the end of *Zarathustra* III). Zarathustra is merely the visionary here, and the disciples are supposed to carry out the plan. In this way, Zarathustra sounds a lot like the young Nietzsche. There is a plan for a renewed culture, but the plan is supposed to be executed by someone else.

The first book of *Zarathustra* ends with Zarathustra exhorting his disciples to go their own way. Rather than finding him, their redeemer, they must find and so redeem themselves, and only when they deny Zarathustra will they find Zarathustra. Again, nothing is explicit, but this may mean that Zarathustra's disciples must learn to love themselves, not him, and by loving themselves, they will then find him in the sense of following his teaching. When they find each other again, they will then be able to celebrate the "great noon." As we have seen, "noon" is a central motif in *Zarathustra*, and it recalls the title of the note in which Nietzsche first pens Zarathustra's name, "noon and eternity" (KSA 9:11[195]). In this same set of notes, Nietzsche associates "noon" with the appearance of the thought of the eternal recurrence (KSA 9:11[148]), and he also speaks of the sun of knowledge wrapped in the serpent of eternity (KSA 9:11[196]).

In elaborating on the concept of the great noon, Zarathustra refers to his speech to the townspeople in the prologue. There, we learned that the human stands between the beast and the *Übermensch*. Here, we are told that the great noon is a moment that "stands in the middle of his way between beast and overman [*Übermensch*] and celebrates his way to the evening as his highest hope for it is the way to a new morning" (ZI "Gift Giving Virtue":3). In this sense, the great noon represents an important turning point in world history. If we follow Nietzsche in associating noon with the eternal recurrence, then the summoning of the eternal recurrence represents an important step in producing the *Übermensch*. It is not, in contrast, the appearance of the *Übermensch* that makes possible the "noon" of the eternal recurrence.

Toward the end of the passage, we learn that the "great noon" is a point in which an individual who "goes under [*der Untergehende*]" blesses "himself for being one who goes over and beyond [*der Hinübergehende*]." As we have seen, "going under" can mean leaving the cave and going down to the town and the people. It can also mean a descent into the earth or some sort of death. Here, "going under" must mean the latter. At the same time, it must be a kind of descent or death that allows for a transformation in the individual that goes under. This is because "going under" is coupled with going "over and beyond." For this reason, I do not think the death implied here can be a biological one. There is no afterlife in which someone who dies can be transformed. Returning to this same life—as the eternal recurrence might suggest—also allows no room for transformation (it is the same life). It is also difficult to see how the going under of a human being could lead to a going over in the sense of producing a distinct entity such as the *Übermensch* (there seems to be no causal connection). Thus, a going under that is coupled with a going over and beyond likely represents a ritual kind of death and rebirth—found in the mystery teachings associated with cults like Dionysus—in which one becomes a child again, and it is this child—born at the great noon in which the eternal recurrence is summoned—that makes it possible for the reborn child to become an *Übermensch*, the this-worldly replacement for the dead God.[27] Thus, the section ends: "'*Dead are all gods: now we want the overman to live.*'—on that great noon" (ZI "Gift Giving Virtue":3).

NOTES

1. A bolded chapter title indicates where I begin the main discussion of a given chapter. I employ this convention to assist readers who may want to consult the discussion of specific chapters.
2. See Parkes (2005:xii). See Aiken (2006) for critical reflections on the connection between Zarathustra and Zoroaster.
3. See both Stern (2008:313) and Tevenar (2013:277).
4. I thank Amelia Randich for helping me craft this language.
5. See Sorgner (2017) for possible connections to contemporary transhumanism.
6. In *Zarathustra* IV, Zarathustra refers to all the higher men gathered in his cave as jesters or *Possenreisser* (ZIV "Ass Festival":2).
7. Hatab (2005:163) also makes such a distinction.

8 See Franco (2022:196) for a discussion of Zarathustra's transition from a solitary hermit to one who rules.
9 See Brobjer (2023: Ch.1) for the connection between *Zarathustra* and the revaluation of values.
10 See KSA10:5[1].178 and KSA 10:4[138] for further references to this concept of a self-moved mover in the *Nachlass* from this time. See Grätz (2024:412) for further discussion.
11 Riccardi (2021:168) uses this chapter to distinguish between two different selves in Nietzsche. The *Selbst* or the "bodily self" is "identical with the structure of one's drives understood as physio-psychologically realized behavioral dispositions." This is in contract to the "I" (*Ich*), which refers to reflective consciousness or mind. Thus, the point of the passage is to say that reflective consciousness is "the direct product of the bodily *Selbst*" and so necessarily dependent on it.
12 See Sinhababu (2022: Ch.7.2) for more on this chapter.
13 This is a clear reference to Protagoras' ancient dictum of *homo mensura*. See Meyer (2014c) for more on Nietzsche's relationship to Protagoras and connections between Nietzsche's perspectivism and Protagoras' epistemology. See Sinhababu (2015: Sec.1.3) for more on subjectivism in *Zarathustra*.
14 In the *Nachlass*, "the spirit of gravity" first appears under the term "genius gravitationis" (KSA 10:3[1].43).
15 See Acampora (2013).
16 See also Nietzsche's "Law against Christianity" at the end of *The Antichrist* (fourth law).
17 See Leiter (2019: Ch.1).
18 See Meyer (2014b) for more on this point.
19 See Meyer (2014:273–275).
20 Such a conception of the human subject is articulated in KSA 10:4[138]: "Every human being is a creative cause of occurrences, a primum mobile with an original movement" (Translation from CWFN 14).
21 Grätz (2024:445) notes that this chapter became a central reference point for early twentieth-century discussions of eugenics and the race-based ideology of National Socialism.
22 As Loeb has pointed out (2010:129), Nietzsche already sketched this idea in section four of *Richard Wagner in Bayreuth*, associating it with the genre of tragedy.
23 In *The Antichrist*, Nietzsche claims that the *missrathen* deserve to perish (A 2).
24 See Stellino (2013) for further reflections on Nietzsche's view of suicide.
25 KSA 10:4[280] indicates that "On Holy Selfishness" or "*Von der heiligen Selbstsucht*" was the original title of the chapter.
26 It is locutions like this that suggest Zarathustra is hoping for the birth of a new species in the *Übermensch* or, more precisely, superhumans in the plural and therefore a Darwinian conception of the *Übermensch*.
27 See Hollinrake (1982:78–89) for a reading of these two terms as a form of death (*Untergang*) but also a rebirth and initiation (*Hinübergang* or just *Übergang*) into the mysteries of Dionysus.

4
THUS SPOKE ZARATHUSTRA II

Unlike *Zarathustra* I, we know that Nietzsche composed *Zarathustra* II with plans for more than just *Zarathustra* II in view. It is at this stage that we know Nietzsche will write a work that includes and even culminates in the teaching of the eternal recurrence, and it is here that the tragic nature of the work takes shape. Indeed, Nietzsche's initial notes from this period include an extensive summary of the basic ideas from *The Birth of Tragedy* (KSA 10:7[7]), and this suggests that he is using his first work as a guide to structure the contents of *Zarathustra* itself. In *Zarathustra* II, there are only hints of the eternal recurrence, as we encounter references to the view in "The Soothsayer" and "On Redemption." However, these hints and the chapters that contain them are vital to the drama of *Zarathustra* as a whole, as the reader is presented with existential problems that will only be resolved in *Zarathustra* III. The function of *Zarathustra* II is to reveal the superficiality of Zarathustra's initial hopes for the birth of an *Übermensch* and to highlight the need for a solution to the problem of revenge against time as both transience (*Vergänglichkeit*) and the past (*Vergangenheit*). These solutions will only come to the fore in *Zarathustra* III.

Even though *Zarathustra* II begins with Zarathustra's terrifying dream, the Apollonian ethos of *Zarathustra* I carries through the opening chapters of *Zarathustra* II. Zarathustra's hopes for an Apollonian *Übermensch* reach their apex in the idyllic "On the Blessed Isles." However, the superficiality of this program and the general ethos of *Zarathustra* I eventually becomes unmasked with the introduction of the problem of revenge in "On the Tarantulas" and the problem of death in "The Tomb Song." The latter is one of three songs that are generally understood as marking a turn toward Dionysian themes in the text, symbolized by Zarathustra's eventual movement from land (Apollo) to the sea (Dionysus). Along the way, we learn that the world is will to power in "On Self-Overcoming," and we are introduced to problems that will eventually require Zarathustra to summon the eternal recurrence. In "On Poets," Zarathustra seems to claim that his own teaching of the *Übermensch* has the problematic status of a poetic fiction, and, in "On Redemption," we are presented with an understanding of human redemption that makes no explicit reference to the *Übermensch*. As *Zarathustra* II closes, Zarathustra realizes that he can no longer rely on others or even the future hope of an *Übermensch* to carry out his redemptive project. If he is going to affirm existence, Zarathustra is going to have to work on himself. This is made clear in the final chapter, "The Stillest Hour," in which Zarathustra is commanded to become a child without shame. *Zarathustra* II ends with Zarathustra weeping as he leaves his friends behind.

4.1 ON THE BLESSED ISLES: CHAPTERS 1–8

The first chapter, "**The Child with the Mirror**," begins by informing us that Zarathustra has returned to his cave and his solitude, and we learn that he has been there for months and even years. Much like the first book, he wakes up one morning and feels compelled to speak. However, rather than stepping out of the cave and speaking to the sun, he now speaks from his bed to his heart.

He narrates a terrifying dream in which a child asks Zarathustra to look into a mirror, and what Zarathustra sees is not himself but "a devil's grimace and scornful laughter." The mirror, an important artifact in Dionysian myth and ritual,[1] forces Zarathustra to turn inward, to reflect on himself and his teaching. This is something that Zarathustra did not do in *Zarathustra* I. Zarathustra interprets the dream as a warning that his teaching is in danger, that it has been perverted by his enemies, and that even his friends are now ashamed of what he has given them. As we know from "On Reading and Writing," Zarathustra's devil is the "spirit of gravity," and Zarathustra may be referring to it here. If this is right, then the spirit of gravity—a figure who comes to represent melancholy and revenge—still haunts Zarathustra's teaching, and Zarathustra has yet to vanquish this foe who now mocks him with scornful laughter.

In response, Zarathustra is overwhelmed with a foolish happiness. He must descend again, plunging his speech and his river of love into the valleys. He will look for his friends, but also his enemies on "the blessed isles." He will mount his horse and carry a spear to hurl against his enemies. Between his thunder and lightning he will "throw showers of hail into the depths." This is all powerful rhetoric, and it suggests that Zarathustra is now overtaken by some non-rational force welling up from the depths of his being. Thus, he speaks of his "wild wisdom" which became pregnant and is giving birth to her young. All of this is reminiscent of Zarathustra's blessing of the cup that wants to overflow in the opening of *Zarathustra* I, and it might also allude to the gift-giving virtue of the final chapter of *Zarathustra* I. It also points forward to the unveiling of Zarathustra's wisdom in *Zarathustra* II, which seems to be that all life is will to power. At the very least, we can say that his wisdom is wild in the sense that it is connected to both passion and longing rather than any sort of contemplative calm.

The title of the next chapter, "**Upon the Blessed Isles**," indicates that Zarathustra has left his cave for these isles. According to Grätz (2024:519–520), the isles represent a poetic utopia or earthly paradise—similar to Elysium—that was a common motif among ancient Greek poets such as Hesiod, Pindar, Homer, Plato, and Lucian.[2] In my view, it represents the highpoint of the Apollonian nature of roughly the first half of the drama. On the island, Zarathustra is giving a speech, but his interlocutors are only identified as his "brothers." Presumably, he is speaking to his friends and disciples who—as suggested by the motto of *Zarathustra* II—have since denied him. However, it is not even certain that he is speaking to anyone at all. He presents his teachings as being ripe and ready to fall from the tree, and he presents himself as the north wind who will help his teachings fall to the ground for harvest. The teaching he has in mind is clearly that of the *Übermensch*, and Nietzsche constructs the speech to refer to the central motif of *Zarathustra* I.

The speech however introduces a new concept that is a variant of the will to power: the will to truth. The will to truth can be understood as a form of Platonic *eros*, the desire that Plato thinks animates all of us, at least initially, to seek out the true, the good, and the beautiful (a variant of this is found at the beginning of Aristotle's *Metaphysics* where he claims that all humans by nature desire to know). On this view, the will to truth amounts to a philosophical process of discovery, one in which anthropomorphic projections are stripped away in a quest to see things as they are in themselves. In contrast, Zarathustra explains that the will to truth means that everything is "changed into what is thinkable for man, visible for man, feelable by man." In other words, satisfying the will to truth means making the world into something intelligible to the human. Indeed, Zarathustra continues by saying that what we call the "world"—and here I take this to mean our "life-world" rather than nature or the natural world discovered through the natural sciences—is something created by us: our reason, our image, our will, our love. Moreover, it is this created life-world that will ultimately be the object of knowledge. In this way, the philosophical quest for knowledge begins with an act of creation and therefore a form of poetry, and the higher human who contemplates reality is, at the same time, one who first creates the reality she contemplates (GS 301).

We also hear from Zarathustra that God is a conjecture and that "God is a thought that makes crooked all that is straight, and makes turn whatever stands." The idea is that God is a concept that becomes the standard for judging nature and human life, and this standard makes the world and the human being appear ugly and fallen. This is a variant of the underlying idea behind Nietzsche's critique of metaphysics: the creation of a second or "true" world inevitably leads to a condemnation of "this" world for failing to live up to the metaphysical world. Indeed, Zarathustra objects to the very idea of a god with a humorous syllogism: "If there were gods, how could I endure not to be a god! *Hence* there are no gods."

Nietzsche also has Zarathustra connect the monotheistic God to the Parmenidean-Platonic notion of being, and he contrasts this notion of being with a natural world of becoming. The contrast between being and becoming is a complex one, and Nietzsche made it a central part of his thinking as early as his reflections in *Philosophy in the Tragic Age*.[3] In "Upon the Blessed Isles," the distinction runs along the lines of "the One," "the unmoved," and "the permanent" (being) versus the realm of time, change, and the impermanent (becoming). According to Zarathustra, the notion of a One or being is evil, and this is presumably because it not only distorts or makes crooked the realm of becoming, but also because it is "misanthropic." That is, it leads to a hatred of the human.

Zarathustra also explains that this talk of the One and the Permanent is a poetic lie and that "the poets lie too much." In contrast, Zarathustra praises parables that speak of "time and becoming," as these can provide a "justification of all impermanence." Here, it seems that Nietzsche wants to cast both being and becoming as "parables" and so forms of poetry. Are they both therefore "lies"? It is not clear whether Zarathustra prefers parables of becoming because they are truer to reality or because they are more life affirming (or possibly both). It is clear that Nietzsche rejects "being" because it distorts the natural world and the human and therefore leads to a hatred of both. But does he also think that "becoming" is a poetic lie? Some have held that he does, that all claims about the world or fundamental ontology are necessarily fictions constructed in our image. The problem with this, however, is that "becoming" must then be a falsification of some further reality that it distorts or misrepresents. But Nietzsche seems to deny that there is or even could be some further reality. Thus, he calls the "flux of things" the "final truth" in an 1881 *Nachlass* note (KSA 9:11[162]).

Having glossed themes of fundamental ontology, Zarathustra then returns to a central theme of *The Birth*: how do we justify suffering and affirm existence? For Zarathustra, the answer is creation. But for creation to occur—and this is also a central point of *The Birth*—suffering and change are needed. The idea that suffering, change, and even death are intimately bound up with creation, joy, and the affirmation of life runs throughout Nietzsche's writings. In an important passage from *The Gay Science*, Nietzsche argues that suffering serves as a necessary springboard to creation, but he also distinguishes between two types of creation that stem from two types of suffering. On the one hand, romantic art emerges from a neediness or lack. On the other hand, Dionysian art emerges from an overfullness of life (GS 370). As a work, Nietzsche's *Zarathustra* seems to represent the latter sort, emerging from the health and exuberance of *The Gay Science*.

We are then introduced to Zarathustra's creative will, a will that wills his destiny. The teaching in "Upon the Blessed Isles" is that the will is a liberator and a joy bringer. "Willing liberates: that is the true teaching of will and liberty." In the *Nachlass* from this time, Nietzsche contrasts willing with feeling and suffering. Whereas the latter creates the feeling of imprisonment, the act of willing can be associated with "freedom of the will" (KSA 10:12[4]).[4] As we will see, this conception of willing and freedom will be problematized in "On Redemption." Here, we are also told that the opposite of willing is not willing, and Zarathustra claims that willing and therefore creating no more is a sign of the great weariness. This weariness recalls the loveless soul of the last human, but even more so the life-denying pessimism of Schopenhauer. Thus, we again see Nietzsche entertaining the central theme of *The Birth*, the affirmation and denial of life, and here again, he points to artistic creation as the means to overcoming life-denying weariness.

The passage ends with Zarathustra speaking of a will to create that pushes him toward the human just as a hammer moves toward stone. Recalling Goethe's description of Prometheus forming men,[5] Zarathustra speaks of liberating a sleeping image from "the ugliest stone." The ugliest stone seems to be the human, and the sleeping image or "shadow" is that of the *Übermensch*. Zarathustra speaks of a hammer—a symbol that Nietzsche often associates with the eternal recurrence—that "rages cruelly against its prison" as "pieces of rock rain from the stone." Here again, the theme of *Zarathustra* I is reprised. Zarathustra will redeem and affirm existence not by loving the human *qua* human, but by loving the human for what the human can become, namely, the *Übermensch*. It is for this reason—the hope of the *Übermensch*—that the gods mean little to Zarathustra now.

With Zarathustra's eye on the *Übermensch*, he is perceived in **"On the Pitying"** as one walking among humans as if they were animals. Here, Nietzsche intimates that Zarathustra has some sort of knowledge, and this knowledge allows Zarathustra to see humans for what they are: animals with red cheeks. The reference to red cheeks is a reference to blushing and therefore shame. Human beings seem to be unique in this respect: They are the only animal which is ashamed of being an animal. Effectively foreshadowing the second essay of the *Genealogy*, Nietzsche has Zarathustra ask how this came about. How is "shame, shame, shame" "the history of man"? Shame is an important topic for Nietzsche, as he connects the overcoming of shame to the project of becoming who one is: "what is the seal of liberation? No longer being ashamed in front of oneself" (GS 275; see also GS 270). As we will see, Zarathustra also links the task of becoming a child to the overcoming of shame at the end of *Zarathustra* II.

Despite the initial emphasis on shame, the passage is, as the title suggests, about pity. Pity is contrasted with both joy and a type of love that transcends pity. As we have noted before, we should understand "pity" as synonymous with Christian love or *agape*. In the passage, Zarathustra expresses his dislike for those who feel pity. In contrast, he claims that humans have "felt too little joy," and this is our "original sin." The contrast between pity and joy points back to the closing aphorisms of *The Gay Science*, in which Nietzsche concludes an extended critique of pity by exhorting us "*to share not suffering but joy*" (GS 338). Near the end of the chapter, Zarathustra claims that pity has brought more suffering in the world than any other folly. Indeed, God's love of humans—his pity for them—is his hell, and this is why God is dead. In contrast, Zarathustra speaks of a great love—likely the *eros* motif we have been tracing throughout the text—that is willing to sacrifice both one's neighbor and oneself. The love of which Zarathustra speaks is likely his love for the *Übermensch*.

In "**On Priests**," Zarathustra describes those who have given their lives to the religion of pity or Christian *agape*, and much of his description foreshadows Nietzsche's portrayal of the power-hungry priest looking for revenge in the *Genealogy*. Here, Zarathustra focuses on two themes: bondage and life-denial. Much like the prisoners in Nietzsche's first portrayal of the death of God in *The Wanderer* (WS 84), the priests here are fettered by their belief in their redeemer, "in fetters of false values and delusive words." They believe they have found an island—this recalls "the blessed isles" of Zarathustra's previous speech—but this island is really a "sleeping monster" of false values that eventually devours the soul. The false values they create are also life-denying values. They invent a god whose essence stands in complete contradiction to human existence. Whereas the Christian God represents a selfless and self-sacrificing love, the human being and indeed all life is characterized by a self-regarding will to power. Thus, the Christian god is represented by a crucified man. Worshiping this god, the priests then live as melancholic corpses, represented by the black they use to clothe themselves.

According to Zarathustra, these priests need to be redeemed from their redeemer and liberated from the bonds the redeemer has created. In this sense, the passage points back to Nietzsche's own project of the free spirit. There, he sought to liberate himself in a systematic fashion from these false beliefs and delusions, and this is something the priests have yet to do. At the same time, the conclusion of Zarathustra's speech gestures toward the redemption offered by the *Übermensch*. In order to "find the way to freedom," one "must be redeemed from still greater ones than all redeemers." Here, the *Übermensch* is presented as this way to freedom. However, Zarathustra remarks: "Never has there been an overman [*Übermensch*]. Naked I saw both the greatest and the smallest man; they are still all-too-similar to each other. Verily, even the greatest I found all-too-human."

The next chapter, "**On the Virtuous**," recalls Zarathustra's speech from the first part, "On the Teachers of Virtue." Here, however, Zarathustra connects his remarks to the fundamental nature of reality. Although he begins by laughing at the virtuous who still want a heavenly reward for their virtue, his main concern is that reward and punishment have been lied into the foundation of things (and therefore into the foundation of the soul). By this, Nietzsche means that notions of good and evil, reward and punishment, have been mistakenly made into cosmological principles. In *Ecce Homo*, Nietzsche tells us that he chose the name Zarathustra to undo what the historical Zoroaster did: imbue the cosmos with notions of good and evil (EH "Destiny":3). In "On the Virtuous," Zarathustra claims to be a "plowshare [*Pflugschar*]" who will uproot these lies that have been both projected into the cosmos and the foundation of souls. The image of the ploughshare is something that Nietzsche used to characterize his own free spirit project on several occasions (EH "Books" HH:2), and it suggests that Zarathustra has been tasked with carrying this project to completion.

Much of the speech consists of Zarathustra describing various mischaracterizations of virtue. As he concludes his speech, Zarathustra emphasizes that he is not speaking to those who lie about virtue. Instead, he is speaking to his friends—or disciples—so that they grow weary of these words of the fools and the liars. Here, Zarathustra makes two important points. First, he tells his disciples that they are too pure for filthy words like "reward, retribution, punishment, and revenge in justice." Eliminating these words from our understanding of the cosmos points back to Nietzsche's critique of Anaximander in *Philosophy in the Tragic Age*[6] and points forward to "the innocence of becoming" that Nietzsche associates with the eternal recurrence in *Twilight of the Idols* (TI "Errors":7). Zarathustra also exhorts his friends to grow weary of saying that selflessness makes an action good. Selflessness is the exact opposite of the healthy self-love Zarathustra preaches in both *Zarathustra* I and III, and it is closely connected with Schopenhauer's morality of pity and so Christian *agape*. In contrast to this self- and life-denying form of morality, Zarathustra claims that the self should be in one's deed just as a mother is in her child. Even though Zarathustra thinks even his friends will react with anger, he promises them they will soon be comforted by new teachings. As Grätz explains (2024:579), the chapter ends by referring to his listeners as children playing with toys near the sea, and the metaphors Zarathustra uses recalls Heraclitus' image of the child that runs throughout Nietzsche's works. As such the chapter implicitly contrasts the reward and punishment cosmology of Anaximander with a playful innocence of becoming he associates with Heraclitus (see KSA 11:26[64]).

In the next two chapters, Zarathustra expresses his contempt for equality. For Nietzsche, the value modernity places on equality—and democracy, the political structure based on equality—is an outgrowth of Christian neighbor love or *agape*, a form of love that stands directly opposed to an upward-directed, ladder-climbing *eros* or will to power. In "**On the Rabble**," Zarathustra turns his critical gaze on the "rabble," and we find him equating the rabble to maggots "in the bread of life." Here, Zarathustra expresses his feelings of nausea (*Ekel*), and he reveals that the desire to be redeemed from such nausea forced him "to fly to the highest spheres" so that he could "find the fount of pleasure again." These great heights, in his "summer noon," preclude "the unclean and their thirst."

The question he raises about the rabble is important, and it, along with Zarathustra's feelings of nausea about the human condition, will reoccur at crucial stages of *Zarathustra*. Specifically, Zarathustra asks: "What? Does life require even the rabble? Are poisoned wells required?" This is a deep question because the chapter begins with Zarathustra comparing life to a "well of joy"; however, he quickly notes that the rabble poison this well. The question that Zarathustra poses is whether the affirmation of joy also requires the affirmation of the rabble that poison it. In response to these thoughts and questions, Zarathustra finds himself nauseated. He cannot even stand the thought of those who haggle for power with the rabble, a seeming reference to Nietzsche's disdain for representative democracy. To get away from this, Zarathustra uses the wings he created with his nausea to fly to "the highest spheres" and drink from the purest wells. In this state of solitude, he plans to build a nest in the tree of the future.

"**On the Tarantulas**" is an important chapter. It is here that we encounter the first robust discussion of revenge, a theme that was briefly referenced in "On the Flies of the Market Place" from *Zarathustra* I and will become central in "On Redemption" in *Zarathustra* II. The black tarantula is a symbol for the way in which revenge darkens the soul,[7] and it uses its poisonous venom to take revenge. Nietzsche holds that the value of equality emerges from the desire for revenge. On this view, human equality is not a self-evident normative truth but rather the offshoot of Christianity, which, as we learn from the *Genealogy*, is itself born of revenge and *ressentiment*. The idea is that we feel hurt when someone makes us feel inferior, and therefore we look to respond by harming them, effectively bringing them back to our level (or even making them subordinate). The doctrine of equality—the claim that we *ought* to be equal—is therefore an act of mass revenge against the elite, a politics of envy on the grandest scale meant to bring down those who are naturally superior, even send them to hell.

As Brusotti (1997: 560) has shown, Nietzsche is engaging with Eugen Dühring in this chapter (Dühring later reappears as the fire hound in "On Great Events").[8] In *Der Werth des Lebens* (1865), Dühring defended, like Nietzsche, a life-affirming philosophy that embraced naturalism and rejected metaphysics. However, Dühring was also a proponent of equality. As Nietzsche has Zarathustra insist more than once, he does "not want to be mixed up and confused with others,"[9] with those who "preach my doctrine of life and are at the same time preachers of equality." As we will see, Nietzsche will have Zarathustra introduce the principle of the will to power in "On Self-Overcoming." The will to power allows Zarathustra to conceive of the world in terms of a hierarchical system of command and obedience. As Grätz explains (2024:670), this directly contrasts with Dühring's concept of a "equality of wills [*Gleichheit der Willen*]" or an "equilibrium of wills [*Gleichgewichts der Willen*]."

Dühring's work is also important because the 1865 edition ends with a chapter titled, "The Transcendent Satisfaction of Revenge." There, he argues that our desire for metaphysics is rooted in the desire for justice which is itself a form of *ressentiment* and revenge.

As an example of this, he points to Kant's postulates of a free will, an immortal soul, and the existence of God. All three are connected to the desire for a transcendent court of justice: we need free will so we can blame others as the cause of a given action; we need an immortal soul so that deeds unpunished in this life will be punished in the next; and we need a god who is the ultimate arbiter of justice. In short, these metaphysical ideas are driven by the desire for revenge for a perceived act of injustice. Of course, this implies that to be liberated from metaphysics (and the desire for it), we must be liberated from revenge. This is the reason why overcoming revenge becomes the focal point of *Zarathustra* II. It is a necessary condition for the acceptance and affirmation of a naturalized conception of the world.

In "On the Tarantulas," Zarathustra presents the demand for justice as a demand for equality and the demand for equality as a form of revenge. Here the tarantulas equate virtue with the will to equality and clamor against all that has power. In effect, this is just a "tyrannomania of impotence," itself rooted in a frustrated desire for power, and it results in a desire of the "good and the just" to punish those who have achieved a certain rank or supremacy. Zarathustra, however, has a different teaching of justice: "men are not equal," and they should not become equal. Instead, they should long for the *Übermensch*, and there should be wars among those fighting for inequality. "Life"—and here we should think of the will to power—wants to climb to new heights, and we should struggle against one another for "power and more power," "like gods." It is this struggle, however, that the tarantulas—themselves motivated by a desire for power— want to punish.

In contrast, Zarathustra promises to deliver the human from revenge, thereby tearing down the webs the tarantula weaves and providing a "bridge to the highest hope, and a rainbow after long storms." The mention of a bridge and a rainbow to the highest hope recalls the language used to describe the *Übermensch* in *Zarathustra* I (ZI "On the New Idol"),[10] and such language is also found in *Nachlass* notes from this time. In one of these *Nachlass* passages, Nietzsche makes it clear that his rejection of equality is bound up with his hope for the *Übermensch*: "Humans should keep becoming ever more unequal—for the sake of the *Übermensch*—that's the way my love itself wants it" (KSA 10:12[43]).[11]

The connection between humanity's redemption from revenge and the *Übermensch* is worthy of some reflection. In *Zarathustra* I, the *Übermensch* is a figure or ideal that helps Zarathustra endure both life and humanity. Very little is said about revenge and its overcoming. Now, however, overcoming revenge is a bridge to the *Übermensch*. Although nothing is clear, the locution suggests that the *Übermensch* results from humanity's redemption from revenge. So understood, the *Übermensch* does not redeem humanity or even help liberate humanity from revenge. Instead, humans must do this themselves. Assuming this is accomplished, the question is then whether a redeemed humanity subsequently produces some distinct entity or being that is the *Übermensch* or whether a redeemed human, one who has overcome revenge, just is or becomes such an *Übermensch*. Because I have difficulty seeing the causal connection that would link a redeemed humanity to the production of a distinct *Übermensch*, I read such passages to mean that whoever redeems him or herself from revenge is on the way to becoming an *Übermensch*. Such an individual would be an *über-Mensch* because she would transcend a human condition plagued by self-disatisfaction and revenge and therefore would be able to affirm life. So construed, Zarathustra would be on the way to becoming the *Übermensch* if he were able to overcome revenge, conquer the spirit of gravity, and affirm existence.

In "On the Tarantulas," there is a clear foreshadowing of the will to power that is presented in some detail in "On Self-Overcoming." This is also true of **"On the Famous Wise Men."** There, Nietzsche is criticizing past philosophers and perhaps even religious founders for their claims to have been driven by and ultimately to have discovered truth. Zarathustra contrasts these famous wise men who pander to the people with free spirits who dwell outside the city, in the woods and the desert. Similar to Nietzsche's critique of self-deceived philosophers of the past in *Beyond Good and Evil* (see BGE 6 and 9), Zarathustra mocks these wisemen for being self-deceived about their own will to truth. Their will to truth is, in fact, an attempt to prove the people right in the things they revere.

According to Zarathustra, the search for truth requires breaking such reverences.

In the third chapter, I claimed that Zarathustra's first speech, "On the Three Metamorphoses," is best understood as referring to Nietzsche's free spirit works from *Human, All Too Human* to *The Gay Science*. In "On the Famous Wise Men," we find evidence that supports this reading. The free spirits are presented as those who, much like the camel, speed into "godless deserts" and eventually, with a "lion-will," conquer all "gods and adorations." The idea of the passage is that only the free spirit, not famous wisemen, can lay claim to a genuine will to truth, and it is a will to truth that requires one to break with the conventions and reverences of the people. However, we should keep in mind that the will to truth will also prove to be insufficient and even deceptive. For what we learn in subsequent chapters of *Zarathustra* II and elsewhere in Nietzsche's writings is that the will to truth is a form of the will to power.

4.2 DESCENDING INTO THE DIONYSIAN: CHAPTERS 9–13

Until now, Zarathustra has provided us with a series of speeches presumably aimed at his disciples who may or may not have fallen victim to a distorted version of his initial teaching. "The Night Song," however, marks a significant break in *Zarathustra* II and, along with the two other songs that follow, an important turning point in the drama of *Zarathustra* as a whole. Although the opening speeches of *Zarathustra* II are less ebullient than *Zarathustra* I and introduce themes, such as revenge, that darken the sky, they nevertheless continue what can be understood as the Apollonian themes and ideas focused mostly around the *Übermensch* of *Zarathustra* I. With the three songs that occupy the center of *Zarathustra* II as well as the two chapters that follow, "On Self-Overcoming" and "On the Sublime," there is a clear shift from the Apollonian to the Dionysian.[12] Whereas *Zarathustra* I begins with the sun shining upon Zarathustra as he steps out from his cave, we now find Zarathustra in the dead of the night. We know that there is something Dionysian about "The Night Song" because Nietzsche points to it as an example of a dithyramb, which is a song sung in honor of Dionysus (EH "Books" Z:7).[13] One of the art forms most associated with Dionysus is dance, and although Zarathustra himself does not dance in these songs, dance is on full display in "The Dancing Song." In "The Tomb Song," Zarathustra confronts, for the first time, the transience of the present and the reality of death, and this will set up a problem that is only solved by the eternal recurrence, which Nietzsche associates with the Dionysian mysteries.

Love also plays an important role in each of these three songs. We have cast both the will to power and the will to truth as forms of *eros* and so love, and in **"The Night Song,"** we learn that the songs of lovers awaken in the night and that Zarathustra's song is the song of a lover. The night song and the imagery of the night can be contrasted with the imagery of the sun at the beginning of *Zarathustra* I. There, Zarathustra speaks of a cup that wants to overflow, which calls to mind an erotic overflowing of psychic energy. Now, Zarathustra presents himself as both a lover and as one who has a "craving for love," and he laments his initial role as a "giver." The problem is that he does not know "the happiness of those who take."[14] Even more troublesome is that he now wants to "hurt" those to whom he gives: "I should like to rob those to whom I give; thus do I hunger for malice." In particular, Zarathustra acknowledges that his loneliness as a giver is mixed with revenge, and therefore his gift-giving virtue is now tired of itself. Thus, "The Night Song" reveals the inadequacy of the standpoint Zarathustra occupied at the beginning of *Zarathustra* I, and it suggests that to overcome this inadequacy he must learn "the happiness of those who take." Otherwise, his gift-giving virtue will be tainted by revenge.

The mention of revenge in "The Night Song" is no small matter, and it is not surprising that the "spirit of gravity," which is presented as "master of the world [*Herr der Welt*],"[15] appears in the next chapter, **"The Dancing Song."** As Brusotti (1997:559) has argued, the spirit of gravity is initially linked to melancholy in *Zarathustra* I, but then takes on a broader dimension in *Zarathustra* II to include revenge. In both cases, melancholy and revenge weigh down the spirit like "gravity" and therefore stand opposed to the light-footed dancing that Zarathustra encounters among the young girls in the forest. Here, Zarathustra himself does not dance, but he does sing a "dancing and mocking song on the spirit of gravity" to accompany the girls who dance with Cupid.[16] In this sense, the song and the dance are meant to combat the life-negating affects that lead to evaluative pessimism and so a condemnation of life and the world.

The song that Zarathustra sings puts him in a three-way conversation with his "wild wisdom," introduced in "The Child with the Mirror," and now Life, who is "changeable and wild and a woman in every way." The song begins with Zarathustra explaining how he was sinking as he looked into the unfathomable, but that "Life" pulled him out with a golden fishing rod. Some have interpreted this to mean that the hitherto boldly striving Zarathustra now finds himself weak, passive, and receptive to life's assistance (Seung 2005:66–76). Here, Zarathustra is almost scolded by wisdom: She reminds him that willing, wanting, and loving makes him praise life. In this way, it seems that the song, which was supposed to mock the spirit of gravity, turns into a mockery of Zarathustra and his inability to fathom the unfathomable.

The introduction of the third woman, Zarathustra's "wild wisdom," makes an already opaque dialogue even more opaque. There is a general lack of clarity about what Zarathustra's wisdom is: Is it a "will to truth" or a desire to fathom the innermost secrets of nature? Or is it something Zarathustra already knows? If the latter, is it that the world is will to power? Or perhaps it is a foreshadowing of the eternal recurrence? The most plausible candidate is that Zarathustra's wisdom is that all life is will to power (a point that will soon be introduced in "On Self-Overcoming").[17] So understood, Zarathustra's wisdom is about life and what life fundamentally is. This, then, would explain why Zarathustra says that Wisdom reminds him so much of Life and that, when Zarathustra speaks of Wisdom, Life insists that Zarathustra is speaking of her.

Although it is supposed to mock the spirit of gravity, the song ends on a rather weighty and depressing note. Zarathustra again finds himself "sinking into the unfathomable" with the sun having set long ago and a chill coming from the woods. Questions are then posed to Zarathustra as to whether he is still alive and, if so, to what end: "Why? What for? By what? Whither? Where? How?

Is it not folly still to be alive?" In short, the life-negating attitudes personified by the spirit of gravity have returned, and they set the stage for further developments in *Zarathustra* II and III.

The juxtaposition of "The Tomb Song" with "The Dancing Song" suggests that Zarathustra cannot mock the spirit of gravity in the way he had planned in "The Dancing Song" because he has not properly confronted the problems associated with change, death, and transience (*Vergänglichkeit*). Indeed, confronting these problems will effectively constitute the remainder of the drama of *Zarathustra* II and III up until "The Other Dancing Song," where Zarathustra himself finally begins to dance. In "**The Tomb Song**," Zarathustra travels to the isle of tombs with the wish to carry an evergreen wreath of life (a symbol that represents the overcoming of death, much like the ivy associated with Dionysus). The death that Zarathustra confronts, however, is not the prospect of his own biological death, but rather the death of "visions and aspirations" of his youth. What were once present moments are now "dead friends" of the past. In short, the problem is that every cherished moment is devoured by time and lost forever to the past. This is the problem of *Vergänglichkeit*. In contrast to moments of the past we regret and wish had been otherwise (*Vergangenheit*), the problem of *Vergänglichkeit* emerges precisely when we love life most.

The passage raises questions as to which visions and apparitions Zarathustra is referring. It could just be memories of a youth long gone. However, it could also be the very vision that inspired the beginning of the drama, namely, his hopes for the creation of a *Übermensch*. It should be kept in mind that some years have passed since he first presented his teaching to the townspeople. In either case, Zarathustra's "enemies" have taken from him something very important and made it hard to affirm existence in the way that he had initially hoped. Worthy of note here is that Nietzsche has Zarathustra refer to the motto of the 1882 edition of *The Gay Science*: "To the poet and the wise man all things are companioned and consecrated, all experiences useful, all days holy, all humans divine."[18] Specifically, Zarathustra points to a time when his purity spoke, "all beings shall be divine to me" and "all days shall be holy to me." This is a "gay wisdom [*fröhlicher*

Weisheit]," according to Zarathustra, but this "gay wisdom" has now left him. Nausea [*Ekel*] is something he vowed to renounce, but here he stands nauseated. And he once wanted to dance, but now he only hears a gloomy horn and a "murderous singer." Thus, his highest hope remains "unspoken and unredeemed."

However, the song ends with a glimmer of hope. Zarathustra asks how he was able to endure and even overcome this and how his soul could rise again out of such tombs. He responds by pointing to something in him that is "invulnerable and unburiable." We learn that this is his will. In the will still lies the possibility of redemption. Thus, Zarathustra ends the song by praising the will that lies within him: "you are still the shatterer of all tombs. Hail to thee, my will! And only where there are tombs are there resurrections." As we will see, the will and its relationship to time and nature will become an important topic in "On Redemption," and the language here foreshadows the language of the final section of "Old and New Tablets" in *Zarathustra* III. It also segues into the all-important speech, "On Self-Overcoming," in which we learn about the will as will to power.

Indeed, **"On Self-Overcoming"** provides the most detailed presentation of the will to power in *Zarathustra*. As I have noted above, the will to power can be understood as a form of *eros*, and the chapter begins by mentioning an alternative form of *eros*, namely, "the will to truth" (Platonic *eros*). The will to truth is traditionally understood as a quest to gaze contemplatively at things as they are, without any interference or alteration from the knowing subject. For Schopenhauer, such contemplation required a completely will-less state in the knowing subject and so a quieting of the will. In "On Self-Overcoming," Nietzsche has Zarathustra quickly invert the relationship between the knowing subject and the known object. The will to truth is really a will "to the thinkability of all beings" or a will to make things, otherwise recalcitrant to knowledge, into something thinkable (we have already encountered this point in "On the Blessed Isles"). Zarathustra appeals to the idea of a mirror, and we can use the mirror to explain this inversion. Whereas the traditional philosophical project aims to mirror reality in the mind or soul of the knowing subject, the new relationship Zarathustra presents is one in which reality is shaped to mirror the knowing subject. In both cases, knowledge occurs when there is a mirroring relationship, and the difference is whether the subject or object takes on the role of the mirror. The other difference is whether the will to truth is animating the project or, as Zarathustra insists, the will to power. As Nietzsche argues elsewhere, the will to truth just is a self-deceived will to power (BGE 9). Thus, rather than having a will to truth that motivates the knower to become like a mirror to reflect reality, Nietzsche presents the will to power as a drive that shapes reality to reflect the knowing subject.

This is Zarathustra's critique of the philosophers. His critique of "the people" is different. They have neither knowingly nor unknowingly projected their values upon the "river of becoming" (note the Heraclitean background of the passage). Instead, they simply take dominant values—projections of the past—to be given—fixed and permanent—and go about their business. However, good and evil are created, and Zarathustra claims that the will to power creates these valuations in all cases. To understand how this is so, Zarathustra feels compelled to articulate his views on life and "the nature of all the living." Specifically, Zarathustra claims that "whatever lives, obeys [*gehorchen*]," and so all living things must either obey themselves or, if they cannot, be commanded [*befehlen*] by something else. Of course, obeying oneself also means being able to command oneself, and Zarathustra emphasizes the responsibility that goes along with such commanding.

According to Zarathustra, the reason life has this structure of command and obedience is because he finds "the will to power" animating all "life." The will to power is a clear modification of Schopenhauer's "will to life," and elsewhere Nietzsche points to at least one important difference between the two notions: whereas the will to life aims at self-preservation, the will to power seeks to discharge its strength, often (but not always) with self-preservation as one important aftereffect (BGE 13). In *Zarathustra* II, we learn that life as will to power always seeks "to overcome itself," and this includes cases in which it sacrifices itself for power. According to Zarathustra, this means that whatever one may create and however much one loves it, one must eventually oppose the creation and so one's own love. The creations that Zarathustra has in mind are "values and words of good and evil." The idea seems to be that although the will to power creates these values, it must eventually break these values to create yet newer values that reach a higher level of power: "And whoever must be a creator in good and evil, verily, he must first be an annihilator and break values."

It is worth pausing here to reflect on the importance of this passage. What we see is the way in which an initial question about the affirmation or denial of life—articulated in *The Gay Science*—eventually forces Zarathustra to reflect upon the nature of fundamental reality. The implication is that the teaching of *Zarathustra* I is superficial. In addition to the sunlight associated with the beauty of the (Apollonian) *Übermensch*, there is also night and the reality of death and destruction (Dionysus). The idea is that if we are going to affirm reality, we must affirm these aspects, too. Indeed, we must also have some sense of what nature is really like, and it is here that Nietzsche introduces us to his Dionysian principle of the will to power.[19] Here, we see the way in which Nietzsche has Zarathustra, immediately after highlighting the reality of death in "The Tomb Song," identify an indestructible and inexhaustible principle at the heart of nature, one that is itself "beyond good and evil" but nevertheless provides a naturalistic explanation of how and why values are ultimately created.

On my reading, **"On Those Who are Sublime"** continues the transition away from the Apollonian features of the opening part of *Zarathustra* toward the Dionysian nature of the last half of Nietzsche's tragedy. Just as the shift from the bright sun (Apollo) to the moon and the night (Dionysus) marks such a transition, the movement from the blessed isles (Apollo) to the sea (Dionysus) does too. "On Those Who are Sublime" begins with a reference to a sea that harbors "sportive monsters." The sublime one that Zarathustra encounters is an ascetic seeker after truth. He has his truths, but they are ugly truths. The claim that the truth is ugly or even deadly is an idea that harkens back to *The Birth* as well as Nietzsche's own quest for truth in *Human*. Here, the sublime one is clothed in torn garments and, like Christ, adorned with thorns. Zarathustra sees no rose (a possible allusion to the rose-wreath crown in *Zarathustra* IV), and the sublime one has yet to learn laughter or beauty. Although nothing is clear, there are possible connections between the sublime one and the ugliest human in *Zarathustra* IV, as we learn in "The Ass Festival" that the latter is wearing "the cloak of the sublime" (ZIV "The Ass Festival":1).

This sublime one is therefore too serious for Zarathustra's taste, and only when the sublime one loses his taste for his sublimity will he be conformable to Zarathustra's taste. Much like the spirit of gravity, he is gloomy and still contemptuous of the earth, and so he needs to be more like a bull that pulls the plowshare. Like Oedipus, he has subdued monsters and solved riddles, but he still has to redeem his own monsters and riddles, thereby "changing them into heavenly children." Thus, he must discard his heroic will and become *beautiful*, such that "power becomes gracious and descends into the visible." He cannot resort to violence and exertion. Instead, he must "stand with relaxed muscles and unharnessed will." When this transformation is complete, the sublime one who has become beautiful will be able to behold his beauty in a mirror, and his soul "will shudder with godlike desires."

The speech ends with a statement that is quite significant for my reading of *Zarathustra*: The soul's secret is that "only when the hero has abandoned her, she is approached in a dream by the overhero [*Über-Held*]." The *Nachlass* contains a variant of this claim: "Dionysus on a tiger: the skull of a goat: a panther. Ariadne dreaming: 'abandoned by the hero, I dream about the super-hero [*Über-Held*].' Keep quiet about Dionysus!" (KSA 10:13[1]).[20] The triangle between the soul, hero, and overhero in the lines from *Zarathustra* can therefore be understood in terms of Ariadne as the soul and Dionysus as the overhero. As we know from the myth, Theseus is the (Apollonian) hero who abandons Ariadne on Naxos, and Dionysus eventually comes to her rescue.

What does all this mean in terms of the text *Zarathustra*? We cannot be sure. However, it could mean this: The heroic will that has been dominant up to this point in the form of the Apollonian *Übermensch* no longer suffices. In other words, the Apollonian is an important part of Zarathustra's overall redemptive strategy, but it is not sufficient. For a complete redemption of the soul, something more than Apollonian imagery and ideals (Theseus) is needed. Specifically, the Dionysian is necessary, and it is necessary because it allows for a direct confrontation with the ugly and disharmonic aspects of existence. Rather than striving to resist these forces, the sublime one becomes beautiful when she acknowledges and accepts these realities. As *Zarathustra* unfolds, we will see Zarathustra learning to acknowledge the force of nature and ultimately learning that redemption comes through what Nietzsche calls a joyous and trusting fatalism. If this is right, we can say that the tragedy of *Zarathustra* becomes decidedly Dionysian from this point on.

4.3 ZARATHUSTRA SPEAKS AGAIN: CHAPTERS 14–17

The next four chapters present us with a series of speeches that, in form, are reminiscent of *Zarathustra* I. However, there is an important shift in the content, and much of the focus can be linked to the introduction of the will to power. In "**On the Land of Education [*Bildung*]**"—originally titled, "Of the Contemporaries"—Nietzsche takes aim at those of his day who consider themselves to be educated, cultured, or cultivated (*gebildet*). According to Zarathustra, such individuals are all frauds decorated with masks of the past. Moreover, they are neutered and impotent and so cannot create anything toward the future. The ideas expressed here recall Nietzsche's early critique of culture and education in works like *The Birth* and *The Untimely Meditations*. Like those critiques, the lack of genuine culture and *eros* in the modern world is connected here with a general condemnation of existence: "Everything deserves to perish."

"**On Immaculate Perception**"—originally titled, "On the Contemplatives"—also attacks the neutered, will-less subject of knowledge. The speech begins with a lament that the moon is neither feminine nor masculine. Nevertheless, the moon is lecherous and dishonest about its lechery. The moon supposedly loves the earth but denies that it does so. This is like the contemplative. The contemplative claims that the highest thing is "to look at life without desire and not, like a dog, with my tongue hanging out […] with a will that has died and without the grasping and greed of selfishness [*Selbstsucht*]." This is what an "immaculate perception" is: it is to lie before something like a mirror and to want nothing of it.

This is clearly Schopenhauer's view of the will-less knowing subject, and Nietzsche excoriates it in a way that anticipates his critique of ascetic ideals in the *Genealogy*. We have just learned that all life is will to power. To say that something living can achieve a state of will-less contemplation is to deny that all life is will to power. Thus, those who idealize such a state present an idea that is both hostile to life and impossible. Indeed, Nietzsche accuses such contemplatives—in much the same way he attacks philosophers of the past in *Beyond Good and Evil*[21]—of being self-deceived. These "sentimental hypocrites" deny that they desire that which they contemplate and yet they are teeming with desire. Even worse is the fact that such contemplatives deny the significance of creation and the will to create. The purest will, according to Zarathustra, is the will that wants to create beyond itself. This goes hand in hand with the teaching in "On Self-Overcoming."

In "**On Scholars**," Nietzsche again has Zarathustra attack a group that wants to "be mere spectators" in everything. That is, they just want to gaze upon and understand life without creating or doing anything beyond that. Similar to *Beyond Good and Evil*, in which Nietzsche attacks scholars (BGE 6) and what he calls "philosophical laborers" (BGE 211), Zarathustra critiques their clockwork methodology and discipline. What they effectively do is take the created works of the past and grind them down into meaningless dust. For this reason, the sheep at the beginning of the speech boasts that "Zarathustra is no longer a scholar."

"**On Poets**" is the last of this group of speeches, and it is an important one for my reading. Zarathustra is now talking to one of his disciples, and he begins by claiming that everything "permanent" is mere parable. The theme is familiar, as the commitment to Heraclitean principles throughout the text entails that there is nothing fixed, sempiternal, or eternal; therefore, all claims that there are such fixed principles are mere parables. However, a disciple who hears this says that Zarathustra always accompanies this teaching with the claim that poets lie too much. Zarathustra responds by acknowledging that they do and, moreover, that he himself is a poet. The striking implication is that Zarathustra also lies too much.

Zarathustra can undoubtedly be construed as a work of poetry, and the character Zarathustra can be understood as a poetic creation. However, the claim here is that Zarathustra is himself a poet and therefore he lies too much. But what poetry has he written or created? Zarathustra claims the poets always believe they have something to say about "things that are between heaven and earth." Moreover, such poets also talk about things *above* the heavens. For instance, all gods are the creations of poets that lift us higher to the clouds. It is there, according to Zarathustra, that we place both gods and *Übermenschen*.

This passage has suggested to some that Zarathustra's poetry consists in the creation of the *Übermensch*, and therefore Zarathustra's concept of the *Übermensch* is itself a poetic lie.[22] So understood, Zarathustra's weariness with the poets and their excessive lying is a weariness with the very idea that had been driving the action of *Zarathustra* thus far, namely, the *Übermensch*. Such a reading would explain why his disciple reacts in anger. After all, Zarathustra's disciples are his disciples because of his teaching of the *Übermensch*. As such, acknowledging that his teaching is a lie would certainly anger his disciples. Despite the disciple's reaction, Zarathustra insists that such poets remain superficial and on "shallow seas"; their thoughts have not penetrated deeply enough and their feelings have not touched bottom. Indeed, this has been a recurring motif throughout the previous chapters. Whereas the teaching of the *Übermensch* takes us up to the heights of bright sunlight, Zarathustra still needs to confront the darkness of night and plunge into the depths of the sea. So understood, Zarathustra is ready to move beyond the Apollonian *Übermensch* for a direct confrontation with Dionysian reality.

As I briefly explained in Chapter 2, Loeb and Tinsley (2019:757–793) offer an alternative reading of the passage. In so doing, they propose that we distinguish between three uses of the term "*Übermensch*": (1) the supernatural use; (2) the superior-individual use; and (3) the superior species use. According to Loeb and Tinsley, the opening part of *Zarathustra* presents the *Übermensch* in the third sense, as the creation of a new species. In "On Poets," Nietzsche is having Zarathustra critique the supernatural use, which Loeb and Tinsley claim is found in German literature and scholarship prior to the introduction of Nietzsche's novel species use. So understood, "On Poets" does not represent a dialectical development over *Zarathustra* I, such that Zarathustra is now expressing dissatisfaction with the ideal that initially drove him down from the cave. Instead, "On Poets" is an attempt to defend a newer version of the *Übermensch* by critiquing an older understanding of the concept.

One of the *prima facia* problems with Loeb and Tinsley's account is that there is nothing in *Zarathustra* (or even in Nietzsche's *Nachlass*) that explicitly develops this contrast. Loeb points to the fact that Nietzsche couples the *Übermensch* with a reference to "gods" in "On Poets," but clearly contrasts the *Übermensch* with the now dead God in *Zarathustra* I. The reader is supposed to infer from this that Zarathustra must be using "*Übermensch*" in two different senses: a sense that he rejects, in which the *Übermensch* is like the fictional gods, and a new sense in which the *Übermensch* is nothing like the gods (this *Übermensch* is supposed to be a replacement for God). Loeb and Tinsley's reading is plausible but not entirely convincing, given that the reader could just as well respond by pointing to the two uses of "god" at work here. In the opening of *Zarathustra*, the dead God is clearly a monotheistic god of a religion like Christianity. In contrast, the reference to "gods and *Übermenschen*" in "On Poets" is clearly a reference to polytheistic gods. Indeed, Loeb and Tinsley connect "On Poets" to Nietzsche's remarks about gods and *Übermenschen* in GS 143, "The Greatest Advantage of Polytheism," and Nietzsche clearly distinguishes between polytheism and monotheism there and the God that has just been declared dead in the preceding aphorisms of *The Gay Science*.

Another problem is that it is not clear that the *Übermenschen* discussed in "On Poets" are "supernatural," as Loeb and Tinsley claim. Zarathustra begins the discussion by referring to those things "*above* the heavens," but then refers to "the realm of the clouds." Surely, polytheistic gods were often placed above the earth and had powers that transcended human abilities, but they were by no means supernatural in the sense of existing beyond space and time. In short, they were just as much a part of nature as humans and animals. In terms of ancient Greek polytheism, which is almost always on Nietzsche's mind, the correlate of the *Übermensch* is the heroes of Homeric epic and even tragedy: Achilles, Agamemnon, Clytemnestra, Odysseus, and Oedipus (GS 143 supports such a reading). Again, these figures may have been supernatural in the sense that they had abilities that went beyond what ordinary humans had (like today's superheroes), but they certainly did not exist beyond nature in a supernatural realm. So understood, Zarathustra's critique here is about the superficiality of the Apollonian world of gods and *Übermenschen*, and it is a critique that again points to the need for a Dionysian solution to the problem of existence. As I explained in the second chapter, I think GS 143 itself points to such a solution: The invention of (Apollonian) *Übermenschen* is a preliminary exercise for the emergence of a self-loving and sovereign individual or what I have identified as the Dionysian *Übermensch* and a new form of nobility.

4.4 THE NEED FOR REDEMPTION: CHAPTERS 18–22

Zarathustra's demand to go beneath the surface and plunge into the depths becomes quite literal—or so goes the rumor—in **"On Great Events."** In a fictional and even fantastical landscape, Zarathustra leaves behind the blessed isles of the *Übermensch* and takes a trip into the underworld or "hell" to confront a "fire hound." The narrator tells us that a ship captain and his crew anchored on an island with a volcano—"the isle of fire"—saw a man flying through the air and heard a voice saying, "It is time! It is high time!" It is claimed that the captain and his crew saw was none other than Zarathustra.

Zarathustra identifies two diseases on the skin of the earth: humans and the fire hound. The fire hound bellows most about freedom, and it is a freedom achieved by revolutionary activity, represented by the fire hound. Zarathustra, however, dismisses these "great events." True revolutions do not occur with the bellowing and smoke of political activity, but rather during the "stillest hours" in which values are revalued and new values are invented. This is not only an obvious reference to the final chapter of *Zarathustra* II but also alludes to a larger project of revaluing values. Although Nietzsche most explicitly associates his latest works (*The Antichrist*) with the revaluation of values, this passage suggests that the "great event" that either constitutes or makes possible the revaluation may occur in Zarathustra's own solitude toward the end of *Zarathustra* III. Such a reading would make sense of *Zarathustra*'s relationship to Nietzsche's later project: It constitutes a silent revaluation that forms the basis for Nietzsche's public attempt—a form of "great politics"—to revalue values in his later works.

Toward the end of the conversation, Zarathustra points to yet another "fire hound." This one, however, has little to do with fire. Instead, it "exhales gold and golden rain." The imagery of gold is something we have already encountered with the golden ball at the end of *Zarathustra* I and life's golden fishing rod in "The Dancing Song," and we will see it again in *Zarathustra* III with the image of a fisherman rowing with golden oars (ZIII "Tablets":3; see also GS 337). In contrast to the ashes and smoke, this fire hound is able to laugh, and it is a laughter made of gold taken from the heart of the earth.

The next two chapters are some of the most important for the drama of *Zarathustra*, and both highlight the way in which Nietzsche is having Zarathustra respond to Schopenhauer's life-denying philosophy. In "On Great Events," we just encountered the idea that human beings are a disease on the skin of the earth, which, as Grätz (2024:773) notes, recalls the opening lines of the second volume of Schopenhauer's *The World as Will and Representation*, where we read that "a film of mildew has generated living beings with cognition" (WWR II:1). In "**The Soothsayer**," we find Zarathustra confronting something akin to the wisdom of Silenus in *The Birth*, in which we learn that the human condition is so miserable that it is best not to be born, not to be at all (BT 3). There, Schopenhauer's philosophy is presented as the modern correlate to the ancient wisdom of Silenus, and Nietzsche is clearly engaging with Schopenhauer in "The Soothsayer," just as he was responding to Schopenhauer in "On Self-Overcoming."[23]

The chapter begins with the soothsayer speaking. He claims to have witnessed "a great sadness descend upon" humankind such that the best grew weary of their works. They have encountered a doctrine: "All is empty, all is the same, all has been!" Everything that has been planted, grown, and harvested now is turning brown and rotting. All work therefore seems to be in vain. The wells have dried up and everything has turned to ashes. People even seem too weary to die. Hearing this, Zarathustra becomes sad and weary, and for three days he does not drink, eat, talk, or sleep. His disciples only wait for him to recover from his melancholy (*Trübsal*).

The most immediate problem expressed here is that it rejects any teleological conception of history and therefore any hope that things will get fundamentally better. Here, one must wonder whether Nietzsche is again having Zarathustra reject the overly hopeful and optimistic program associated with the *Übermensch*. Whatever the *Übermensch* is or whatever hope he will bring, he will not be able to change the character of existence in any fundamental way. The other idea that produces melancholy is that everything that comes to be must pass away. Nothing is permanent. Everything is subject to the power of time and the law of change. In short, everything is transient (this is the problem of *Vergänglichkeit*). Moreover, as Grätz (2024b:453) points out, Nietzsche penned an 1881 note in which he associates the soothsayer with the idea that the world is nothing but "*Fatum*" or fate and therefore a teaching of the "unfreedom of the will" (KSA 9:15[12]). For these reasons, individuals who hear this doctrine conclude that everything is in vain: no project is worthwhile; everything is fated; nothing can be changed; and life is not worth living.

Whether this teaching is meant to apply to Zarathustra's own teaching of the *Übermensch* is not entirely clear. However, it is worth noting that Zarathustra refrains from offering a triumphant response to the soothsayer's wisdom in the form of a redemptive *Übermensch* offering a better future. In this sense, Zarathustra seems to agree that his teaching of the *Übermensch* will not change anything. Thus, he suffers from melancholy and falls into a deep sleep. However, "The Soothsayer" also gives an account of Zarathustra's dream, and the interpretation of the dream given by Zarathustra's favorite disciple is revealing. Specifically, the dream thematizes the problem of transience (*Vergänglichkeit*) by making Zarathustra into a watchman and guardian of tombs. As Zarathustra sits alone at the mountain castle of death, he tries to open some gates but fails. As he is trying, a roaring wind rips through and opens the gates, and suddenly a coffin bursts open and spews out "a thousandfold laughter." The laughter frightens Zarathustra and eventually wakes him up. According to Zarathustra's most beloved disciple, there is meaning in this dream. The disciple tells Zarathustra that he himself is both the wind and the coffin full of laughter. Thus, Zarathustra will eventually laugh at death and frighten "all the night watchmen and guardians of tombs." The reference to laughter seems to foreshadow both the shepherd's laughter that is "no human laughter" from "On the Vision and the Riddle" in *Zarathustra* III and the laughing lion that arrives at the end of *Zarathustra* IV. It also points back to the jester who skips over the tightrope walker in the prologue of *Zarathustra* I. Given these associations, one may speculate that Zarathustra's ability to laugh will result from his ability to teach the eternal recurrence, a teaching that directly responds to the problem of transience and is associated with both Zarathustra's *going under* and his *going over*.

Whereas "The Soothsayer" can be said to highlight the problem of transience or *Vergänglichkeit*, "**On Redemption**" can be understood as highlighting the problem of the past or *Vergangenheit*. It is one of the most important chapters in all of *Zarathustra*, as it again highlights the inadequacy of Zarathustra's initial redemptive strategy and points to a new type of redemption. In a scene that parodies Jesus' role as a miracle worker and redeemer (Grätz 2024:803), Zarathustra is confronted by a series of "cripples" in the ordinary sense of the term: individuals who cannot hear, see, or walk in addition to a hunchback. But Zarathustra quickly points to another type of cripple, the inverse cripple. Inverse cripples are human beings who have developed one aspect of themselves so much that it becomes a detriment to and cripples the rest of their person. In this way, they have failed to cultivate a sense of wholeness or personhood that Nietzsche lauds in early works like *History for Life* and *Schopenhauer as Educator*. Zarathustra therefore walks among "fragments and limbs and dreadful accidents—but no human beings." Because of this, Zarathustra only knows how to live with an eye to the future. He simply cannot endure the present and the past.

The emphasis on the need for genuine human beings and even the redemption of human beings is a striking contrast to Zarathustra's attitude in *Zarathustra* I. There, he had nothing but contempt for the human being and only found value in the human being insofar as the human was a bridge to the *Übermensch*. Now he is concerned with the redemption of the human and making genuine or whole human beings. In this way, Zarathustra's thoughts on redemption are now much closer to the ideal articulated in "the 'humaneness' of the future" in *The Gay Science* (GS 337), where Nietzsche gestures toward a god-like human who can incorporate and embrace all the laughter and tears, sorrows and joy of human history. Indeed, Zarathustra announces here his hope for the future that resembles the ideal of GS 337: To "create and carry together into one what is fragment and riddle and dreadful accident." Indeed, this is what Zarathustra now calls redemption: "To recreate all 'it was' into a 'thus I willed it.'" As we learn in *Ecce Homo*, Zarathustra's redemptive task is also Nietzsche's redemptive task (EH "Books" Z:8).

Zarathustra's revised understanding of redemption also includes a revised understanding of the will and its relationship to time and nature. Specifically, he points back to his teaching from "On the Blessed Isles," where he claimed that creation provided "the great redemption from suffering" and the justification of all impermanence (*Vergänglichkeit*). On this view, the will is a "liberator and joy bringer." In "On Redemption," Zarathustra specifically refers to his teaching that the will is a "liberator and joy-bringer." However, he quickly adds that "the will itself is still a prisoner." Here, we learn that the will is limited by the "it was," which "is the name of the will's gnashing of teeth and most secret melancholy." The melancholy results from a sense of powerlessness (just as revenge and *ressentiment* are said to result from a sense of powerlessness in the first essay of the *Genealogy*). The reason is that the will cannot break two things: "time" and "time's covetousness."

In my view, these two things are equivalent to what I, following Brusotti (1997), have called *Vergangenheit* and *Vergänglichkeit*.

By "time [*Zeit*]," I take Zarathustra to mean the impossibility of going back in time to change the past and so the problem of *Vergangenheit*. By "time's covetousness [*Zeit Begierde*]," I understand Zarathustra to mean the way in which the continual flow of time devours and destroys the present and so the problem of *Vergänglichkeit*. There is a third problem that may also render the will powerless. Until now, there has been little reflection on the will's relationship to nature. Instead, Zarathustra has presented us with a vision of a seemingly autonomous will, something that potentially echoes the ideas of Max Stirner, and its ability to achieve some sort of redemption through creative willing (this is what Seung calls the Faustian *Übermensch*). Here, however, we learn that we must disabuse ourselves of any conception of a will that stands over and above and so free from nature. Instead, the will is fully enmeshed with both nature and history or the "it was." Thus, if the will is going to be "free" or even liberate and redeem anything at all, it must first be reconciled with both time and the causal chain of events that constitutes nature.

In "On Redemption," the will is cast as a prisoner of time and nature, and in trying to escape this prison, the will becomes a fool and tries to redeem itself foolishly. Suffering, the will looks to wreak revenge on all that suffers in a similar way. Thus, the will takes revenge for its inability to go backward, and Zarathustra makes the surprising claim that revenge just is "the will's ill will against time and its 'it was.'" Here the *"spirit of revenge"*—likely synonymous with the "spirit of gravity"—then looks to make suffering (and wanting to make suffer) into a form of punishment. In this way, revenge cloaks itself with a "hypocritical lie" and begins to see itself as executing a form of justice, thereby creating a "good conscience for itself." The idea of punishment as a response to suffering then begins to take on cosmological dimensions. Here, "all life" is construed as a punishment: Everything that has come to be also passes away because it *deserves* to pass away. Transience or passing away is therefore seen as an act of justice, atoning for the initial sin of coming to be. As Gary Shapiro (2017) has pointed out, this is precisely the vision of the cosmos that Nietzsche attributed to Anaximander and associates with Schopenhauer in *Philosophy in the Tragic Age*, and Nietzsche contrasts this vision with his own

Heraclitean understanding of the cosmos that celebrates artistic play and affirms existence beyond categories of sin, punishment, and retribution.[24]

As we learn from the next line, this conception of the cosmos orders things "morally according to justice and punishment." In this sense, it is clearly not a Heraclitean world of innocence beyond good and evil. As such, we see that moving beyond good and evil requires an overcoming of the revenge that generates this interpretation of the world. If this does not happen, one will seek redemption behind or beyond the world: "alas, where is redemption from the flux of things and from the punishment called existence?" The worry here is that justice and punishment are eternal, too. So construed, existence itself becomes a punishment, such that everything again becomes "deed and guilt." The only way out of this situation is for willing to become not willing. This, of course, is the essence of Schopenhauer's evaluative pessimism and what Nietzsche calls nihilism. It is also what Zarathustra calls a "fable of madness."

In contrast to "The Soothsayer," which emphasizes the problem of transience (*Vergänglichkeit*), the problem in this chapter is primarily one of the past or *Vergangenheit*. As I argued in the second chapter, the solution that Nietzsche devises to solve the problem of the past is backward willing. In this passage, Zarathustra explains how he has led his listeners away from the madness of his predecessors. He has done this by pointing to the creative nature of the will. Without the will, the "it was" is merely a fragment, a riddle, and an accident. This repeats language that Zarathustra has already used, and we can now see that the task of the creative will is to unite together all of the "it was(es)" into "one" by saying not only "thus I willed it" but also "thus I will it" and "thus shall I will it." The will, however, has yet to learn all this. It has yet to be taught a "reconciliation with time and something higher than any reconciliation [*Versöhnung*]." In a rather cryptic closure to the speech, we are told that the will to power aims precisely at that which is higher than any reconciliation. To do this, the will must learn to will backwards [*Zurückwollen*].[25]

I have already laid out a rough framework for understanding backward willing in Chapter 2, but there are a few more details that need to be filled in here. In particular, it is worth focusing on what it means to transform an "it was" not only into "thus I willed it" but also "thus I will it; thus shall I will it." For some, like Richard Elliott (forthcoming), Nietzsche's stress on the past tense version of this claim, "thus I willed it," means that we are supposed to think of a past event, an "it was," and transform that past event into something that I willed at the time it occurred (this is the reason for the past tense expression, "thus I will*ed* it").[26] The example Elliott gives, taken from Anderson (2005), is Jimmy Carter's experience of losing the 1980 Presidential election. At the time he experienced the election, Carter certainly could not be said to have willed or wanted it. According to Elliott, it is not enough to say that Nietzschean redemption for Carter would be attaining a later standpoint in which he wills this past event even though he did not will it at the time it happened. Such a reading only makes sense of the present-tense formulation, "thus I will it." It does not, however, make sense of the past-tense formulation, "thus I willed it." To transform an "it was" into a "thus I willed it," we must be able to say that Jimmy Carter willed, at the time of its occurrence, his loss in the 1980 election. However, since he cannot go back and change his attitude about the election at the time he lost, it seems that the only way Carter can engage in this sort of backward willing is to falsify what actually happened. As Elliott notes, however, this is a problem because it amounts to a form of self-deception that Nietzsche would likely find objectionable. Thus, Elliott concludes that "Nietzsche's positive account for redeeming a human life runs into a problematic rut" (forthcoming).

As much as Elliott should be praised for forcing us to tend carefully to the language Nietzsche has Zarathustra employ in the passage, I think the unresolved problems that this reading creates forces us to consider an alternative reading of what it means to transform an "it was" into "thus I willed it" (past tense). First, it should be noted that the "it was" is not something that is inherently negative or unwanted (Elliott treats it as if it is). Instead, the "it was" is a brute fact to which no valence, positive or negative, is assigned. Indeed, and this is a second point, there is nothing, for Nietzsche, that is inherently good or bad (GS 301); instead, the value we assign to something is always a matter of interpretation.

With these principles in hand, we can now make sense of what it takes to transform an "it was" into "thus I will it" (now). We take either a brute fact (an "it was") or even an "it was" that we previously wished had not happened and change it into something that I now wish to have happened ("thus I will it"). Here, we can even imagine "a tremendous moment [*einen Ungeheuren Augenblick*]" (GS 341) in which we find ourselves so in love with existence that we transform every "it was" (all the preceding events leading up to that moment) into something to which one says, "thus I will it." In terms of *The Gay Science*, we can say that this transformation is equivalent to *amor fati* or a love of the world for what it is without exception (GS 276). Whereas fate represents all the brute facts of the "it was," *amor* or love represents the positive and affirmative attitude—something greater than a mere reconciliation with the past—that one has toward the "it was" and therefore it is equivalent to saying, "thus I will it."

But what about the past tense formulation, "thus I willed it"? Must this mean what Elliott takes it to mean? I don't think so. Whereas Elliott thinks it must mean we will an event at the time it happens, all that "thus I willed it" requires is that willing some past event must have occurred *at some point* in the past and so at some point prior to an ever-changing "now." It does not require that the point in the past in which I will an event be at the same time the event occurred. In terms of the Jimmy Carter example, it only requires Carter to reach a standpoint *at some point in his life* such that he can now say, "thus I willed it." For instance, Carter will have achieved this if he came to terms with his 1980 loss in 1990, such that he can "now" (in 2024) look back on 1990 and say that he willed or affirmed his 1980 loss. In terms of *The Gay Science*, the goal is to reach a *moment* in life in which we can affirm the past, and we can now look back on that affirmative moment and say, "thus I willed it." On this reading, the past tense can be understood as a retrospective reflection on a moment in one's life in which one said "yes" to everything. The "thus I willed it" therefore does not need to occur at the same time a given event occurs.

Although this makes sense of how we might understand "thus I willed it," the idea that we should only have a moment in which we affirm everything might be too limited. Here it is worth noting that Zarathustra presents this idea of redemption in terms of the past, present, and future, and that doing this in all three tenses is the goal of the creative will. What Nietzsche *might* have in mind here is that affirmation does not have to be limited to a mere moment—a point in time in which one reaches the mountaintop of affirmation and then must inevitably come down. Instead, the goal is to reach a continued state in which one has climbed the mountain ("thus I willed it"), remains (now) on the mountaintop ("thus I will it"), and has every intention of staying on the mountaintop as much as possible in the future ("thus shall I will it"). Here, we would have a continuous state of willing the "it was" and a plan to continue this into the indefinite future, but nevertheless a starting point in time in which the "it was" was transformed into the "thus I willed it." Of course, if one were able to achieve such a condition, one would not only be able to will the eternal recurrence, but one would also want to will the eternal recurrence, as it would eternalize the repetition of all the events to which one has said and still says, "thus I will it."

"On Redemption" ends with remarks that deepen the drama and shift the focus to Zarathustra's internal struggles with his own teachings. The reader is told that Zarathustra himself is shocked by what he has just said. But he quickly recovers by effectively laughing it off. He remarks that being among people is difficult because silence is so different for one, like himself, who is so garrulous. The hunchback, however, then asks why Zarathustra speaks differently to the crippled humans than to his disciples. After some exchange, we learn that Zarathustra is indeed speaking differently to the cripples than to his disciples, but it is also suggested that Zarathustra speaks differently to his disciples than to himself. The upshot seems to be that there is a lot more going on *within* Zarathustra than what he is communicating to others, and this points toward "the stillest hour" in which Zarathustra returns to his solitude.

In "**On Human Prudence**," we encounter one of the last significant discussions of the *Übermensch* in *Zarathustra* (after this the word is only mentioned), and it is a discussion much more ambivalent than Zarathustra's presentation of the *Übermensch* in *Zarathustra* I. In my view, this is a consequence of the shift from the Apollonian to the Dionysian that has taken place since "The Night Song" in *Zarathustra* II, and it points forward to Zarathustra's eventual identification as the teacher of the eternal recurrence (not the teacher of the *Übermensch*). Thus, the passage begins with a discussion of Zarathustra's double will, one that looks up toward the *Übermensch* and one that grasps onto and is nevertheless bound to the human. That fact that Zarathustra now feels bound to the human is, of course, a significant shift from his initial longing for the *Übermensch* and only the *Übermensch*.

Because of his double will, he lives "blind among men" as if he did not know them. His prudence is effectively a series of strategies to be able to associate with otherwise unpalatable human beings. Because he shuddered when he saw even the best of human beings naked—and so for who they really were—he "grew wings" (*eros*) to fly off into distant futures toward the creation of the *Übermensch*. In short, he wants to go to a realm in which it is shameful not to be naked, not to be disguised. In other words, he wants to go to a world in which it is shameful to feel ashamed. Thus, when he approaches the human, he must see them in disguise, just like the "good and the just." Moreover, he also wants to sit among them in disguise. Because Zarathustra still clings to the human, but the human is something intolerable to behold, he must employ this bit of prudence. However, the unexpressed hope here seems to be a hope for a human that is tolerable to behold such that he no longer needs to exercise his prudence. In my view, it will become Zarathustra's task in the final chapters of *Zarathustra* to become just such a human, one without shame.

"**The Stillest Hour**" is a crucial chapter for my interpretation. Zarathustra now retreats into his cave and his solitude. His initial attempt to teach the people his doctrine of the *Übermensch* failed in the prologue, and now it seems that his attempt to teach his disciples has failed as well. Indeed, we have seen that Zarathustra has had to revise his teaching of the will and redemption to address the problems of time and the past. It now seems that Zarathustra can rely less and less on the creation of an *Übermensch*. Instead, he is forced to turn more and more toward himself (recall that Zarathustra seems to have created the *Übermensch* out of his own inability to confront the eternal recurrence). The only way to address the problems articulated in chapters like "The Soothsayer" and "On Redemption" is for Zarathustra to find satisfaction within himself, transform the "it was" into "thus he willed it," and prepare himself to become the teacher of the eternal recurrence. It is here that the drama of *Zarathustra*, in Oedipus-like fashion, turns back on Zarathustra himself.

The stillest hour is the name of an "awesome mistress," and in this stillest hour Zarathustra begins to dream. Here the hand on the clock of life moves forward—likely toward the midnight bell of "The Other Dancing Song" in *Zarathustra* III—and Zarathustra's heart takes fright. In the dream, something speaks to him—Seung claims it is lady Life (2005:111)—without voice: "You know it, Zarathustra." The voice here is like the voice in "On Great Events," which tells Zarathustra that, "it is time! It is high time!" In both cases, the command seems to be compelling Zarathustra—almost as a matter of inner necessity—to accept a fate that he still wants to resist. Indeed, the voiceless voice indicates that Zarathustra does not want to move forward, and it commands him not to hide in defiance. Zarathustra insists that he wants to follow the command, but he also insists that he does not have the strength to undertake the task being commanded.

Such a reading is evidenced by the phrase that Zarathustra then hears next: "What do you matter? [*Was liegt an dir?*]" This phrase and its variants recur throughout Nietzsche's free spirit works, and it is generally linked to a passion for knowledge that Nietzsche develops in *Daybreak*. What is important about this passion for knowledge is that it becomes so great that the individual is willing to sacrifice him or herself to attain it. "What do you/I matter" is a phrase that can be traced back to the Stoics, and it stresses the relative insignificance of the individual in relation to the larger whole. As Jamie Parr explains, this attitude can be linked to the "joyous and trusting fatalism" that Nietzsche describes in *Twilight of the Idols* (2022:115). There, we learn that "only the particular is loathsome, and that all is redeemed and affirmed in the whole." As Nietzsche writes, this is "the highest of all possible faiths: I have baptized it with the name of *Dionysus*" (TI "Skirmishes":49). This attitude contrasts with the Christian view that places extreme significance on the life of the individual and so heightens the terror associated with death. It also corresponds with the meaning Nietzsche attributes to the tragic in *Richard Wagner in Bayreuth*: In order to liberate the individual from the anxiety caused by time and death, "the individual must be consecrated to something higher than himself" (RWB 4).

If this is right, then the phrase "what do you matter" in "The Stillest Hour" is meant to remind Zarathustra that there is something greater than himself and that his own existence is rather insignificant in comparison. This, of course, is precisely the teaching of tragedy as Nietzsche understands it. At the essence of tragedy is the concept of fate and the corresponding idea that the individual does not control her own destiny. Instead, nature does, and the individual is nothing more than a piece of nature or fate. Indeed, tragedy not only teaches that individuals are entirely natural beings, but also that in the end there are no individuals at all. Instead, there is only an interconnected web of nature. This can be used to explain what Zarathustra means to "go under." He must, qua individual, merge with and submerge himself into nature and become part of nature or fate. Thus, when Zarathustra speaks his word—presumably the word of the eternal recurrence—he will also break on his word. At the same time, his will merges with the necessity that defines nature. In my view, this is why Nietzsche ends the aphorism in which he first refers to the eternal recurrence with the question: "When may we begin to '*naturalize*' humanity in terms of a pure, newly discovered, newly redeemed nature?" (GS 109).

The final portion of "The Stillest Hour" is also important for my interpretation, as it points back to Zarathustra's first speech, "On the Three Metamorphoses," in at least two respects. First, Zarathustra claims that he lacks the "lion's voice for commanding," and this raises the question as to whether Zarathustra is referring here to the lion of the second metamorphoses. As I explained in Chapter 2, I think we need to distinguish between the lion of the second metamorphoses and the lion that has the ability to command others in society and politics (as represented by the laughing lions of *Zarathustra* IV). Whereas the former precedes the final metamorphoses into the child, the latter is something that emerges once the standpoint of the child has been achieved.

In this passage, Zarathustra's claim that he lacks the lion's voice for commanding refers to the lion in the second sense, one capable of legislating values for a larger community. So understood, the reference here to commanding great things foreshadows Nietzsche's philosophers of the future in *Beyond Good and Evil* (BGE 211).

At the same time, the voiceless voice insists that the world is guided by "thoughts that come on doves' feet." This points back to "On Great Events" in which we learned that true revolutions come through the quiet moments of solitary thinking, not through political action. Indeed, there is reason to think that one of these great events will occur in Zarathustra's cave as he calls forth the eternal recurrence at the end of *Zarathustra* III. Zarathustra nevertheless insists that he feels a sense of shame about taking on this role. In response, the voiceless voice instructs him to "become as a child and without shame." In "On the Three Metamorphoses," the child is connected to innocence, and in "The Stillest Hour," the voiceless voice orders Zarathustra to become a child precisely because the child is "without shame." The idea that Zarathustra, a mere human, should overcome his sense of shame is quite striking. In "On the Pitying," we learned that the human is a shameful thing and therefore could only be tolerated in disguise (in comparison to a land in which gods are ashamed of wearing clothes and so being disguised). Thus, for Zarathustra to become without shame would amount to Zarathustra making himself tolerable to behold. In so doing, he will have accomplished something that no human has ever accomplished and in this sense could be considered an *Übermensch*. If we look at *The Gay Science*, this is no small feat. There, the ultimate seal of liberation is "no longer being ashamed in front of oneself" (GS 275), and this is directly connected to the leitmotif of Nietzsche's larger oeuvre: "you shall become who you are" (GS 270). So construed, the command to become a child in "The Stillest Hour" now focuses on Zarathustra's personal transformation (he must become ripe), and his personal transformation will be bound up with his willingness to take on the role of teaching the eternal recurrence, which is the subject matter of *Zarathustra* III. However, he will need to do this alone, and *Zarathustra* II ends with Zarathustra weeping loudly as he leaves his friends behind.

NOTES

1 The child Dionysus was looking into a mirror when he was captured by the Titans and ripped to pieces.
2 See Groff (2021) for an Epicurean reading of the blessed isles.
3 See Meyer (2014c: Ch.1) for more on this point.
4 I thank Grätz (2024:533–534) for pointing this out.
5 Vivarelli (2018) points to a biography of Michelangelo by Herman Grimm as a possible inspiration for this passage.
6 See Shapiro (2017) for more on this point.
7 As Grätz (2024:596) points out, there are also notes that connect the tarantula to (evaluative) pessimists or people who teach the "worst world" (KSA 10:13[3, 17]).
8 See KSA 10:7[21] for a connection between Dühring and equality.
9 This is also a central theme of Nietzsche's *Ecce Homo* (EH "Pref":1).
10 I thank Melanie Shepherd for noting that there might be a connection between "rainbow bridges" and Valhalla in Wagner's *Das Rheingold*. Grätz (2024:207) also highlights the connection.
11 Translation from CWFN 14.
12 See Gooding-Williams (2001:160–182) for further remarks on the Dionysian nature of these songs.
13 See Pickard-Cambridge (1962: Ch.1) for more on the dithyramb.
14 My translation. Here, Kaufmann translates "*das Glück des Nehmenden*" as "the happiness of those who receive." This is clearly an alternative translation of "*Nehmenden*" that is less than faithful to the original. As Grätz (2024:627) notes, Nietzsche goes on to claim that stealing is even more holy than taking in the *Nachlass* (KSA 10:12[1.140]).
15 This phrase invites comparisons to the new nobility that Nietzsche eventually presents as "rulers of the earth [*Herrn der Erde*]." See KSA 11:25[247] and KSA 11:35[72]. The contrast suggests a battle between a world ruled by those animated by revenge and those who have overcome revenge.
16 The child holding the mirror at the beginning of *Zarathustra* II might also be Cupid.
17 Here I agree with Lampert (1986:105).
18 This is found in the Kaufmann (1974:27) translation of *The Gay Science*.
19 The connection to Dionysus is made explicit in the *Nachlass* (see KSA 11:38[12] and KSA 13:24[1]).
20 Translation from CWFN 14.
21 See GS 301 for a similar critique.
22 See Tom Stern (2008). Lampert (1986:129) presents a similar reading.
23 There is undoubtedly some relationship between the soothsayer and Schopenhauer. However, Janaway (2022) argues that the relationship is a complex one. As Grätz (2024:787) explains, there is a *Nachlass* note that connects the soothsayer of *Zarathustra* IV to a "black pessimism"; this again points in the direction of Schopenhauer. See also Kerkman (2017).

24 We know from an 1884 note that Nietzsche is still thinking in these terms: "The major problems surrounding the *value of becoming* formulated by Anaximander and Heraclitus—in other words, the decision whether a moral or aesthetic valuation is permitted in general in relation to all these problems" (KSA 11:26[64]). Translation from CWFN 15.
25 Grätz (2024:816) points to Nietzsche's discussion of a "retroactive force [*rückwirkende Kraft*]" that great human beings exert in GS 34. This may also shed more light on Nietzsche's concept of backward willing.
26 If KSA 10:17[38] is Nietzsche's attempt to explain backward willing (and it may not be, even though Brusotti (1997:572–573) claims that it is), then Elliott is misunderstanding the concept and the nature of redemption. In the note, it explicitly states that we must want something afterward which we previously did not want.

5

THUS SPOKE ZARATHUSTRA III

Immediately upon the publication of *Zarathustra* II in July 1883, Nietzsche began working on a continuation in *Zarathustra* III. As Nietzsche makes clear in his letters, he considers *Zarathustra* III to be the most important book of the entire text. It is the "grand finale of [his] symphony" (KSB 6:485), and it concludes with Zarathustra summoning the eternal recurrence, thereby marking the end of Zarathustra's "going under" and therefore Nietzsche's tragedy. It begins with Zarathustra leaving behind his disciples and the blessed isles to return to his cave and his solitude. It also begins with Zarathustra having a prevision of what turns out to be his own struggle with the spirit of gravity and the nausea he must overcome before he can summon the eternal recurrence. The intervening chapters, beginning with "The Return Home," are vitally important for understanding Zarathustra's eventual transformation into someone who can summon the eternal recurrence. There, he realizes that he must learn to love himself to overcome revenge and defeat the spirit of gravity. In coming to this realization, he also begins what might be called a silent revaluing of values in "On the Three Evils" and "On Old and New Tablets." The latter chapter concludes with Zarathustra's identification of himself with nature and cosmic necessity and therefore marks a point at which Zarathustra is approaching the ideal of *amor fati* (GS 276).

In the final four chapters, Zarathustra is ready to summon the eternal recurrence. Thus, we find Zarathustra confronting his nausea about the recurrence of the "small human" in "The Convalescent" in a way that recalls the shepherd's battle with the snake that chokes him in "On the Vision and the Riddle." As Lampert notes, Zarathustra's redemption is obscured by the fact that his acceptance of the eternal recurrence largely happens offstage, narrated by his animals (1986:156). Although obscure, we know that Zarathustra's summoning of the eternal recurrence is coupled with the appearance of a "nameless one" who is none other than Dionysus in "On the Great Longing." This sets up a concluding scene in which Zarathustra's soul declares his love for eternity. In this way, Zarathustra gives an affirmative answer to the question that the demon originally posed at the end of the fourth book of *The Gay Science*: can one be so well disposed toward oneself and life so as "*to crave nothing more fervently*" than the eternal recurrence of this world (GS 341)?

5.1 ZARATHUSTRA SETS SAIL: CHAPTERS 1 AND 2

Zarathustra III begins with Zarathustra climbing a mountain on his way to the other coast to depart from the island. During his wandering and his climb, Nietzsche has Zarathustra present a most startling realization: "In the end, one experiences only oneself" (ZIII "The Wanderer"). Zarathustra has been in strange lands and scattered among all things and accidents, but now everything returns to him and his own self. The drama thus far has been about Zarathustra trying to communicate his teaching of the *Übermensch* first to the townspeople and then to selected disciples. After his experiences in *Zarathustra* II, Zarathustra now understands that the problems he finds with the world are ultimately rooted in and experiences of his own self. Thus, if he is going to find redemption, he must ultimately find redemption within himself. Again, we see the way in which the drama of *Zarathustra* parallels the tragedy of Sophocles' *Oedipus Rex*.

Zarathustra also notes that he is on his way to "greatness," and this is a greatness in which peak and abyss unite, where the ultimate danger is also an ultimate refuge. This suggests that Zarathustra's quest for the heights of greatness is ultimately bound up with his "going under." As the first chapter of *Zarathustra* III, "**The Wanderer**," unfolds, we encounter evidence for such a reading. He recognizes both his "lot [*Loos*]" and his "destiny [*Schicksal*]"—terms closely associated with tragic fate—and he recognizes that his destiny is the source of loneliness, where everything comes back to himself. It is his destiny to go down to the sea. This descent to the sea is a descent into "pain," and Zarathustra characterizes his pain as black and sorrowful. The descent can also be characterized as a move away from the Apollonian world of individuation, represented by the blessed isles, toward a Dionysian world of will, suffering, and the dissolution of individuation, represented by the sea. Because it entails the loss of his own individuation, Zarathustra shudders before the task that lies ahead of him. The fact that everything now weighs on Zarathustra's shoulders—coupled with the fact that he must also leave his disciples or friends—causes him to weep bitterly.

"**On the Vision and the Riddle**" is one of the most important chapters of the book, and it can be understood as bringing together the various existential threats that were developed in *Zarathustra* II. It begins with Zarathustra on a boat at sea, having departed from the blessed isles. He is among other sailors—fellow travelers on the sea—but he remains silent for two days. Eventually he begins to speak, and in so doing he speaks of a "riddle," "the vision of the loneliest" (again "riddle" recalls the tragedy of *Oedipus Rex*). Zarathustra tells of his quest to climb a rocky mountain but laments that he is burdened by the "spirit of gravity," a dwarf and his archenemy that keeps pulling him down toward the abyss. The spirit of gravity insists that every stone thrown high must inevitably fall; it is a law of gravity. The spirit of gravity's point, however, is not just about upward and downward motion. Instead, it can be connected to the cyclical and necessary oscillation between opposites such as pleasure and pain, joy and suffering, peace and war, life and death. These things do not exist without their opposites, and nature exhibits a cycle in which everything transforms into its opposite and back again, just as everything that goes up must come down.

The thought of the spirit of gravity still weighs on Zarathustra, and it even makes him sick. However, he responds to this sickness by calling on his courage, and his courage forces him to confront the dwarf: "Dwarf! It is you or I!" This courage enables Zarathustra to overcome every pain, even human pain, which supposedly is the deepest. According to Zarathustra, courage even slays pity or *Mitleid* (synonymous with Christian *agape*). Pity is a suffering from another's suffering, and this is why it is "the deepest abyss." Courage is also said to slay even death itself. This is quite a striking claim. It is one thing to face death with courage. It is another thing for courage to slay or conquer death. Although this seems impossible, we are given a clue as to how this is supposed to work. A courage that attacks can look at death and say: "Was *that* life? Well then! Once more [*Noch ein Mal*]!" As we will see, this is the name of the song sung near the end of both *Zarathustra* III ("The Other Dancing Song":3) and *Zarathustra* IV ("The Drunken Song":12).[1]

The mention of "Once more" suggests that courage alone is not sufficient, and this phrase indicates that this death-slaying courage is connected to the eternal recurrence. That is, wanting life again is to want it to recur, and wanting it to recur forever is to want its eternal recurrence. Thus, Zarathustra must eventually find the courage to summon the eternal recurrence, and, as Zarathustra's confrontation with the dwarf continues, something resembling the eternal recurrence comes to the fore. Zarathustra again presents the dwarf with the claim that it is either "you or I," and he insists that the dwarf cannot handle his most "abysmal thought." He elucidates this abysmal thought by pointing to a "gateway [*Thorweg*]" that represents the present "moment [*Augenblick*]."[2] From this gateway proceed two paths that extend for an eternity, presumably a path that runs infinitely back into the past and a path that runs infinitely into the future. The question that Zarathustra poses is whether these two paths contradict each other or run opposite each other for eternity.

A curious feature of the dialogue is that the dwarf responds by claiming that "all that is straight lies" and that "time itself is a circle." It is curious because the dwarf seems to be presenting, or at least foreshadowing, the abysmal thought that Zarathustra thinks will banish the dwarf, i.e., the eternal recurrence. However, the dwarf's claim that time itself is a circle is neither exactly what Zarathustra himself presents nor is it exactly Nietzsche's conception of the eternal recurrence. For time to be a circle, time itself would be finite and repetitive. However, we know from Nietzsche's *Nachlass* that a central premise in one of his arguments for the truth of the eternal recurrence is that time is infinite (KSA 9: 11[202]; KSA 13: 14[188]). On this view, time itself cannot be a circle; instead, a finite number of events create a circular repetition of these same events within infinite time. The idea is that if time runs infinitely backwards and infinitely forwards, then the finite number of events that constitute the course of nature must have already occurred—and not just once but an infinite number of times—and they must also occur again—and not just once but an infinite number of times. Taken together, such a view amounts to the eternal recurrence of these same events.

Such a reading is supported by Zarathustra's explanation of the view. Rather than arguing that time is a circle, he asks whether it must not be the case that the events that are happening now must not have happened before: "And this slow spider, which crawls in the moonlight, and this moonlight itself, and I and you in the gateway, whispering together, whispering of eternal things—must not all of us have been there before?" And then he asks whether we must not also return to the same moment in the future: "And return and walk in that other lane, out there, before us, in this long dreadful lane—must we not eternally return?" Thus, the position has to do with the recurrence of events within time; it is not a claim about the nature of time itself.

So far, the view seems straightforward enough. However, some other things that Zarathustra says complicate matters. First, Zarathustra asks whether this "moment" returns. This is different from asking whether the events happening at this moment will return. However, it may be that any given moment of time just is whatever event occurs at that time, such that time is nothing more than a succession of events. That said, Zarathustra's elucidation of this point indicates that the events of the moment are what returns, e.g., the spider's crawl, the whispering of eternal things, and not the moment itself. This brings us to a second point. Zarathustra suggests not just that the things that *do* happen have already happened and will happen again, but that whatever *can* happen has already happened and will happen again. So construed, the view is not that there is one chain of events among many possible chains that constitutes nature, which is then continuously repeated. On this view, nature would be like a single musical symphony—just one of many possible symphonies that could have been created—that is repeated endlessly. Instead, Zarathustra presents the view that nature plays through every possible musical note and combination of notes before it begins to repeat itself again. In other words, nature consists of a cycle of all possible musical compositions. This, of course, makes an already implausible view even more implausible, but it does correspond to the proofs that Nietzsche experimented with in his notes. The idea is that the events within time are finite—precisely because the number of forces that constitute nature are finite—and therefore with infinite time, the music box of nature will repeat itself again, even if the music box must run through all possible notes and all their possible combinations.

Zarathustra introduces yet another point that is crucial for understanding the eternal recurrence. Specifically, he asks: "are not all things knotted together so firmly that this moment draws after it *all* that is to come?" This claim implies determinism. That is, there is a tight, unbreakable, and even necessary link between one event in time and the next event (and the next and the next and so on). And just as this moment effectively contains within it "*all* that is to come," each previous moment—prior to the present moment—can be said to contain "*all* that is to come." Thus, by extension, this moment not only entails all subsequent moments but is also entailed by all previous moments. In short, each moment contains within it every other moment both present and past. Thus, Zarathustra's claim that everything is knotted together entails a strict determinism in which neither the past nor the future can be changed, and because it is true for the cosmos it is also true for an individual such as Zarathustra.[3] It is the acceptance of this predetermined cosmos that constitutes the essence of the tragedy of *Zarathustra* and ultimately forces Zarathustra to accept the idea that he cannot fundamentally alter the course of nature or who he is or what he does. It is this thought that terrifies Zarathustra.

Just as he finishes presenting the idea that everything must eternally return, Zarathustra hears a dog howl. The howling of the dog, in turn, creates a flashback for Zarathustra to his distant childhood when he first heard a dog howl in this way. The dog is howling in the stillest midnight or hour, a time in which there is a full moon and everything is still.[4] The dog is howling from pain, and Zarathustra experiences pity in response to the dog's howling. Amidst the howling of the dog, the dwarf seems to have disappeared, and Zarathustra is not sure if he is dreaming or waking up. Suddenly Zarathustra finds himself next to a young shepherd, and the dog returns, still howling, whining, and jumping, effectively crying for help. The shepherd is having spasms and writhing in pain. A black snake has crawled into his mouth and fastened its teeth on his throat. Zarathustra sees the dread and nausea (*Ekel*) on his face. Zarathustra struggles to pull out the snake, but to no avail. The only option is for the shepherd to bite off the head of the snake, and something comes from within Zarathustra that has him exhorting the shepherd to do just this: "Thus it cried out to me—my dread, my hatred, my nausea, my pity, all that is good and wicked in me cried out of me with a single cry." Toward the end of the chapter, we learn that the shepherd has indeed taken Zarathustra's counsel and bitten off the snake's head. As soon as he does, the shepherd is transformed: "no longer human—one changed, radiant, *laughing*! Never yet on earth has a human being laughed as he laughed! O my brothers, I heard laughter that was no human laughter."

Based on the text alone, the meaning of Zarathustra's encounters with the dwarf and the shepherd is far from clear. Indeed, Zarathustra himself invites his fellow seafarers to unriddle this riddle and interpret his vision. Zarathustra claims that it is a "foreseeing," and he goes on to inquire into the identity of the shepherd and the one "who must yet come one day." No answer is given, but "On the Convalescent" indicates that the young shepherd represents Zarathustra himself, and the young shepherd's battle with the nausea-inducing snake represents what will be Zarathustra's own battle with all the negative emotions that can emerge in the process of trying to summon and affirm the eternal recurrence. If this is right, we can also say that as a result of this battle, Zarathustra will be transformed into something capable of producing a laughter that is no longer human. This suggests, first, that Zarathustra himself will become something like an *Übermensch* (no longer human). If this is right, then we also have reason to associate this (Dionysian) vision of the *Übermensch* with laughter, something largely absent from Zarathustra's first description of the *Übermensch* (with the exception of the laughter of the jester). The fact that Zarathustra himself might soon become capable of such laughter gestures toward the laughing lions that appear at the end of *Zarathustra* IV. It also points forward to the conception of nobility and the philosopher of the future in *Beyond Good and Evil*, where Nietzsche risks an order of rank among philosophers according to their ability to laugh (BGE 294) and associates such philosophers with Dionysus (BGE 295).

5.2 ON THE WAY HOME: CHAPTERS 3-8

In "**On Involuntary Bliss** [*Von der Seligkeit wider Willen*]," Zarathustra travels across the sea away from the blessed isles gave him the time to overcome the pain and bitterness he felt about these riddles. He is now presented as "triumphant," ready to face his (tragic) "destiny [*Schicksal*]." Here, the narrative turns even further inward, as Zarathustra speaks of the "afternoon of [his] life." He also speaks of the companions that he always sought, but now he realizes that he must create such companions or children himself. For the sake of these children, Zarathustra's task now is to "perfect himself [*vollenden*]." Self-perfection entails a "great love to oneself," which is also a sign of pregnancy. It also means evading one's happiness and offering oneself "to all unhappiness." For this task, Zarathustra is ready, and we again hear the refrain of *Zarathustra* II that "it is high time!" Specifically, it is time for

Zarathustra to confront his abysmal thought "without trembling anymore." For this, he might discover the "prankish bearing of the lion" and the "lion's voice to summon" it.

Here again, the focus is now on Zarathustra and his own perfection. The reason Zarathustra needs to perfect himself is so that he can summon his "abysmal thought." It is striking to note the absence of any explicit reference to the *Übermensch*. Rather than directing his love toward some future redeemer, Zarathustra is focused on preparing himself for the eternal recurrence and ultimately his own redemption. That said, Zarathustra does refer to his children, and he mentions that a great love of oneself is a sign of pregnancy. These children could very well be the kind of individuals capable of creating an *Übermensch* or, in fact, *Übermenschen* themselves. Thus, Zarathustra compares such children to trees and claims that "where such trees stand together there are blessed isles." Here, we should not overlook the fact that *Zarathustra* III ends with Zarathustra wanting to have children with the woman Eternity and that *Zarathustra* IV ends with an impending return of Zarathustra's children.

In "**Before Sunrise**," Zarathustra sings praises to the heaven above and "the abyss of light." According to Löwith (1997:72), the "abyss of light" reflects the unity of "peak and abyss" in "The Wanderer." In *Ecce Homo*, Nietzsche claims that "Before Sunrise" employs "the language of the dithyramb," and he juxtaposes the happiness of this passage with the melancholy of the other dithyramb, the "Night Song" in *Zarathustra* II. Rather than being weighed down by the heaviness of night, Zarathustra explains here that he wants nothing more than to fly up to the heavens. He learns from the heavens that "whoever cannot bless should *learn* to curse." However, Zarathustra explains that he is "one who can bless and say Yes into all abysses" and that he has become one "who blesses and says Yes." Specifically, he wants "to stand over every single thing as its own heaven, as its own round roof, its azure bell, and eternal security." Here all things are baptized in "the well of eternity" and "beyond good and evil." Saying "yes" to all things recalls the task of *amor fati* in *The Gay Science* (GS 276), and baptizing things in the well of eternity foreshadows the end of *Zarathustra* III.

The phrase "beyond good and evil" is not only significant because it becomes the title of Nietzsche's next work but also because the concept is closely associated with the eternal recurrence. Here, "beyond good and evil" is linked to overcoming the idea that nature has purposes. Thus, Zarathustra teaches that "over all things stand the heaven Accident [*Zufall*], the heaven Innocence [*Unschuld*], the heaven Chance [*Ohngefähr*], the heaven Prankishness [*Übermuth*]." The idea is that by removing purposes from nature, morality is overcome. For Nietzsche, the problem with moral judgment is that it wants the world to be other than it is, and it effectively burdens the world with categories of sin and punishment. By eliminating purposes and morality, we can speak of an "innocence of becoming," and this sort of innocence can lead to a "heavenly cheer" and make all things "*dance* at the feet of chance." Indeed, the purity of this heaven for Zarathustra is not a moral purity. Instead, it is a "dance floor for divine accidents" and "a divine table for divine dice and dice players." The language of dance recalls Zarathustra's earlier claim that he would only believe in a god (like Dionysus) who can dance. The language of an innocence beyond good and evil also recalls Nietzsche's affinity for Heraclitus' cosmology as well as that of the Heraclitean child.

Again, the lack of any reference to the *Übermensch* as a redeemer is striking. Zarathustra is now the one who will bless the earth, and what he is going to bless are things like accident and chance. This is doubly striking for two reasons. First, the general thrust of *Zarathustra* I is that humanity needs a purpose or goal, and the goal that Zarathustra gives them is that of the *Übermensch*. Zarathustra's presentation of nature as purposeless does not necessarily conflict with the goal of the *Übermensch*. Indeed, they are quite compatible: because nature lacks purpose, human beings must create a goal for which they strive. What does conflict with the previous teaching of the *Übermensch* is that Zarathustra is now blessing chance and accident themselves such that he is turning nature into a divine dancefloor. That is, Zarathustra is gesturing toward a standpoint in which dance expresses pleasure in chance and accident themselves and therefore a pleasure in the lack of a goal. Indeed, this also seems to conflict with the message of redemption in *Zarathustra* II. This is because we are told that redemption consists of carrying "together into One what is fragment and riddle and dreadful accident." There redemption is not found through blessing accidents themselves, but rather through an interpretation that gives each accident significance and meaning in terms of a larger, unifying narrative. Whether this blessing of accident is supposed to be a new form of redemption or whether it is meant to supplement the redemption that gives meaning to accident is not entirely clear, but subsequent chapters in *Zarathustra* III suggest that Zarathustra still holds on to key teachings from "On Redemption."

In "**On Virtue that Makes Small**," Zarathustra is on land again, and although he is headed to his cave, he nevertheless encounters human beings, if only from a distance. Here he considers whether human beings have become greater or smaller while he was away. He concludes that everything has become smaller! Zarathustra locates the reason for their smallness in their "*doctrine of happiness and virtue*." According to Zarathustra, these small humans want "contentment [*Behagen*]." Zarathustra's critique of this view not only recalls his critique of the teachers of virtue in *Zarathustra* I but also his attack on the passionless "last man" in the prologue. Similar to his other critiques in *Zarathustra* I, such as his critique of the "preachers of death," Zarathustra links this conception of happiness to the virtues of "those who serve," pity, and ultimately renunciation. All of this can be understood as targeting Schopenhauer's ethics of pity, resignation, asceticism, and life negation.

Like Schopenhauer, Zarathustra proclaims himself to be the godless one. However, he rejects this ethics of resignation. Such an ethic does not stem from virtue, but rather from the vice of cowardice. In contrast, Zarathustra is courageous and strong enough to embrace the sort of world described in "Before Sunrise." Here we are told that Zarathustra cooks "chance [*Zufall*]" in his pot, and it is only when it is cooked thoroughly does it become his food. Cooking here is likely a metaphor for interpretation, and the idea is that interpretation effectively "cooks" the facts of one's present and past so that they can be digested as a coherent whole.[5] The idea of giving meaning to chance and accident by weaving them together into a coherent narrative recalls the notion of backward willing from *Zarathustra* II, and it suggests that this way of redeeming chance and accident is still alive in *Zarathustra* III. As I explained in the second chapter, this can also be linked to Nietzsche's early notion of a plastic power to transform and incorporate into oneself what is past and foreign (HL 1). In this passage, Zarathustra's will enables him to confront and ultimately subordinate the force of chance. It is for this reason that the passage concludes with Zarathustra's teaching: "Do whatever you will, but first be such as are *able to will*." Here again, this echoes the importance of the strength of will and even the will to power that played a key role in *Zarathustra* II.

The title of "**Upon the Mount of Olives**" is clearly a biblical reference, and although the Mount of Olives plays a role in both the Old and New Testament, it is likely that Nietzsche is trying to compare Zarathustra's journey to the time Jesus spent there. Specifically, it allowed Jesus to stand outside the city of Jerusalem, and it was only a few days before his crucifixion that he wept over the fate of Jerusalem from the Mount of Olives. In contrast, Zarathustra's mount of olives is a place that allows him to laugh and mock the cold winter (possibly a symbol for death), even as we sense his impending confrontation with the eternal recurrence. This mocking prankishness emerges from a sense of courage and a joy in existence, and it can be coupled with a silence that is "one's indomitable solar will." His silence and his concealment protect him from the "grudge-joys" and "drudge boys" that surround him. These individuals have *pity* for Zarathustra's accidents. In contrast, Zarathustra welcomes accidents and embraces them as innocent little children. Here again, we encounter the idea that chance and accident can be embraced in themselves, in all their innocence. In the end, Zarathustra's winter loneliness is an "escape *from* the sick," and the "sunny nook" of Zarathustra's mount of olives allows him to sing and "mock all pity."

Continuing to make his way back to his cave, Zarathustra passes by numerous towns, and in "**On Passing By**," Zarathustra comes upon a great city. Outside this city is a "foaming fool" whom the people call "Zarathustra's ape." Zarathustra's ape exhorts Zarathustra to "spit on the city gate and turn back." The city is filled with "revolting verbal swill" of newspapers and "public opinions." If there is virtue here, it is a servile virtue, where everyone serves the prince. But ultimately, the prince serves the real god, which is the gold of the shopkeepers. In short, the city is a place in which everyone, including the rulers, obeys their desire for gold and wealth. It is for these reasons that Zarathustra must despise the city.

Zarathustra, however, is nauseated by the speech of the one they call Zarathustra's ape.[6] He despises that his ape despises. If one despises, one must despise out of love, not hate, and Zarathustra's ape is a hater. Indeed, Zarathustra calls the ape his "grunting swine," and his grunting is a result of a hatred rooted in a desire for revenge. Revenge, of course, is a leitmotif of *Zarathustra* II, and it is something that Zarathustra seeks to overcome. The problem with Zarathustra's ape is that he is still attached to the city and fixated on the perceived deficiencies of its inhabitants. In contrast, Zarathustra rejects both the city and the ape's disgust for the city. There is nothing to love in the city, and where there is nothing to love, Zarathustra teaches that "one should pass *by*."

Just as we see Zarathustra's teaching being distorted and ultimately falling into the mouth of his ape, so too do we learn that any followers he may have had have fallen back into their old ways in "**On Apostates [*Von den Abtrünnigen*]**." Zarathustra is back in the town of the Motley Cow, the place where he gave many of his speeches about the *Übermensch* in *Zarathustra* I. Whatever ears the citizens of the Motley Cow may have had for his teaching, Zarathustra now sees that they have, in the meantime, "become pious again." Before, they "lifted their legs like dancers, cheered by the laughter" in Zarathustra's wisdom. Now, however, some are crawling back to the cross, presumably conquered by the spirit of gravity.

Zarathustra identifies cowardice as the cause of this. Cowardice contrasts with the courage that Zarathustra eventually calls upon to confront the spirit of gravity and affirm the eternal recurrence. It is the cowardly devil from within that urges these individuals to believe that there is a god. In so doing, they want to become like little children again and pray to this god, where submissive obedience becomes a central virtue. Here, faith—not proof—makes blessed. In contrast, Zarathustra suggests that he will one day laugh himself to death when he sees asses drunk and night watchmen doubting God. This is similar to how the old gods—and here he likely means the gods of the ancient world—came to an end. They laughed themselves to death once it was said that "there is one god" and that "thou shalt have no other god before me!" Although opaque, such remarks foreshadow the ass festival in *Zarathustra* IV, where Zarathustra will teach the higher men, who are also exhibiting pious tendencies, how to laugh.

5.3 BACK TO THE CAVE AND A REVALUATION OF VALUES: CHAPTERS 9–12

In "**The Return Home**," Zarathustra finally ends his wanderings and returns to his cave and his solitude. He is now where he was when the drama first started in the prologue of *Zarathustra* I. In my view, this is what Nietzsche has in mind when he writes to Köselitz that *Zarathustra* III circles back to the beginning of *Zarathustra* I (KSB 6:499).[7] As Grätz (2024b:183) notes, Zarathustra's homecoming is less about returning to his cave as it is returning to himself and being at home with himself. The chapter begins with Zarathustra speaking to Solitude (personified) and declaring solitude his home (not necessarily his cave). Responding to Zarathustra, Solitude explains that in solitude one "can talk freely about everything and pour out all the reasons" and that one "may talk fairly and frankly to all things." This contrasts with Zarathustra's attempt to speak among the people, where "all speech is in vain." Solitude also references various points in Zarathustra's journey thus far. First, we are reminded of Zarathustra standing near a corpse in the forest (presumably in the prologue of *Zarathustra* I), claiming that it is more dangerous to be among men than animals. Zarathustra is also reminded of "The Night Song," when he asked whether it is not more blessed to "take [*Nehmen*]" than to give and to steal still more blessed than to "take [*Nehmen*]."[8] According to Solitude, Zarathustra was then forsaken during his stillest hour, when he was driven away from himself with the words, "speak and break."

Toward the end of the speech, Zarathustra identifies his two greatest dangers, "to spare and to pity [*Schonen und Mitleiden*]."[9]

All humans want pity and want to be spared, but Zarathustra's care and concern for humans have caused him harm. He had to disguise and mistake himself to be among them, to be something other than he is. He even had to take revenge on himself. Recalling the passage from "On the Flies of the Market Place," Zarathustra claims that he is covered with "the bites of poisonous flies and hollowed out like a stone by many drops of malice." The most poisonous of these flies were those who call themselves "good" (this recalls Zarathustra's reflections on the "good and the just"). In response to these bites, Zarathustra had to remind himself that "everything small is innocent of its smallness." Now, however, things are much better. He can again "breathe mountain freedom" as his nose "is delivered from the smell of everything human."

The next three chapters are very important. If there is a revaluation of values in *Zarathustra* itself, it arguably occurs in "On the Three Evils," "On the Spirit of Gravity," and "On Old and New Tablets." "**On the Three Evils**" begins with Zarathustra recounting a dream. Zarathustra pictures himself beyond the world and yet holding the scales that measure the world. Now awake from his dream, Zarathustra places "the three most evil things on the scales" and weighs them. These three things are (I refer to the German because of the difficulty of translation): *Wollust*, *Herrschsucht*, and *Selbstsucht*. Kaufmann translates these as: "*sex, the lust to rule, selfishness*." However, it is worthwhile to offer a comment on each. *Wollust* is not to be understood as merely sex or sexual activity, but rather the desire for sexual intercourse. In this sense, the best translation seems to be "lust," as such a translation associates the concept with one of the seven deadly sins (*Wollust* is the German for the deadly sin *luxuria*). *Herrschsucht* is a compound word made up of *Herrsch* and *Sucht*. *Herrsch* is derivative of the verb "*herrschen*," which means to rule or dominate. One might think that *Sucht* is derivative of the verb, "*suchen*," which means to seek, but it is best translated as "addiction" or "obsession," and therefore linked to *süchtig* (addicted). So understood, a literal translation of *Herrschsucht* is an addiction to or obsession with ruling or power. In turning to *Selbstsucht*, we can analyze the word in a similar fashion. *Sucht* means addiction, and *Selbst* means self. Put together, we have an addiction to the self.

Selbstsucht was traditionally thought of as an unhealthy or even pathological addiction to the self (a form of narcissism), and it can be connected to the chief of the deadly sins, namely, pride. For Schopenhauer, *Selbstsucht* is the root of *eros* and the opposite of Christian love or *agape* (WWR I:67).

So understood, we can see how *Wollust*, *Herrschsucht*, and *Selbstsucht* have been denigrated in the Western tradition by comparing them not only to some of the deadly sins within the Christian tradition but also to the views of Plato. Here, we can turn to Plato's *Republic* to sharpen the contrast. A central theme of the *Republic* is *eros*, and the question is whether *eros* is directed toward the intellectual realm of the Forms or toward political power and ultimately personal immortality. The character types in which these two forms of *eros* are embodied are the philosopher (Socrates) and the tyrant (Alcibiades), respectively. Importantly, the tyrant can be said to be animated by all three of these "evil" passions that Zarathustra wants to revalue. The sexual impulses (*Wollust*) of the tyrant are highlighted throughout the dialogue, and it is most prominent in the description of the tyrant in *Republic* IX. By definition, the tyrant is driven by a lust to rule and an addiction to power (*Herrschsucht*), and this is sharply contrasted with the philosopher's reluctance to rule in *Republic* I. Finally, the *Selbstsucht* of the tyrant is less pronounced, but a case can be made that self-love or selfishness effectively transforms the desires of the tyrant into a matter of right, where the tyrant feels himself entitled, as a matter of justice, to get what he wants.[10]

What is striking about Zarathustra's attempt to revalue these passions is that there is no explicit mention of the will to power in "On the Three Evils." However, as Grätz points out (2024b:207), Nietzsche's initial draft for the chapter did mention "will to power" among the three evils. Moreover, each of these "evils" can be readily understood as a manifestation of a desire for power (the most obvious of these is *Herrschsucht*). If this is right and we take the further step in thinking of the will to power as a form of *eros*, we can see how *Zarathustra* is directly engaging with the argument of Plato's *Republic*. Whereas the will to truth is the philosophical form of *eros*, the will to power can be understood as a form of both poetic and tyrannical *eros* (an *eros* that Plato denigrates and devalues). To solidify this connection, we can further note that the *Republic* also links the tyrannical form of *eros* to the notion of *pleonexia* (the desire to have more), introduced in *Republic* I, and the *Nachlass* shows that Nietzsche also understood the will to power as a form of *pleonexia* or the "desire to have more [*Mehr-haben-wollen*]" (KSA 13:14[65]).

The purpose of drawing out this contrast between Nietzsche and Plato is to show just how much Zarathustra's revaluation of these passions can be understood as an attempt to overturn a tradition that historically deemed such passions "evil." In the text itself, Zarathustra provides a series of statements about both *Wollust* and *Herrschsucht* that fail to amount to any straightforward revaluation of these values. We are reminded, however, that in "The Gift-Giving Virtue" at the end of *Zarathustra* I, Zarathustra "pronounced *selfishness* [*Selbstsucht*] blessed, the wholesome, healthy selfishness that wells from a powerful soul." Such a soul is "powerful" and "beautiful, triumphant, refreshing" and around it "everything becomes a mirror." The body of such an individual is both "high" and "persuasive," and it is a dancing body, where the dance is a "parable and epitome" of "the self-enjoying soul [*die selbst-lustige Seele*]" (it also has clear connections to Dionysus). Zarathustra calls this "self-enjoyment of such bodies and souls" virtue.

Casting *Selbstsucht* as a form of "self-enjoyment [*Selbst-Lust*]" or an essential feature of a "self-enjoying soul" is worthy of reflection. First, it makes sense of the idea that *Selbstsucht* is a form of self-addiction or self-indulgence. Here, an individual who loves him or herself can be said to take pleasure in his or her own existence. In this sense, one can be said to get "high" on oneself or one's own life. Although typically condemned, we can see how a feeling about oneself offers a powerful response to evaluative pessimism, as it implicitly holds that there is at least one thing in existence that makes life worth living: me, myself, my soul! Regardless of what the world is like, it is nevertheless the case that life is worth living because *I* am living it. Indeed, Zarathustra's comments indicate that such self-enjoyment expresses itself in dance (one recalls here the final dance of *Zorba the Greek*). Although Zarathustra himself could not dance in "The Dancing Song," we have seen that Zarathustra would only believe "in a god who could dance" (ZI "On Reading and Writing"). This god is none other than Dionysus, and we will eventually find Zarathustra himself dancing at the end of *Zarathustra* III, where Dionysian metaphors and imagery are prevalent.

It is from this standpoint of self-enjoyment that the soul can protect itself in its own "sacred groves" and banish "from its presence whatever is contemptible" and "cowardly." It finds contemptible whatever "worries, sighs, and is miserable," and it "despises all wisdom that wallows in grief." Such a wisdom "blooms in the dark, a nightshade wisdom, which always sighs: all is vain." The mention of a night wisdom that declares the vanity of all things is a reference to the wisdom of the soothsayer and so Schopenhauer's philosophy of evaluative pessimism. So construed, Zarathustra's account of the self-enjoying soul and so *Selbstsucht* is *the* antidote to such pessimism. Interesting here is that Zarathustra's prescription for overcoming pessimism now corresponds much more with the ideas Nietzsche presents in *The Gay Science*. There, Nietzsche not only chides those who deprive *Selbstsucht* of its good conscience (GS 328), but he also argues that the one thing needful for the human being—the one thing needed to overcome revenge—is to attain satisfaction with oneself (GS 290).

The "blessed selfishness" that Zarathustra praises "spits" on everything servile. Such servility can come in the form of being servile to a god or servile to the opinions of others along with the social mores upheld by the "good and the just." Again, we can see the deep hostility of this ethic to a Christian virtue such as humility as well as an ethic of service that derives from the Christian concept of neighbor love. Indeed, Zarathustra singles out the sham wisdom of the priests. They are world-weary with "womanish and servile" souls. It is their trickery that has played tricks on selfishness. In contrast to selfishness, these "world-weary cowards" tried to make themselves "selfless." To overthrow the reign of this priestly evaluation, Zarathustra promises a judgment day of the "great noon." This will come on the day when someone "proclaims the ego wholesome and holy, and selfishness [*Selbstsucht*] blessed."

As one can see, "On the Three Evils" is a pivotal chapter in *Zarathustra*. It presents a recipe for overcoming the life-denying pessimism that haunts much of the text, and this recipe does not require a commitment to the truth of the eternal recurrence or the hope for an *Übermensch*. Instead, the recipe lies in the revaluation of three evils, most notably a revaluation of the Christian condemnation of self-love.

That "On the Three Evils" is a crucial moment in the text is supported by the fact that Zarathustra finally confronts his archenemy in the next chapter, "**On the Spirit of Gravity**," and he appeals to self-love and self-enjoyment in so doing. Recall, the spirit of gravity is the dwarf from "On the Vision and the Riddle," and therefore Zarathustra's overcoming of the spirit of gravity represents his victory over the negative forces that appeared with the first robust presentation of the eternal recurrence. To speak about his archenemy, Zarathustra feels compelled to sing (an important correlate to Dionysian dance). Zarathustra's song begins by exhorting humans to fly, as this will effectively remove all boundary stones. The flight of the bird is said to defy gravity (even though it technically does not) and therefore the spirit of gravity. The flight imagery also recalls the wings of *eros* and its upward movement. Moreover, we learn that self-love is a necessary condition for learning how to fly: "but whoever would become light and a bird must love himself." Taken together, the idea is that self-love and self-enjoyment overcome the spirit of gravity and propel the spirit into flight. Again, the contrast between this prescription and the opening of *Zarathustra* could not be starker. In the latter, Zarathustra taught the townspeople to love the *Übermensch*; the human is only lovable as a means to producing an *Übermensch*. Here, Zarathustra sings that the human must learn to love herself, and it is through this self-love that the spirit of gravity will be defeated.

Like "On the Gift-Giving Virtue," Zarathustra notes that there are healthy and unhealthy forms of self-love.[11] The healthy sort of self-love, which has clear associations with ancient Greek *eros*, allows one to be alone with oneself such that one "need not roam" (as Zarathustra had been doing prior to his homecoming). Such roaming suggests a self that looks outside of itself, perhaps looking for the love that it does not feel for itself, either from another human being or from a deity that is all love. Zarathustra associates this sort of roaming with Christian "neighbor love."[12]

Zarathustra, however, acknowledges that his teaching cuts against the doctrine of "good" and "evil." Specifically, the spirit of gravity orders that children should be taught not to love themselves. This teaching leads to the idea that "life is a grave burden," and humans then carry this burden on their shoulders, just as Zarathustra was carrying the spirit of gravity on his shoulders in "On the Vision and the Riddle." The burden is caused by individuals trying to live up to ethical standards that are different from or even contrary to what they themselves fundamentally are. By failing to be what one ought to be, individuals begin to hate themselves, and this makes life a grave burden. This contrasts with the idea that Zarathustra puts forward: a healthy individual seeks to discover one's own "good" and "evil." It is through this discovery that one "reduces to silence the mole and dwarf" who claim, "good for all, evil for all."

Going beyond good and evil, however, does not mean going beyond good and bad (a point Nietzsche makes in the first essay of the *Genealogy*). Zarathustra calls those who approve of everything the "omni-satisfied." The omni-satisfied taste everything but have no taste in the sense of having no ability to discriminate between good and bad for oneself (ultimately one's taste can be reduced to judgments about what satisfies and increases the will to power). Chewing and digesting everything is equivalent to braying "Yea-Yuh" to everything (this foreshadows "The Ass Festival" in *Zarathustra* IV). In contrast, Zarathustra honors those tongues that are "choosy," which "have learned to say 'I' and 'yes' and 'no.'" For instance, Zarathustra says "no" to those mummies and ghosts who are enemies of the body. He also finds "parasites" revolting. Parasites are those who are not able to love but yet want "to live on love." According to Zarathustra, this is *his* taste, and he is no longer ashamed of his taste. His taste, however, is not the one and only way. Thus, the passage ends with "'this is *my* way; where is yours?' [...] For *the* way—that does not exist."

It is worth pausing to reflect on the significance of this passage. Zarathustra is effectively reducing all moral judgments to aesthetic judgments of taste. According to Nietzsche, the difference between moral judgments and aesthetic judgements of taste is that moral judgments purport to be universal and make claims of objective truth; in contrast, aesthetic judgements are based on subjective preference and make no claims to universality (KSA 9:11[79]; see also GS 335). Unlike aesthetic judgments, moral judgments are said to correspond to or be based on something that transcends the individual self. This ground can be in nature, some universal truth about human rationality, claims about the intrinsic value of pleasure and avoidance of pain, or ultimately God's will. Nietzsche, however, rejects the idea that there is anything in nature, God, human beings, etc., that could make moral judgments true. Even though past moralists and religious figures, such as Zoroaster, believed themselves to be making objective, universal claims about good and evil, they were really projecting their judgments of taste onto a world beyond themselves. For Nietzsche, aesthetic judgments create tablets of "good" and "evil," and tablets of good and evil are the foundation of what is then called morality (KSA 9:11[78]). However, in reducing morality to aesthetic judgments, Nietzsche is aware that it makes each individual's taste the Protagorean "measure of things" (KSA 9:11[79]). Because the taste of each individual is rooted in the specific physio- and psychological facts about that individual (KSA 9:11[112]), each individual will have his or her own taste or "way."

It is from this standpoint of embracing self-love and establishing one's own taste as a measure of value that Zarathustra speaks in "**On Old and New Tablets**." The opening line of the text provides some clue as to where things stand with a possible revaluation of values: "Here I sit and wait, surrounded by broken old tablets and new tablets half covered with writing." However, it is not clear whether Zarathustra has broken the old tablets and begun to construct his own (new) tablets or whether these are just the old tablets of the past and some new tablets recently half-written, perhaps by the world-weary. In either case, Zarathustra is now waiting for his hour to "go under." In this instance, "going under" means for him to go down to human beings yet again. This is importantly different from the type of "going under" that ends "The Convalescent," which is something that happens in his cave alone with his animals.[13] Indeed, the going under that goes down among humans is marked by "the laughing lion with the flock of doves," and there is no such sign in "The Convalescent," where Zarathustra's "going under" happens when he is alone in his cave. Instead, this sign of a laughing lion finally comes at the end of *Zarathustra* IV, where Zarathustra decides to leave his cave and presumably go among humans again.[14]

"On Old and New Tablets" is divided into 30 sections and much of it recounts Zarathustra's odyssey thus far. In fact, Zarathustra is now biding his time until his going under and so he talks to himself "as one who has time." He learns nothing new from anyone, and so he tells himself to himself ("Tablets":1).[15] The story he tells begins with substantive evidence for reading *Zarathustra* as a text that moves "beyond good and evil." Zarathustra narrates how he confronted the conceit of the wise, the masters of virtue, the saints, the sages, the poets, and the world-redeemers for all claiming that they know the nature of good and evil. He contrasts their Socratic ignorance (i.e., they do not know that they do not know) with his own "ethics" of creativity. This ethic states that creativity gives humans a goal, and it is with this goal that anything at all can be dubbed good or evil ("Tablets":2).

Zarathustra also narrates how his "wild wisdom" took him to distant places "where gods in their dances are ashamed of all clothes" (this recalls Zarathustra's remarks in "On Human Prudence" from *Zarathustra* II). It is also a place "where all becoming seemed to [him] the dance of gods and the prankishness of gods, and the world seemed free and frolicsome and as if fleeing back to itself." In such a world, "necessity" is "freedom itself playing happily with the sting of freedom." Much of this contrasts with a spirit of gravity—the personification of melancholy and revenge—that created notions such as "consequence and purpose and will and good and evil." ("Tablets":2). Here again, we see Zarathustra stressing the idea that we can take pleasure in a purposeless world beyond good and evil.

In the third section, Zarathustra explains how he came upon the idea or "word" of the *Übermensch*. This is the idea that the human must be overcome and that the human "is a bridge and no end." Here Zarathustra mentions the "great noon," which refers to the end of *Zarathustra* I where the human is said to stand in the middle between beast and the *Übermensch* and points forward to his summoning of the eternal recurrence. As Zarathustra continues, he recounts his teaching on redemption and the need to "carry together into One what in man is fragment and riddle and dreadful accident." Doing so would lead to a better future that would redeem all that "*has been.*" This is accomplished by recreating "all it was" into "Thus I will it! Thus I shall will it!"

So much for what Zarathustra taught others. Now he claims that he is waiting for his own redemption. Once he is redeemed, he can then go again to humans, to go under, "dying." Whether this is a biological death that never occurs in the extant four parts of *Zarathustra* or whether this is the ritual death of the psyche that Zarathustra undergoes at the end of *Zarathustra* III is not clear. In any case, Zarathustra will give his richest gift, like the sun which bears inexhaustible riches and makes it such that "even the poorest fisherman still rows with golden oars" ("Tablets":3). The mention of making even "the poorest fisherman row with golden oars [*der ärmste Fischer noch mit goldenem Ruder rudert*]" are the exact words that Nietzsche uses to describe the "'humaneness' of the future" in *The Gay Science*. There Nietzsche speaks of a "new nobility," one in which such nobles become god-like in their ability to bless all that has been and all that will be (GS 337). The direct reference to this passage suggests that Zarathustra himself will become this god-like human and a "new noble."

In the fourth section, Zarathustra presents a new tablet. This new tablet is derived from his love of the farthest, which could be a reference to his love of the *Übermensch*. The tablet or command is the opposite of neighbor love: "*do not spare your neighbor.*" We have already seen in "The Return Home" that the temptation to spare humanity constitutes one of Zarathustra's two great dangers (pity is the other). The human is something that needs to be overcome, and sparing the neighbor would prevent humanity from overcoming itself. The reason for thinking that Zarathustra has the *Übermensch* in mind is that he mentions the "jester" or *Possenreisser*, the very figure that skipped over the tightrope walker—sending him to his eventual death—as Zarathustra was presenting his teaching of the *Übermensch* in the prologue

("Tablets":4). In the *Nachlass*, Nietzsche presents Zarathustra as the *Possenreisser* who sends the tightrope walker to his death, which is another reason for thinking that Zarathustra himself is on his way to becoming an *Übermensch* (KSA 10:16[88]).

In section five, Zarathustra explicitly mentions "noble souls" and he provides some insight into their character. According to Zarathustra, such souls do not want something for nothing. They are always thinking of giving in return ("Tablets":5). Zarathustra's talk of giving in return for receiving seems to be connected to his idea that "the firstling is always sacrificed." Zarathustra goes on to say that he and his brothers are such firstlings, ready to "bleed at sacrificial altars." This willingness to be sacrifices is something Zarathustra praises. This shows that such noble characters do not exist merely to preserve themselves. Instead, they are willing to "go under" ("Tablets":6).

Much of this passage sounds as though Zarathustra is praising those who are willing to die (in the biological sense) for a good cause. However, we are also told that by going under such souls also "cross over [*sie gehen hinüber*]" As I have explained before, it is hard to make sense of a going under that is also a crossing over in terms of a biological death. Since there is no afterlife, it could at best mean somehow crossing over to the beginning of one's repeated life. But a crossing over seems to imply a crossing over to something higher and thereby tied to some sort of initiation into a new life. For this reason, I think that both "going under" and "crossing over" suggest a willingness to sacrifice one's current self for a new self that has been transformed in some significant and fundamental way. As I have previously noted, this idea is central to several religions, including Christianity and the worship of Dionysus, and there are reasons for thinking that Zarathustra's own going under amounts to a "crossing over" into the mysteries of Dionysus. Indeed, Nietzsche's theory in *The Birth of Tragedy* is based on the idea that tragedy is rooted in sacrifice ritual and that it is through the destruction of the individual hero on stage that the chorus and the audience are initiated into the Dionysian mysteries.

There is another curious feature of the sixth section that is worthy of discussion. In the first section, Zarathustra claims that he is now talking to himself, telling himself to himself ("Tablets":1). At the beginning of section four, Zarathustra implies the absence of any "brothers" to carry down his new tablet into the valley ("Tablets":4). However, in section six, Zarathustra now addresses his "brothers," and he continues to do so throughout much of the remainder "On Old and New Tablets." This is a curious feature of the text, and Loeb (2010) has used this discrepancy to argue that we can situate the events of *Zarathustra* IV somewhere between the third and sixth sections of "On Old and New Tablets." According to Loeb, the action of *Zarathustra* IV begins with Zarathustra alone in his cave at the beginning of "On Old and New Tablets," but it ends with a return of Zarathustra's disciples. As an analeptic satyr play, the dramatic events of *Zarathustra* IV explain how Zarathustra begins "On Old and New Tablets" by speaking to himself but then addresses his brothers in the latter three-fourths of the chapter. The short answer is that his disciples have joined him between the third and sixth sections, and these disciples will remain with him to witness his tragic suicide at the end of *Zarathustra* III.

Zarathustra's repeated mentions of his brothers is undoubtedly a puzzling feature of the text. Equally puzzling, however, is that there are no other indications in the remaining chapters of *Zarathustra* III that other humans are present with Zarathustra (only his talking animals are present). It is also puzzling that "On Old and New Tablets" begins with Zarathustra explaining that he is going to tell himself to himself. Because this ends the first section, it seems intended to govern the entirety of "On Old and New Tablets," not just the first section. Thus, it would be surprising to think that years have passed by the time we get to the sixth section and Zarathustra is now talking to a group of disciples who have joined him unannounced (a lacuna only filled in by the privately distributed *Zarathustra* IV). Instead, it seems that he is still telling himself to himself.

This leaves us with the task of explaining why Zarathustra refers to his "brothers" in nearly every other section. The most plausible answer has been given by Lampert: It is an "imagined audience of brothers" (1986:204). Other commentators have gone on to suggest that Zarathustra is imagining this to occur in the future, and Loeb has responded by arguing that verb tenses in the speech do not support an imagined future audience (2010:126ff.). The problem is that there is no reason to think that he is necessarily imagining some *future* audience. Instead, he is just imagining that an audience is present at the time he is speaking, even if this audience might, in the future, play some role in fulfilling his hopes for a new nobility. Indeed, Zarathustra's reference to his absent brothers at the beginning of section four—"but where are my brothers"?—seems to be the reason why Zarathustra would be thinking of and so addressing such (imagined) brothers in subsequent sections even though they remain absent throughout all of "On Old and New Tablets."

Returning to "On Old and New Tablets," the noble souls that Zarathustra imagines stand in contrast to the "the good" or "*good men*." The good try to prevent the creation of new values in part because they believe that "good" and "evil" are rooted in nature ("Tablets":7). In short, such individuals deny the Heraclitean idea that "everything is in flux." Instead, they have a "winter" doctrine in which everything is said to stand still, presumably also the categories of "good" and "evil." Zarathustra, however, points to "the thawing wind, a bull that is no plowing bull, a raging bull, a destroyer who breaks the ice with wrathful horns." Nothing is explicit, but there are close associations between the bull and Dionysus, and it is likely that Nietzsche again has Dionysus in mind. In any case, Zarathustra points out that broken ice also breaks bridges, and bridges symbolize the notions of good and evil that supposedly stand above the flux ("Tablets":8). Because there have only been illusions, not knowledge, about "good and evil" ("Tablets":9), it is time to "break the old tablets!" ("Tablets":10).

As the section unfolds, Zarathustra again calls for a "*new nobility.*" These new nobles must oppose the "rabble" that have a very limited sense of history, a history that only goes back as far as the grandfather. Nothing is explicit, but we can again think back to Nietzsche's description of new nobles in *The Gay Science* who make human history their own history (GS 337). Indeed, just as Nietzsche describes these new nobles as having god-like feelings in *The Gay Science*, Zarathustra associates these nobles with the thought that "there are gods, but no God" ("Tablets":11). Even though these nobles look far back into the past, this is done for a future-oriented project. Such nobles should leave their fatherlands, but in turn create a land for their children. In their children they will compensate for being children of their fathers and eventually use the future to redeem the past ("Tablets":12).

These new nobles will also break the tablets written by the "world-weary." The world-weary are those who, like the soothsayer, claim that "all is vanity," that there is no point to living ("Tablets":13). Similarly, there are those who point to some filth in the world to claim that the world itself is filthy. In response to the nausea this produces, Zarathustra acknowledges that there is indeed much to overcome ("Tablets":14). However, this should not lead one to "renounce the world," as "the pious afterworldly" do ("Tablets":15), or claim that one should not desire or will because nothing is worthwhile ("Tablets":16). These are all tablets created by weariness, and Zarathustra exhorts his new nobles to break these tablets and "maxims of those who slander the world" ("Tablets":15). According to Zarathustra, it is willing that liberates and creates ("Tablets":16).

Zarathustra then speaks of the way in which he is moving ever higher up the mountain until there are fewer and fewer with him. Here, he warns against "parasites" following him up the mountain. These parasites feed off the weariness of such mountain climbers. However, Zarathustra then describes a soul that is capable of withstanding and even nourishing such parasites. Such a soul has the longest ladder because it reaches both up and down. It is also the most comprehensive soul because it can roam farthest from itself. It is also the most necessary soul because "out of sheer joy" it "plunges itself into chance; the soul which, having being, dives into becoming." Thus, it is "the soul which loves itself most, in which all things have their sweep and countersweep and ebb and flood" ("Tablets":19).

The language is not exact, but the description of this soul again recalls Nietzsche's description of the "new nobility" and god-like soul in *The Gay Science* (GS 337). *Nachlass* notes shed further light on Zarathustra's description of this type of soul. In one note, Nietzsche runs through a list of adjectives that describe this soul, all of which appear in section 19 of "Tablets":

The most comprehensive, the wisest, the most necessary, the soul that has being, the soul that possesses. At the end of the note, Nietzsche adds something that does not appear in the published version of *Zarathustra*: "The soul for which everything is a game" (KSA 10:17[41]).

This latter remark suggests a clear connection between the child of the "Three Metamorphoses" from *Zarathustra* I and the most comprehensive soul described here. In other *Nachlass* notes, we find evidence for associating this soul with the *Übermensch*. In one, Nietzsche again describes what he calls the "highest soul." Such a soul is "the most comprehensive," the "most necessary" in that it plunges into accidents, a soul that has being but falls in love with becoming. Such a soul is in love with itself—a key motif in previous chapters of *Zarathustra* III—and therefore in love with everything. For this reason, this soul experiences everything as a game. Nietzsche then speaks of redemption from chance by transforming something that was merely allowed to happen in the past ("it was") into something that one now wants ("thus I will it"). Toward the end, we read that "after this, *out of happiness for superhumans [Übermenschen]*, Zarathustra relates the **secret** that everything recurs," and then Zarathustra is said to die (KSA 10:20[10]).[16]

Although the note suggests some connection between the *Übermensch* and the "highest soul," the connection itself is not clear. Is it that the highest soul just is the *Übermensch*? So understood, Zarathustra's happy anticipation of the *Übermensch* is at the same time a happy anticipation of a soul that makes possible Zarathustra's summoning of the eternal recurrence. On another reading, the "highest soul" just is a soul capable of summoning the eternal recurrence, and it is the summoning of the eternal recurrence—and so the existence of such a soul—that will eventually give birth to the *Übermensch*. On this reading, Zarathustra would then be the embodiment of this highest soul, and it is Zarathustra's summoning of the eternal recurrence that initiates a future in which the *Übermensch* can appear.

It is worth reflecting on these matters because Nietzsche devotes significant space in *Ecce Homo* to discussing the type of soul he describes in "On Old and New Tablets." A striking feature of Nietzsche's account in *Ecce Homo* is that he claims that Zarathustra achieves and embodies this *"supreme type"* of being. Moreover, Nietzsche claims that through Zarathustra's achievement, the concept of the *Übermensch*, which is equated with overcoming the human condition, has "become the greatest reality." In other words, Zarathustra is both the soul Zarathustra describes in section 19 of "Tablets" as well as the *Übermensch*. Finally, after quoting extensively from "On Old and New Tablets," Nietzsche then goes on to claim that this description of the highest soul is *"the concept of Dionysus himself."* What makes Zarathustra Dionysian is that he can bear the heaviest fate—perhaps the "greatest weight" of the eternal recurrence—and yet still be "the lightest and most transcendent." This light-footed transcendence is exemplified by the fact that Zarathustra is a dancer, a clear mark of the Dionysian (EH "Books" Z:6).

Nietzsche's claim that Zarathustra himself becomes a supreme type of being and even the *Übermensch* was written retrospectively in 1888, and it does not exactly map onto what we find in the text. In *Zarathustra* III, mentions of the *Übermensch* are very few (there are only three), but one passage presents the *Übermensch* as Zarathustra's hope for the future and not something that Zarathustra himself is or is soon to become. Specifically, toward the end of "On Old and New Tablets," Nietzsche again has Zarathustra assign sharply divergent gender roles to men and women, with the former being fit for war and the former being fit for giving birth (both however are fit for dance and laughter) ("Tablets":23–24). He then speaks of marriage. Recalling the ethos of *Zarathustra* I, Zarathustra claims that a healthy marriage has the aim of producing something *"higher,"* and given his love for the *Übermensch*, this is precisely what his marriage counseling must be ("Tablets":25). Based on this passage, it still seems as though Zarathustra is one thing and the *Übermensch* is another. That is, Zarathustra still longs for and is in love with the *Übermensch*.

Nevertheless, "On Old and New Tablets" closes with no further mention of the *Übermensch*. Instead, Zarathustra again emphasizes the idea that the "good and the just" stand in the way of the creation of new values ("Tablets":26–27), and he then issues an exhortation to break the tablets of the good and the just ("Tablets":28). To do this, creators of values must "become hard," and this is the new tablet that Zarathustra erects ("Tablets":29). Finally, Zarathustra calls upon his will, which is his own necessity, the destination of his soul, and his destiny. It also marks a great victory ("Tablets":30).

The final two sections of "On Old and New Tablets" deserve special attention. As I noted above, there are reasons for thinking that the final chapters of *Zarathustra* III either contain an initial attempt at a revaluation of values or prefigure Nietzsche's later revaluation of values. The final two sections of "On Old and New Tablets" take on importance in this respect because both can be linked to Nietzsche's 1888 works which are intimately bound up with his revaluation project. On the one hand, Nietzsche concludes *Twilight of the Idols* by quoting all of section 29 of "Tablets." As Brobjer has pointed out, the title of the section is "The Hammer Speaks," and the "hammer" is a clear reference to the eternal recurrence and therefore the central doctrine of *Zarathustra* (2023b: Ch.5.8). Brobjer also points out that Nietzsche had planned to conclude *Ecce Homo* by quoting the entirety of section 30 of "Tablets" (2021: Ch.4.2). The title of the final chapter of *Ecce Homo* is "Why I am a Destiny," and the title itself suggest a union between the individual soul and cosmic necessity or fate. Indeed, the placement of both passages at the end of Nietzsche's own work indicates a close continuity between Nietzsche and Zarathustra. Such continuity is supported by the fact that in the section just before "The Hammer Speaks" in *Twilight of the Idols*, Nietzsche declares himself—not Zarathustra—to be the last disciple of the philosopher Dionysus and "the teacher of the eternal recurrence" (TI "What I Owe":5).

Seung has also stressed the importance of the final section of "Tablets" (2005:159–160). He claims that everything prior to this section has been merely a retrospective account of what Zarathustra has already done and taught. The final section is different. It sets the stage for the final act of Zarathustra in which he unites his own will with cosmic necessity and becomes the teacher of the eternal recurrence. As Seung points out, one notable feature of the section is that it begins with Zarathustra addressing his will (rather than his "brothers"). This implies a distinction between Zarathustra and his will. His will is his "*own* necessity," the "destination of his soul," and his "destiny [*Schicksal*]." This will is both in him and over him. For Seung, this means two things. First, the will is something that controls Zarathustra; it is not something that Zarathustra controls. Second, Zarathustra's claim that the will stands both in and over him effectively links his will to nature and even the larger cosmos. This is further supported by Zarathustra's mention of an "inexorable solar will [*unerbittlicher Sonnen-Wille*]" toward the end of the passage. The "solar" or "sun" will is much bigger than a particular individual. Indeed, it may be a reference to something like the will to power and so the driving cosmological force of all life.

The text of section 30 of "Tablets" provides important evidence for my claim that Zarathustra's eventual summoning of the eternal recurrence and corresponding "going under" amount to a death of a non-natural concept of the self in which the self merges with nature, necessity, and fate. By "diving into becoming" like the most comprehensive soul and merging with fate, Zarathustra himself is naturalized, and it is the naturalization of the self that constitutes the essence of the tragic nature of *Zarathustra*. Indeed, this notion of a naturalized humanity is something that Nietzsche foreshadows in the passage in which he first mentions the eternal recurrence in *The Gay Science*. Thus, Nietzsche ends "Let us Beware," with the question: "When may we begin to '*naturalize*' humanity in terms of a pure, newly discovered, newly redeemed nature?" (GS 109). There is no mention of Zarathustra, but another passage from the *Genealogy* suggests that Zarathustra (or Nietzsche) will be the one who redeems humanity by merging with nature or reality: Such a redeeming man will not be free from reality; instead "it is only his absorption, immersion, penetration *into* reality, so that, when he one day emerges again into the light, he may bring home the *redemption* of this reality." Such an individual will—once he has effectively died and then been reborn as a naturalized being—redeem us both from the moral ideal and the nausea and nihilism that grow from it (GM II:24).

5.4 ZARATHUSTRA'S INITIATION INTO THE DIONYSIAN MYSTERIES: CHAPTERS 13–16

Lampert writes that "the last four chapters of part III of *Thus Spoke Zarathustra* contain the event for the sake of which the whole book exists" (1986:210). Indeed, we saw that *The Gay Science* introduced the idea of the eternal recurrence with a question as to whether one can affirm the thought or whether one would be crushed by it. The 1882 edition of *The Gay Science* then ended with the phrase "incipit tragoedia" and the opening lines of *Zarathustra*. However, *Zarathustra* begins with a program for creating the *Übermensch*, not an attempt to affirm the eternal recurrence, and it is only toward the end of *Zarathustra* II that we encounter any substantive hints of the eternal recurrence. Until this point, *Zarathustra* III is largely about Zarathustra returning to his solitude and "perfecting himself" so that he can summon and affirm the eternal recurrence.

In "**The Convalescent**," Zarathustra is presented as one who, as a convalescent, has overcome the sickness that has plagued humanity. The sickness that has plagued humanity is personified in the spirit of gravity, and the spirit of gravity represents melancholy and revenge. Revenge results from the inability to change the unwanted parts of the past (*Vergangenheit*) and to prevent time from devouring the present (*Vergänglichkeit*). Melancholy results from the insight that nothing will ever change, that all is the same, all is in vain. Both melancholy and the first form of revenge stem from a common desire for things to be different than they are. The cure for these infirmities, therefore, requires an overcoming of wanting things to be different than they are, and this is achieved when an individual is satisfied with and therefore able to love herself (GS 290). In short, Zarathustra's convalescence and so his health and nobility go hand in hand with the healthy form of self-love he extolled in "On the Three Evils" and "On the Spirit of Gravity."

It is from the standpoint of self-love and self-satisfaction that Zarathustra is now able to transform the "it was" into "thus I willed it." By identifying with nature and fate, he is able to expand his own self-love into a gift-giving virtue that includes all things. As noted above, the ability to transform the "it was" into "thus

I willed it" is a necessary condition for the affirmation of the eternal recurrence. This is because the eternal recurrence entails that every event in the world is already determined. Thus, things cannot be otherwise, and therefore the affirmation of the eternal recurrence entails a love of fate (*amor fati*). However, the more Zarathustra loves both past and present events, the more he will lament their passing. Thus, the transience (*Vergänglichkeit*) of all things can still be a source of revenge. The solution to this problem is the eternal recurrence. Although things come to be and pass away, they will nevertheless return again and again. In other words, the eternal recurrence is the thought that stamps being onto a world of becoming (KSA 12:7[54]) and thereby provides a solution to the problem of transience (KSA 10:4[85]). So understood, we can see a trajectory in which Zarathustra's perfection of himself ultimately leads to a deep longing to eternalize and immortalize nature.

In a scene that recalls Wagner's *Siegfried* when Wotan calls upon Erda (see Brusotti 1997:608), "The Convalescent" begins with Zarathustra waking up in his cave, letting out a terrible roar that frightens his animals. Zarathustra then calls out, "Up, abysmal thought, out of my depth!," and he emphasizes that he is the one calling up the thought: "Zarathustra, the godless, summons you! I, Zarathustra, the advocate of life, the advocate of suffering, the advocate of the circle; I summon you, my most abysmal thought!" It is his abyss that is speaking, and he is turning his "ultimate depth inside out into the light." In other words, Zarathustra is bringing to consciousness a subterranean or unconscious wisdom ("The Convalescent":1).

Upon speaking these words, Zarathustra collapses, almost as if he is dead. He then awakens, but in a pale, trembling, and sickly state. He remains like this for almost seven days. In the meantime, his animals tend to him, giving him food. Once Zarathustra had taken a bite of an apple (a likely reference to the Garden of Eden), his animals decide to speak to him. Zarathustra responds in turn, and eventually the animals—not Zarathustra—provide an account of the eternal recurrence. The animals claim that they think like Zarathustra, and for them, "all things themselves are dancing." On this account,

> everything goes, everything comes back; eternally rolls the wheel of being. Everything dies, everything blossoms again; eternally runs the year of being. [...] Everything parts, everything greets every other thing again: eternally the ring of being remains faithful to itself. In every Now, being begins; round every Here rolls the sphere There. The center is everywhere. Bent is the path of eternity.
>
> ("The Convalescent":2)

There are three important ideas built into the animals' presentation of the eternal recurrence. First, there is the concept of the "year of being." The idea is that just as the earth's movement around the sun and the seasons it produces constitute a single year in which there is a cycle of life and death, so too is there a cosmic year in which everything blossoms and blooms, everything dies out, and then everything is repeated. Even if our best physics tells us that the universe is sliding toward an eventual "heat death," the eternal recurrence holds that the cycle of nature will nevertheless start again (this possibility is not ruled out by our best science).[17] The second point comes last in the animals' description, but it is worth noting here as a corrective to the previous point. It would be wrong to think that there is an end that is also the beginning to the universe such as the point when the universe reaches a heat death and then the process somehow "starts" over again. Zarathustra's animals reject such a view because it preserves a remnant of a linear conception of time where there is a beginning and an end to the process. Instead, the eternal recurrence entails that there is no starting point or center. Every "now" is a new beginning and yet not a new beginning. Finally, we learn that this circular conception of nature makes it a self-enclosed and self-contained entity. There is nothing beyond the circle of being—such as a god—responsible for starting or bringing the process to an end. Instead, it exists and continues eternally, and, like God, it explains itself. This is why the eternal recurrence plays a crucial role in completing the system of naturalism: It eliminates the need for positing an external deity to explain the existence of the cosmos as well as its beginning and end.

After hearing the animals' description of Zarathustra's teaching, Zarathustra calls them "buffoons and barrel organs!" One could read this as Zarathustra lashing out at them for getting his teaching wrong.[18] However, it seems that Zarathustra is accusing his animals of not fully grasping how this teaching profoundly affected his being; the animals, in contrast, seem to be immune to the psychological effects of such a view (they are incapable of experiencing nausea and revenge). Zarathustra explains that during the seven days between now and when he first called up his "abysmal thought" he was battling the "monster [*Unthier*]" that crawled down his throat and suffocated him. Zarathustra's tale recalls the shepherd's battle with the snake in "On the Vision and the Riddle," and just like the shepherd, Zarathustra claims that he bit off the head of the snake and spewed it out. Even now, Zarathustra is still recovering from this battle, "still sick" from his "own redemption [*Erlösung*]." For Zarathustra, the problem with the animals is that they watched all this, perhaps taking a perverse pleasure in Zarathustra's sufferings.

Although "The Convalescent" repeats the scene in "On the Vision and the Riddle," now with Zarathustra battling the snake, "The Convalescent" marks an important advance. Specifically, we learn more about the things that are "choking" Zarathustra. First, it is "the great disgust with man." Second, it is the soothsayer's claim that "all is the same, nothing is worth while." As the passage unfolds, there is some ambiguity about what exactly chokes Zarathustra. Much of the focus is on the fact that the "small man" eternally recurs. Although the language is not the same, the reference to the "small man" recalls "On Virtue that Makes Small" in *Zarathustra* III as well as the "last man" that Zarathustra critiques in the prologue of *Zarathustra* I.

This brings us to the first ambiguity. Zarathustra begins by speaking of his disgust with "the human," but he then switches to a certain type of human, the small human. We see this sort of equivocation here: "Alas, man [*der Mensch*] recurs eternally! The small man [*der kleine Mensch*] recurs eternally!" The question is whether Zarathustra's disgust is merely with a certain subset of humans, namely, small humans, or all humans and so humanity as such. As the passage continues, we find evidence that supports the latter interpretation. Specifically, Zarathustra claims that even the greatest humans are "all-too-similar" to the smallest humans, "even the greatest all-too-human." The idea is that the set of small humans is equivalent to the set of all humans, and therefore Zarathustra's disgust with the small human is really a "disgust with humans [*Überdruss am Menschen*]" and ultimately a "disgust with all existence."[19]

The other ambiguity is what the snake is supposed to represent. On the standard interpretation, the snake represents Zarathustra's *disgust or nausea* about the eternal recurrence of the small human or even humanity itself. Loeb, however, has argued that the snake (which he translates as serpent) represents "the eternally recurring small human" (2010:151, 154). This interpretive difference is significant. If the snake represents Zarathustra's *disgust or nausea* (with the human), then biting off the head of the snake—and spitting it out—represents Zarathustra's overcoming of his *disgust or nausea* (with the human). If, as Loeb has it, the snake represents *the (small) human*, then biting off the head of the snake amounts to Zarathustra's negation of "the future existence of small humans." So rather than overcoming the negative emotions of disgust and nausea that Zarathustra has toward the (small) human (the standard reading), Loeb's reading has Zarathustra devising a plan to eliminate "humankind's *present* existence" (2010:162).

But how could one "eradicate" the human or humanity? Here Loeb admits that Zarathustra cannot undo the existence of human beings in the past and therefore he must accept their eternal recurrence. However, Loeb argues that the future in this current cycle is nevertheless "open to change" (2010:155). Thus, the new future that Zarathustra hopes to initiate is one in which humanity is supplanted by a new species of *Übermenschen*. But how does Zarathustra propose to do this? According to Loeb, the eternal recurrence is a selective doctrine. That is, most humans cannot bear its weight and will be crushed by the very thought of it. Thus, Zarathustra can "initiate the self-destruction of present-day humankind" by calling up the thought of the eternal recurrence. As Loeb explains, "confronted with the thought of an eternally recurring 'it was,' the human being therefore has no choice but to act on his immeasurably greater longing for death and select himself out of existence" (2010:165).

As one can see, there is a lot hanging of how we interpret Zarathustra's biting off the head of the snake. One obvious concern with Loeb's reading is its appalling consequences. On this view, the eternal recurrence is not a test or even a means by which a human being can affirm life. Instead, the teaching effectively becomes a gas chamber for humanity. Although this is enough to motivate an alternative reading, developing such a reading is not just a matter of charity. Specifically, Loeb's future-directed project of replacing humans with *Übermenschen* does little to address the two issues that nauseate Zarathustra: the recurrence of the (small) human and the thought that "all is the same, nothing is worthwhile." A program of eugenics in the name of a better future flies in the face of the claim that "all is the same," and it does nothing to address the *recurrence* of the (small) human: No matter what better future Zarathustra may envisage, the (small) human will still return. In contrast, if there is going to be redemption, it must come in the form of Zarathustra transforming the "it was" into something that he wills, and the focus here seems to be on the "it was" of the (small) human. In so doing, Zarathustra can effectively respond to the second source of his nausea: the idea that all is the same. By willing the past, Zarathustra will now embrace, even celebrate, an idea that eternalizes the way reality was, is, and will be. What was an objection to existence—that "all is the same"—now becomes a source of joy.

But what is it about the human that Zarathustra finds so disgusting? The answer seems to be that the human is a vengeful animal (unlike all other animals), and this revenge stems from a desire for the world to be other than it is. Animated by revenge, the human being turns these instincts inward, becoming "the cruelest animal against himself." Thus, he blames himself for all that he finds wrong in the world, and he invents concepts such as "sinner" and "cross-bearer" and "penitent." As we saw in previous chapters, the vengeful human projects categories of good and evil into the foundations of things and conceives all existence as a system of sin, punishment, and retribution. This is all madness, and it nauseates Zarathustra.

It is important to understand, however, that Zarathustra's disgust with the small human is just a particular instance of this vengeful attitude. And it is not just that he wishes that the small human did not exist. Instead, he wishes that all of humanity had not existed. Indeed, the problem goes deeper. If the hatred of the small human is really a hatred of humanity, then this hatred extends to Zarathustra himself, and it is Zarathustra's hatred of his own self that chokes him when he thinks that he, and all those like him, must return again and again.[20] It is here, then, that we can see how a dissatisfaction with one's self generates a longing for revenge and how others will inevitably be the victims of this revenge (GS 290). In other words, if Zarathustra cannot overcome his disgust with himself, this self-dissatisfaction can lead to fantasies about exterminating all humanity.

On this reading, the psychological battle that Zarathustra is waging within himself as he confronts his role as the teacher of the eternal recurrence is effectively a struggle to expand the love he has attained for himself in the previous chapters to encompass all of human history. Even if other humans are vengeful creatures, he must overcome the revenge he feels about the presence of such vengeful creatures. Instead, they must be understood as part of a larger whole that has produced his own being. Thus, by loving himself, he can also love the chain of causes that has produced the thing that he now loves. At its height, the love of self transforms into a love of fate (*amor fati*).

As he is describing his struggles and overcoming his disgust with the (small) human, his animals stop him from speaking further. Instead, they counsel him to learn from the songbirds how to sing. Zarathustra quickly silences them, but he effectively agrees that singing is indeed a comfort for the convalescent. Again, the animals try to silence him, now recommending that he fashion himself a new lyre and compose new songs in honor of his role as "*the teacher of the eternal recurrence.*" As we know, Nietzsche associates the eternal recurrence with the Dionysian mysteries of ancient Greece, and it is therefore no surprise that the animals counsel Zarathustra to turn to the two art forms most closely associated with the Dionysian chorus of tragedy, song and dance.

The description of the eternal recurrence that we then get from the animals is the most detailed in all of Nietzsche's published works. Here, they mention several features of the doctrine that we have already encountered. All things recur eternally, and this includes ourselves. There is a great year that resembles the earthly year. One great year is equivalent to one cycle of all events. This great year is like an hourglass that turns over and over. Again, it is emphasized that this teaching applies to ourselves. Just as the events of the great year repeat themselves, we too repeat the very lives that we lead again and again.

The stress on the implications the eternal recurrence has for oneself is one reason why it is so difficult for Zarathustra to accept the doctrine. Those who read the doctrine as an existential test focus on the fact that Zarathustra has to come to terms with the prospect that he will live his self-same life over and over again. However, the cosmological version also has significant implications for the self, and it seems to entail some sort of death. Thus, Zarathustra speaks of dying and vanishing and of a soul that is as "mortal as the body," and this is combined with the idea that he will come again to the self-same life. When he speaks his word, he will also break of his word, and as a proclaimer of the eternal recurrence, he will perish. Thus, Zarathustra's summoning of the eternal recurrence amounts to an end to "Zarathustra's going under" (ZIII "The Convalescent":2).

In my view, Zarathustra's summoning of the eternal recurrence amounts to a death of a non-natural conception of the self, and this best explains why the animals couple Zarathustra's summoning of the eternal recurrence with a "going under" that amounts to this type of death. One reason for resisting the biological reading of this death is that there doesn't seem to be any causal connection between the summoning of a cosmological idea and the biological death of a given individual. That is, how exactly does Zarathustra die in a biological sense? Does he become so overwhelmed that he can no longer breathe? Perhaps he goes into cardiac arrest? Perhaps, like Empedocles, he jumps into a volcano? But none of this is portrayed in *Zarathustra*. Another reason for resisting this reading is that Nietzsche later sketched plans to have Zarathustra die (biologically) in additional parts. But if Nietzsche is sketching such plans after publishing *Zarathustra* III, he cannot have understood *Zarathustra* III as including some implied depiction of Zarathustra's biological death. Thus, rather than thinking of Zarathustra's death in the biological sense, it is best understood as a "going under" that is also a "going over," and it is the "going under" of a non-naturalized conception of the self to a "going over" to a naturalized self initiated into the mysteries of Dionysus. So understood, *Zarathustra* follows the idea of *The Birth of Tragedy*: it is through tragedy that individuation is overcome and the human being is reunited with others and nature herself.

Evidence for thinking that Zarathustra's going under can be understood in terms of being initiated into the mysteries of Dionysus can be found throughout the final chapters of *Zarathustra* III. For instance, "Ariadne" was the original title of "On the Great Longing."[21] Correspondingly, the original title of the third stanza of "On the Seven Seals" was "Dionysus." Here, there is reason to equate Ariadne with the soul to which Zarathustra speaks in "On the Great Longing" and to recall the way in which Dionysus the overhero or *Über-Held* is supposed to approach the soul once the hero (Theseus) has abandoned it. The important upshot of these two titles is that they provide evidence that the final chapters of *Zarathustra* III amount to Zarathustra's initiation into the mysteries of Dionysus. We know that Nietzsche associates the eternal recurrence with the ancient Greek mysteries (KSA 10:8[15]) and that he presented Greek tragedy as rooted in the mysteries (BT 10). As Nietzsche explains in *Twilight of the Idols*, it is in these mysteries that "the Hellene guaranteed himself [...] *eternal* life, the eternal return of life; the future promised and hallowed in the past; the triumphant Yes to life beyond all death and change" (TI "What I Owe":4).

The presence of Dionysus at this stage of the text also provides important evidence for reading *Zarathustra* as a tragedy. In *The Birth*, Nietzsche presented tragedy as a quasi-initiation ritual into the mysteries of Dionysus. The idea that Nietzsche articulates in his first work is that tragedy is supposed to confront the reality of death and yet point beyond death to an inexhaustible source of nature. In that work, Nietzsche relied on the metaphysical framework of Schopenhauer, positing an indestructible "*Ur-Eine*" or an original unity that supposedly underlies all of nature. By confronting the destruction of the individual on the tragic stage, the spectator experiences the inexhaustibility of nature beyond all individuation (BT 16). On my reading, the eternal recurrence of *Zarathustra* takes over the function that Nietzsche originally ascribed to the *Ur-Eine* in *The Birth*. By eternalizing nature, we look beyond the death of any one individual, knowing that nature continues forever and that the individual, now merged with nature, will eternally return. In the *Twilight of the Idols*, this is precisely what Nietzsche describes as the tragic effect:

> Saying Yes to life even in its strangest and hardest problems, the will to life rejoicing over its own inexhaustibility even in the very sacrifice of its highest types—*that* is what I called Dionysian, *that* is what I guessed to be the bridge to the psychology of the *tragic* poet. Not in order to be liberated from terror and pity [...] but in order to be *oneself* the eternal joy of becoming [...] that joy which included even joy in destroying.
>
> (TI "What I Owe":5)

"**On the Great Longing**" begins with Zarathustra addressing his soul. The chapter initially had the title "Ariadne" (KSA 14:324), the mythical Cretan princess who saved Theseus from the minotaur but was then left by Theseus on Naxos only to be rescued by Dionysus. We have seen that, immediately following the dream sequence in "On the Vision and the Riddle" at the beginning of *Zarathustra* III, Zarathustra was tasked with perfecting himself, and this self-perfection went hand in hand with a self-love that was identified as the gift-giving virtue in *Zarathustra* I. In "On the Great Longing," Zarathustra now presents himself as the great liberator of the soul and one who has taught it many things to achieve such perfection. Most notably, Zarathustra claims to have "even strangled the strangler that is called 'sin.'" The concept of sin is directly tied to notions of good and evil. By overcoming sin, Zarathustra has moved the soul into a new innocence that recalls the child of "On the Three Metamorphoses." Along with this, Zarathustra has removed from the soul any temptation to obey, bow, and revere the "lord." Instead, he named his soul—as he does at the end of "On Old and New Tablets"—both "cessation of need [*Wende der Noth*]" and "destiny [*Schicksal*]." Zarathustra repeats "destiny" twice, and it again points to the idea that Zarathustra is fusing his soul with nature and necessity. For these reasons, Zarathustra now presents his own soul as "more loving and comprehending and comprehensive" than any other soul. Such language points back to "the most comprehensive soul" in section 19 of "Tablets," the passage that Nietzsche identifies in *Ecce Homo* as providing us with "*the concept of Dionysus himself*" (EH "Books" Z:6).

We also know from *Ecce Homo* that Nietzsche presents Zarathustra's own soul as this most comprehensive soul that "loves itself most" and "having being dives into becoming" (EH "Books" Z:6), and, in the second half of "On the Great Longing," we encounter language which indicates that Zarathustra's soul is now "diving into becoming" and merging with necessity. The perfected soul now suffers from its own overfullness and has a melancholic longing for "the vintager and his knife." Just as Ariadne is the soul, the vintager and his knife are clear references to Dionysus, and therefore we see that the "great longing" presented in this chapter is nothing other than Ariadne's longing for Dionysus. As Grätz notes (2024b:358), one variant of the chapter presents the vintager as the "over-hero [Über-Held]," and we know from "On the Sublime" in *Zarathustra* II as well as supporting *Nachlass* notes (KSA 10:13[1]) that this "over-hero" is Dionysus.

Weeping is presented as one way of responding to the melancholy of the soul, but it is suggested that all weeping is a lamentation, and all lamentation an accusation (presumably against life). Thus, rather than weep and thereby accuse life, Zarathustra instructs his soul to sing. Such singing will silence all seas and allow for the arrival of Dionysus by boat, who is now referred to as "the nameless one." The repeated references to Dionysus' diamond knife that will cut the overripe grape from the vine have suggested to some, like Loeb, that Zarathustra is himself preparing for a biological death in the final songs of *Zarathustra*. But if the cutting of the vine represents a death, it is a death of Zarathustra's soul, and this death seems to be at the same time a union with Dionysus. On this reading, the cutting of the grape from the vine represents a union with all of nature and the moment in which the gift-giving virtue of self-love is now spread to the rest of the cosmos, just as the setting of the sun pours its inexhaustible riches into the sea, allowing even the poorest fisherman to row with golden oars (GS 337).

As Lampert notes (1986:233–234), this chapter provides a direct response to the problem presented in "The Night Song" in *Zarathustra* II. There, the gift-giving virtue of Zarathustra's soul was secretly mixed with both malice and revenge. This is because it did not know the happiness of those who received. Much has changed, however, since "The Night Song." Zarathustra's soul (Ariadne) has received much from Dionysus, and the question now is which one should be thankful. At the end of the chapter, the answer seems to be both: the soul now sings for having learned "the happiness of those who receive," and Zarathustra is now thankful for the song of his soul.

Thankfulness or gratitude is the exact opposite of revenge and therefore symbolizes the final overcoming of the spirit of gravity that prevented Zarathustra from dancing in "The Dancing Song" in *Zarathustra* II. Because Zarathustra has now overcome the melancholy and revenge that produces the spirit of gravity, there is a significant difference between "The Dancing Song" in *Zarathustra* II and "**The Other Dancing Song**" in *Zarathustra* III.[22] In the latter, Zarathustra both learns to dance and finds himself reconciled with the woman Life. Indeed, the song begins with Zarathustra looking into the eyes of Life with his foot frantic to dance. The frantic and frenzied nature of the dance recalls the intoxication that Nietzsche associates with Dionysian art in *The Birth of Tragedy* as well as Zarathustra's early remark that he could only believe in a god who can dance.

What follows is a description of a cat and mouse game of dance that Zarathustra and Life play as they approach and flee each other. Like Dionysus, Zarathustra takes on the role of the hunter, and Life is now the hunted. Zarathustra is aggressively pursuing her, and he looks to capture this "witch." He then threatens to make her both dance and cry. He will do this with his whip, which he has not forgotten. The whip will make Life keep time as she dances. Life, however, responds rather playfully, entreating Zarathustra not to crack his whip so frightfully. She reminds Zarathustra that they are much alike. They have both found their island—this recalls the island of Naxos (Lampert 1986:236)—and their meadow "beyond good and evil." They therefore should not bear a grudge toward each other. Indeed, they should like or even love each other. What Life likes and even loves about Zarathustra is his wisdom, and it even makes her a bit jealous. Without such wisdom, Life would not find Zarathustra so loveable.

There is a problem, however. Life accuses Zarathustra of not being faithful to her. She knows that he is thinking of leaving her soon when a bell Zarathustra can hear from his cave strikes midnight. Thus, she insists that she knows Zarathustra wants to leave her soon. Here, we encounter a much-discussed scene between Zarathustra and Life. Zarathustra responds to Life's accusations by first acknowledging that he plans to leave her and, second, that he also presumably knows something that will mitigate his departure. After whispering this in her ear, Life is shocked about what Zarathustra claims to know. Nevertheless, Life and Zarathustra are now reconciled, gazing into each other's eyes. Then they weep, and we are told that Life is now dearer to Zarathustra than all his wisdom. Any accusation against Life has now been overcome, and the spirit of gravity is most certainly vanquished.

But what does Zarathustra whisper in Life's ear? This has been the subject of much scholarly controversy and rightly so. Unfortunately, we can only speculate. Michael Platt (1988) offers a few conjectures, ultimately settling on Zarathustra whispering, "I shall return." Lampert argues that Zarathustra whispers, "I will eternally return" (1986:238). Maudemarie Clark speculates, "to affirm life one must also affirm death" (1990:263). Loeb defends a suggestion that Platt offers but ultimately rejects: "you want to leave me" or "you want me to leave you" (2010:79). Finally, Gabriel Zamosc devotes an article to defending the idea that Zarathustra whispers, "yes, but you also know that you carry my child, you are pregnant" (2015b:245).

Although the text places constraints on any interpretation, there is a clear underdetermination by the text in this case, and so any answer will be speculative. Here, it only seems reasonable to follow Clark's claim that whatever is whispered must have something to do with the eternal recurrence (1990:263). Some, like Zamosc, have wondered why Zarathustra would whisper this, given that the doctrine has been openly discussed in previous scenes.

In response, it should be kept in mind that nowhere has Zarathustra tried to teach the doctrine to anyone, including Life. Instead, he has merely summoned it or called it into consciousness. Moreover, Nietzsche thinks of this teaching as a "mystery doctrine" associated with Dionysus. As such, it is something revealed to those who are initiated into these mysteries and only shared among those who have been initiated. If we assume that Life is already privy to these mysteries, then her surprise at what Zarathustra whispers is perhaps a surprise that he knows about the mysteries associated with the eternal recurrence.

Whatever Zarathustra whispers will also likely have something to do with responding to the problem of death, destruction, and the transience of all things. On the one hand, this could amount to Zarathustra telling Life something about him. As noted above, these conjectures largely have to do with Zarathustra applying the teaching of the eternal recurrence to himself, such that he reminds Life that he will come again or eternally return. On the other hand, Zarathustra could be whispering something to Life about Life, something that Life knows (because it is about her) but no one else supposedly knows. Of course, it could be that he says something about both himself and Life.

Nietzsche may have offered us a clue to what is whispered in one of his *Dithyrambs of Dionysus* (which were originally titled, *Songs of Zarathustra*), "Fame and Eternity." As Hollingdale explains, "Fame and Eternity" records the "four stages on Zarathustra's path to enlightenment" (1984:93) and "the third and fourth poems transport us to the end of Part Three of *Zarathustra*" (1984:94). In "Fame and Eternity," we find a phrase that is very similar to the phrase Zarathustra speaks just before he whispers into the ear of Life. In "The Other Dancing Song":2, the German phrase that Zarathustra utters is: "*aber du weisst es auch* [but you also know it]." In "Fame and Eternity," it is: "*aber du weisst es ja* [but you indeed know it]." In the latter, Zarathustra begins by addressing "the highest star of being" and he ends by declaring his love for "eternity." What "the highest star of being" or "eternity" is supposed to know ("*aber du weisst es ja*") is that Zarathustra loves her for the same reasons that others—like Socrates—hate her. These reasons are twofold: (1) that she is eternal (*ewig*) and (2) that she is necessary (*nothwendig*). The poem ends with Zarathustra declaring that he is the "eternal Yes of being."

Could this be what Zarathustra whispers in Life's ear in "The Other Dancing Song"? In "Fame and Eternity," Life is never mentioned, and this may be a reason to avoid using the dithyramb to make sense of what Zarathustra whispers. However, there is an interesting transition that takes place from the end of "The Other Dancing Song" to the last chapter of *Zarathustra* III, "The Seven Seals." There we find Zarathustra proclaiming his love for and wanting to marry Eternity, not Life. This raises some questions: Is Zarathustra now in love with yet another woman? Or is there some relationship between Life and Eternity?

Here I follow both Lampert (1986:238) and Loeb (2010:80) in holding that Life and Eternity are the same woman under different names. If this is right, when Zarathustra declares his love for eternity at the end of "Fame and Eternity," he is also declaring his love for the woman "Life." It also gives us reason to think that when Zarathustra explains why he loves Eternity in "The Seven Seals," he is also giving us a clue as to what he whispers in Life's ear. It is he alone who loves Life because Life is both "eternal" and "necessary." These may sound like strange reasons to love Life, but it seems that Zarathustra is in love with a world that always is (eternal) and cannot be otherwise (necessity). In this sense, he is someone who loves necessity in the form of fate (*amor fati*) and eternity in the form of the eternal recurrence. In this way, he distinguishes himself from all others who—like the vengeful Socrates—would hate Life precisely for these reasons. On this reading, the reason why they weep together at the end of "The Other Dancing Song" is that they have finally been reconciled in the fullest sense. The tears they shed are therefore tears of joy, and they are shed because Life is now dearer to Zarathustra than his wisdom had ever been. This, then, points toward the union between Zarathustra and Life under the name "Eternity" in "The Seven Seals."

Before this union in "The Seven Seals," the final section of "The Other Dancing Song" ends with a song sung on the twelve tolls of the bell at midnight. The song begins by awakening midnight, just after counseling humans to "take care." The wisdom here is something deep and potentially disturbing. The depth of the wisdom is emphasized with the fifth, sixth, and seventh tolls of the bell. Again, the idea is that there is a sort of superficiality that goes along with day and daylight, which is perhaps a symbol for consciousness or even life itself. In contrast, nighttime is deep, much like the unconscious and even death, and along with the depth of the world comes the suffering that both Schopenhauer and Nietzsche think are ineluctable features of existence. Such suffering is referred to with terms such as "woe" and "agony." At the same time, we learn that "joy [*Lust*]"[23] is deeper than agony. Similarly, we learn that "woe" or "pain [*Weh*]" implies or implores "decay [*Vergeh*]" or transience.[24] But here again, we learn that just as joy is deeper than any suffering, joy [*Lust*] desires not death or transience, but rather "eternity [*Ewigkeit*]." The stanza of the eleventh bell repeats this: "wants deep, wants deep eternity."

In "The Drunken Song" of *Zarathustra* IV, we are provided with what is effectively a commentary on this song, and we learn there that the name of the song is "Once More [*Noch ein Mal*]."[25] The theme of "once more" is clearly associated with the eternal recurrence, and this comes to the fore toward the end of the song where we learn that all joy wants eternity, "deep eternity." In short, finding pleasure or joy in the world is deeper than the suffering or agony of the world, and therefore rather than wanting the world to perish (as evaluative pessimists do), this sort of joy longs to immortalize or eternalize the world. In this way, the relationship between joy [*Lust*] and eternity in the conclusion of "The Other Dancing Song" corresponds to the understanding of the relationship between the past (*Vergangenheit*) and transience (*Vergänglichkeit*). The more we love the "it was" (*amor fati*) and therefore the chain of events that constitutes nature (*Vergangenheit*), the more we long for the eternalization of these events (thereby overcoming *Vergänglichkeit*). In terms of ancient Greek poetry (and expressed by Diotima in Plato's *Symposium*), the conclusion of *Zarathustra* III follows the idea that the ultimate object of love or poetic *eros* is immortality. Expressed in terms of *Zarathustra*, the ultimate object of the will to power (a form of poetic *eros*) is the eternal recurrence of all things (the mystery teaching of Dionysian worship).

It is also worth noting the close connection between the themes in this song and the central idea of *The Birth of Tragedy*. In the penultimate section of that work, Nietzsche explains how tragedy provides an aesthetic justification of existence by appealing to the phenomenon of musical dissonance. Specifically, musical dissonance shows that we can find great joy even in the deepest pain and therefore shows that we can love life even though it includes suffering and death (BT 24). Although not mentioned explicitly by Nietzsche, the most important example of musical dissonance is Wagner's "Tristan chord" at the beginning of *Tristan and Isolde*. Nietzsche praises *Tristan and Isolde* in both *The Birth of Tragedy* (BT 21) and *Richard Wagner in Bayreuth* (WB 8), and Vivarelli (2017) has shown that much of the vocabulary used in "Once More" (e.g., *Acht, Nacht, Tag, erwacht*) comes from *Tristan and Isolde*. Because Nietzsche considers this opera to be Wagner's tragedy *par excellence*, we have further evidence for thinking that *Zarathustra* is Nietzsche's own tragedy.

Before we leave behind "Once More" or Zarathustra's "Midnight Song," it is necessary to address the question of whether Zarathustra dies in some sense with the tolling of the twelfth bell at midnight. The answer is that we simply do not know, and Nietzsche left us with very little, if anything, to help us resolve the matter. Nevertheless, Loeb has argued that, despite his convalescence, Zarathustra's confrontation with the eternal recurrence has left him "a shattered man." In confronting the abysmal thought, Zarathustra "inflicts tremendous suffering upon himself, and by these means ultimately brings about his own death" (2010:77). According to Loeb, this death occurs exactly with the last toll of the bell at midnight, and it is represented by the silence that follows it (2010:80).

To be sure, there are hints in the surrounding text that support such a reading. At the end of section two of "The Other Dancing Song," Life links the striking of the bell to Zarathustra's desire to leave her. The most natural reading of Life's accusation is that Zarathustra therefore wants to die (thus leaving Life). We have also seen that these final chapters depict Zarathustra's "going under" ("The Convalescent":2). Since this is clearly not a "going under" in the sense of going down among the people, it is best understood as a tragic "going under" that is often associated with death and destruction. We also know from "The Stillest Hour" (*Zarathustra* II) that when Zarathustra speaks his word—presumably an allusion to the eternal recurrence—he will also "break" and perhaps die from his word. Finally, there is a long poetic tradition that associates the striking of the midnight bell with death. Whereas Loeb points to Goethe's *Faust* (2010:42–43), Daniel Conway (2008) discusses John Donne's poem, "For Whom the Bell Tolls." As Vivarelli explains (2017:312), Nietzsche also couples night with death in his discussion of *Tristan and Isolde* in *Richard Wagner in Bayreuth* (WB 8; also see Nietzsche's discussion of Isolde's "metaphysical swansong" in BT 22).

If *Zarathustra* were to end entirely with the tolling of the twelfth bell (coupled with the silence that follows it), the evidence for reading the conclusion of "The Other Dancing Song" in this way would be significant. However, *Zarathustra* does not end on this note. Instead, *Zarathustra* III concludes with Zarathustra expressing his love for and his desire to have children with Eternity (he therefore seems to be alive and well), and *Zarathustra* IV then continues the narrative with a much older Zarathustra as its protagonist. Although Loeb's reading of *Zarathustra* IV as an analeptic satyr play offers a way to reconcile Zarathustra's continued existence after the tolling of the twelfth bell, we have seen that it is not easy to fit the action of *Zarathustra* IV within the narrative of "On Old and New Tablets" and there is evidence from the *Nachlass* that speaks against the idea that Nietzsche staged Zarathustra's death at the end of *Zarathustra* III. Finally, scholars such as Del Caro (2011:84) have noted the tension between this reading of the conclusion of *Zarathustra* III, in which Zarathustra is said to commit suicide with the tolling of the twelfth bell, and the idea that *Zarathustra* is supposed to be, in some deep sense, a life-affirming work. Indeed, the fact that a "Yes and Amen Song" follows upon "Once More" suggest that just as joy is deeper than any agony, Zarathustra's love for eternity can overcome the reality of death and transience implied by the tolling bells at midnight.

It is for these reasons that I think we should understand the transition from the tolling twelfth bell at midnight to "The Yes and Amen Song" as a transition from Zarathustra's "going under" to Zarathustra's "going over." That is, it is meant to represent a threshold experience that is part of Zarathustra's initiation into the mysteries of Dionysus. On this reading, Zarathustra "dies" at midnight in the sense that he has an ecstatic experience of the world beyond "the principle of individuation." Like the ecstatic experience at "noon," Zarathustra feels himself to be at one with nature. However, unlike "noon," in which he is fully conscious of himself and his union with the world, he loses himself and his conscious "I" in the midnight experience and unites with a natural world. Feeling himself united with and even identical to nature, he can now experience the eternal process of creation and destruction as a child-like game that nature plays with herself (BT 24; PTAG 7; ZI "On the Three Metamorphoses").

This union with nature also results in a longing to have children with Eternity, and this longing is clearly expressed in "**The Seven Seals or: The Yes and Amen Song.**" The third section of the song initially bore the title, "Dionysus" (KSA 14:325), and readers like Del Caro (1988:138) have used this to argue that "The Seven Seals" is a dithyramb to Dionysus.[26] This is further evidence for thinking that Zarathustra has been initiated into the mysteries of Dionysus and now feels at one with the god. The title of the chapter is a clear reference to the apocalypse described in the book of Revelations in the Bible, and it is meant to provide an alternative to these apocalyptic fantasies. Just as such apocalyptic fantasies evince the life- and world-denying character of Christianity, the new seven seals of *Zarathustra* commit one to the eternal repetition of this world, thereby exhibiting the life-affirming culmination of the text. As Lampert has pointed out, "The Seven Seals" effectively moves through the various roles that Zarathustra has taken on in the text. Thus, in each of the seven stanzas, we find Zarathustra "celebrating himself serially as soothsayer, destroyer, creator, bringer of harmony, seafarer, dancer, and finally, supremely, flier." All of these prove his fitness to marry Life and so Eternity (1986:241) and evidence his final overcoming of the spirit of gravity.

Interestingly, Zarathustra first presents himself as a soothsayer. The soothsayer was a figure that Zarathustra encountered in his journeys, but the soothsayer was also a figure that Zarathustra opposed in at least one sense. That is, Zarathustra clearly opposes the life-denying conclusions the soothsayer drew from his insight that "all is the same, all has been!" At the same time, Zarathustra's acknowledged role as the teacher of the eternal recurrence has him embracing this very idea, i.e., "all is the same, all has been!" Here, Zarathustra also presents himself as the redemptive flash of the lightning bolt and someone pregnant with lightning bolts. We know from the prologue that Zarathustra had originally associated the lightning bolt with the *Übermensch*, but also that the youth in "On the Tree on the Mountainside" in *Zarathustra* I claimed that Zarathustra was this lightning bolt. Has Zarathustra himself therefore become an *Übermensch*? Perhaps, but the text is not clear. What is clear is that he lusts after "the nuptial ring of rings, the ring of recurrence," and that he only wants children from Eternity.

In the second stanza, Zarathustra speaks of his wrath. He mentions bursting tombs, a possible reference to "The Tomb Song." He talks about moving "boundary stones," something he links to teaching humans how to fly in "On the Spirit of Gravity." He claims that he has rolled old and broken tablets, which is a clear reference to "On Old and New Tablets." He then speaks about using a broom to sweep away "the cross-marked spiders." These cross-marked spiders are a symbol of Christian revenge (see "On the Tarantulas" in *Zarathustra* II), and Zarathustra then speaks of his love for old churches as tombs of gods. Such language recalls Zarathustra's first mention in the prologue of the death of God, and now Zarathustra claims that he enjoys sitting "on broken churches." Thus, he again lusts after "the ring of rings, the ring of recurrence."

In the third stanza, Zarathustra extolls his role as a creator. In so doing, he connects his creative activity to an understanding of the universe that includes descriptors such as accident (*Zufall*), dice, and dance. In "On Redemption," Zarathustra speaks of redeeming humanity from accident, and in "On the Virtue that Makes Small," Zarathustra proclaims himself to be the godless one who cooks chance (*Zufall*) in his pot. Herein lies his creativity: he is able to take accidents and weave them into an interpretation that lends them meaning and significance. As I have argued, this is precisely what Zarathustra means by "backward willing" in "On Redemption." At the same time, the idea of associating the world with a game of dice played by the gods gestures toward the ability to find pleasure in meaningless play. The conception of the world as a game of dice has already been presented in "Before Sunrise," and this notion can also be found in Nietzsche's late *Nachlass* in which he articulates his "new world-conception" with the eternal recurrence as its centerpiece (KSA 13:14[188]). The notion of play can be linked to the Heraclitean child of "On the Three Metamorphoses," and dance immediately associates this world-conception with the arts of Dionysus. This might explain why "Dionysus" was the original title of the stanza (KSA 14:325).

In the fourth stanza, Zarathustra speaks of blending various opposites together: "if my hand ever poured the farthest to the nearest, and fire to spirit, and joy to pain, and the most wicked to the most gracious." This blending or weaving together of opposites includes the union of "good with evil." The unity of opposites is a Heraclitean principle that can be found in the penultimate section of *The Birth* in Nietzsche's discussion of musical dissonance and the life-affirming powers of tragedy (BT 24). It then receives a fuller treatment in *Philosophy in the Tragic Age of the Greeks*, and Nietzsche makes this his own principle at the beginning of both *Human, All Too Human* (HH 1) and *Beyond Good and Evil* (BGE 2). The latter text is significant because Nietzsche understands *Zarathustra* as moving us to a standpoint beyond good and evil, and this stanza provides evidence for linking Zarathustra's teaching of the eternal recurrence to beyond good and evil.

In the fifth stanza, Zarathustra presents himself as a seafarer fond of the sea, driven to undiscovered waters. *Zarathustra* III began with Zarathustra descending to the sea, leaving behind the blessed isles. The imagery of the sea however predates even *Zarathustra*. At the end of *Daybreak*, Nietzsche speaks of birds flying farther and farther until everything is open sea (D 575). In the section preceding the announcement of the death of God in *The Gay Science*, Nietzsche equates the sea with the "horizon of the infinite" (GS 124). The horizon is now infinite because of the death of God and the elimination of his shadow (GS 125). Nietzsche returns to this theme in the opening aphorism of the fifth book of *The Gay Science*, which was added to the 1887 edition. There, after discussing the death of God, Nietzsche writes:

> At long last the horizon appears free to us again, even if it should not be bright; at long last our ships may venture out again, venture out to face any danger; all the daring of the lover of knowledge is permitted again; the sea, *our* sea, lies open again; perhaps there has never yet been such an 'open sea.'
>
> (GS 343)

In the penultimate stanza, Zarathustra presents himself as a dancer capable of laughter. We have already noted the close connection between dance and Dionysus. It again attests to the lightness of a soul that has overcome the spirit of gravity. This is also true of laughter, which is something closely associated with the worship of Dionysus that will take centerstage in *Zarathustra* IV. In this stanza of "The Seven Seals," we learn that "in laughter all that is evil comes together, but is pronounced holy and absolved by its own bliss." It is through the blessing of laughter that everything becomes light, and with this lightness one not only learns to walk, then run, and then dance, but also how to fly. A soul capable of flight is a soul that has vanquished the spirit of gravity, and it is with a soul capable of flight—and here again we can think of the wings of *eros*—that Zarathustra wants to have children with the woman Eternity.

The final stanza emphasizes both flight and song. Specifically, Zarathustra speaks of a "bird-wisdom" closely connected to freedom (we can also think of the "Songs of Prince Free Bird" at the end of the 1887 edition of *The Gay Science*). This bird-wisdom proclaims that there is no above and no below, an implicit reference to the idea that there is no center of the universe now that God has died. Along with the lightness that allows the soul to fly, Zarathustra commands his soul to "Sing! Speak no more!" The spoken word is heavy, and singing is more fitting for aeronautics of the spirit. Like dance, Nietzsche associates song with Dionysus, and here again we can think of the dancing and singing of the Dionysian chorus of an ancient Greek tragedy. Thus, the tragedy of *Zarathustra* III ends with Zarathustra singing his love for Eternity and eternal life, which, according to *The Birth*, is the ultimate point of tragedy (BT 16).

NOTES

1 Nietzsche also considered using "Once more [*Noch ein Mal*]" as a title for one of the closing chapters of *Zarathustra* III (KSA 11:22[8], 23[10]).
2 See Salaquarda (1989) for more on the "*Ungeheure Augenblick.*" Loeb (2010: Ch.3) argues that this represents the moment of death. I am not convinced that "moment" necessarily means "moment of death" or "the last moment of life" or that Nietzsche is trying to imply this here.
3 Seung (2005) emphasizes this point throughout his study. Loeb (2002:97f.) holds that the future is still open to change.
4 Löwith (1997:70) interprets the howling of the dog as a foreshadowing of the higher men's cry of distress.
5 I thank Scott Jenkins for bringing this to my attention.
6 See Groff (2004) for further reflections on Zarathustra's ape and Groff (2022) for reflections on how this chapter cuts against Nietzsche's seeming pretensions for a great politics.
7 See Loeb (2010:201) for a different interpretation of this letter.
8 Here again, Kaufmann seemingly mistranslates "*Nehmen*" as "receive."
9 This is my translation of "*Schonen.*"
10 See Meyer (2014b) for more on this point.
11 See Ioan (2021) and Owen (2009) for further reflections on self-love in relation to Zarathustra and *amor fati*.
12 Indeed, Nietzsche's portrayal of Jesus, as a knower of the heart, at the end of BGE 269 suggests that the psychological essence of Christianity consists in the inability to love oneself and therefore a corresponding need for someone or something to provide this love. At its height, this need culminates in the invention of a God that is all love.
13 Grätz (2024b) has identified several instances in "On Old and New Tablets" in which Nietzsche alludes to or quotes from Hölderlin's *Death of Empedocles*. To recall, Hölderlin's unfinished drama was the inspiration for one of Nietzsche's earliest attempts to write his own tragedy in the early 1870's. Grätz finds such allusions in sections 3 (254–255), 8 (262), 12 (270), 21 (288–291), and 26 (300). The mere fact that the model for Nietzsche's early attempt at his own Empedocles tragedy is now playing such a significant role near the climax of *Zarathustra* provides further support for the idea that Nietzsche understands *Zarathustra* to be his own tragedy.
14 See my discussion in chapter two of Loeb's (2010) alternative reading of the text.
15 The parallels to Nietzsche's own attempt to tell himself to himself in *Ecce Homo* are striking.
16 Translation taken from CWFN 14.
17 See Mack (2021).
18 See Clark (1990:256) for a version of such a reading.
19 Loeb (2010:156) favors this latter interpretation.
20 As Seung (2005:168) observes, "Zarathustra's great disgust with man is his great disgust with himself."

21 See EH "Books" Z:8 for Nietzsche's remarks about the presence of Ariadne and Dionysus in *Zarathustra*.
22 "Vita Femina" was the original title of the chapter, which is the same title as GS 339 (KSA 10:324).
23 I use Kaufmann's translation of "*Lust*" as "joy," even though "pleasure"—as the opposite of "pain" or "*Weh*"—might work better in some cases in this context.
24 Kaufmann renders this as "go." This loses the close connection between *vergehen* and *Vergänglichkeit* or transience.
25 The song is also called "O Man, Take Care," "The Midnight Song," and "Zarathustra's Roundelay." See Grätz (2024b:381–382) for more on the multiplicity of titles.
26 I borrow this point from Grätz (2024b:351 and 391). Grätz notes that Del Caro mistakenly held that "Dionysus" was the original title for the entire chapter rather than just the third stanza.

6
THUS SPOKE ZARATHUSTRA IV

It is now common for all four parts of *Zarathustra* to be published together as one unit. This, however, was not always the case. During his lifetime, Nietzsche only released the first three parts of *Zarathustra* to the larger public, even when he published them together as a single volume in 1887. *Zarathustra* IV was not released to the public until 1892 as a separate work and only in 1893 did it appear as part of the four-volume edition that we now know today (Grätz 2024b:418–419). Thus, even though the text still falls under the same name and the main character remains the same, there is something fundamentally different about *Zarathustra* IV. Indeed, Nietzsche took a break of about nine months between the completion of *Zarathustra* III in January of 1884 and beginning work on *Zarathustra* IV in the fall of 1884. In terms of content, one difference is that the tragedy of *Zarathustra* I–III is now over, and therefore it is written from the standpoint of Zarathustra having been initiated into the mysteries of Dionysus at the end of *Zarathustra* III. That is, Zarathustra has undergone a ritualized death, and he now feels himself to be reborn as a person now at one with nature and necessity. As such, he experiences himself as a child that has recaptured the "innocence of becoming" and gone "beyond good and evil."

In ancient Greek theater, the playfulness of the child was best expressed in the genre of the satyr play. Satyr plays did deal with serious matters, but the seriousness often dissolved into laughter and absurdity. During the height of ancient Greek theater in fifth-century Athens, tragic playwrights were required to submit a tetralogy of three tragedies and a concluding satyr play. The content of the satyr play was often, but not always, related to the tragedies that preceded it. Unfortunately, very few satyr plays survive. Perhaps the best example of we have of a satyr play submitted along with a tragic trilogy of related content is Aeschylus' *Proteus*, of which we only have fragments, that was submitted along with his *Oresteia*. Very little is known about the *Proteus*, but it seems to have told a story of Menelaus' journey home from the Trojan wars that parodies Agamemnon's tragic homecoming in which he is killed by his wife, Clytemnestra, upon his arrival (this begins the tragedy of the *Oresteia*).[1]

Zarathustra IV does have serious content, but as Nietzsche's own satyr play, it is nevertheless written in the "mood" of a comic "Mr. Sausage [*Hanswurst*]" (KSB 7:573). The serious matter at hand is the temptation of pity, and it is generated by the distinction between Zarathustra's standing as one who has been initiated into the mysteries of Dionysus (perhaps an aged papa Silenus) and the buffoonish higher men (satyrs) who are seeking him out. In *Zarathustra* III, we saw Zarathustra fleeing the poisonous rabble into solitude because he had to perfect himself. Even though he was able to achieve this and eventually summon the eternal recurrence, his solitude is now coming to an end. Thus, the question is how he will respond when he is confronted by others, especially those who seek his help and see him as their redeemer. Will he feel pity? Or will he remain true to himself and his work? Either way, there is an air of humor that pervades the action, and even though Zarathustra is open to taking on this role, the desperation with which the higher humans pursue Zarathustra as their supposed redeemer is reminiscent of Monty Python's *Life of Brian* in which a crowd of followers desperately pursue an unsuspecting Brian in hopes that he may redeem them.

The threat of pity comes from the fact that the higher human beings have not overcome the nausea and disgust they feel about themselves. For this reason, they are all characterized, both in Nietzsche's notes and in *Zarathustra* IV, as *missrathen*, which can be translated as "ill-constituted" or "failures." This, then, is the essence of the cry of distress from the higher human beings, and they are all seeking out Zarathustra as a figure who might be able to help relieve their distress. Because Zarathustra is an example of being well-constituted or *Wohlgerathenheit*, they see Zarathustra as something like their redeemer. Unlike the *missrathen* higher humans, Zarathustra is able to love himself and therefore is a convalescent. But rather than loving themselves, the higher humans now want to be loved by Zarathustra. In other words, they want Zarathustra's pity or love in the sense of Christian neighbor love or *agape*. Although Zarathustra is trying to avoid the temptation of pity, he nevertheless invites them all back to his cave for a celebration. It is at this celebration, one that parodies the last supper of Christ and culminates in an ass festival, that even the ugliest man says that he is satisfied with his whole life and is willing to say to death, "once more."

Zarathustra IV ends with a sign that comes to Zarathustra. The sign is in the form of laughing lions with doves that, as we are told in "On Old and New Tablets" from *Zarathustra* III, signals Zarathustra's time to leave the solitude of his cave and go down among humans again. Here, the laughing lion represents the ability to command, and there is reason to think that when Zarathustra steps out of the cave in the morning, he is now ready to go among men again, just as he did in the prologue of *Zarathustra* I. The difference, however, is that he is now ready to rule, rather than merely preach the *Übermensch* in the marketplace. This is because Zarathustra has since become ripe. Therefore, he can now engage in his work, which is nothing less than legislating a revaluation of values. Because this is something that Nietzsche himself undertakes in his later works, this reading implies a continuity between Nietzsche and Zarathustra. Just as the figure of Zarathustra emerges from Nietzsche's efforts in his free spirit works, Nietzsche continues the work of Zarathustra in his post-*Zarathustra* writings. However, he will do so by donning the "second mask" of Dionysian theater (BGE 278). In his 1888 works, Nietzsche will take on the role of a *Hanswurst* and write as "the grand old eternal comic poet of our existence" (GM "Pref":7).

6.1 ENCOUNTERS WITH THE HIGHER HUMANS: CHAPTERS 1–9

Zarathustra IV begins with months and years having passed since Zarathustra expressed his love for eternity in *Zarathustra* III. Zarathustra has spent his time in solitude and his hair has since turned white. The whiteness of his hair may suggest some sort of wisdom or even more speculatively that he is playing the role of Papa Silenus. In "**The Honey Sacrifice**," Zarathustra's animals find him outside his cave staring out over the sea and abysses, and they ask him if he is looking out for his happiness. In a move that foreshadows the end of the text, Zarathustra insists that he is no longer concerned with his happiness; instead, he is concerned with his work.

However, Zarathustra acknowledges that he is overflowing with happiness—a claim that points back to the gift-giving virtue presented at the end of *Zarathustra* I. His happiness is "heavy," and it seems to be oozing out of him like "melted tar." However, Zarathustra soon corrects himself. His animals claim that he is becoming yellower and darker—much like a grape ready to fall from a tree—and Zarathustra responds by acknowledging that he has honey—not tar—in his veins. This makes his blood thicker and his soul calmer. Nothing is clear, but the honey in Zarathustra's veins seems to be the result of his ripening, perhaps even his transfiguration that took place in confronting the eternal recurrence. In particular, the honey in his veins might be a result of the self-love he was able to achieve in the time he spent in solitude starting with "The Return Home" in *Zarathustra* III and therefore be a sign of his gift-giving virtue. We also know from *The Birth of Tragedy* that Nietzsche associates honey (and milk) with the Dionysian experience of overcoming the principle of individuation and uniting with nature and other individuals:

> Just as the animals now talk, and the earth yields milk and honey, supernatural sounds emanate from him, too: he feels himself a god, he himself now walks about enchanted, in ecstasy, like the gods he saw walking in his dreams.
>
> (BT 1)

Whatever the honey may represent, Zarathustra's animals recommend that he climb even higher on the mountain. Zarathustra agrees, and he claims that he can make a "honey sacrifice" up there. But this turns out to be only a ruse. Zarathustra has climbed the mountain to be able to speak more freely. He now admits that his "sacrifice" is really a squandering of the riches he has saved up in his soul. As for the honey he requested from his animals, that was bait. Here he compares himself to both a hunter and a fisher, and, in turn, he compares the human world to a rich sea full of human fish ready to be caught. The background to this is undoubtedly biblical, as it recalls Jesus' instruction to his disciples to become fishers of men.[2] Zarathustra is now such a fisher, and he has a golden rod that he will cast into the human abyss, fishing for his own disciples.

As Zarathustra's subsequent remarks make clear, there is a political dimension to Zarathustra's role as a fisher. He is looking for "new nobles" who will form a new caste of humans that function as "rulers of the earth [*Herrn der Erde*]" (KSA 11:25[134], 25[137], 35[72], 39[3]). Here, however, Zarathustra highlights the attributes that have made this political activity possible. As a fisher, he is someone who reels in and raises up, someone who disciplines and cultivates. He can do all this because he once counseled himself: "become who you are [*Werde, der du bist*]."

The importance of becoming who one is for Nietzsche's overall project cannot be overstated. It was the central theme of his early meditation, *Schopenhauer as Educator*,[3] and it became the leitmotif of Nietzsche's free spirit project. Specifically, Nietzsche seems to have executed in the free spirit works the very project he articulated, in theory, in *Schopenhauer as Educator* (see Meyer 2019). Importantly, the phrase of becoming who one is appears at the end of both books three and four of *The Gay Science* (GS 270, 335), and a variant is the subtitle to his 1888 *Ecce Homo*. Zarathustra's claim to have counseled himself to undertake this project thereby suggests a continuity between Nietzsche's own project and the achievements of his fictional character Zarathustra.

Zarathustra's remark should be understood as a claim to have achieved a certain level of cultivation such that he can now engage in the project of disciplining and breeding other human beings. That is, there is a sense in which he is ready to legislate. Nevertheless, he still resists the idea that he must go down to the people at this time. Here again, he uses the phrase of going under in the sense of going down to society: "I am still waiting for the sign that the time has come for my descent; I still do not myself go under, as I must do, under the eyes of men." The sign here likely refers to "the laughing lion with the flock of doves" that is mentioned at the end of *Zarathustra* II ("The Stillest Hour") and at the beginning of "On Old and New Tablets" in *Zarathustra* III. As we know, this sign will finally come to Zarathustra at the end of *Zarathustra* IV.

For now, Zarathustra claims that any men, any fish, must come up to him, which is an inversion of his initial going down at the beginning of *Zarathustra* I. Now, he has patience, and he will wait until his destiny calls. He is quite confident that his great *Hazar* will come one day. That is, Zarathustra will have a kingdom that will last a thousand years. This is in the distant future, but this distant hope stands "on eternal ground, on primeval rock." Again, nothing is clear, but the eternal ground on which Zarathustra's kingdom stands seems to be his teaching of the eternal recurrence. It is this teaching that will create a rank order of human beings and separate out those who are well-constituted (*wohlgerathen*) from those who are ill-constituted (*missrathen*). It is the former who will come to rule the earth. The latter, in contrast, will not be fit for rule. Indeed, they may even perish in response to the eternal recurrence. Important here is that these *missrathen* will soon populate the scene in *Zarathustra* IV, and Zarathustra will have to overcome the temptation to pity these individuals.

As Zarathustra waits for this sign, all he wants to do is "laugh, laugh" with his "wholesome sarcasm." He wants to send down from high mountains his "mocking laughter." It is this emphasis on laughter that provides evidence for reading *Zarathustra* IV as a satyr play and an interlude between the drama of *Zarathustra* III and the great politics of the post-*Zarathustra* works. In line with the motto at the beginning of *Zarathustra* III, Zarathustra now seems to be looking down from an elevated position. Having climbed the highest mountains, he can laugh "at all tragic plays and tragic seriousness" (see also ZI "On Reading and Writing"). For now, the glitter of this laughter will be bait for "the most beautiful human fish." Here he wants to fish out from the human sea only that which belongs to him. It is for these humans that he is waiting on high. Thus, he wants such humans to bite his fishing rod. Unfortunately, these are not the humans that are seeking him out.

In "**The Cry of Distress**," we encounter the first of a series of characters that invade Zarathustra's solitude and tempt him to his great sin, "pity." He is sitting again on the stone outside his cave, and he suddenly finds the old soothsayer standing next to him. Here, the reader is reminded that the soothsayer is the one who taught that "all is the same, nothing is worth while, the world is without meaning, knowledge strangles" (ZII "The Soothsayer"). Zarathustra recalls his encounter with the soothsayer and eventually welcomes him. The soothsayer, however, warns the cheerful Zarathustra that waves of melancholy will soon be approaching his cave. To recall, melancholy is what initially defines Zarathustra's archenemy, the spirit of gravity.

Listening more carefully, Zarathustra eventually hears the cry of distress about which the soothsayer is warning. It comes from the black sea—the color presumably represents melancholy. Zarathustra explains that this distress will tempt him to his final sin, and the soothsayer declares that he knows what that is: pity. Indeed, the soothsayer is there to seduce him to the final sin of pity. Here it is important to note two things. First, the fact that pity threatens Zarathustra points to a difference between Zarathustra and all those seeking him out. Whereas they suffer from precisely what Zarathustra had to battle in *Zarathustra* I–III (an initial inability to be at home with himself), Zarathustra no longer suffers from melancholy or revenge. Instead, the threat to Zarathustra comes in the form of the sympathetic feelings he may develop for the plight of those who have not or cannot overcome the feelings of discontent they have for themselves and the spirit of gravity that this creates. Second, the soothsayer is a character who largely represents Schopenhauer and his philosophy, and we know that pity lies at the heart of Schopenhauer's ethics. That is, it is pity for another's suffering and discontent that opens the door to Schopenhauer's larger project of the negation of the will or nihilism and therefore opposes Zarathustra's standpoint of life affirmation.

It is at this point that the soothsayer introduces us to the higher human (*der höhere Mensch*). Like many concepts in *Zarathustra*, just what constitutes a higher human is not clear. Loeb and Tinsley have argued that Nietzsche defines these higher human beings as those who are able to rule over others and have an overwhelming inclination to do this to the best of their ability. Inferior or lower human beings lack this ability and the corresponding desire. On this reading, the idea of the higher or superior human being is closely connected with Zarathustra's teaching of the will to power, understood by Loeb and Tinsley as the insatiable desire to dominate and control other human beings (2022:512). The goal of these higher humans is to facilitate the "self-overcoming of humankind" to create a race of *Übermenschen*. However, there are also failed higher human beings (the *missrathen*), and these are the higher humans that gather around Zarathustra in *Zarathustra* IV. According to Loeb and Tinsley, these higher human beings are filled with self-loathing because they have in some way failed to fulfill their true nature, which is to rule over other human beings (2022:517).

Although Loeb and Tinsley should be applauded for trying to explain exactly what it means to be a higher human being, I do not find their definition entirely convincing. The textual evidence they provide is sometimes tangential, and I see no reason why the will to power or the ability to rule is a distinguishing feature of higher humans. The desire for power is characteristic of everyone, even though some may be made sick by internal conflict and division, and all of us seem to have the ability to rule over others in some respect. All parents rule over their children, at least initially, and even the ascetic can be understood as attempting to rule herself. Finally, although the characters that appear in *Zarathustra* IV do suffer from self-loathing, there is little evidence that this is caused by their failure to rule over human beings in the way that Zarathustra demands. Instead, if there is a connection here, it seems to be the reverse of what Loeb and Tinsley argue. These ill-constituted (*missrathen*) higher humans are incapable of ruling precisely because they are filled with self-loathing. In the language of the *Genealogy*, these ill-constituted humans say, "I am sick of myself!" (GM III:14). In contrast, a well-constituted higher human like Zarathustra is capable of ruling precisely because he has learned to love himself. In the language of *Beyond Good and Evil*, Zarathustra exhibits the "egoism" (BGE 265) and "self-reverence" (BGE 287) characteristic of the noble soul.

Although I disagree with important features of Loeb and Tinsley's account, my own account overlaps with theirs in significant respects and is supported by some of the textual evidence they provide. Again, nothing is clear,[4] but I think we can start by contrasting higher humans with two types that play important roles in *Zarathustra* I–III: (1) the good and the just and (2) the last humans. What is characteristic of the former group is that they rule society by upholding and enforcing the conventions of that society simply because they are conventions. In contrast, higher humans all seem to stand above or beyond conventional society or are at least critical of the conventions that the good and the just enforce. In this sense, the saint that Zarathustra meets in the prologue of *Zarathustra* I is a higher human. Blind obedience to convention also characterizes last humans, but what is distinctive about last humans is their relative lack of disturbance about the human condition and the potential meaninglessness of existence. Thus, they exhibit a cow-like contentment with existence and therefore are immune to proclamations from figures like the madman (GS 125) and the soothsayer. In contrast, higher humans all exhibit a longing for something more and can therefore suffer from the kind of existential nausea about human existence that plagued Zarathustra in the first three parts of the text (see KSA 11:29[8]).

According to this understanding, Zarathustra is just as much of a higher human as the higher humans that eventually gather in his cave (this is also Loeb and Tinsley's view). However, unlike the ill-constituted higher humans that seek out Zarathustra for meaning and redemption (KSA 11:31[2]), Zarathustra is a well-constituted higher human.[5] The difference between a well-constituted and an ill-constituted higher human is the extent to which self-love or, as Loeb and Tinsley call it, self-loathing characterize their respective souls. Because Zarathustra is capable of self-love and can therefore "redeem" himself, he is capable of living in solitude in his cave and he does not seek out anyone else for comfort or even redemption. In contrast, the ill-constituted higher humans seek out someone like Zarathustra precisely because they are discontent with and nauseated by themselves. Ultimately, they want Zarathustra to provide them with the love they cannot feel for themselves. In short, they want Zarathustra's pity and love, and this is why they cry out in distress (KSA 11:26[289]; 31[8]).

Because pity is his greatest temptation and his "final sin,"[6] Zarathustra is troubled by the possible arrival of these higher humans. Indeed, he is "seized with horror." To compound this, the soothsayer utters more dire warnings. He insists that there is little happiness to be found in Zarathustra's cave. Even if he dances, he is the last gay (*frohe*) man. Such happiness cannot be found among hermits and their caves. Perhaps it can be found on the blessed isles. But again, the soothsayer insists that "all is the same, nothing is worth while, no seeking avails, nor are there any blessed isles any more" (ZIV "The Cry of Distress").

Zarathustra, however, gathers his courage and offers a strident response to the soothsayer. He insists that there are still blessed isles, and he blasts the soothsayer as a "raincloud in the morning" drenched with melancholy. Zarathustra now welcomes the higher humans to come to him in his realm. In this realm, higher humans will "not come to grief." Indeed, Zarathustra now plans to leave his cave and search for these higher humans in the surrounding forest. In the meantime, the soothsayer plans to wait in Zarathustra's cave for his return. In response, Zarathustra promises to make him both cheerful and gay once he returns. When he does, even the soothsayer will dance.

In the "**Conversation with the Kings**," Zarathustra does not have to search long to find the first of the higher humans. Here he encounters two kings wandering in his realm. The scene recalls the three kings or wisemen (Magi) on their way to visit the infant Jesus in Bethlehem. So interpreted, the implication is that Zarathustra—or the higher human whom the two kings are seeking—is the new redeemer, and he is now being sought by those looking to be redeemed. However, the two kings have brought with them an ass who happens to be carrying some skins of wine. The appearance of the ass, as well as the wine, is setting the stage for the later ass festival, and all of this gives the scene a comical atmosphere like Monty Python's *Life of Brian*.

When Zarathustra stumbles upon the kings, they do not recognize him as Zarathustra, even though they later claim to be, like Zarathustra, looking for "the higher man." Prior to recognizing Zarathustra, the two kings engage in a dialogue about their current situation. The king on the left worries that the hermit might have lost all manners, being away from society. The king on the right, however, responds by noting that they are trying to flee so-called "good manners" and "good society." Those who call themselves noble and good are actually "false and foul through and through." Accordingly, the noblest species today is the peasant, and they claim that the peasant should actually rule. What now rules is the motley "mob hodge-podge," and this is what the two kings are trying to escape.

Much like Zarathustra in the earlier parts of *Zarathustra* III, the kings claim to suffer from "nausea [*Ekel*]" (notice that Zarathustra makes no such complaints). They not only loathe the current situation but also themselves. It is possible to read this self-loathing—as Loeb and Tinsley do—as a failure of the two kings to take control of the mob. Here, we might infer that it is their lack of power that disgusts them. However, I read it differently. The two kings claim that they themselves have become "false, overhung and disguised with ancient yellowed grandfather's pomp, showpieces for the most stupid and clever and anyone who haggles for power today." The falsity here rests on that fact that they "are not the first and yet must represent" the masses, and this is what causes them disgust. That is, it is the fact that they are rulers but they themselves are not worthy of ruling. Thus, they end their remarks but asking, "what do we kings matter now?"

What underlies the kings' self-loathing is not that they do not rule, but that their rule and their position is not founded on the virtue Zarathustra extolls and connects to the "eternal ground" of the eternal recurrence. Indeed, Zarathustra points out to them that it was he who once asked about the value of kings. In response to their self-loathing, the kings claim that they are now seeking "the higher man," as the higher human is the one who is higher than they and therefore the one who truly deserves to rule: "for the highest man shall also be the highest lord on earth." The problem, therefore, is not that they have failed to exercise power. The problem is that they do not deserve to exercise power. Only the higher human (presumably of the well-constituted sort) deserves this. Because the higher human does not rule, even the mob can see that the rule of these kings is fraudulent. Thus, the mob becomes more and more strident, now claiming that they alone are virtue.

In the second section of "Conversation with the Kings," the king on the right now claims that they were searching for Zarathustra (the implication is that Zarathustra is the higher human for whom they were seeking). Evidently, they had heard about the scene from "The Child with the Mirror," and they were scared that Zarathustra had "the mocking grimace of a devil." However, they were pierced with Zarathustra's teachings (such as his claims about a good war), and it made them feel like frauds. To cure this feeling, they felt they had to find Zarathustra. Upon hearing this, Zarathustra invites them to his cave, letting them know that they should wait there as he continues his own quest to find "the higher man."

In "**The Leech**," Zarathustra encounters another figure that will eventually join him in his cave, "*the conscientious in spirit*" (this was the original title of the chapter (KSA 14:331)). Zarathustra comes across this figure by literally stepping on him. In fright, Zarathustra responds to the cries of this man by beating him more. Once he realizes what he is doing, he laughs and asks for forgiveness. There is some back and forth between Zarathustra and the man about whose realm it is. Insisting that it belongs to him, Zarathustra seems to compare himself to a god: "I am who I must be. I call myself Zarathustra." That is, Zarathustra is the one who is, the one who is real, genuine, and self-grounded. In short, he is the one who has become who he is.

Upon learning that it is Zarathustra who has stepped on him, the man is immediately transformed (the reaction is like someone encountering Jesus but to comic effect). Here he cries out: "*Who* else matters to me any more in this life but this one man, Zarathustra"? But then he adds: "and that one beast which lives on blood, the leech?" It is the leech who has caused his arm to bleed. But now he is confronted with an even greater leech: Zarathustra himself.

At this point, the man identifies himself as "*the conscientious in spirit*." Again, much is obscure, but there are reasons for thinking that this individual embodies what Nietzsche has called the "intellectual conscience" (GS 2). This is something that Nietzsche himself endorsed in his free spirit writings, and the honesty (*Redlichkeit*) of which this man speaks is also a key feature of Nietzsche's free spirit project. It is this honesty that forms the basis for this individual's commitment to science and his view that he would rather "know nothing than half-know much."

There are also reasons to think that this individual embodies the very asceticism and the related will-to-truth that Nietzsche criticizes in *Zarathustra* and in a work like the *Genealogy*. In the latter, Nietzsche describes the ascetic as a manifestation of "life *against* life" (GM III:13). Here, the leech is seduced by Zarathustra's claim that "spirit is the life that itself cuts into life." Despite this attribution to Zarathustra, there is reason to think this is precisely what makes this person in need of healing. In contrast to the conscientious in spirit, Nietzsche's own free spirit project culminated in the self-overcoming of this very idea. With the death of God in *The Gay Science*, one no longer had to place life in service of knowledge. Instead, both truth and falsity could be placed in service of a larger project that has life affirmation as its goal (BGE 4). Because he has yet to overcome the ascetic ideal and therefore eliminate all the shadows of God, the conscientious in spirit is still in need of healing, and Zarathustra therefore sends him up to his cave.

In "**The Magician**," we also encounter a figure who is characterized as an ascetic of the spirit. However, the magician does not initially present himself as such. Just as the soothsayer is often associated with Schopenhauer, there are reasons for associating the magician with Richard Wagner. As Grätz (2024b:515) notes,

Nietzsche refers to Wagner as an "old magician" in an 1882 letter to Köselitz (KSB 6:276). Although the magician is therefore also seen as an artist, the title of "magician" suggests an ability to create an appearance that is also an illusion. In this sense, the term is meant to be derogatory, and Zarathustra effectively unmasks the magician, revealing him for what he truly is (the critique here recalls the critique in "On Poets" in *Zarathustra* II). Before doing this, the convulsing maniac of a magician launches into what looks to be an extended dithyramb devoted to "the unknown god," i.e., Dionysus. Indeed, Nietzsche would later authorize a version of this poem for publication in his own name in his collection of *Dithyrambs of Dionysus* under the title, "Ariadne's Complaint," and Dionysus is explicitly named there. Here it is important to recall that Nietzsche identified the dithyramb as an important precursor to both tragedy and the satyr play in *The Birth of Tragedy* (BT 5 and 7) and that he characterized the fourth book of plans for a proto version of *Zarathustra* as a dithyrambic celebration of an eternally recurring life (KSA 9:11[197]).

In response to this dithyramb, Zarathustra beats the magician with a stick like he did with the leech. He calls him an "actor," a "counterfeiter," and a "liar from the bottom." Here again, one thinks of Nietzsche's interpretation of Wagner, as he repeatedly presents him as a "first-rate actor" (CW:8). The idea is that the magician's artistic creations are not genuine. They do not represent true passions or convictions. In this sense, he is a fraud, just like the two kings. The magician, however, admits as much: "I did all this only as a game." The magician claims that he was playing the role of the ascetic of the spirit, which is defined as someone in whom the spirit turns against itself, and this asceticism is again linked to a sort of death from "science" and "conscience."

Zarathustra, however, accuses the magician of being deceptive here, too. He is an ascetic of the spirit to some degree, and this is revealed by the one thing genuine in him, his nausea. Here again, Zarathustra had to confront such nausea as he was being choked by the snake of the small man, and Zarathustra overcame this nausea by overcoming his disgust with himself. So construed, the magician's nausea is a product of his own disgust with himself. Like the two kings, the magician feels that he is a fraud: "everything about me is a lie"; even his art nauseates him.

The magician's belief that he is a fraud in turn drives him to seek out one who is "genuine, right, simple, unequivocal, a man of honesty, a vessel of wisdom, a saint of knowledge, a great human being" ("The Magician":2). For this, Zarathustra gives him credit. However, the magician responds by insisting that he seeks Zarathustra. Here again, we encounter the difference between a Zarathustra who has overcome his self-disgust and those who are disgusted with themselves and therefore life. Nevertheless, Zarathustra resists the magician's claim that he embodies the greatness the magician seeks, insisting that he himself has never "seen a great human being." In so doing, he invites the magician up to his cave.

Zarathustra's next encounter in "**The Retired**" is with the last pope (the original title included an explicit mention of "the pope" (KSA 14:334)). The last pope is wandering through the woods looking for "the last pious man." This is a reference to the saint Zarathustra encountered at the beginning of *Zarathustra* I. Because the saint had been living in the forest, the saint had not heard about the death of God. Thus, he was still pious, and this is why the last pope refers to him as the last pious man. The last pope had been searching for the last pious man because he can no longer rejoice in his god, for that god has died. He is retired, and his memories are the only thing he has. The problem is that the last pope has since discovered that the old saint has died, too. Now, the last pope seeks Zarathustra, "the most pious of all those who do not believe in God."

In their conversation, Zarathustra explains that God died of his pity for man (in this sense, Zarathustra's temptation is the very thing that killed God). It was a man, not a god, on the cross, and thus God's love of humankind became his hell. The idea seems to be that God sacrificed himself out of love for humans who were not able to love themselves. In this sense, this type of selfless love—represented by the crucified Christ—culminates in the self-sacrificial death of the lover. As Nietzsche says in *Beyond Good and Evil*, this type of love seeks death (BGE 269). The last pope, however, corrects Zarathustra. He claims that in having served God, he knows the dead God better than Zarathustra. Not only was his son born of adultery, but it is also wrong to speak of the dead God as a God of love. The last pope points out that this god wanted to be a judge. A loving God, however, would not be a God of reward and retribution. Here again, this remark points forward to the first essay of the *Genealogy*, where we are told that the all-loving God of Christianity was really born of hate, evidenced by the fact that Christian love also created hell (GM I:15).

In their exchange, the last pope also claims that Zarathustra is the most godless because he himself believes in a god. This paradoxical utterance likely refers to Zarathustra's commitment to Dionysus, a god closely tied to nature and the celebration of the earth. It is this commitment that makes Zarathustra honest and leads him beyond good and evil. For this reason, Zarathustra is predestined "for blessing from eternity," and the last pope wants a scent of this blessing. Thus, he wants to be a guest in Zarathustra's cave. Zarathustra welcomes him, but also worries that he will not be able to remove his melancholy now that the old god is "thoroughly dead."

"**The Ugliest Man**" is a chapter that stands out among all of Zarathustra's encounters. Although it has only one section, it is lengthy, and the scenery changes as Zarathustra approaches the ugliest man. Zarathustra enters the valley of "Snake's Death," where there is no grass, trees, birds, or even animals. Here the ugliest man is presented as more like a monster than a human being. Upon seeing him, Zarathustra is tempted by pity. However, we are told that Zarathustra immediately resists this temptation, as his "face becomes hard."

Part of what makes the ugliest man so ugly is that he is the murderer of God. According to Zarathustra, the ugliest man killed God because God saw just how ugly he really was. Here again, the idea seems to be that the ideal of God is what makes the human ugly and shameful, and we feel an even greater sense of shame when we imagine this ideal looking down upon and judging us. Thus, the ugliest man expresses this desire to kill God as a form of "revenge against the witness." Again, revenge stems from self-dissatisfaction (GS 290; GS 359), and God is presented here as one source of this self-dissatisfaction and therefore the object of revenge.

Here, however, it seems that killing God has made the ugliest man even uglier. That is, he seems to be much like the pale criminal from *Zarathustra* I who was no longer equal to the deed after the fact. In this sense, the ugliest man is made ugly by the fact that he has not done what is necessary to justify this deed. In *The Gay Science*, we are told that humans must become gods to justify the murder of god (GS 125). In contrast, the ugliest man has yet to overcome the human condition, and he therefore suffers from what he has done.

In fleeing society, the ugliest man is fleeing the pity of others. Zarathustra is the one he seeks because he does not pity the ugliest man. Zarathustra also knows what it feels like to be the murderer of God. According to the ugliest man, Zarathustra teaches that "pity offends the sense of shame." This contrasts with the virtue that rules supreme among the people. This indicates that they have no respect "for great ugliness, for great failure [*Missrathen*]." The elevation of pity is the result of Jesus's preaching (although Jesus is not explicitly mentioned). Zarathustra, however, has warned against this error. All creators must be "hard" in the sense that they are above pity. Indeed, "all great love is over and above its pity."

Here again, Zarathustra instructs the ugliest man to find refuge in his cave. As he is departing from the ugliest man, he reflects on the human condition, noting just how ugly the human is. But he also remarks that he has "been told that man loves himself," and he wonders just "how great must this self-love be!" In contrast to this self-love, there is also much contempt. According to Zarathustra, the ugliest man is both a great lover and a great despiser. For this reason, it looks as if the ugliest man is "the higher man" whose cry Zarathustra heard. Although this is not explicit, such a characterization makes the ugliest man the exact opposite of the last human, a figure who has neither great love nor great contempt. Zarathustra loves this great contempt, but nevertheless ends by noting that man "is something that must be overcome."

A much softer tone is set for Zarathustra's encounter in "**The Voluntary Beggar**." He initially feels something "warm and alive" that is refreshing, but this turns out—with comic effect—to be cows. But Zarathustra hears a human voice among the cows, and it turns out to be a "peaceful man and sermonizer on the mount." Although Loeb and Tinsley have argued that this is David Friedrich Strauss (2022:521–522), in line with their view that all these higher humans must be Nietzsche's contemporaries, Weaver Santinello's claim that the voluntary beggar is Jesus or a Jesus-like ascetic seems more plausible (2005:51ff.). This sermonizer is seeking happiness on earth, and he wants to learn this from the cows. The problem with human beings, according to the sermonizer, is that they are afflicted by melancholy and nausea (again, the very things that afflicted Zarathustra in the first three books), and he thinks we can cure these ailments by learning from cows how to "chew the cud."

After speaking his piece, the voluntary beggar only then begins to wonder about the identity of his interlocutor, and at this point he realizes it is none other than Zarathustra. Important here is that Zarathustra is presented as "the man without nausea" and "the man who overcame the great nausea." In my view, all of this indicates that Zarathustra has already confronted his feelings of nausea about the small man and affirmed the eternal recurrence, as he does at the end of *Zarathustra* III. In this way, Zarathustra now stands above humanity, as the one man who is not afflicted with melancholy and nausea. Indeed, it is for this reason that the voluntary beggar greets Zarathustra as a kind of redeemer, kissing the hand of Zarathustra and having eyes filled with tears.

The voluntary beggar explains his reasons for fleeing society to live among the cows. He tried giving and preaching charity among the "mob," but the mob is in the process of revolting, and this mob rejects even his charity. The rich, however, are even worse. Much like the two kings, the voluntary beggar is nauseated by such individuals. Thus, he has decided to live among the cows.

The cow is not an insignificant figure in Nietzsche's philosophy. As Seung has noted, Nietzsche compares the Buddhist to a "perfect cow" in the late *Nachlass* (Seung 2005:258). In his earliest reflections on history, Nietzsche characterized the cow as a blissful animal who lives without a sense of self and therefore without historical memory (the cow is fully immersed in the moment, chewing the cud as it were):

> consider the cattle, grazing as they pass you by: they do not know what is meant by yesterday or today, they leap out, eat, rest, digest, leap about again, and so from morn till night and from day to day, fettered to the moment and its pleasure or displeasure, and thus neither melancholy nor bored.

In contrast, the human is plagued by the "it was," "that password which gives conflict, suffering and satiety access to man so as to remind him what his existence fundamentally is—an imperfect tense that can never become a perfect one" (HL 1). The voluntary beggar's wish to learn from the cows is therefore a desire to live unhistorically. The idea seems to be that we can overcome the nausea and melancholy that plagues humanity by becoming unhistorical and therefore inhuman (like a cow).

In *History for Life*, Nietzsche looks at alternative ways for the human to deal with the problem of history, and we have seen that the problem created by the "it was" stands at the center of the drama of *Zarathustra*. Indeed, the voluntary beggar's enthusiastic response to Zarathustra suggests that Zarathustra himself is the one who has redeemed himself from the problem of history. Rather than spending time among the cows, Zarathustra instructs the voluntary beggar to consort with his eagle and his serpent in his cave. In turn, Zarathustra leaves the beggar to continue his search for the one crying out in distress.

In **"The Shadow,"** Zarathustra encounters what will be the last of his invitees for his own "last supper." As Zarathustra is chasing off the voluntary beggar to his cave, his shadow calls him out and demands that he stop. Zarathustra initially ignores the shadow. But the shadow then chases after him, and this creates a ridiculous situation. Eventually, Zarathustra stops and demands to know who the shadow is. The shadow claims that he is also "a wanderer," but a wanderer who has lost his goal and his home. In this sense, he is like the "Eternal Jew," even though he might be neither eternal nor a Jew. The wanderer claims to have been with Zarathustra as he ventured into what is forbidden and overthrew all reverences, thus coming to believe that "nothing is true, all is permitted."

Like the other characters, the wanderer exhibits a sense of psychic and spiritual desolation. After finding the truth (and being kicked by it), he is no longer concerned about truth. He no longer loves anything, and therefore wonders why he should love himself. Nothing really pleases him, and he has no goal. He is trying to find his home, but he has no home: "O eternal everywhere, O eternal nowhere, O eternal—in vain!"

Interesting here is that Zarathustra characterizes his shadow as a "free spirit and a wanderer." At the end of *Human, All Too Human* (HH 638) and then most obviously in *The Wanderer and His Shadow*, Nietzsche presented himself both as a free spirit and a wanderer with a shadow. Free spirits and wanderers are figures who leave behind the conventions of the city in search of the truth (like the camel of the first metamorphosis). This, however, makes them homeless. Interesting here, however, is the juxtaposition and the contrast between Zarathustra and his shadow. Although both live outside of the city and Zarathustra was even presented as a wanderer in the first chapter of *Zarathustra* III, we know that Zarathustra, unlike his shadow, has made his own home and therefore is at home with himself in his cave in "The Return Home" in *Zarathustra* III. As we know from that chapter, Zarathustra made his cave his home by learning to enjoy his own solitude and his soul. If this is right, it seems to follow that this is something the shadow has not learned. This lack of self-love or even self-loathing is what makes all the higher humans that Zarathustra encounters in *Zarathustra* IV ill-constituted (*missrathen*) higher humans. Thus, Zarathustra again directs the shadow to his home, his cave, where he promises to have dancing in the evening, something that occurs when one learns to take pleasure in oneself.

6.2 A DRUNKEN INTERLUDE AT NOON: CHAPTER 9

It is interesting to reflect on the juxtaposition between Zarathustra sending his shadow to his cave and his experience in "**At Noon**." Noon, of course, is the time when shadows are minimized or even disappear. Based on what we know from Nietzsche's plans for

Zarathustra and his reflections on the eternal recurrence in the *Nachlass*, the importance of this chapter cannot be overstated. Indeed, we hear in *Zarathustra* I that the "great noon" stands in the middle between the beast and the *Übermensch*, and we know that Nietzsche considered giving the whole of *Zarathustra* IV the title, "Noon and Eternity" (KSA 11:31[30]).

We can elevate the significance of the passage by comparing it to an aphorism from *The Wanderer and His Shadow*. In *The Wanderer*, Nietzsche temporarily adopts a form of Epicureanism to confront the loss of the metaphysical world in the opening stages of *Human*. The Epicureanism he adopts takes the form of focusing on the "closest things" such as food, clothing, shelter, and the simple pleasures of daily life. However, toward the end of the work we find an aphorism with the title, "At Noon." The description of noon very much resembles what we find in *Zarathustra* IV. It consists of a repose "that can last for months or years." The sun is shining above, and Pan, the companion of Dionysus, is sleeping. All of nature has an expression of eternity on its face, and nothing troubles the soul. Thus, Nietzsche writes that it is "a death with open eyes." However, the aphorism ends, somewhat abruptly, by noting how this individual is sucked back into life, and along with life comes "desire, deception, forgetfulness, destruction, transience [*Vergänglichkeit*]" (WS 308).

Although it provides us with a striking image of "noon," the passage points to one of the problems that Epicurean philosophy fails to solve: the problem of transience and ultimately death. For the Epicureans, these realities are non-realities precisely because we never experience our own transience. When I am, death is not; when death is, I am not. However, one cannot escape the present awareness we have of our own transience, and this is something Epicurean philosophy does not solve. The difference between the passage from *The Wanderer* and "At Noon" in *Zarathustra* is that Zarathustra now experiences noon from the perspective of having incorporated the eternal recurrence. As I argued in previous chapters, one of the chief functions of the eternal recurrence is to provide a solution to the problem of transience [*Vergänglichkeit*] by eternalizing the cycle of nature. Because Nietzsche links the eternal recurrence to Dionysus, we can say that Dionysus provides the solution to the problem of transience that the Epicurean could not solve, and it thereby provides a more robust experience of noon that is now coupled with "eternity" in *Zarathustra* IV.

In the narrative of *Zarathustra* IV, Zarathustra's experience of noon is rather sudden and surprising. He has just encountered a series of intruder-like figures in his "realm," and very little is done to transition to this mystical experience. After running both with and from the voluntary beggar and his shadow, we learn that it is now noon, "when the sun stood straight over Zarathustra's head." At this time, Zarathustra encounters an old tree wrapped with a grapevine with yellow grapes hanging from it in abundance. This a clear allusion to Dionysus, and as Grätz (2024b:616 and 632) notes, the chapter likens Zarathustra's experience to a "strange drunkenness" and so an experience of Dionysian intoxication and ecstasy. Indeed, Nietzsche first described the noontime experience in "The Dionysian Worldview" (a precursor to *The Birth of Tragedy*) in which he appeals to Euripides' *Bacchae* to describe such a moment. Of particular interest is that Nietzsche describes this moment as one in which milk and honey flow from nature and nature celebrates its reconciliation with humans (DW 1).

In "At Noon," Zarathustra is tempted to break off a grape, but he is overcome by an even stronger desire to sleep during the noon hour. Here Zarathustra speaks to his heart: "Still! Still! Did the world become perfect just now?" With the world having become perfect, Zarathustra asks if his soul will sing. The question immediately recalls the closing chapters of *Zarathustra* III where Zarathustra commanded his soul to sing rather than to cry in response to his melancholy. Here, however, Zarathustra's soul does not sing, possibly because he no longer feels such melancholy. Noon is now drinking "an old brown drop of golden happiness," and his happiness laughs.

Zarathustra then remarks that he seems to have fallen into the well of eternity. The world has become perfect, round and ripe, comparable to a golden ring and a "golden round ball" (an image familiar from the final chapters of *Zarathustra* I). In terms of the arc of the text, it seems that Zarathustra has reached—or is continuing to enjoy—his moment of ripeness such that he is now ready to go down among humans once again (ZIII "Tablets":1–3). That is, he is ready for his sign to come at the end of *Zarathustra IV*. What therefore stands between this noontime experience and this sign is his "last supper" with the higher humans gathered in his cave.

It is worth reflecting on the notions of "noon" and "eternity" and what it means for the world to have become perfect. We know from *Twilight of the Idols* that Nietzsche understands *Zarathustra* to be the work in which the appearance-reality distinction is overcome (TI "Fable"). This means that there is no longer any metaphysical world that lies behind or exists in addition to the natural or apparent world. This is part of the reason why Nietzsche takes *Zarathustra* to be such a significant text: the teachings of the eternal recurrence and the will to power complete a system of naturalism, thereby eliminating the metaphysical world and making the natural world the only world. On this understanding, "noon" represents a moment in which this world is experienced as the only world, where the shadow (and so "appearance") is eliminated. In contrast to "midnight," noon is a time in which consciousness and even self-consciousness is at its peak. Just as there is no distinction between the world and appearance, there is no distinction between the self and its shadow.

What about eternity? Noon is not only a time in which there is no appearance-reality distinction, but also a time in which there is no desire for the world to be other than it is. For this to be the case, Zarathustra must overcome any revenge against the past (*Vergangenheit*) and love his fate. In so doing, he can experience the world as perfect. Without the eternal recurrence, such an experience is threatened by the recognition of the transience (*Vergänglichkeit*) of everything temporal (this is precisely what undercuts the experience of "noon" in *The Wanderer*). Because the mystery doctrine of the eternal recurrence imposes being onto becoming, it eternalizes the cycle of change and transience, forever preserving the noontime experience. In contrast to *The Wanderer*, where we have a noontime experience destroyed by transience, we now have, in light of the eternal recurrence, an experience of not just "noon" but "noon and eternity."

6.3 ZARATHUSTRA'S FEAST: CHAPTERS 10–18

No matter how long he felt himself to have slept, Zarathustra still has to get up, and he will now move from utter solitude to associating with humans once more. In "**The Welcome**," we find Zarathustra returning to his cave in the late afternoon, now with all the higher humans gathered there, and it is from his cave that he hears a "great *cry of distress*." This time it is not from a single individual; instead, it comes from all the voices in the cave. Going into the cave, he finds the men sitting there, with the ugliest man wearing a crown and two crimson belts. However, it is a party filled with melancholy, and the spirit of gravity pervades the atmosphere.

Indeed, Zarathustra initially addresses these higher humans as "you who despair [*Ihr Verzweifelnden*]"! Despair is repeated throughout the discourse, and it harkens back to Nietzsche's initial confrontation with despair at the end of the first chapter of *Human*. There, Nietzsche concludes the chapter by identifying despair as a possible response to the free spirit's discovery that there is no metaphysical world or higher purpose that guides humanity (HH 31, 33, 34). Nietzsche dodged the threat of despair in that work by suspending judgment on the value of life. Here, it again characterizes the psychological disposition of everyone in the cave except Zarathustra. The idea is that between *Human* and *Zarathustra* IV, Nietzsche has, through his free spirit project and now through his son, Zarathustra, conquered this life-negating affect as a possible response to the death of God and the loss of the metaphysical world. However, these free-spirited higher humans are still affected by it, and herein lies the discrepancy between Zarathustra and those gathered around him. As we have noted above, they are all ill-constituted higher humans who are sick of themselves. It is for this reason that these higher humans have sought out Zarathustra, the one who has learned to love himself.

We also encounter here the first inklings of the spirit of laughter that will eventually pervade the rest of *Zarathustra* IV, thereby giving reason to read it as a satyr play. Specifically, Zarathustra claims that he feels a sense of prankishness in the presence of these ill-constituted higher humans, and he feels strong enough to cure them, at least for the night, of their despair in his dominion. Indeed, he claims that these cries of distress must be met by someone who must come, "someone to make [them] laugh again, a good gay clown [*Hanswurst*], a dancer and wind and wildcat, some old fool." In the context of *Zarathustra* IV, this seems to be gesturing toward Zarathustra. However, it is not clear whether Zarathustra ever takes on the role of a *Hanswurst* in *Zarathustra* IV.[7] In the context of Nietzsche's later works, it is important to note that Nietzsche presents himself as such a *Hanswurst* in his 1888 writings and letters (EH "Destiny":1; KSB 8:1240), and therefore Zarathustra's claim could be understood as a proleptic reference to Nietzsche's later activity. Nevertheless, the implicit claim here is that laughter and comedy provide a direct response to feelings of despair, something that finds support from Nietzsche's reference to Baubo at the end of the preface to the 1887 edition of *The Gay Science* (GS "Pref":4). In Greek mythology, Baubo is known for cheering up Demeter as she was in despair about the abduction of Persephone. In comic fashion, Baubo does this by revealing her genitalia to Demeter, moving her to laughter.

The higher humans are all refreshed to hear Zarathustra's promise that no one in his home or region will come to despair. As the king on the right explains, even beholding Zarathustra makes them feel better, as they are now done with their cries of distress. The king on the right also explains what makes them feel so refreshed. Zarathustra has a strong and lofty will (this recalls the "solar will" of "Tablets":30),[8] much like a tall and strong tree, and it is this strong tree that stretches out its branches for its "*own* dominion," a commander and triumphant. This tree is also refreshing to the *missrathen* or the ill-constituted higher human. Because Zarathustra is such a refreshing sight, they all long for Zarathustra, and they now ask: "who is Zarathustra?" Without Zarathustra, they would again despair of the soothsayer's words: "Life is no longer worth while, all is the same, all is in vain." For these reasons, there are many who will soon be coming to Zarathustra's cave, pulling him out of his solitude. And because he has transformed the higher humans now in his cave, there will soon come those even better than these higher humans (this is a reference to Zarathustra's children near the end of *Zarathustra* IV).

Zarathustra is taken aback by all this veneration, but after a bit, he decides to tell his guests what he really thinks about them. They are all higher humans, but they are not high and strong enough for him. His guests are still sick, and as such, they still want to be spared (*Schonen*). In "The Return Home" from *Zarathustra* III, Zarathustra lists *Schonen* next to pity as one of his great dangers. It is therefore not surprising that he tells his guests that he shows no consideration, not even to his warriors. He also tells them that he needs smooth mirrors for his teaching, but there is much in them that is "crooked and misshapen." As such, they are mere bridges, and he hopes that yet even higher humans will climb right over them.

Zarathustra is therefore not waiting for his guests. Indeed, the buffoonish nature of his guests is intimated when the king on the left cracks a joke about Zarathustra's desire to speak in "clear" German. Instead, Zarathustra is waiting for someone else (his children), and when these others come, he will "go down [*niedersteigen*] for the last time." His guests are signs, however, that such higher humans are on their way. Unlike his guests, the coming humans are "*not* the men of great longing, of great nausea, of great disgust," and "the remnant of God." Instead, the coming humans are more triumphant and cheerful. These "*laughing lions* must come." Here, Zarathustra chides his guests for not knowing anything of his children, and he insists that his children are on their way to his cave. These are his "highest hope"!

As we can see, the closing part of "The Welcome" points back to the first section of "On Old and New Tablets" in *Zarathustra* III and points forward to the final chapter of *Zarathustra* IV, "The Sign." In the former, Zarathustra is waiting for his sign to go down (*Niedergang*) and go under (*Untergang*), as he wants to go among humans once more: "the laughing lion with the flock of doves." In "The Welcome," Zarathustra explains that this sign is coming, and in "The Sign," the laughing lion and the doves finally come to Zarathustra, both signs that Zarathustra's children are near.

In between "The Welcome" and "The Sign," we are treated to an evening festival in Zarathustra's cave. It begins with "**The Last**

Supper," and it is here that the playful spirit of the satyr play comes to the fore. Zarathustra's prophetic speeches may be well and good, but the soothsayer soon interrupts to point out one very important fact: he is hungry, and Zarathustra invited them for supper! This is followed by a parenthetical remark that Zarathustra's animals are now afraid that the soothsayer—on account of his enormous hunger—will soon want to eat them. The soothsayer then insists that he is also thirsty, and water will not be enough. He wants wine, as that will provide some convalescence and health. Fortunately, it turns out that the kings' ass has been carrying wine all along. The only thing they lack now is bread!

As Higgins (1987:204) notes, the last supper—and the chapters that follow in *Zarathustra* IV—is clearly meant to parody both the last supper of Jesus and his disciples as well as the dinner party that Plato dramatizes in the *Symposium*, which scholars have also noted contains a satyr play (Usher 2002). The title alone makes it an obvious play on Jesus' last supper, and the references to bread and wine make it even more obvious. Of course, the purpose here is not to drink the blood and eat the body of Christ, doing this in remembrance of his sacrificial death. Instead, they are going to gorge themselves on food and drink, slaughtering two lambs for their enjoyment. Here it should not be overlooked that Jesus is also understood as the "lamb of God." Possible references to Plato's *Symposium* also abound. For instance, one can readily connect Zarathustra's alertness in the early morning with Socrates' ability to stay up all night. There are further inversions. For instance, the soothsayer insists that he cannot live on speeches alone, needing food instead. In contrast, the *Symposium* focuses on speeches. Indeed, the *Symposium* begins with a general agreement that there will be no drinking—and certainly no dancing girls—because the guests are hungover from the night before. In contrast, "The Last Supper" already points to the excessive consumption of both food and wine and the drunkenness that ensues.

That said, there are speeches given at Zarathustra's last supper, and the speeches focus "**On The Higher Man**," the title of the next multipart chapter. In terms of its length, the chapter parallels "On Old and New Tablets" near the end of *Zarathustra* III. Both chapters begin with Zarathustra recounting his previous activity and teachings. In "The Higher Man," Zarathustra begins by referring to his initial folly: He first went to the marketplace, but when he spoke to all, he spoke to none (this seems to explain the subtitle of the book, "A book for all and none"). At this point, he was almost like the dead tightrope walker who had fallen from the rope. However, he avoided this fate by turning his back on the market and the mob. The mob insists that everyone is equal, that everyone is equal before God, that there are no higher humans. This, Zarathustra thinks, is wrong, and this is why he counsels his higher humans to flee the marketplace ("Higher Man":1).

God, however, has died, and Zarathustra repeats a line that runs throughout Nietzsche's thought: the death of God undermines the doctrine of equality. Thus, God's death leads to the resurrection of the higher human. Indeed, with the coming of the "great noon," it is now possible for the "higher man" to become "lord [*Herr*]." This statement is then followed by the claim that, "God died: now *we* want the *Übermensch* to live." The juxtaposition of these two statements suggests that Nietzsche is now equating a certain type of higher human—as one who replaces God as "lord"—with the *Übermensch*—who was also supposed to replace God. Of course, it cannot be the case that the ill-constituted or failed (*missrathen*) higher humans gathered in his cave are examples of the *Übermensch* who will become rulers of the earth (*Herr der Erde*). However, there are reasons for thinking that higher humans, like Zarathustra, who are well-constituted (*wohlgerathen*), can indeed take on this role and therefore that such higher humans are now equivalent to the *Übermensch* (ZIV "Higher Man":2).

In the next section, Zarathustra repeats the idea that he does not love the human as such: "not the neighbor, not the poorest, not the most ailing, not the best." This again repeats his rejection of Christian neighbor love. Instead, he loves the human insofar as he is both a going over (*Übergang*) and a going under (*Untergang*). The higher humans gathered around him are great despisers, and this gives Zarathustra hope. However, the current situation, one in which the mob rules, creates much nausea (*Ekel*). Indeed, a *Nachlass* note indicates that a higher human is distinguished by the nausea he feels about the fact that the masses and their contentment rule today (KSA 11:29[52]). The masses want the human to be preserved the best, the longest, and most agreeably. These people and this attitude constitute the great danger for the *Übermensch* (ZIV "Higher Man":3).

After highlighting the need for courage (ZIV "Higher Man":4) and even "evil" (ZIV "Higher Man":5), Zarathustra again insists that he is not there to make the higher humans more comfortable. His mind and his longing "are directed toward the few, the long, the distant." For this reason, their sufferings matter little to him. Indeed, they have not yet suffered enough. Unlike Zarathustra, they only suffer from themselves. They, however, do not suffer from the human as such. In contrast, Zarathustra claims to have suffered from the human, and this is precisely what he had to overcome at the end of *Zarathustra* III (ZIV "Higher Man":6).

Toward the latter half of the section, Zarathustra begins to instruct the higher humans on how they can contribute to the cause. First, he insists that if they are going to "go high," they must use their own legs. They should not let someone or something else carry them up (ZIV "Higher Men":10). They should also avoid doing things for the sake of the neighbor. This is again a warning against Christian "neighbor love," and Zarathustra rejects this as a virtue of "the little people." As such, they have neither the right nor the strength for their "egoism [*Eigennutz*]." This egoism is a sign of pregnancy, and everything should be focused on what one loves, the child, not the "neighbor" (ZIV "Higher Man":11).[9]

Toward the end of the section, Zarathustra begins to speak of the failures of the higher human beings. Zarathustra has often seen the higher humans fail (*missreith*) because they "have not learned to gamble and jest as one must gamble and jest." Because they have failed, there is reason to think that they themselves are failures (*missrathen*) and therefore that the human being is a failure (*missrathen*). Because of these failures, Zarathustra counsels these higher humans to learn to laugh at themselves "as one must laugh." Interestingly, Zarathustra does not counsel himself to laugh at himself and therefore he is not the object of laughter here. Much is still possible, and the earth is rich "in little good perfect things, in what has turned out well [*an Wohlgerathenem*]!" The golden ripeness of these things heals the heart, and "what is perfect," perhaps like Zarathustra, "teaches hope" (ZIV "Higher Man":14–15).

Zarathustra knows that laughter has been traditionally condemned, especially within Christianity and by Christian ascetics.[10] Here, we only need to think of Jorge de Burgos from Umberto Eco's *The Name of the Rose* to grasp the historical tension between laughter and Christianity. Indeed, Zarathustra is counseling higher humans to respond to, even redeem, their failures—what might also be called "sins"—by laughing about them. It is for this reason that Christianity counsels, "woe unto those who laugh." Those who laugh about their sins stand in no need of God's love and forgiveness, and therefore such laughter renders God superfluous. For Zarathustra, it is laughter, not Christ, that washes away the sins of the world.

Along with laughter, Zarathustra encourages his higher humans to dance: "but whoever approaches his goal dances." By dancing, one can run right through the melancholy of the swamp. Thus, we hear Zarathustra exhorting his higher humans: "Lift up your hearts, my brothers, high, higher! And do not forget your legs either. Lift up your legs too—you good dancers; and better yet, stand on your heads" (ZIV "Higher Man":17). This is followed by Zarathustra claiming that he is the only one strong enough to pronounce laughter holy: "This crown of him who laughs, this rose-wreath crown: I myself have put on this crown, I myself have pronounced my laughter holy" (ZIV "Higher Man":18) Here again, the reference to a rose-wreath crown contrasts sharply with Christ's crown of thorns: The former signifying a life-affirming attitude; the latter signifying death and the denial of life. The upshot is that Zarathustra is now crowning himself as the new redeemer who will replace an other-worldly redemption through Christian love with a this-worldly redemption through Dionysian laughter.[11]

The entire speech to the higher humans concludes with Zarathustra lamenting that these higher humans have not learned to dance. It should not matter, he explains, that they are *miss-rathen*; there is still much that is possible. Thus, they must also learn to laugh over themselves. "Lift up your hearts, you good dancers, high, higher! And do not forget good laughter. This crown of him who laughs, this rose-wreath crown: to you, my brothers, I throw this crown. Laughter I have pronounced holy; you higher men, *learn* to laugh!" (ZIV "Higher Man":20). The call for higher humans to learn to laugh can be connected to the laughing lions that appear at the end of *Zarathustra* IV. Whereas these ill-constituted higher humans must *learn* to laugh, the laughing lions are, like Zarathustra, both well-constituted and ripe. What this suggests is that the capacity for laughter is essential feature of the well-constituted individuals or nobles for whom Zarathustra is waiting. It is therefore no coincidence that Nietzsche closes his chapter on nobility at the end of *Beyond Good and Evil* by establishing a rank order of noble philosophers according to the rank of their laughter (BGE 294).

Zarathustra's sanctification of laughter would seem to set the stage for the centerpiece of the satyr play in "The Ass Festival." However, "**The Song of Melancholy**" begins with Zarathustra stepping out of the cave to get some fresh air and be alone with his animals (evidently, the *missrathen* guests are stinking up the place). As soon as he does this, the magician steps forward, claiming to be possessed by his "melancholy devil" and the "adversary of this Zarathustra." This devil is present for all those who suffer from "*the great nausea*." These are people who call themselves things like free spirits or ascetics of the spirit or the great longers for whom the old god is dead and "for whom no new god lies as yet in cradles and swaddling clothes." Although not explicit, this melancholy devil can be none other than the spirit of gravity, an entity that still threatens these higher humans, and the lack of a "new god" seems to be a reference to none other than Dionysus.

The magician then launches into a song that takes the form of a dithyramb (a version of this song appears in Nietzsche's *Dithyrambs of Dionysus* as "Only a Fool! Only a Poet!"), hoping to draw the nauseated higher humans in the cave into the snares of his "melancholy lust." As Grätz remarks (2024b:726), the poem thematizes the relationship between truth and poetry (or the poetic "I"), where the poet is presented as a "fool" who is "banished from the truth" (ZIV "The Song of Melancholy":3). It is for this reason that the conscientious in spirit—the one who prizes truth above all—resists the charms of the magician. In "**On Science**," he quickly grabs the harp from the magician and demands that Zarathustra return to the cave to let in "fresh air." He protests that the magician is trying to seduce everyone into falsity and deception, and therefore he should not make any speeches about truth (there is much about truth in his song). The conscientious in spirit then counsels all free spirits to guard against such magicians, as their artistic magic will mean an end to their freedom.

The appeal to free spirits, along with the conscientious spirit's association with truth and science, recalls the interplay between Wagner's art, on the one hand, and truth and science, on the other hand, in Nietzsche's own free spirit project. In particular, Nietzsche turned to an ascetic-like quest for truth and the methods of scientific discovery in *Human* to resist the charms and even reject outright the kind of art in which the magician now traffics. In so doing, he achieved a certain sort of freedom from art and the snares of the magician. However, this opposition between science and art is peculiar to *Human*, and it is a stage of the free spirit that Nietzsche eventually transcends, evidenced by the fact that *Zarathustra* is Nietzsche's own work of art.

At the same time, the self-description Nietzsche has the conscientious in spirit provide also reveals the insufficiency of the standpoint of truth and science that this spirit inhabits. Specifically, the conscientious of spirit claims that he is different from all the other higher humans gathered in the cave. Whereas they all seek "more thrill, more danger, more earthquakes," he has come to Zarathustra for more security. He wants security because he is afraid. Indeed, the conscientious in spirit claims that fear is the basic instinct of humans, and it is from fear that his own virtue has grown, namely, science (*Wissenschaft*). Here, *Wissenschaft* can mean the natural sciences, but it can also be understood more broadly as any activity that aims to create a systematic body of knowledge. The idea seems to be that through *Wissenschaft* we can understand and more importantly control things that are otherwise foreign and threatening. This is the essence of *Wissenschaft*, and this account suggests that there is nothing noble about it.

At this point, Zarathustra returns to the cave, throwing roses at the conscientious man's so-called truths. Based on the ending of "The Higher Man," the roses symbolize laughter, and Zarathustra is said to laugh at the truths of the conscientious in spirit. Nothing is clear, but Zarathustra's gesture here suggests that comic laughter is the means to overcome the opposition between deceptive art and truth-seeking science. Thus, we are told that the conscientious in spirit is a fool, and Zarathustra is too. According to Zarathustra, fear is the exception in the history of the human. Instead, it is courage and adventure that constitutes human's "whole prehistory." Zarathustra is then about to explain the nature of courage when it is spiritualized and combined with the pride of the eagle and a serpent's wisdom. However, the higher humans interrupt with cries of Zarathustra's name, and they all start laughing, including the magician. He now acknowledges that the evil spirit is gone, and he wonders if he was the one who created him.

According to Grätz (2024b:753), commentators have speculated that Zarathustra was going to name a science that is based on courage and mixed with laughter "a gay science" (GS 327). This makes some sense. There seems to be a dialectic between art and science in chapters "The Song of Melancholy" and "Science." Whereas art is objectionable to the conscientious in spirit because it fails to tell the truth, the science and the related will to truth of the conscientious in spirit turns out to be rooted in fear and therefore nothing noble. In contrast, Zarathustra laughs at the truths of conscientious man and points to a different kind of science. Although he does not explicitly connect this science to art, it is explicitly connected to laughter. However, if it is connected to art, this "laughing science" would point to something like comedy, a genre in which art becomes conscious of itself and the deceptions it produces.

The threat of melancholy—and so the spirit of gravity—still pervades the cave in "**Among Daughters of the Wilderness**," and this is why the wanderer (Zarathustra's shadow) begs Zarathustra to stay. The old pope looks like he has fallen into melancholy and, if Zarathustra leaves, the kings will too. It is here that we see the shadow emphasizing the difference between Zarathustra and the higher humans gathered in Zarathustra's cave. Having defeated the spirit of gravity in *Zarathustra* III, Zarathustra is now the one who brings in fresh air (a sign of his *Wohlgerathenheit* and his having overcome his *nausea*).[12] In this way, he is very much their redeemer. At the same time, the wanderer claims that the fresh air Zarathustra brings reminds him of an old song he composed "among daughters of the wilderness." As a wandering "European," he was among "Oriental girls" and far "away from cloudy, moist, melancholy Europe." It is this song that the wanderer then sings for the group, and we are told that he does it with a roar. This is a likely reference to the well-constituted laughing lions that will soon come, and the song represents a turning point in the general mood of those gathered in Zarathustra's cave.

In "**The Awakening**," the wanderer's song comes to an end, and "the cave all at once became full of noise and laughter." Their gaiety pleases Zarathustra, although he remains distant from them. He takes their laughter as a "sign of convalescence," which reminds us of Zarathustra's convalescence near the end of *Zarathustra* III, and the chapter title suggests some kind of religious redemption or revival like "The Great Awakening" in the United States (see Grätz 2024b:774). Talking with his animals, he explains that they have overcome their cry of distress. They have learned to laugh, even though Zarathustra emphasizes that it is not his laughter they have learned. For this reason, the day marks a triumph. Specifically, "*the spirit of gravity*" is retreating. His guests have learned to laugh at themselves, and they are now filled with new hopes. As a result, their nausea is retreating and the burden from their souls is lifting. Most importantly, they are becoming grateful (*dankbar*), and their gratitude will make them invent festivals to celebrate the occasion. Gratitude is precisely the emotion that Nietzsche expresses about his own life at the beginning of *Ecce Homo*, and such gratitude is the exact opposite of the revenge and *ressentiment* that produces the spirit of gravity (ZIV "The Awakening":1).

In the second section of "The Awakening," Zarathustra's happiness is interrupted by the way in which the cave suddenly becomes deathly still and filled with smoke and incense. Returning to the cave, Zarathustra finds the higher humans worshipping the ass in a type of religious ceremony, evidenced by their kneeling and praying. At this point, the ugliest man begins leading the higher humans in a litany designed to glorify the ass. The ass is praised for, among other things, bearing the suffering of the world, always saying "yes" (presumably even to life), and for having a kingdom of innocence beyond good and evil ("The Awakening":2). It is here that the satyr play of *Zarathustra* IV reaches its apex.

"**The Ass Festival**" begins with Zarathustra trying to stop the litany. He jumps into the middle of the guests and asks whether they have all gone mad. He then turns to the last pope, the shadow, the magician, the conscientious in spirit, and the ugliest man to inquire into how they could possibly do this given all they have learned. All of them provide different justifications for their actions. The last pope seems to have a habitual need to worship *something*, and he claims it is most fitting to worship an ass. The conscientious man claims that if there is a god, then the ass is its most credible form (one can clearly believe what one sees). The shadow blames the ugliest man, as he is the one who killed god.

When Zarathustra finally turns to the ugliest man, we encounter an explanation that is key to interpreting the overall significance of the ass festival in *Zarathustra* IV. He explains that only Zarathustra knows best whether God still lives or lives again or whether he is thoroughly dead (in the "Retired," it is said that God is "thoroughly dead"). At the same time, he points to Zarathustra's own teaching that "whoever would kill most thoroughly, *laughs*" and that "not by wrath does one kill, but by laughter." The implication is that the ugliest man—who appears to be transfigured—has organized this festival so that the higher humans—especially the last pope—can laugh about their own latent desire to worship something and their secret wish to revert to the "metaphysical comforts" of the old god (see BT "Pref":7). The way to overcome this tendency, and thereby to kill God most thoroughly, is to mock it, to laugh about the very idea of worshipping a god in any form ("The Ass Festival":1). This, I think, is the meaning and purpose of the ass festival; it is here that we can clearly say, "*incipit parodia.*"

It seems, then, that Zarathustra has fallen for a prank of sorts instigated by the ugliest man. Whether the others are in on the prank or whether they too are subject to the ugliest man's tricks and are indulging their pious tendencies is unclear. On the one hand, Zarathustra calls them all "roguish fools" and "jesters [*Possenreisser*]" and accuses them of dissembling. On the other hand, he claims that they delighted in becoming like little children again, which means that they became "pious [*fromm*]" by praying to God. It is by becoming little children in this sense that they can enter the kingdom of heaven. However, Zarathustra says that "we have no wish whatever to enter into the kingdom of heaven: we have become men—*so we want the earth*" ("The Ass Festival":2). Here, we see that whatever piety these higher humans exhibit, it is a piety that inverts Christianity and is likely connected to Dionysus.

The "Ass Festival" concludes with Zarathustra addressing the higher humans as his "new friends." He claims that they have all blossomed and become "gay [*fröhlich*] again." This implies that they have all—at least temporarily—conquered the spirit of gravity. He then suggests that their blossoming requires "*new festivals*, a little brave nonsense, some divine service and ass festival, some old gay fool of a Zarathustra, a roaring wind that blows your souls bright." The mention of new festivals points back to Zarathustra's earlier claim in "The Awakening" that new festivals will be created to celebrate a newly found gratitude among the higher humans. This ass festival is therefore a sign of their convalescence. When they celebrate this ass festival again, they should do it both for themselves and "in remembrance" of Zarathustra ("The Ass Festival":3).

6.4 ZARATHUSTRA'S FINAL FAREWELL: CHAPTERS 19 AND 20

The penultimate chapter of *Zarathustra* IV is "**The Drunken Song.**"[13] It has a clear connection to the final section of "The Other Dancing Song" at the end of *Zarathustra* III. Indeed, it seems to elaborate on and reveal the meaning of the twelve bells that symbolize Zarathustra's initiation into the mysteries of Dionysus. It begins with Zarathustra leading the higher humans, in particular the ugliest man, out of the cave into the night, where they all stand together in silence. Here, we learn that Zarathustra now takes a liking to these higher humans, even though his liking remains unarticulated.

At this point, the ugliest man begins to speak. He claims that for the first time he is satisfied that he has lived his whole life, and he concludes from this that "living on earth is worth while." Zarathustra's festival is the reason for his newfound love of life. Now he is ready to say to death: "Was *that* life?" "Well then! Once more [*Noch ein Mal*]!" We have already encountered this exact phrase in the first section of "On the Vision and the Riddle" (*Zarathustra* III) in which Zarathustra, at least indirectly, is confronting his own nausea about the human and existence itself. There we learn that courage is something that can slay even death, and the idea of saying "once more" to death clearly associates this courage with summoning and incorporating the eternal recurrence.

Given the relationship between Zarathustra and the ugliest man, it is difficult to see how Loeb's analeptic reading of *Zarathustra* IV could hold. The ugliest man's willingness to say "once more" to death indicates his willingness to affirm the eternal recurrence of his existence. If this is the case and *Zarathustra* IV is an analeptic satyr play, then the ugliest man's affirmation of the eternal recurrence would occur before Zarathustra's own confrontation with the idea at the end of *Zarathustra* III. However, it seems clear that Zarathustra relates to the ugliest man and the other men in a way that indicates he stands on higher spiritual or psychological ground than they do. In short, he has already overcome his nausea about humanity and affirmed the eternal recurrence, and he is now helping the otherwise ill-constituted higher humans achieve at least a temporary convalescence and so approximate his own affirmative standpoint.

Having expressed his willingness to live life again, the ugliest man now encourages the other higher humans to respond to death in the same way. Here we are told that when the higher humans heard this question, they became aware that they too had convalesced. They also recognized that Zarathustra was responsible for their convalescence, and they all sought to express their gratitude in their own way. Even the soothsayer was dancing with joy (something promised in "The Cry of Distress"), and he was perhaps full of wine (here the narrator speaks as if there were chroniclers of the event, much like the events of Plato's *Symposium* that were narrated as recollections). The ass is also reported to have danced, perhaps as a result of the ugliest man having given him wine. But in the end, we do not know for sure, and the narrator dismisses such concerns about accuracy with Zarathustra's proverb (related to the Stoic "what do I matter?"): "What does it matter [*Was liegt daran*]?" (ZIV "Drunken Song":1).

As the ugliest man is saying all this, Zarathustra stumbles, almost as if he is drunk, and the higher humans help hold him up. Then he hears a bell; it is the bell of midnight. Thus, he encourages his higher humans to wander with him into the night (ZIV "Drunken Song":2). It is here that Zarathustra seems to reveal the secrets of his own initiation process that took place at the end of *Zarathustra* III. Such a reading is supported by the fact that each of the subsequent sections ends with a quotation from the third section of "On the Great Longing." In the third section of "The Drunken Song," we thus find the words associated with the first bell, "O man, take care!" (ZIV "Drunken Song":3).

The secretive nature of what Zarathustra is going to reveal is stressed in the next part, where he says he would rather die than reveal what his "midnight heart thinks now." However, this is followed by: "Now I have died. It is gone." The hour in which he freezes is approaching, and he wants to know who has the heart for it. The "it" seems to refer to the task of becoming rulers or "lords of the earth [*Herr der Erde*]" (ZIV "Drunken Song":4). The reference to the "lords of the earth" occurs at least three times in "The Drunken Song," and it is worth discussing in more detail. A certain form of preparatory politics is clearly at work in *Zarathustra* IV. The book begins with a reference to Zarathustra's kingdom of a thousand years (ZIV "The Honey Sacrifice"), and this seems to be connected to the "work" that Zarathustra plans to undertake once he leaves the cave at the end of *Zarathustra* IV. The importance of the phrase "*Herr der Erde*" is evidenced by the fact that Nietzsche had considered it for the title of a book (KSA 11:34[202]). In another note, he connects the idea of producing *Übermenschen* to a ruling race that he calls "*die Herrn der Erde*" (KSA 11:35[72]), and he argues that these rulers of the earth are supposed to replace the dead God (KSA 11:39[3]). The phrase also appears in a draft for the final section of *Zarathustra* IV, "The Sign." There he explicitly states that the higher humans gathered around him are ill-constituted human beings (*missrathen*) and therefore are not worthy of becoming rulers of the earth. In contrast, he points to the lion as a "well-constituted [*wohlgerathenen*]" symbol for the type of human being that can take on this role (KSA 14:344). Given that Nietzsche, in *Ecce Homo*, presents the *Übermensch* as an exemplar of *Wohlgerathenheit* and that Zarathustra is such an *Übermensch*, it would follow that Zarathustra is the only one in the cave fit to become a ruler of the earth. However, Zarathustra never explicitly takes on this role in *Zarathustra*. Instead, he points to his coming children, and there are reasons to associate these children with the kind of nobility Nietzsche describes in the final chapter of *Beyond Good and Evil*.[14]

The fifth part of "The Drunken Song" begins with a reference to Zarathustra's work. The higher humans who have surrounded him have indeed danced, but Zarathustra wants to know if they have flown. The deep night confronts them with the task of redeeming even the dead, and Zarathustra asks, "why does the worm still burrow"? The combination of a burrowing worm—a symbol for revenge (see "the worms of vengefulness" in GM III:14)—and the task of redeeming the dead point to the demanding task of affirming the eternal recurrence. To recall, if we are going to redeem the tombs of the past (*Vergangenheit*), it is necessary to want the past to recur. However, if we want the past to be different from what it was and therefore still harbor feelings of revenge vis-à-vis the "it was," we will not be able to affirm the eternal recurrence. Based on what Zarathustra says here, one wonders if the higher humans are indeed up to the task of affirming the eternal recurrence.

In section six of "The Drunken Song," the mood shifts. Zarathustra appeals to his "sweet lyre." All the pains of the past (of fathers, grandfathers, etc.) have torn into him, and the speech has grown ripe like Zarathustra's heart. As something ripe, it is ready to die of happiness. This ripeness brings a smell, and it is the smell of eternity. This is "the drunken happiness of dying at midnight" ("Drunken Song":6). In section seven, Zarathustra wants day to leave him, as he wonders whether the world has become perfect just now. In saying this, he explicitly connects this experience to those who shall be "the lords of the earth." These rulers of the earth are the "midnight souls who are brighter and deeper than any day" (ZIV "Drunken Song":7). In other words, these seem to be souls who can generate their own light and meaning for an otherwise dark and meaningless world.

In section eight, we learn that, despite the depths of "woe," all *"joy is deeper yet than agony."* In section nine, Zarathustra speaks as the vintager Dionysus to his vine, rather than to his soul as a vine about Dionysus at the end of *Zarathustra* III,[15] and we learn that what has been perfect and ripe (the two seem to be synonymous) "wants to die." This is why the vintager's knife is blessed, a claim that is a clear allusion to the vintager's knife and so Dionysus in "On the Great Longing" from *Zarathustra* III. In contrast, we also learn that unripe things still want to live, and this desire to live is then associated with "woe." It is suffering things, not perfect things, that want to live, and they want to live so they can be ripe and perfect. Those who are imperfect want heirs and children; they do not want themselves. In contrast, joy "does not want heirs, or children." This is because "joy wants itself, wants eternity, wants recurrence, wants everything eternally the same" (ZIV "Drunken Song":9).

There is a lot to unpack here. On the one hand, we have already encountered in other parts the language of death and "the drunken happiness of dying at midnight" (ZIV "Drunken Song":6). It is this kind of language that has led Loeb to argue that Zarathustra dies in a biological sense at the end of *Zarathustra* III. However, the language here seems to be more along the lines of a psychic death and a transformation of the soul. In part four, Zarathustra claims to have died, but in claiming this, it is obvious that he has not died in the biological sense. Instead, the idea seems to be that everything ripe wants to eternalize all things. This follows if ripe or perfected things also experience joy in their state of perfection. So understood, perfected or ripe things are ready to be wedded with eternity, and just as an individual might be said to die in the process of uniting in marriage with another individual, we can say that the everyday soul or psyche dies with its union to nature and eternity. In the language of *The Birth of Tragedy*, we would thereby have a Dionysian experience of the overcoming of the principle of individuation.[16] Such an ecstatic and intoxicating experience corresponds to the theme of "drunkenness" that runs throughout the song.

The tenth section begins with Zarathustra asking the higher humans about who or what exactly he is: A soothsayer? A dreamer? A drunkard? The list goes on, but he follows this up with the claim that "just now my world became perfect; midnight too is noon; pain too is a joy; curses too are a blessing; night too is a sun." We have already seen that the world became perfect for Zarathustra in "At Noon," and here we wonder whether he is describing the experience of midnight he has at the end of *Zarathustra* III or whether he is experiencing a perfect world once more. Either way, we should not overlook the significance of the claim that the perfection of the world is a state in which "pain too is a joy." The claim recalls the final lines of the *Hymn to Life*, which Nietzsche interprets as meaning that "pain is *not* considered an objection to life" (EH "Books" Z:1). It also follows Nietzsche's early discussion of musical dissonance in *The Birth*. There, he argues that musical dissonance reveals the way in which even pain can produce joy, and he uses this to ground his larger claim that tragedy can ultimately affirm a world characterized by meaningless suffering (BT 24).

The last half of the section begins with a question as to whether one has ever said "yes to a single joy [*Lust*]."[17] If one has, then one has also said "yes too to *all* woe." Taken on its own, this claim is rather surprising. One might think Zarathustra is saying that just as joy requires some affirmation of pain, joy requires some experience of suffering (and therefore affirming one requires the other). But the claim is stronger: it is that we say yes to all suffering when we say yes to just a single joy. The basis for this claim is clearly rooted in a key element of the cosmological theory of the eternal recurrence (an element that could be true even if the cosmological theory is not). It is the idea that "all things are entangled, ensnared, enamored" such that the affirmation of any part requires the affirmation of the whole. If one wants to affirm existence, then the task is to have that "tremendous moment [*ungeheure Augenblick*]" in which one can say yes to that moment and so everything. Indeed, it is by saying yes that one wants to eternalize that moment, "*for all joy wants—eternity*," and in wanting to eternalize the moment one wants to eternalize all things. (ZIV "Drunken Song":10).

In wanting the eternity of all things, all joy wants itself. But in wanting itself, it wants the ring of all things. Here Zarathustra asks what joy does not want, and the answer seems to be nothing: "it wants love, it wants hatred, it is overrich, gives, throws away, […] so rich is joy that it thirsts for woe, for hell, for hatred, for disgrace, for the cripple, for *world.*" In saying this, Zarathustra specifically addresses the higher humans and their woes, referring to them as "you failures [*Ihr Missrathenen*]!" Indeed, he claims that all joy longs for the ill-constituted (*nach Missrathenem*). This is because in wanting itself, joy also wants agony and presumably even what is ill-constituted.

Here again it is worth pausing to reflect on these claims. There are number of different types of humans that appear in *Zarathustra*: the last human, the small human, the higher human, and the *Übermensch*. In the above passage, we find Zarathustra claiming that the experience of joy longs for the higher humans that Zarathustra is addressing. These higher humans, however, are *missrathen*. Although there are reasons for differentiating between the small human and these ill-constituted higher humans, it seems that Zarathustra's claim that joy longs for the *missrathen* could also include a longing for even the small human (either as a form of being *missrathen* or something similar to being *missrathen*). In this sense, the song that Zarathustra sings is a song of "Once More [*Noch ein Mal*]," and this "once more" includes the recurrence of small and ill-constituted humans (ZIV "Drunken Song":11–12).

"**The Sign**" is the final chapter of *Zarathustra* IV. Zarathustra wakes up the next day and emerges from his cave. Like the opening of *Zarathustra* I, he addresses the star, asking if it would not be angry that those for whom it shines are not out to enjoy its gifts in the early morning. However, unlike the opening of *Zarathustra* I, Zarathustra himself is now presented as "glowing and strong as a morning sun that comes out of dark mountains." The imagery is significant. Whereas Plato, in the *Republic*, associates the sun with the Form of the Good and so a proto version of a monotheistic god, Nietzsche now presents Zarathustra as such a sun, and although he addresses the great star as he does in *Zarathustra* I, he now seems to embody some version of the teaching in the prologue.

In other words, Zarathustra is presented in ways that associate him with an *Übermensch* who now replaces the dead God.

Unlike the higher humans, Zarathustra is also awake, and Zarathustra quickly concludes from this that the higher humans who are sleeping are not his proper companions. Zarathustra is waiting for someone else to go to his work, and these higher humans do not understand his signs. Burnham and Jensinghausen (2010:198) see here a possible allusion to Plato's *Symposium*, which concludes with Socrates outlasting almost all the guests at the party. As previously noted, Plato's *Symposium* is also thought to contain within it a satyr play (Usher 2002). Interestingly, Plato's satyr play ends with Socrates lecturing the tragedian Agathon and the comedian Aristophanes on why a good poet can write both genres. Although speculative, there are reasons to think of this as an allusion to Plato's own activity such that the satyr play of the *Symposium* is an "interlude" between the tragedy of the *Phaedo* and the (political) comedy of his *Republic*. As I see it, *Zarathustra* IV has the same function. It is an interlude between Nietzsche's tragedy of *Zarathustra* I–III (itself a response to Plato's *Phaedo*) and the political comedy of his later works, which, in turn, can be understood as a response to Plato's *Republic*.

The idea that *Zarathustra* IV is gesturing toward some sort of political comedy—one in which law-giving and laughter go together—is suggested by the signs that finally come to him in this chapter in almost mystical fashion. He is suddenly surrounded "by innumerable swarming and fluttering birds" that appear like a cloud over him, a cloud of love. Then he reaches out his hand, and it goes into a thick warm mane. Then he hears the roar of the lion, and both the lion and the doves express their affection for Zarathustra. Zarathustra is changed, and he announces that "the sign is at hand." The lion laughs.

Many commentators hold that the appearance of the lion in *Zarathustra* IV correlates to the second of the three metamorphoses Zarathustra outlined at the beginning of *Zarathustra* I (see Burnham and Jensinghausen 2010:198). In my view, there are several reasons to reject this association. Unless Loeb's analeptic reading is correct, this would mean that Zarathustra himself never achieves the child-like state he associates with the third metamorphosis. However, there is significant textual evidence for connecting the innocence of the child with the teaching and incorporation of the eternal recurrence, which occurs at the end of *Zarathustra* III. Moreover, the transformation of the lion only makes possible a battle with God or the dragon that represents all created values hitherto. If Zarathustra only now (at the end of *Zarathustra* IV) is transforming into the lion, he still has to confront and kill God. This is problematic because the entirety of *Zarathustra* presupposes the death of God, and it is for this reason that I locate the first and second stages of the three metamorphoses outside *Zarathustra* itself. As for the (re-)appearance of the lion at the end of *Zarathustra* IV, the lion now stands for the ability to command or legislate within society (not in the desert), and this seems to be what Zarathustra sets out to do as he leaves his cave at the end of *Zarathustra* IV.

I have also argued that we have reason to connect the laughing lion surrounded by doves to comedy. Although this could mean that it is a proleptic reference to Nietzsche's own comedy, it could also be a reference to Heinrich Köselitz's (Peter Gast) comic opera, *The Lion from Venice* (see Meyer 2018:156–157), which Nietzsche was very eager to promote during this time. The title of Köselitz's opera provides a potential clue for understanding the symbolism here because we know that the lion is a symbol for Venice, and there is a bronze statue of the lion in the Piazza San Marco. The square is also known for its doves, and, as Grätz notes (2024b:842; also see 658–660), Nietzsche speaks of the "doves of San Marco" in the poem, "My Happiness," from the "Song of Prince Vogelfrei" in the appendix to the 1887 edition of *The Gay Science*.

In any case, the sign that Zarathustra has been given is that Zarathustra's children are near. These children could be the disciples that he cultivated in the opening books of *Zarathustra* or they could be the children that he longed to produce with eternity at the end of *Zarathustra* III. They could also be both: Zarathustra's true disciples just are the children he produces with eternity. What is clear is that these children are different from the higher humans now surrounding Zarathustra. Indeed, when the higher humans awake and come out of the cave, the lion greets them with a savage roar.

Zarathustra now claims to have understood what happened in the past twenty-four hours. The cry of distress was from the higher humans, and this was part of the soothsayer's ploy to tempt him to his final sin. This final sin was pity for the ill-constituted higher humans. Now, however, he has no concern for such pity, just as he has no concern for his happiness. He is now concerned with his work. Everything is now coming together. The lion is there, the children are near, and Zarathustra is ripe. It is morning, and noon will soon come. Thus, Zarathustra leaves his cave, "glowing and strong as a mountain sun that comes out of dark mountains." Thus ends *Zarathustra*.

There is no explicit mention of Zarathustra's "going under" here. But the trajectory of the ending seems to indicate that Zarathustra now plans to "go under" in the sense of going "among men once more" (ZIII "Tablets":1). We know from the *Nachlass* that Nietzsche understood the final chapter to represent Zarathustra's "farewell to the cave" and a "tearing himself away from solitude" (KSA 11:29[14]).[18] To recall, he fled into solitude in *Zarathustra* III because he needed to find his own redemption and to attain a right relationship with himself and nature. Because he still needed to work on himself, larger society was seen as a threat and a source of poison. In *Zarathustra* IV, Zarathustra is forced to associate with humanity again, and he must confront the temptation to "pity." He was able to overcome this with the laughter he preached to the higher humans. Thus, he is now ready to go down once more.

In this sense, *Zarathustra* IV takes us back to Zarathustra's going under—in the sense of going to the people—in the prologue of *Zarathustra* I. There, Zarathustra preached the *Übermensch* to a crowd of people unwilling to embrace his message. In response, Zarathustra limited himself to preaching to a small number of disciples and pinned his hopes on the creation of an *Übermensch* on them. However, as *Zarathustra* progressed, Zarathustra came to realize that his hopes for the future ultimately depend on him and that before he can teach anyone anything, he must himself incorporate and embody his own teachings. This eventually occurs in *Zarathustra* III, and if we follow Nietzsche's remarks in *Ecce Homo*, Zarathustra himself has become a Dionysian *Übermensch* by reconciling himself to the eternal recurrence and its implications. Thus, what is different about Zarathustra's descent at the end of *Zarathustra* IV is that rather than having a vision of some future being, he himself is now a well-constituted higher human or *Übermensch* ready to become a "ruler of the earth." Thus, when he goes among men again, he will not preach the need for an *Übermensch*. Instead, he himself will become a philosopher-legislator and attempt nothing less than a political— rather than a merely private—revaluation of values.

Of course, the problem is that Zarathustra's career largely comes to an end with *Zarathustra* IV. I say "largely" because Zarathustra does appear at key moments in texts such as *Beyond Good and Evil* (see the "Aftersong"), the *Genealogy* (GM II:25), *The Antichrist* (A 53–54), and *Dithyrambs of Dionysus*. Nevertheless, if we are to understand the unfinished "work" of Zarathustra to be the revaluation of values, then it must be the case that Nietzsche is taking on this work himself. This is because Nietzsche either begins or completes this work with the composition of *The Antichrist*. Although Nietzsche seems to differentiate himself from Zarathustra in GM II:25,[19] we have seen reasons for thinking that Zarathustra is a son or second self of Nietzsche and thus there can be movement from one to the other. In GM III:24, for instance, Nietzsche speaks of the coming redeemer as "this Antichrist and antinihilist; this victor over God and nothingness," and although he identifies Zarathustra as this redeemer in the next section, we know that Nietzsche also describes himself as the antichrist in his latest works and letters. Similarly, just as he describes Zarathustra as the highest type of *Wohlgerathenheit* in *Ecce Homo*, the purpose of *Ecce Homo* is to present Nietzsche as a well-turned-out person who is uniquely positioned to revalue values. In this sense, there is a close relationship, if not a continuity or even identity, between Nietzsche and Zarathustra, and the tragedy and satyr play of *Thus Spoke Zarathustra* play a crucial role in transitioning from Nietzsche's free spirit works to the project that drives his post-*Zarathustra* writings and culminates in a Dionysian comedy.

NOTES

1 See Sutton (1984) for more on Aeschylus' satyr play.
2 Grätz (2024b:339) points to Matthew 4:18–20.
3 As Blue explains (2016:275–276), Nietzsche used this motto, taken from Pindar's *Second Pythian Ode*, as early as 1867 when he used it as an epigraph for his prize-winning paper on Diogenes Laertius.
4 Grätz (2024b:425) expresses doubts about developing a single definition that captures all the higher humans that appear in *Zarathustra* IV.
5 I understand a well-constituted higher human to be equivalent to both Nietzsche's "new nobles" (KSA 11:31[2]) and what I have called the Dionysian *Übermensch* (these could also be equivalent to Zarathustra's children at the end of *Zarathustra* IV). In contrast, Loeb and Tinsley try to distinguish between the *Übermensch* and a well-constituted higher human like Zarathustra. By this point (1885), the idea that Nietzsche is holding onto a concept of the *Übermensch* that is distinct from a well-constituted higher human or new noble is rapidly fading. Even if one can extract such a distinction from the notes of this time (I am not convinced that one can), Nietzsche will soon (1887) insist that the *Übermensch* just is a higher type of human (KSA 12:9[154]; 10[17] and KSA 13:11[413]). KSA 13:11[413] provides the clearest evidence for this view. KSA 12:10[17] does refer to the *Übermensch* as a stronger "*Art*," which could be translated as "species," but it seems clear that Nietzsche is using "*Art*" as a synonym for "*Typus*" or "type" of human (he also refers to the *Übermensch* as a "*Gleichniß*" or "metaphor" in the note). Since Loeb and Tinsley agree that Zarathustra is a well-constituted higher human (2022:517), the equation of such a human with the *Übermensch* would make sense of why Nietzsche presents the *Übermensch* as a form of *Wohlgerathenheit* (being well-constituted) (EH "Books":1) and Zarathustra as an *Übermensch* (EH "Books" Z:6) in *Ecce Homo*.
6 As Grätz (2024b:462) points out, this is a clear inversion and parody of Jesus' own temptations. Since pity is equivalent to Christian neighbor love, Zarathustra's greatest "temptation" and "final sin" is Christianity itself.
7 Grätz (2024b:646) claims that Zarathustra does take on this role in a preliminary draft of the chapter.
8 Grätz (2024b:655) notes that Zarathustra's "solar will" is explicitly referenced in a preliminary draft to "The Welcome."
9 Grätz (2024b:698) points to a *Nachlass* note in which "*Selbstsucht*" is used instead of "*Eigennutz*" (KSA 10:12[1].195). This connects the "egoism" here to the self-love that Zarathustra pronounced holy in *Zarathustra* I and III.
10 See Halliwell (2008: Ch.10) on the historical opposition between Christian asceticism and laughter.
11 See BT "ASC":7 for Nietzsche's association of this passage with "the Dionysian monster" Zarathustra.
12 See GM III:14 for the opposition between *Wohlgerathenheit* and bad air (which is also connected to nausea).

13 Kaufmann's translation of this chapter is based on an earlier version of the text in the *Großoktav-Ausgabe* in which the title of this chapter is "Das trunkene Lied." This translates easily as "The Drunken Song." The title of the chapter in the *Kritische Gesamtausgabe* is "Das *Nachtwandler-Lied*," which translates as "The Somnambulist Song" or perhaps "The Sleepwalker Song." For the purposes of continuity in using Kaufmann's translation, I will refer to this chapter as "The Drunken Song."
14 As Grätz notes (2024b:819), Nietzsche associates these "rulers of the earth" with the idea of a "lawgiver of the future [*Gesetzgeber der Zukunft*]" in a *Nachlass* note (KSA 11:35[9]). Developing this point, one can also connect the "lawgiver of the future" to the "philosophers of the future," who are also "lawgivers" in *Beyond Good and Evil* (BGE 211) and then link these lawgivers to a conception of nobility at the end of *Beyond Good and Evil*. So understood, the nobles of *Beyond Good and Evil* are the "rulers of the earth" in *Zarathustra*.
15 See Grätz (2024b:824) for more on this point.
16 Grätz (2024b:828) links the breaking of the heart at the end of section 11 to the overcoming of the principle of individuation.
17 As noted in chapter five, I have reservations about Kaufmann's translation of "*Lust*" as "joy," but defer here because other translations have other drawbacks. "Pleasure" is perhaps the best alternative.
18 Translation from CWFN 15.
19 Loeb emphasizes (2010:225) the significance of this passage, claiming that Zarathustra is the only one strong enough to overcome the forces of nihilism and affirm the eternal recurrence, whereas Nietzsche himself is too weak to do so. Loeb develops this idea in his reading of *Ecce Homo* (2021).

7
THE PHILOSOPHICAL SIGNIFICANCE OF *ZARATHUSTRA*

In the opening chapters, I made the case for the significance of *Zarathustra* in relation to Nietzsche's larger project. The idea is that if we read *Zarathustra* as a tragedy (and a satyr play), then *Zarathustra* is essential for understanding Nietzsche's larger project, and therefore if understanding Nietzsche's larger project is important, then understanding *Zarathustra* will also be important. In this concluding chapter, I want to say something about the philosophical significance of *Zarathustra* as a standalone work, and I will do so from two different philosophical perspectives. First, I want to invite the reader to think about philosophy as a live conversation among figures in the history of philosophy. Here, I will situate *Zarathustra* in relation to Plato's *Phaedo*, arguing that the naturalism of *Zarathustra* is meant to reclaim a truly tragic way of thinking about both life and death, one that does away with the metaphysics and morality introduced in the *Phaedo*. Second, I want to put *Zarathustra* in conversation with

DOI: 10.4324/9781315209470-7

contemporary philosophy. Elsewhere, I have done this by arguing that *Zarathustra* is the work in which Nietzsche completes a system of naturalism and therefore can be understood in relation to contemporary work on naturalism (Meyer 2022). Here, I want to extend this idea by arguing that the fatalism entailed by the eternal recurrence amounts to a rejection of what contemporary philosophers call a libertarian conception of free will and a corresponding notion of moral responsibility, and the drama of *Zarathustra* revolves around Zarathustra's willingness and ability to overcome this conception of himself and his agency. At the same time, Nietzsche develops, in his later writings, a conception of freedom that is compatible with the fatalism of Zarathustra. Although this type of freedom has rightly been compared to the compatibilist conceptions of freedom in the Stoics and Spinoza,[1] I conclude by noting that Nietzsche wants to connect his conception of freedom to Dionysus and by arguing that Nietzsche presents himself as having achieved this type of freedom in the centerpiece of his Dionysian comedy, *Ecce Homo*.[2]

7.1 NIETZSCHE'S *ZARATHUSTRA* AND PLATO'S *PHAEDO*

The idea that *Zarathustra* can be understood in relation to Plato's *Phaedo* is not new. For instance, Loeb provides an extensive discussion of the *Phaedo* in his work on *Zarathustra*. It is also not without textual support. The starting point for Loeb's analysis is Nietzsche's discussion of Socrates' attitude toward life and death in GS 340, "The dying Socrates." The position of the aphorism is significant, as it immediately precedes the introduction of the eternal recurrence in GS 341 and then the introduction of Zarathustra in GS 342. As such, there are reasons for following Loeb in holding that Nietzsche intends to contrast the attitudes of Socrates and Zarathustra toward life and death. Whereas Socrates is presented in the *Phaedo* as someone who wants to escape life and welcomes death, Zarathustra is presented as someone who loves life and eventually wills the eternal recurrence of his existence and the world (2010:45).

Before getting into specifics, it is important to have a larger framework in place by which one can contrast Plato and Nietzsche with respect to these two characters and these two works. In *The Birth of Tragedy*, Nietzsche claims that Socrates and Plato represent a significant break with the worldview that gave rise to the glories of ancient Greek culture, which reached its zenith in fifth-century Athens. Although Socrates lived during this time and is presented by Plato as trying to save Athenian culture from degeneration, Nietzsche holds that Plato (with Socrates as a character in his dialogues) tried to do this by reworking the philosophical, ethical, and political foundations of the entire culture. In this way, philosophers like Socrates, Plato, and even Aristotle were not providing a philosophical articulation of the views that underpinned ancient Greek civilization. Instead, they were introducing new principles that were entirely foreign to the previous way of thinking, and this only accelerated the destruction of an already declining culture. This, then, is one reason why Nietzsche identifies Socrates as the one responsible for the death of tragedy in his first work.

This is Nietzsche's view, but there are independent reasons for giving it serious consideration. Plato's attempt to expel the poets from his ideal city in the *Republic*, not to mention his attacks on both pre-Platonic philosophers and the sophists, provides evidence for Nietzsche's claims. By way of the *Republic*, the reader is led to believe that Plato and Socrates, not Homer and the tragedians, should be the true teachers of Athenian youth. Applied to the *Phaedo*, there are reasons for thinking that the work constitutes Plato's attempt to offer a new way of thinking about life and death, the nature of the soul, and the relation between the soul and the body. More specifically, it is an attempt to replace a way of thinking about these matters that was embedded within the tragedies that were performed in honor of Dionysus and were arguably modeled on the "mysteries" associated with the god (see BT 10). To be sure, Plato's account of Socrates' death in the *Phaedo* is, in some sense, "tragic," but because it attacks some of the fundamental assumptions of Dionysian tragedy, the work can be understood as Plato's anti-tragic tragedy. It is a tragedy in the broad sense that it presents a character facing his impending death; it is anti-tragic in that it introduces ideas foreign and even antithetical to what Nietzsche would call the "tragic worldview." Indeed, it introduces metaphysical principles of the soul and the world that provide comfort for Socrates and possibly his friends in facing the reality of death.

What exactly constitutes this "tragic worldview" is open for debate, but here Plato and Nietzsche would likely agree: the tragic worldview presents the human being as a fully naturalized entity subject to forces beyond her control.[3] As an "anti-tragic" tragedy, Plato's *Phaedo* sets out to de-naturalize the human being by sharply dividing the soul from the body and presenting the former as an immortal principle that exists beyond death. In short, Plato reconceived of how the tragic Greeks thought about death by introducing metaphysical principles of both an immortal soul and eternal Forms that are the true objects of knowledge.[4] Because we ultimately long for knowledge of these Forms and because sense perception is a hindrance to such knowledge, the philosopher or lover of knowledge will long for death, which is presented as a process by which the soul separates from the body. Here, the Platonic *eros* for knowledge, which Nietzsche calls the will to truth, is at the same time an *eros* for death or *thanatos*. So understood, philosophy is a preparation for death (64a). Thus, the life of the body, along with sense perception, can be understood as a hindrance to what we really want, and therefore it is a kind of disease. This, then, is why Plato presents Socrates as owing Asclepius a cock at the end of the dialogue; Socrates wants to thank Asclepius for giving him the cure for the disease of life.

There are important features of the *Phaedo* which indicate that Plato is trying to overturn principles that are, first, found among his predecessors and, second, that Nietzsche is trying to revive. The first is the Heraclitean principle of the unity of opposites. In both the *Phaedo* and the *Republic*, Plato attacks this principle, insisting on a strict separation of opposites (see *Phaedo* 103a–c and *Republic* 475d–476b). Here, Plato agrees that the unity of opposites holds for the sensible world. However, he insists that the sensible world cannot constitute true reality because it violates the principle of non-contradiction. Thus, there must be a suprasensible or metaphysical world in which opposites are strictly separated and is intelligible to reason alone. The strict separation of opposites gives rise to his doctrine of the Forms, entities that conform to the logical principle of identity (A=A) and exist in and for themselves.

Nietzsche begins both *Human* and *Beyond Good and Evil* by identifying the problem of opposites as the fundamental problem of philosophy. In contrast to Plato, Nietzsche rejects the division of opposites that historically led to the tradition of metaphysics that Plato (and Parmenides) initiated. In *Beyond Good and Evil*, Nietzsche explicitly attacks Plato for his invention of both an immortal soul and the Form of the Good (BGE "Pref"). In *Human*, Nietzsche insists on a historical philosophy that also implies the Heraclitean principle of becoming (HH 1; KSA 14:119). As I have argued elsewhere, this principle provides the foundation for a "tragic worldview." This tragic worldview is also a naturalistic worldview which does away with any conception of transcendent metaphysics, and it establishes the foundation for a worldview that *Zarathustra* both completes and to which it responds. Because it puts an end to the metaphysical world, Nietzsche associates *Zarathustra* with the "great noon" and the overcoming of the "true world" and so the appearance-reality distinction (TI "Fable").

In the *Republic*, Plato links the unity or separation of opposites to two different types of lives. Whereas genuine philosophers separate opposites and focus their energies on acquiring knowledge of the Forms, there are persons similar to genuine philosophers whom Plato calls lovers of sights and sounds. These pseudo-philosophers focus on the sensible world and reject the separation of opposites. Interestingly, Plato also accuses these pseudo-philosophers of running around to all the Dionysian festivals at which tragedies and comedies are performed (475d). The idea is that Plato is consciously responding to a worldview embedded within the art forms of tragedy and comedy associated with Dionysus.

In the *Phaedo*, we encounter a similar sort of distinction. There, Plato insists that those who practice philosophy in the right sort of way are the true Bacchants (rather than those who attend Dionysian festivals) (69c–d). Thus, the "true mysteries" are the mysteries that Plato associates with the practice of philosophy as he construes it. Rather than celebrating a this-worldly existence, philosophy is an ascetic practice in which one turns away from the body and the sensible world and turns toward an immortal soul that uses pure reason to grasp metaphysical Forms. The contrast between these "true mysteries" of Platonic philosophy and the "mysteries" that Nietzsche associates with Dionysus and the teaching of the eternal recurrence could not be greater.

Plato links these sorts of ascetic practices to a dualism between soul and body and establishes the soul as the ruler over the body. Here we see the emergence of something similar to what contemporary philosophers call a libertarian conception of free will (discussed below). Although the soul is affected by various desires and emotions through the body, the rational part of the soul can ultimately choose to endorse or resist acting on these desires and emotions. Indeed, the fact that the soul can exercise control over the body is one reason Socrates gives in the *Phaedo* for rejecting an epiphenomenal understanding of the soul as a harmony produced by the body (94b–c). If the soul is like a harmony, then the soul cannot exercise control over the body, just as a musical harmony cannot exercise control over the strings that produce it. However, Socrates takes it as a given that the soul can exercise control over the body, and he concludes that the soul therefore cannot be a harmony.

Socrates also makes this point by highlighting his dissatisfaction with naturalistic explanations of the cosmos. Although he found in Anaxagoras' writings a principle of Mind (*nous*) that could be the basis for understanding a cosmos ordered for the best, he was disappointed to learn that it played no explanatory role in Anaxagoras' system (98b). Importantly, Socrates explains his disappointment by highlighting the causal role his own mind plays in directing the movements of his body. According to Socrates, there are two reasons he is sitting in jail: first, the Athenians, after deliberating, decided to condemn him; second, after deliberating, he judged it best to remain in prison and endure the penalty (98d–e). In short, Socrates' tragic death is not a result of a nonrational fate or machinations of the body, but rather the product of choices human beings made based on what they thought was best. Of course, this also means that the Athenians can be held morally responsible for killing a man who devoted his life to the pursuit of truth and the cultivation of virtue.

In contrast to the fate of Oedipus, the ability of the soul or mind to determine how one acts makes it possible for one to choose the kind of life one will ultimately lead, and Plato links this choice of lives to a post-death judgment day in the concluding myth of the dialogue. The underlying idea of the dialogue is that philosophy detaches us from the body and therefore the natural world. The more we indulge in the desires of the body, the more we nail ourselves to the natural world (83d). Moreover, the pursuit of bodily pleasures—unlike the pursuit of intellectual pleasures—also gives rise to conflict. This is because the possession and consumption of material objects that satisfy bodily desires excludes others from the enjoyment of those same objects and therefore leads to competition for scarce resources. Thus, strong physical desires can lead to acts of theft, violence, murder, and tyranny, all of which pollute the soul in this life. However, because the soul is immortal, death will not purify the polluted soul (107c–d). Instead, souls are subjected to judgment in the afterlife, and those who have committed monstrosities are thrown into Tartarus forever. In contrast, those who "have lived an extremely pious life are freed and released from the regions of earth as from a prison," and those who "have purified themselves sufficiently by philosophy live in the future altogether without a body" (113d–114c). It is here that we see a close connection between an emerging concept of free will and notions of reward and punishment, and the idea is that the true reward for living a good life is an escape from earthly life altogether. This is why the philosopher does not lament death, but rather welcomes it like a cure for a disease (118d). In short, this is why Socrates' death is not tragic.

The "life-denying" ethos of the *Phaedo* is undeniable, and it sharply contrasts with the "life-affirming" ethos that Nietzsche attributes to pre-Socratic culture in general and tragedy in particular. From a Nietzschean perspective, we can say that the *Phaedo* effectively creates a framework that will evolve into the nihilism that Schopenhauer promotes and Nietzsche ultimately rejects. For Schopenhauer, the important point of a work like the *Phaedo* is not the bliss that a morally good soul will experience once it passes on to the afterworld, but rather the idea that the soul can be liberated from the suffering of this world. In other words, Plato and Schopenhauer agree that the natural world of the body is something from which we need to be liberated (like a prison), and they both agree that we can either remain condemned to a this-worldly existence by affirming the will or seek to liberate ourselves from such a state by engaging in an ascetic renunciation of bodily desire.

Zarathustra can be understood as a response to this general framework and to the *Phaedo* in particular. Here, we can see how *Zarathustra* tries to undo, in systematic fashion, much of what Plato does in the *Phaedo*. As early as *Zarathustra* I, we are told that "god is dead" and encounter attacks on any idea of a metaphysical "*Hinterwelt*." Robust notions of a soul that in some way controls the body are immediately replaced with the body and unconscious desires controlling the "soul" and any sort of conscious reasoning. Good and evil, we are told, are not grounded in a metaphysical reality, but rather are creations of a will to power. The asceticism of the *Phaedo* is also rejected. Later in the text, Zarathustra replaces the "will to truth" (Platonic *eros*) with a will to power and revalues self-love and sexual desire by making them into necessary and positive features of life. Finally, the philosophical task of *Zarathustra* is not to prepare for death by slowly separating the soul from the body, but rather to immerse oneself in nature and necessity and to create such a lust for life that one wants it to repeat forever. Thus, the tragedy of *Zarathustra* I–III ends with Zarathustra proclaiming his love for eternity, not drinking hemlock and slowly leaving behind the body and the natural world.

7.2 *ZARATHUSTRA*, FREE WILL, AND THE METAPHYSICS OF REVENGE

One important difference between Plato's *Phaedo* and Nietzsche's *Zarathustra* centers on the notion of free will. Whereas the *Phaedo* establishes a framework that allows humans to choose the type of life they will live—either pursuing the pleasures of the body or turning toward the rational longings of the soul—the drama of *Zarathustra* revolves around the difficulties that Zarathustra faces in abandoning this conception of himself and merging with both nature and necessity. The will does not exist outside or above nature. Instead, it is embedded within a chain of historical causes that determine both the present and the future. For Nietzsche, the true mystery teaching is that the will must will the eternal recurrence, and the eternal recurrence entails an already predetermined world and therefore reinforces the idea of tragic fate. What Zarathustra must be willing to give up, therefore, is the idea that he can control his destiny and shape the world. What he wins back, however, is the "innocence of becoming," a world free from guilt and punishment and conceptions of good and evil. In terms of the *Phaedo*, Zarathustra's teaching of the eternal recurrence shuts down any possibility of escaping the "prison" of this world. For Zarathustra, however, this is a welcomed event. The world is not a prison, but our true home and a proper object of love and veneration. It is in this sense that Zarathustra remains true to the earth.

For Zarathustra to teach the eternal recurrence, he must overcome his revenge against the past (*Vergangenheit*). That is, he must overcome his desire for the world to be other than it is. As Scott Jenkins has pointed out, Nietzsche attributes to the dying Socrates a desire for revenge near the end of GS 340: "Did a Socrates need such revenge?" (2019:236). Plato's Socrates wanted the world to be other than it is. However, the world can't be otherwise. Thus, he suffered from life, and because he suffered from life, he wanted to die. To give meaning to his death wish, Plato's Socrates invented a metaphysical world. This, of course, is the exact opposite of Zarathustra: Zarathustra loves himself, and therefore he loves life, and because he loves life, he embraces the eternal recurrence to immortalize his life and all of nature. In this way, he puts the stamp of being onto becoming and remains "true to the earth."

Importantly, Nietzsche penned an extensive note in 1887 explaining the connection between metaphysics and revenge. The title of the note is "On the Psychology of Metaphysics." Nietzsche lists various inferences that move from the existence of a so-called apparent world to a metaphysical world—inferences on full display in Plato's *Phaedo* that include the inference of being from becoming and the true world from the apparent world. Nietzsche then argues that suffering "inspires these conclusions." That is, transcendent metaphysics is based on false inferences rooted in human suffering. Thus, it is a longing for a metaphysical world—not its actual existence—that explains why people have invented and still believe in such a world. For this reason, Nietzsche claims that "the *ressentiment* of metaphysicians against actuality is creative here" (KSA 12:8[2]).

The connection between metaphysics and revenge (or *ressentiment*) is not original to Nietzsche. Eugen Dühring—one of Nietzsche's primary interlocutors on the topic of the eternal recurrence as well as his reflections on equality and revenge in "On the Tarantulas" of *Zarathustra* II—devotes the concluding chapter of the 1865 edition of *The Value of Life* (*Der Werth des Lebens*) to discussing the "transcendent satisfaction of revenge." Like the first essay of Nietzsche's *Genealogy*, Dühring explains that the "feeling for revenge is essentially a ressentiment [*ein Ressentiment*], a reactive feeling, i.e., it belongs with revenge in the same species of feelings" (1865:219). And like Nietzsche, Dühring warns against constructing metaphysical systems that attempt to provide a "transcendent satisfaction of revenge" (1865:234). He even uses the phrase "let us beware [*Hüten wir uns*]" in this context, which is the title of the aphorism in which Nietzsche first mentions the eternal recurrence in his published works (GS 109).

According to Dühring, our drives have a profound impact on what we believe. In the case of metaphysics, even though we may not have evidence to support our beliefs in such concepts, our drives and desires can nevertheless compel us to hold such beliefs. For Dühring, the desire to retaliate against a perceived wrong, i.e., revenge, is such a drive, and it lies behind our continued belief in metaphysical concepts. Indeed, Dühring claims that all three of Kant's postulates—God, freedom of the will, and the immortality of the soul—have been constructed to provide a transcendental satisfaction of revenge (Kant connects all three to the categorical imperative). The cornerstone of this type of thinking is the notion of "metaphysical guilt," which is only possible through "metaphysical freedom." In short, we need a robust concept of free will, one which transcends the laws of nature. We then need to believe in the continued existence of the guilty party, even beyond death. Thus, we need to believe that the soul is immortal so that the individual cannot escape punishment for his or her misdeeds (like the concluding myth of Plato's *Phaedo*). Finally, we need to believe in a metaphysical judge to determine and administer such a punishment. This, of course, is God. In sum, it is our dissatisfaction with the natural world that keeps us in the snares of these metaphysical beliefs (1865:230).

In Kant's view, the most important of these metaphysical beliefs—the cornerstone for the entire edifice—is freedom of the will. Indeed, it can be argued that much of Kant's theoretical philosophy—most notably the distinction between phenomenal and noumenal realms—is designed to preserve a conception of freedom that makes moral responsibility possible by allowing the human being to transcend the causal network of nature. In the *Genealogy*, Nietzsche targets this view, arguing that it is a product of slave morality, which itself is a product of *ressentiment* (GM I:13).[5] On this view, a metaphysical "doer" is added to the "deed," and this doer can then be the subject of praise or blame for performing a particular deed. Nietzsche, however, insists that we are no different from animals, and just as we do not saddle beasts of prey with a sense of guilt for being beasts of prey, we should not do the same to humans, especially those nobles who are the target of the slaves' *ressentiment*. This not only falsifies nature (adding a fictitious "doer"), but also creates in humans a sense of guilt and bad conscience that unfolds into a life-denying asceticism and nihilism.

In contemporary philosophical debates, the kind of free will that Nietzsche associates with slave morality is known as a libertarian conception of free will (more specifically, it is a form of "agent-causal libertarianism"). Libertarian free will is typically understood to be incompatible with the idea that everything is determined. Libertarians usually hold that if an agent has free will, that agent must have the freedom to act otherwise than they do (O'Connor 2022). For this reason, agents cannot be determined to act in the way that they do. Most libertarians also hold that there is an agent—a doer—that plays some causal role in determining an otherwise undetermined deed. It is for this reason that libertarians believe that how we act is ultimately "up to us," and this, in turn, makes us "ultimately responsible" for who we are and what we do (see Kane 1998:32–33). This, of course, is precisely the conception of free will that Nietzsche associates with the *ressentiment* of slave morality in the *Genealogy*.

Not everyone who believes in free will, however, is a libertarian. Instead, compatibilists argue that free will is compatible with causal determination. That is, it is possible to hold that we are both determined to act in the way that we do and that the action emanated from a free will. Here, it should be noted that the attempt to show the compatibility between free will and determinism is usually an attempt to preserve the intuition that we can hold agents morally responsible for their actions. In short, both libertarians and compatibilists are in the business of showing that we can hold individuals morally responsible, even though they disagree about whether free will and moral responsibility are compatible with determinism. The motivating idea behind compatibilism is that the alternative—known as "hard determinism"—comes at a very high price, and some philosophers have argued that we just cannot take seriously positions which deny moral responsibility and "the radical changes that it would involve" (Waller 2011:1)

One of the philosophers who cannot take the denial of moral responsibility seriously is P.F. Strawson. In a well-known paper, "Freedom and Resentment" (2020), Strawson argues that even if the thesis of determinism were true, we neither could nor should abandon the idea of moral responsibility in our interpersonal relationships. Interpersonal relationships require reactive attitudes of praise and blame—most notably "resentment"—and giving up these reactive attitudes because of determinism would destroy these interpersonal relationships. The idea is that it matters, in interpersonal relationships, whether others do harm or benefit by accident, indifference, or intention, and when we are done harm by others out of indifference or intention, we react differently than when it is done by accident. In the former cases, we hold them morally responsible, and we respond accordingly. Making this sort of distinction when dealing with others is something we cannot escape, even if determinism were true.

The parallel between Strawson's argument and Nietzsche's rejection of a morally responsible agent in the *Genealogy* is quite striking: Both link the idea of moral responsibility—albeit in different ways—to the reactive attitude of resentment (and, for Nietzsche, revenge). However, they reach radically different conclusions. Strawson's argument relies on the idea that our everyday commonsense world *would not* and even *should not* be changed or disrupted by scientific, cosmological, or philosophical speculations about the truth of determinism. In contrast, Nietzsche rejects the everyday world that Strawson takes as a non-negotiable given, seeing it as a product of the psychology of a certain type of person (the slave) that has become dominant in modern Europe, and he thinks that we need to reorder ourselves and our world on the basis of a purely naturalistic understanding of the human being as well as a deterministic cosmos that does away with moral responsibility.

So understood, Nietzsche can be placed alongside recent theorists—such as Derk Pereboom and Bruce Waller—who not only think that we can get along without moral responsibility, but also that the world would be better off if we did. Although Waller makes it clear that he is attacking the entire system of moral responsibility, "root and branch" (2011:2), there are ways in which Nietzsche's critique of moral responsibility is even more thoroughgoing. Nietzsche wants to attack a system of moral responsibility and an entire metaphysical worldview that emerged to support it (as outlined by Dühring), and in so doing, he wants to upend the commonsense worldview that Strawson takes to be fundamental. This, I think, is why Nietzsche likens Zarathustra's attempt to go "beyond good and evil" by teaching the eternal recurrence to an initiation ritual into the mysteries of Dionysus. Just as one is supposed to be radically transformed by accepting Christ as one's savior, Nietzsche believes that one's entire self will be transformed by the acceptance of a natural and deterministic world order that does away with libertarian free will and a corresponding sense of moral responsibility. At the same time, the acceptance of such a worldview is not easy to do, and it requires that we first overcome the revenge and *ressentiment* that have been identified as the root of our desire to hold others, and even ourselves, morally responsible. Indeed, it is this difficulty that shapes the dramatic arc of *Zarathustra* and offers a possible explanation as to why Nietzsche decided to present the teaching of the eternal recurrence in the form of a tragic drama.

It is interesting to note that Pereboom connects his own project of rejecting moral responsibility directly to Spinoza and indirectly to the Stoics (he says nothing about Nietzsche). As I explained in Chapter 2, Seung argues that although *Zarathustra* begins by proclaiming what he calls a "Faustian *Übermensch*" (a version of libertarian free will), the drama ends with a "Spinozian *Übermensch*" in which the will identifies with cosmic necessity (2005:xviii). Not only does Nietzsche associate Spinoza's denial of free will with his own philosophy in a letter from 1881 (KSB 6:135),[6] but he also points to the Stoics as offering a cosmology that has affinities with his own doctrine of the eternal recurrence (EH "Books" BT:3). Donald Rutherford has also stressed Nietzsche's kinship with Spinoza and the Stoics on the topic of freedom and free will. Although he rejects libertarian versions of free will that are "perpetuated by defenders of a 'moral world-order,'" Nietzsche nevertheless endorses a conception of freedom that is compatible with the affirmation of fate (2011:512). According to Rutherford, actions are said to be free when they "reflect the inherent power of an agent" rather than "the power of external forces." As such "freedom is the condition in which an individual's power is least constrained by external things and maximally expressive of a principle of action internal to the agent herself" (2011:514).

I think this is largely right, but what gets overlooked in Rutherford's treatment is the important role that Dionysus and the Dionysian art forms of tragedy and comedy play in Nietzsche's understanding of freedom. To be sure, Rutherford refers to the affirmation of fate on a handful of occasions, but only once connects this to Zarathustra and Dionysus (and he never mentions tragedy). On the reading of *Zarathustra* I have advanced here, the purpose of Nietzsche's Dionysian tragedy is to overcome our commonsense tendency to attribute moral responsibility to agents for their actions, thereby affecting a catharsis not of pity and fear, as Aristotle would have it, but a catharsis of the guilt we might feel about our own actions as well as the desire to hold others morally responsible for theirs. In terms of ancient Greek tragedy, this is why Nietzsche places so much stress on *Oedipus at Colonus* in *The Birth of Tragedy*. Oedipus' actions were already "in the cards," and the true teaching of Oedipus' story is that he must accept, rather than resist, his allotted fate (BT 9). Even though his deeds are horrific, Oedipus is not to be blamed for them, as fate governs all things. This is part of what Nietzsche means by an "aesthetic justification" of the world, and why he writes that, in tragedy, "all that exists is just and unjust and equally justified in both" (BT 9). At the same time, the acceptance and affirmation of fate is only the first step on the road to a naturalized form of freedom, and it would be a mistake to think that the tragedy of *Zarathustra* is the work in which this freedom is achieved. In the next section, I sketch reasons for thinking that Nietzsche presents himself as having achieved this alternative form of freedom in *Ecce Homo*,[7] which I understand to be the centerpiece of Nietzsche's own Dionysian comedy.

7.3 FROM TRAGIC FATE IN *ZARATHUSTRA* TO COMIC SELF-CREATION IN *ECCE HOMO*

At the risk of complexifying matters, I want to conclude this work by sketching how the affirmation of fate in the tragedy of *Zarathustra* relates to Nietzsche's positive conception of freedom in comedy by looking at the issue through the lens of what Leiter (2001) has dubbed the "paradox of fatalism and self-creation." What will become clear is that whatever understanding of self-creation Nietzsche endorses, it cannot be a libertarian conception that is incompatible with fatalism. As we have seen, Rutherford has argued that there is a conception of both freedom and self-creation that is compatible with Nietzsche's fatalism, and I will sketch reasons for thinking that Nietzsche presents himself as having realized these in the centerpiece of his comedy, *Ecce Homo*. So understood, the so-called "paradox of fatalism and self-creation" will be resolved by linking each element of the paradox to the two most important poetic genres associated with Dionysus. Whereas we are forced to confront the truth of fatalism in the tragedy of *Zarathustra*, the comedy of Nietzsche's 1888 works allows for the artistic construction of a self that aligns with and embraces nature and what one fundamentally is.

According to Leiter, the paradox of fatalism and self-creation goes something like this. On the one hand, prominent interpreters of Nietzsche, such as Richard Rorty and Alexander Nehamas, have attributed to Nietzsche a strong notion of self-creation, one that seems to have few constraints (2001:281–283). This strong sense of self-creation seems to rely on a libertarian conception of free will: persons must freely choose (without being determined by other causes) what they will become, and they must be able to causally effect the self they create. Although Leiter does not mention *Zarathustra*, there is a way in which the "Faustian" or "Apollonian" conception of the *Übermensch* in *Zarathustra* I and II provides textual support for this reading: a form of *creatio ex nihilo* is the means by which suffering is redeemed (ZII "Blessed Isles") and new values are created (ZI "Thousand and One Goals"). On the other hand, there are multiple passages in which Nietzsche emphasizes fate and the way in which the individual is a piece of necessity or *fatum*. Although Leiter bases his evidence on other texts in Nietzsche's corpus, we have seen that the eternal recurrence entails a fatalism that takes centerstage in *Zarathustra* II and III. Because the stress on fate clearly contradicts the libertarian understanding of self-creation, Leiter resolves the paradox by arguing that Nietzsche is primarily committed to fatalism and any talk of self-creation must be understood in a different and attenuated way (2001:319). Although I want to provide a more robust reading of Nietzsche's views on freedom and self-creation, Leiter is right to hold that however we understand Nietzsche's emphasis on creation in *Zarathustra* and elsewhere, it must be reconciled with the naturalism and fatalism that dominate the latter part of the text.

We can get a sense of how these might be reconciled by looking at a key passage that has been used to support both strong notions of self-creation and Leiter's emphasis on fatalism. The passage occurs near the end of the fourth book of *The Gay Science* and bears the title, "Long live physics!" (GS 335). Here, Nietzsche calls on individuals to create themselves: "we, however, *want to become those we are*—human beings who are new, unique, incomparable, who give themselves laws, who create themselves." Nietzsche then connects the idea of becoming who one is to a clear modification of the Kantian project of achieving freedom in the sense of autonomy or self-legislation. Rather than self-legislating a moral law that is universally valid for everyone, the "law" which one gives to oneself is, for Nietzsche, a rule of *taste* that both expresses what one is and shapes who one is. In this way, giving an aesthetic law to oneself goes hand in hand with the idea, expressed earlier in the text, of giving style to one's character (GS 290).

However, Leiter also notes that the next lines of the passage emphasize the need to reconcile this project of self-creation with necessity and therefore the notion of *amor fati* already announced in GS 276. Thus, Nietzsche writes: To achieve this goal of self-creation, "we must become the best learners and discoverers of everything that is lawful and necessary in the world: we must become *physicists* in order to be able to be *creators* in this sense." The idea is that a clear comprehension of nature and necessity is a condition for self-creation. Hitherto, values, ideals, and even the self were constructed in a way that contradicted nature. Now, the task is to create a self—as well as the values and ideas that give shape to a self—that accords with nature and so aligns with the idea of *amor fati*. Expressed in language that Nietzsche employs elsewhere in *The Gay Science*, we must "'*naturalize*' humanity in terms of a pure, newly discovered, newly redeemed nature" (GS 109).

In *Twilight of the Idols*, Nietzsche combines the ideas of self-creation and *amor fati* with an understanding of freedom in his description of Goethe. According to Nietzsche, Goethe not only "disciplined himself to wholeness" and "*created himself*," but he is also a "spirit who has *become free*" and "stands amid the cosmos with a joyous and trusting fatalism" (TI "What the Germans Lack":49). Much is open to interpretation here, but I want to suggest that Nietzsche is presenting us with two distinct, yet related, notions of freedom, both of which conform to Rutherford's analysis. On the one hand, we read of a "spirit who has *become free*" and so exhibits a joyous and trusting fatalism. In my view, this animates Nietzsche's free spirit project, one grounded in the idea of *Schopenhauer as Educator* that we first need to liberate ourselves from everything foreign to our natures and external to ourselves. This process of liberation includes a liberation from the false belief that we are distinct from nature, and it therefore culminates in the joyous and trusting fatalism of *Zarathustra*, in which "only the particular is loathsome, and that all is redeemed and affirmed in the whole" (TI "Skirmishes":49). Nevertheless, the condition of losing the particular in a redeemed whole is not the same as disciplining oneself to wholeness and creating oneself. In my view, this is where a second type of freedom comes into play. The affirmation of fate is a necessary condition for the individual to create herself in a way—to use Rutherford's language—that is "maximally expressive of a principle internal to the agent herself." In this way, "becoming free" (in the free spirit works) and affirming fate (in *Zarathustra*) are necessary steps toward a new type of freedom and the construction of a new self that aligns with nature rather than social conventions or metaphysical beliefs.

The passage from *Twilight of the Idols* ends on a somewhat puzzling note: Nietzsche claims that this joyous and trusting fatalism, which redeems and affirms everything in the whole, is something that he has baptized with the name Dionysus. It is puzzling because Nietzsche then goes on to say that Goethe did not understand Dionysus and therefore did not understand the Greeks (TI "What I Owe":4). However, it is far less puzzling when we apply the idea to Nietzsche's own writings. As we have seen, subtle references to Dionysus run throughout the final moments of *Zarathustra* III where Zarathustra exhibits his joyous and trusting fatalism by teaching the eternal recurrence. Toward the end of the *Twilight of the Idols*, Nietzsche confirms this connection. There, he tells us that in the Dionysian mysteries, the Greeks gave the greatest expression to the "will to life" and they guaranteed themselves "*eternal* life" and "the eternal return of life" (TI "What I Owe":4). They celebrated procreation and sexuality, and they even pronounced pain holy. Nietzsche associates all of this with the psychology of the tragic poet—alluding back to *The Birth*—and then proclaims himself to be both the "last disciple of the philosopher Dionysus" as well as the teacher of the eternal recurrence (TI "What I Owe":4).

The upshot of this is that Dionysus—and not so much Goethe, Spinoza, or the Stoics—provides the key to understanding how freedom and self-creation can be reconciled with a teaching of fate and necessity. By emphasizing his own discipleship to Dionysus,

Nietzsche is also indicating that he himself is the one who will best realize a type of freedom and self-creation that is compatible with nature, fate, and necessity. Again, one might infer—and *Twilight of the Idols* lends some support for this reading—that all of this is achieved in Nietzsche's own tragedy of *Zarathustra*. Although *Zarathustra* is a central part of Nietzsche's Dionysianism and the place in which Nietzsche's "son," Zarathustra, is reconciled with nature and fate, I think we need to turn to *Ecce Homo*, where Nietzsche presents himself as a "disciple of the philosopher Dionysus" (EH "Pref":2), to find the place in which Nietzsche presents himself as having realized the ideals of freedom and self-creation that he outlines in his previous writings.

The aforementioned passage from *The Gay Science* supports this move. In addition to outlining a project of self-creation and stressing the need to become discovers of everything lawful and necessary in the world, Nietzsche first refers to a "we" who "*want to become those we are*" (GS 335). This idea or ideal is central to *Schopenhauer as Educator*, and Nietzsche makes a variant of the phrase the subtitle of *Ecce Homo*, "How One Becomes What One Is." Indeed, the variant used in the subtitle suggests that one of the purposes of *Ecce Homo* is for Nietzsche to explain how he achieved the ideal originally expressed in *Schopenhauer as Educator* and then foreshadowed in *The Gay Science*. Because Nietzsche combines the idea of becoming who one is with a notion of self-creation and a form of autonomy in GS 335, we have reason to believe that *Ecce Homo* is the work in which Nietzsche presents himself as a human being who is "new, unique, incomparable" and who has given himself laws and created himself (GS 335).

So understood, *Ecce Homo* is not only the work in which Nietzsche presents himself as having realized the ideals of freedom and self-creation but also the work in which these ideals come together with his self-proclaimed discipleship to Dionysus. We know that in addition to being the god of tragedy, Dionysus was also the god of comedy, and I have argued elsewhere that *Ecce Homo* should be understood as the *parabasis* of Nietzsche's own comedy (Meyer 2012, 2018). On this reading, the tragedy of *Zarathustra* prepares the way for the Dionysian comedy of Nietzsche's late works. Such a reading makes sense of the fact that Nietzsche repeatedly mentions comedy alongside tragedy in the 1882 edition of *The Gay Science* (GS 1, 107, 153) and then supplements "incipit tragoedia" of GS 342 with "incipit parodia" in the 1887 edition of the text (GS "Pref":1). Of course, if Nietzsche's later writings contain a Dionysian comedy, then it makes sense of the way in which *Zarathustra* IV is both an interlude and a satyr play, as satyr plays have been understood as a transitional genre between tragedy and comedy. That is, *Zarathustra* IV is the interlude between the tragedy of *Zarathustra* I–III and the comedy of Nietzsche's 1888 works.

Although it might sound strange to think that Dionysian comedy—Aristophanes provides us with the only full-length plays that still survive—is the arena in which Nietzsche's ideals of freedom and self-creation are realized, the genre both acknowledges the human being's status as a fully natural being and stresses the way in which human beings create the values and conventions that structure their lived realities and even themselves. What the genre also implies is that there is no objective grounding for these structures and thus the comic poet is free to both deconstruct and then reconstruct social conventions and personal identities over the course of his plays (this is why Plato found comedy to be an equally dangerous counterpart to tragedy). The laughter generated by Dionysian comedy often derives from the destruction of reverences, the overturning of conventions, and the psychological subordination of others through humor and jokes. As Nietzsche has Zarathustra remark in *Zarathustra* IV: "not by wrath does one kill, but by laughter" (ZIV "The Ass Festival").

The destruction of these reverences and the limitations they place on the psyche creates a form of freedom that clears space for genuine self-creation. That is, we can use humor to overcome the tendency to think of ourselves in ways that conform to social conventions and the narratives others tell about us, and it opens up a space for the comic poet to tell her own story and who she fundamentally is. Nietzsche's pushback against forces that would have him be other than who he is can be found in the *agon* he enacts in his late writings with figures like Socrates, Paul, and Wagner. The attack on Socrates in *Twilight of the Idols* ("The Problem of Socrates") is reminiscent of Aristophanes' attack on

Socrates in the *Clouds*. Although his late attacks on Wagner in both *The Case of Wagner* and *Nietzsche contra Wagner* seem to be a mere airing of grievances later in Nietzsche's life, they begin to make sense when understood as part of Nietzsche's comedy. That is, they are attempts to use humor and even malice to undo the psychological grip that even the deceased Wagner held over him. In antiquity, *onomasti komodein* was the technical term used to describe comedy's penchant for *ad hominem* attacks on and comic abuse of notable individuals. Of course, Nietzsche's own *ad hominem* tendencies, especially in his later works, have been well documented (Solomon 2003: Ch.1). Finally, Nietzsche's *agon* with Paul is part of a larger war he is waging with Christianity, and this war reaches its apex with his "Law against Christianity" at the end of *The Antichrist* in which he redates the calendar from September 30, 1888, to "the first day of year one."

For my purposes, the most notable feature of Dionysian or Old Comedy is the *parabasis*, a moment in the play in which the dramatic action stops and the chorus leader directly addresses the audience either on behalf or in the name of the comic poet. It is important because the content of the *parabasis* is often autobiographical. As one scholar writes about the comic poet Aristophanes, "virtually an entire biography, purporting to be historical, has accreted to [Aristophanes] over the centuries on the basis of his parabases" (Rosen 2000:23). At the same time, the *parabasis* offers a highly stylized and rhetorically inflated *persona* of the comic poet. This is why scholars also speak of the "construction of the comic self" in these parabases (Rosen 2000). In so doing, comic poets would often boast of their own prowess and belittle their poetic rivals to comic effect. In the *parabasis* of the *Clouds*, Aristophanes asserts his superiority not only by attributing to himself the virtues of *sophia* (wisdom) and *sōphrosynē* (cleverness) but also by claiming to have been nurtured by Dionysus himself. The parallels to Nietzsche's *Ecce Homo* should be clear: With chapter titles such as "Why I am so Wise" and "Why I am so Clever," he presents himself as a comic *Hanswurst* (EH "Destiny":1), a satyr, and "a disciple of the philosopher Dionysus" (EH "Pref":2). What is often taken to be Nietzsche's autobiography is really an exercise in what I call comic self-definition. That is, Nietzsche is not aiming to write an autobiography in the sense of writing a straightforward story of his life. Instead, he sets out to state definitively who he is: "*Hear me! For I am such and such a person. Above all, do not mistake me for someone else*" (EH "Pref":1).

The title of the final chapter of *Ecce Homo*, "Why I am a Destiny," is worthy of some reflection, and it allows us to conclude by returning to some of the key themes in *Zarathustra* and speculating on the connection between these two works. In addition to being both "wise" and "clever," Nietzsche also claims to be a "destiny [*Schicksal*]." In *Ecce Homo*, the primary meaning of the chapter title seems to be that Nietzsche's works, ideas, and even his person are an unavoidable destiny for the future of humankind. Thus, he claims to break human history into two: "One lives before him, or one lives after him" (EH "Destiny":8). However, the claim to be a destiny can also be understood as Nietzsche asserting the identity of his constructed "I" with nature and fate [*Schicksal*]. So understood, we can see how the tragedy of *Zarathustra* becomes a necessary condition for the creation of his comic *persona* in *Ecce Homo*. This is because the central upshot of *Zarathustra* is the naturalization of the self, such that an "old" or non-naturalized self dies and one is then reborn like a child reconciled with nature. The child at the end of *Zarathustra* III and into *Zarathustra* IV is therefore a "new beginning" and a precondition for the game of (self-)creation (ZI "Three Metamorphoses"). It is only in the comic *parabasis* of *Ecce Homo* that we encounter a new self or *persona*, one that is created not according to social conventions or metaphysical concepts, but in accord with nature, necessity, fate, and what one fundamentally is. Here, the reflectively conscious self ("who one is") is aligned with its innermost nature and the constellation of drives and affects that constitutes the bodily self ("what one is").[8] By creating and being determined by values that are "maximally expressive of a principle internal to the agent herself," this reflective self or *persona* has also attained the kind of freedom that Nietzsche attributes to Goethe (TI "Skirmishes" 49). Because the narrative that defines who he is (the first-person of the reflectively conscious self) aligns with what he is (the third-person bodily self or constellation of drives and affects), Nietzsche does not want himself or the world to be any different from what they are. Thus, he presents himself as having achieved the ideal of *amor fati* (EH "Clever":10), and he presents himself as someone who cannot help but be grateful—the opposite of revenge and *ressentiment*—for his entire life:

> On this perfect day, when everything is ripening and not only the grape turns brown, the eye of the sun just fell upon my life: I looked back, I looked forward, and never saw so many and such good things at once [...]: *How could I fail to be grateful to my whole life?*
>
> (EH "Pref")

NOTES

1 Here it should be noted that the only way in which Nietzsche could be considered a "compatibilist" has to do with the possible compatibility between determinism and a certain type of freedom. As Forester (2019:389) notes, Nietzsche is not a compatibilist in the sense of holding the compatibility between determinism and moral responsibility. Nietzsche clearly appeals to the former (among other considerations) to reject the latter. Also see Riccardi (2017) for an overview of Nietzsche's views on free will.
2 As Löwith (1997:122) points out, the young Nietzsche wrote two early essays on fate and freedom of the will: "Fate and History" and "Freedom of the Will and Fate."
3 See Halliwell (1996) for the view that Plato is responding to an entire worldview embedded within tragedy.
4 To be sure, Plato had predecessors, such as the Pythagoreans, in these respects.
5 For an earlier and important account of this, see Williams (2006).
6 An indirect reference to Spinoza's philosophy is included in Nietzsche's initial sketch of a proto version of *Zarathustra* in 1881, where he includes the phrase "*chaos sive natura*," a clear variation on Spinoza's "*deus sive natura*" (KSA 9:11[185]).
7 See Acampora (2013b) for a reading of *Ecce Homo* in line with this claim.
8 See Riccardi (2021: Ch.8) for the distinction between these two types of selves, a distinction he bases on the chapter, "On the Despisers of the Body" in *Zarathustra* I. Here it is worth noting that, on this model, it is not always the case that the reflectively conscious self adequately expresses and so aligns with the bodily self. In these cases, which are more often the rule rather than the exception, one would not be what one is. Instead, the narrative that the reflectively conscious self creates—the "who one is"—would be the product of both the bodily self (and so an expression of what one is) and socio-cultural forces that shape one to be other than what one is.

APPENDIX

THE WORKS OF FRIEDRICH NIETZSCHE: AN INTERPRETATION[1]

I. The Rebirth of Tragedy at Wagner's Festival in Bayreuth (1872–1876)

   A. *The Birth of Tragedy out of the Spirit of Music* (1872 and 1886)[2]
   B. Two important unpublished essays:[3]

      1. *On Truth and Lie in an Extra-Moral Sense* (1873)
      2. *Philosophy in the Tragic Age of the Greeks* (1873)

   C. Untimely Meditations (1873–1876):

      1. *David Strauss, the Confessor and the Writer* (1873)
      2. *On the Uses and Disadvantages of History for Life* (1874)
      3. *Schopenhauer as Educator* (1874)
      4. *Richard Wagner in Bayreuth* (1876)

II. The Tragedy and Comedy of Life or How Nietzsche Becomes Who He Is (1878–1888)

   A. The Free Spirit and Nietzsche's Rebirth of Tragedy (1878–1885)
      1. The Free Spirit (1878–1882)

         a. The Cycle of *Human, All Too Human I and II* (1886)

            i. *Human, All Too Human* (1878)
            ii. *Assorted Opinions and Maxims* (1879)
            ii. *The Wanderer and His Shadow* (1880)

            b. *Daybreak* (1881 and 1887)
            c. *Idylls from Messina* (1882)
            d. *The Gay Science I–IV* (1882 and 1887)
        2. The Rebirth of Tragedy (1883–1885)
            a. The Tragedy: *Thus Spoke Zarathustra I–III* (1883–1884)
            b. The Satyr Play: *Thus Spoke Zarathustra IV* (1885)[4]
    B. The Philosophy of the Future and the Rebirth of Old Comedy (1886–1888)
        1. Prelude to a Philosophy of the Future (1886–1887)[*]
            a. *Beyond Good and Evil: A Prelude to a Philosophy of the Future* (1886)
            b. *The Gay Science V* (published with the republication of *The Gay Science* I-IV in 1887)
            c. *On the Genealogy of Morals: A Polemic* (1887)
        2. The Rebirth of Old Comedy and a Revaluation of Values (1888)[5]
            a. The Comic Agon
                i. *The Case of Wagner: A Musician's Problem* (1888)
                ii. *Twilight of the Idols or How One Philosophizes with a Hammer* (1888)
                iii. *The Antichrist: A Curse upon Christianity* (1888)
                iv. *Nietzsche contra Wagner: From the Archives of a Psychologist* (1888)
            b. The Comic Parabasis: *Ecce Homo: How One Becomes What One Is* (1888)
        3. *Dithyrambs of Dionysus* (1888–1889)

NOTES

1 The divisions marked here are my own. The works are not listed in exact chronological order. Some minor works are excluded. For a complete list of Nietzsche's works along with publication dates and publishers, see KSA 14:22ff.
2 Nietzsche published a second edition of the text in 1874 and again in 1878.
3 Because these are unpublished essays, these dates listed are those of composition, not publication.
4 This is the year of composition. Nietzsche never published this work during his productive career.
5 For the 1888–1889 works, I provide the dates of composition, not the year of publication.

---

[*] The prefaces Nietzsche added in 1886-1887 to his previous works should also be included here.

BIBLIOGRAPHY

Acampora, Christa Davis (2006). "On Sovereignty and Overhumanity: Why It Matters How We Read Nietzsche's *Genealogy II:2*." In *Nietzsche's "On the Genealogy of Morals": Critical Essays*, ed. C. Davis Acampora, 147–161. New York: Rowman & Littlefield Publishers.
——— (2013). *Contesting Nietzsche*. Chicago: Chicago University Press.
——— (2013b). "Beholding Nietzsche: *Ecce Homo*, Fate, and Freedom." In *The Oxford Handbook of Nietzsche*, ed. K. Gemes and J. Richardson, 363–385. Oxford: Oxford University Press.
Aiken, David Wyatt (2006). "Nietzsche's Zarathustra: The Misreading of a Hero." *Nietzsche-Studien* 35:70–103.
Alderman, Harold (1977). *Nietzsche's Gift*. Athens: Ohio University Press.
Alfano, Mark (2019). *Nietzsche's Moral Psychology*. Cambridge: Cambridge University Press.
Anderson, R. Lanier (2005). "Nietzsche on Truth, Illusion and Redemption." *European Journal of Philosophy* 13(2):185–225.
——— (2022). "Friedrich Nietzsche." In *The Stanford Encyclopedia of Philosophy*, ed. E. Zalta (https://plato.stanford.edu/entries/nietzsche/).
Ansell-Pearson, Keith (1992). "Who is the *Übermensch*? Time, Truth, and Woman in Nietzsche." *Journal of the History of Ideas* 53(2):309–331.
——— (2005). "The Eternal Return of the Overhuman: The Weightiest Knowledge and the Abyss of Light." *Journal of Nietzsche Studies* 30:1–21.
Ansell-Pearson, Keith and Marta Faustino (2022). "Philosophy as a Way of Life in *Thus Spoke Zarathustra*." In *Nietzsche's* Thus Spoke Zarathustra*: A Critical Guide*, eds. K. Ansell-Pearson and P. Loeb, 41–61. Cambridge: Cambridge University Press.

Ansell-Pearson, Keith and Paul Loeb (eds.) (2002). *Nietzsche's* Thus Spoke Zarathustra: *A Critical Guide*. Cambridge: Cambridge University Press.

Babich, Babette (2012). "Nietzsche's Zarathustra and Parodic Style: On Lucian's *Hyperanthropos* and Nietzsche's *Übermensch*." *Diogenes* 58(3):58–74.

Beiser, Frederick (2016). *Weltzschmerz*. Oxford: Oxford University Press.

Bennholdt-Thomsen, Anke (1974). *"Also sprach Zarathustra" als literarisches Phänomen*. Frankfurt: Athenäum-Verlag.

Berkowitz, Peter (1995). *Nietzsche: The Ethics of an Immoralist*. Cambridge, MA: Harvard University Press.

Bleeckere, Sylvain de (1979). "'Also sprach Zarathustra': Die Neugestaltung der 'Geburt der Tragödie'." *Nietzsche-Studien* 8:270–290.

Biles, Zachary (2011). *Aristophanes and the Poetics of Competition*. Cambridge: Cambridge University Press.

Bishop, Paul and Roger H. Stephenson (2005). *Friedrich Nietzsche and Weimar Classicism*. Rochester, NY: Camden House.

Blue, Daniel (2016). *The Making of Friedrich Nietzsche: The Quest for Identity, 1844–1869*. Cambridge: Cambridge University Press.

Brinton, Crane (1948). *Nietzsche*. Cambridge, MA: Harvard University Press.

Brobjer, Thomas (2008). "*Thus Spoke Zarathustra* as Nietzsche's Autobiography." In *Nietzsche's* Thus Spoke Zarathustra: *Before Sunrise*, ed. J. Luchte, 29–46. London: Continuum Publishing.

––––––– (2021). *Nietzsche's Ecce Homo and the Revaluation of All Values: Dionysus versus Christian Values*. London: Bloomsbury Academic.

––––––– (2023). *The Close Relationship between Nietzsche's Two Most Important Books*. London: Palgrave Macmillan.

––––––– (2023b). Twilight of the Idols *and Nietzsche's Late Philosophy*. London: Bloomsbury Academic.

Brusotti, Marco (1997). *Die Leidenschaft der Erkenntnis: Philosophie und ästhetische Lebensgestaltung bei Nietzsche von* Morgenröthe *bis Also sprach Zarathustra*. Berlin: De Gruyter.

––––––– (2016). "Unsere letze Dankbarkeit gegen die Kunst: Die Druckbogen der *Fröhlichen Wissenschaft* und Nietzsches Abschied von seiner 'Freigeisterei'." In *Nietzsche zwischen Philosophie und Literatur*, ed. K Grätz and S. Kaufmann, 199–220. Heidelberg: Universitätsverlag Winter.

––––––– (2019). "Die Autonomie des 'souveränen Individuums' in Nietzsches *Genealogie der Moral*." *Nietzsche-Studien* 48:36–48.

Burnham, Douglas and Martin Jesinghausen (2010). *Nietzsche's* Thus Spoke Zarathustra. Bloomington, IN: Indiana University Press.

Calder III, W. M. (1985). "The Lion Laughed." *Nietzsche-Studien* 14:357–359.

Cauchi, Francesca (1998). *Zarathustra contra Zarathustra: The Tragic Buffoon*. London: Routledge.

Clark, Maudemarie (1990). *Nietzsche on Truth and Philosophy*. Cambridge: Cambridge University Press.

Clayton, John Powell (1985). "Zarathustra and the Stages on Life's Way. A Nietzschean Riposte to Kierkegaard?" *Nietzsche-Studien* 14:179–200.

Conway, Daniel (1988). "Nietzsche's *Zarathustra* as Political Irony." *Political Theory* 16(2):257–289.

——— (1989). "Overcoming the *Uebermensch*: Nietzsche's Revaluation of Values." *Journal of the British Society for Phenomenology* 20(3):211–224.

——— (1990). "Nietzsche contra Nietzsche: The Deconstruction of *Zarathustra*." In *Nietzsche as Postmodernist: Essays Pro and Contra*, ed. C. Koelb, 91–110. Albany, NY: SUNY Press.

——— (2008). "For Whom the Bell Tolls." *Journal of Nietzsche Studies* 35/36:88–104.

Crawford, Claudia (1995). *To Nietzsche: Dionysus, I Love You! Ariadne*. Albany, NY: State University of New York Press.

Creasy, Kaitlyn (2020). *The Problem of Affective Nihilism in Nietzsche: Thinking Differently, Feeling Differently*. London: Palgrave

——— (2022). "Nietzsche on the Re-Naturalization of Humanity in *Thus Spoke Zarathustra*." In *Nietzsche's* Thus Spoke Zarathustra*: A Critical Guide*, eds. K. Ansell-Pearson and P. Loeb, 225–246. Cambridge: Cambridge University Press

Danto, Arthur (1965). *Nietzsche as Philosopher*. New York: Columbia University Press.

Del Caro, Adrian (1988). "Symbolizing Philosophy: Ariadne and the Labyrinth." *Nietzsche-Studien* 17:125–157.

——— (2011). "Zarathustra is Dead, Long Live Zarathustra!" *The Journal of Nietzsche Studies* 41:83–93.

——— (2014). "Zarathustra vs. Faust, or Anti-Romantic Rivalry among Superhumans." In *Nietzsche on Art and Life*, ed. D. Came, 143–162. Oxford: Oxford University Press.

D'Iorio, Paulo (2014). "The Eternal Return: Genesis and Interpretation." *Lexicon Philosophicum: Journal for the History of Texts and Ideas* 2:41–96.

——— (2016). *Nietzsche's Journey to Sorrento: Genesis of the Philosophy of the Free Spirit*, trans. S. M. Gotelick. Princeton, NJ: Princeton University Press.

Djurić, Mihailo (1979). "Die Antiken Quellen der Wiederkunftslehre." *Nietzsche-Studien* 8:1–16.

Dühring, Eugen (1865). *Der Werth des Lebens: Eine philosophische Betrachtung*. Breslau: Verlag der Eduard Trewendt.

——— (1875). *Cursus der Philosophie als streng Wissenschaftlicher Weltanschauung und Lebensgestaltung*. Leipzig: L. Heimann's Verlag.

Easterling, P. E. (1997). "A Show for Dionysus." In *The Cambridge Companion to Greek Tragedy*, ed. P. E. Easterling, 36–53. Cambridge: Cambridge University Press.

Elliott, Richard (2022). "Why 'All Joy Wills Eternity'." In *Joy and Laughter in Nietzsche's Philosophy: Alternative Liberatory Politics*, eds. M. McNeal and P. Kirkland, 85–104. London: Bloomsbury.

——— (forthcoming). "Eternal Recurrence, 'On Redemption' and the Risk of Self-Deception."

Fink, Eugen (2003). *Nietzsche's Philosophy*. Trans. G. Richter. New York: Continuum.

Flucher, Elisabeth (2022). *Philosophische Seiltänze: Zur poetischen Argumentation in Nietzsches Also Sprach Zarathustra."* Paderborn: Brill Fink.

Forester, Michael (2019). "Nietzsche on Free Will." In *The New Cambridge Companion to Nietzsche*, ed. T. Stern, 374–396. Cambridge: Cambridge University Press.

Förster-Nietzsche, Elisabeth (1929). "Introduction." In *Thus Spake Zarathustra*, trans. T. Common, 9–21. New York: The Modern Library.

Franco, Paul (2022). "The Great Politics of *Thus Spoke Zarathustra*." In *Nietzsche's Thus Spoke Zarathustra: A Critical Guide*, eds. K. Ansell-Pearson and P. Loeb, 187–204. Cambridge: Cambridge University Press.

Gadamer, Hans-Georg (1988). "The Drama of Zarathustra," trans. H. Heilke. In *Nietzsche's New Seas: Explorations in Philosophy, Aesthetics, and Politics*, eds. M. A. Gillespie and T. B. Strong, 220–231. Chicago: The University of Chicago Press.

Gooding-Williams, Robert (1990). "Zarathustra's Three Metamorphoses." In C. Koelb, *Nietzsche as Postmodernist: Essays Pro and Contra*, 231–245. Albany, NY: SUNY Press.

——— (2001). *Zarathustra's Dionysian Modernism*. Palo Alto, CA: Stanford University Press.

——— (2011). Review of *The Death of Zarathustra* by Paul S. Loeb. In *Notre Dame Philosophical Reviews*. April 4, 2011: https://ndpr.nd.edu/reviews/the-death-of-nietzsche-s-zarathustra/

Grätz, Katharina (2017). "Portofino in der Schweiz? Textgenese und Deutungsperspektiven von Nietzsches Gedicht 'Sils Maria'." In *Nietzsche und die Lyrik: Ein Compendium*, eds. C. Benne and C. Zittel, 283–298. Stuttgart: J. B. Metzler Verlag.

——— (2024). *Kommentar zu Nietzsches Also sprach Zarathustra I und II*. In *Historischer und kritischer Kommentar zu Friedrich Nietzsches Werken*, Vol. 4/1. Berlin: De Gruyter.

——— (2024b). *Kommentar zu Nietzsches Also sprach Zarathustra III und IV*. In *Historischer und kritischer Kommentar zu Friedrich Nietzsches Werken*, Vol. 4/2. Berlin: De Gruyter.

Groddeck, Wolfram (1997). "Die 'Neue Ausgabe' der 'Fröhlichen Wissenschaft': Ueberlegungen zu Paratextualität und Werkkomposition in Nietzsches Schriften nach 'Zarathustra'." *Nietzsche-Studien* 26:184–198.

——— (2016). "Das Nachtlied. Dithyrambisch reflektierte Rede in *Also sprach Zarathustra*." In *Nietzsche zwischen Philosophie und Literatur*, ed. K. Grätz and S. Kaufmann, 413–424. Heidelberg: Universitätsverlag Winter.

Groff, Peter (2003). "*Amor Fati* and *Züchtung*. The Paradox of Nietzsche's Nomothetic Naturalism." *International Studies in Philosophy* 35(3):29–52.

——— (2004). "Who is Zarathustra's Ape?" In *A Nietzschean Bestiary: Animality Beyond Docile and Brutal*, eds. C. Davis Acampora and R. R. Acampora, 17–31. Lanham, MD: Rowan and Littlefield.

——— (2021). "Zarathustra's Blessed Isles: Before and After Great Politics." *Journal of Nietzsche Studies* 52:135–163.

——— (2022). "'Is the Sea Not Full of Verdant Islands?': Zarathustra on Passing by the Great City." In *Joy and Laughter in Nietzsche's Philosophy: Alternative Liberatory Politics*, eds. M. McNeal and P. Kirkland, 65–84. London: Bloomsbury.
Guay, Robert (2002). "Nietzsche on Freedom." *European Journal of Philosophy* 10:302–27.
Haase, Marie-Luise (1984). "Der *Übermensch* in *Also Sprach Zarathustra* und im Zarathustra-Nachlass 1882–1885." *Nietzsche-Studien* 13:228–244.
——— (1994). "Zarathustra auf den Spuren des Empedokles und eines gewissen Herrn Bootty." In *"Centauren-Geburten". Wissenschaft, Kunst und Philosophie beim jungen Nietzsche*, eds. T. Borsche, F. Gerrantana, A. Venturelli, 503–523. Berlin: De Gruyter.
Halliwell, Stephen (1996): "Plato's Repudiation of the Tragic." In *Tragedy and the Tragic*, ed. M. Silk, 332–349. Oxford: Clarendon Press.
——— (1998). *Aristotle's Poetics*. Chicago: The University of Chicago Press.
——— (2008). *Greek Laughter: A Study of Cultural Psychology from Homer to Early Christianity*. Cambridge: Cambridge University Press.
Han-Pile, Beatrice (2011). "Nietzsche and Amor Fati." *European Journal of Philosophy* 19(2):224–61.
Hatab, Lawrence J. (1988). "Laughter in Nietzsche's Thought." *International Studies in Philosophy* 20(2):67–79.
——— (2005). *Nietzsche's Life Sentence: Coming to Terms with Eternal Recurrence*. London: Routledge.
——— (2018). "What Kind of Text is *Zarathustra*?" *The Agonist* 11(2):1–7.
Havas, Randall (2013). "The Overman." In *The Oxford Handbook of Nietzsche*, eds. K. Gemes and J. Richardson, 645–671. Oxford: Oxford University Press.
Heidegger, Martin (1967). "Who is Nietzsche's Zarathustra?" *Review of Metaphysics* 20(3):411–431.
Heller, Erich (1973). "Zarathustra's Three Metamorphoses. Facets of Nietzsche's Intellectual Biography and the Apotheosis of Innocence." *Salmagundi* 21:63–80.
Hellwald, Friedrich von (1874). *Culturgeschichte in ihrer natürlichen Entstehung bis zur Gegenwart*. Augsburg: Lampart & Co.
Higgins, Kathleen M. (1987). *Nietzsche's Zarathustra*. Philadelphia, PA: Temple University Press.
Hollingdale, R. J. (1984). "'Introduction' and 'Notes'." In *Dithyrambs of Dionysus*, Friedrich Nietzsche, trans. R. J. Hollingdale, 7–18 and 85–95. London: Anvil Press Poetry.
Hollinrake, Roger (1982). *Nietzsche, Wagner, and the Philosophy of Pessimism*. New York: Routledge.
Huddleston, Andrew (2019). "The Value of Our Values: Nietzsche" In *A Companion to Nineteenth-Century Philosophy*, ed. J. Shand, 339–364. London: Blackwell.
——— (2020). "Nietzsche's Aesthetics." *Philosophy Compass* 15(11):1–9.

Ioan, Razvan (2021). "Self-Love in Nietzsche's *Thus Spoke Zarathustra*." *The European Legacy* 26(5):505–518.

Janaway, Christopher (2007). *Beyond Selflessness: Reading Nietzsche's Genealogy*. Oxford: Oxford University.

——— (2022). "Zarathustra's Response to Schopenhauer." In *Nietzsche's* Thus Spoke Zarathustra: *A Critical Guide*, eds. K. Ansell-Pearson and P. Loeb, 83–103. Cambridge: Cambridge University Press.

Jenkins, Scott (2012). "Time and Personal Identity in Nietzsche's Theory of Eternal Recurrence." *Philosophy Compass* 7(3):208–217.

——— (2019). "Nietzsche's Psychology of Metaphysics (Or, Metaphysics as Revenge)." In *Nietzsche's Metaphilosophy*, eds. P. Loeb and M. Meyer, 227–246. Cambridge: Cambridge University Press.

——— (2020). "The Pessimistic Origin of Nietzsche's Thought of Eternal Recurrence." *Inquiry* 63(1):20–41.

——— (2022). "Zarathustra's Great Contempt." In *Nietzsche's* Thus Spoke Zarathustra: *A Critical Guide*, eds. K. Ansell-Pearson and P. Loeb, 168–186. Cambridge: Cambridge University Press.

Johnson, Dirk (2019). "*Zarathustra:* Nietzsche's Rendezvous with Eternity." In *The New Cambridge Companion to Nietzsche*, ed. T. Stern, 173–194. Cambridge: Cambridge University Press.

Kane, Robert (1998). *The Significance of Free Will*. Oxford: Oxford University Press.

Katsafanas, Paul (2022). "What Makes the Affirmation of Life Difficult?" *In Nietzsche's* Thus Spoke Zarathustra: *A Critical Guide*, eds. K. Ansell-Pearson and P. Loeb, 62–82. Cambridge: Cambridge University Press.

Kaufmann, Walter (1974). *Nietzsche: Philosopher, Psychologist, Antichrist*. Princeton: Princeton University Press.

Kerkman, Jan (2017). "Die Einkreisung der schwarzen Schlange: Zur Figur des Wahrsagers im *Zarathustra*." In *Nietzsche als Dichter*, eds. K. Grätz and S. Kaufmann, 245–272. Berlin: De Gruyter.

Knortz, Karl (1906). *Nietzsche's* Zarathustra: *Eine Einführung*. Halle: Verlag von Hugo Peter.

Lampert, Laurence (1986). *Nietzsche's Teaching: An Interpretation of* Thus Spoke Zarathustra. New Haven, CT: Yale University Press.

Leiter, Brian (1992). "Nietzsche and Aestheticism." *Journal of the History of Philosophy* 30(2):275–290.

——— (2001). "The Paradox of Fatalism and Self-Creation in Nietzsche." In *Nietzsche*, eds. B. Leiter and J. Richardson, 281–321. Oxford: Oxford University Press.

——— (2002). *Routledge Philosophy Guidebook to Nietzsche on Morality*. London: Routledge.

——— (2013). "Nietzsche's Naturalism Reconsidered." In *The Oxford Handbook of Nietzsche*, eds. K. Gemes and J. Richardson, 576–598. Oxford: Oxford University Press.

——— (2019). *Moral Psychology with Nietzsche*. Oxford: Oxford University Press.

Loeb, Paul S. (1998). "The Moment of Tragic Death in Nietzsche's Dionysian Doctrine of Eternal Recurrence: An Exegesis of Aphorism 341 in *The Gay Science*." *International Studies in Philosophy* 33(3):131–143.

——— (2000). "The Conclusion of Nietzsche's *Zarathustra*." *International Studies in Philosophy* 32(3):137–152.

——— (2001). "Time, Power, and Superhumanity." *Journal of Nietzsche Studies* 21(1):27–47.

——— (2002). "The Dwarf, the Dragon, and the Ring of the Eternal Recurrence: A Wagnerian Key to the Riddle of Nietzsche's Zarathustra." *Nietzsche-Studien* 31:91–113.

——— (2004). "Zarathustra's Laughing Lions." In *A Nietzschean Bestiary: Becoming Animal Beyond Docile and Brutal*, ed. Christa Davis Acampora and Ralph R. Acampora, 121–139. Lanham, MD: Rowman & Littlefield.

——— (2006). "Finding the *Übermensch* in Nietzsche's *Genealogy of Morality*." In *Nietzsche's "On the Genealogy of Morals": Critical Essays*, ed. C. Davis Acampora, 163–176. New York: Rowman & Littlefield Publishers.

———(2008). "The Gateway-Augenblick." In *Nietzsche's* Thus Spoke Zarathustra: *Before Sunrise*, ed. J. Luchte, 91–108. London: Continuum Publishing.

——— (2010). *The Death of Nietzsche's Zarathustra*. Cambridge: Cambridge University Press.

——— (2013). "Eternal Recurrence." In *The Oxford Handbook of Nietzsche*, eds. K. Gemes and J. Richardson, 645–671. Oxford: Oxford University Press.

——— (2018). "The Colossal Moment in Nietzsche's Gay Science 341." In *The Nietzschean Mind*, ed. P. Katsafanas, 428–447. London: Routledge.

——— (2021). "Ecce Superhomo: How Zarathustra Became What Nietzsche Was Not." In *Nietzsche's "Ecce Homo"*, eds. N. Martin and D. Large, 207–234. Berlin: De Gruyter.

——— (2021b). "Nietzsche's Heraclitean Doctrine of the Eternal Recurrence of the Same." *Nietzsche-Studien* 50:70–101

——— (2022). "What does Nietzsche Mean by 'the Same' in His Theory of Eternal Recurrence?" *Journal of Nietzsche Studies* 53:1–33.

——— (2022b). "Nietzsche's Solution to the Problem of Change." In *Nietzsche's Thus Spoke* Zarathustra: *A Critical Guide*, eds. K. Ansell-Pearson and P. Loeb, 125–147. Cambridge: Cambridge University Press.

Loeb, Paul S. and David F. Tinsley (2019). "Translators' Afterword." In *CWFN* 14:717–798.

——— (2022). "Translators' Afterword." In *CWFN* 15:475–532.

Löwith, Karl (1997). *Nietzsche's Philosophy of the Eternal Recurrence of the Same*. Trans. H. Lomax. Berkeley: University of California Press.

Mack, Katie (2021). *The End of Everything (Astrophysically Speaking)*. New York: Scribner.

Magnus, Bernd (1978). *Nietzsche's Existential Imperative*. Bloomington: Indiana University Press.

———. (1983). "Perfectibility and Attitude in Nietzsche's '*Übermensch*'." *The Review of Metaphysics* 36(3):633–659.

Marsden, Jill (2005). "Sensing the Overhuman." *The Journal of Nietzsche Studies* 30:102–114.

Martin, Clancy (2008). "Thus Spoke Zarathustra." In *Notre Dame Philosophical Reviews*. February 6, 2008: https://ndpr.nd.edu/reviews/thus-spoke-zarathustra/

McNeil, Beavis (2021). *Nietzsche and Eternal Recurrence*. London: Palgrave MacMillan.

Meier, Heinrich (2017). *Was ist Nietzsches Zarathustra?* Munich: C. H. Beck.

Meyer, Matthew (2002). "The Tragic Nature of Zarathustra." *Nietzscheforschung* 9:209–218.

——— (2004). "*Human, All Too Human* and the Socrates Who Plays Music." *International Studies in Philosophy* 36(3):171–182.

——— (2006). "The Three Metamorphoses of the Free Spirit." *International Studies in Philosophy* 38(3):49–63.

——— (2012). "The Comic Nature of *Ecce Homo*." *Journal of Nietzsche Studies* 43(1):32–43.

——— (2014). "The Ancient Quarrel between Philosophy and Poetry in Nietzsche's Early Writings." In *Nietzsche's Value as a Scholar of Antiquity*, eds. A. Jensen and H. Heit, 197–214. New York: Bloomsbury Academic.

——— (2014b). "Peisetairos of Aristophanes' *Birds* and the Erotic Tyrant of *Republic* IX." In *The Political Theory of Aristophanes*, eds. J. J. Mhire and B.-P. Frost, 275–302. Binghamton, NY: SUNY Press.

——— (2014c). *Reading Nietzsche through the Ancients*. Berlin: De Gruyter.

——— (2015). "Nietzsche's Naturalized Aestheticism." *British Journal for the History of Philosophy* 23(1):138–160.

——— (2018). "The Divine Hanswurst: Nietzsche on Laughter and Comedy." In *Humor, Comedy, and Laughter in 19th-Century Philosophy*, ed. L. Moland, 153–173. New York: Springer.

——— (2018b). "Nietzsche's Ontic Structural Realism?" In *The Nietzschean Mind*, ed. P. Katsafanas, 365–380. London: Routledge.

——— (2019). *Nietzsche's Free Spirit Works: A Dialectical Reading*. Cambridge: Cambridge University Press.

——— (2019b). "Review of *Friedrich Nietzsche and European Nihilism* by Paul van Tongeren." *Notre Dame Philosophical Reviews* (3 September 2019): https://ndpr.nd.edu/reviews/friedrich-nietzsche-and-european-nihilism/.

——— (2022). "Nietzsche's Naturalism and Thus Spoke Zarathustra." In *Nietzsche's Thus Spoke* Zarathustra: *A Critical Guide*, eds. K. Ansell-Pearson and P. Loeb, 104–124. Cambridge: Cambridge University Press.

Moles, Alistair (1990). *Nietzsche's Philosophy of Nature and Cosmology*. New York, NY: Peter Lang.

Montinari, Mazzino (2003). *Reading Nietzsche*, trans. G. Whitlock. Urbana, IL: Illinois University Press.

Nehamas, Alexander (1985). *Nietzsche: Life as Literature*. Cambridge, MA: Harvard University Press.

——— (2012). "For Whom the Sun Shines. A Reading of Also sprach Zarathustra." In *Friedrich Nietzsche: Also sprach Zarathustra*, ed. V. Gerhardt, second edition, 123–142. Berlin: Akademie-Verlag.

O'Connor, Timothy (2022). "Free Will." In *Stanford Encyclopedia of Philosophy*, ed. E. Zalta: https://plato.stanford.edu/entries/freewill/.
Owen, David (2009). "Autonomy, Self-Respect, and Self-Love: Nietzsche on Ethical Agency." In *Nietzsche on Freedom and Autonomy*, eds. K. Gemes and S. May, 197–222. Oxford: Oxford University Press.
Parkes, Graham (1994). *Composing the Soul: The Reaches of Nietzsche's Psychology*. Chicago, IL: University of Chicago Press.
——— (2005). "Introduction." In *Thus Spoke Zarathustra: A Book for Everyone and Nobody*, ed. and trans. G. Parkes, ix–xxxiv. Oxford: Oxford University Press
——— (2008). "The Symphonic Structure of *Thus Spoke Zarathustra*: A Preliminary Outline." In *Nietzsche's* Thus Spoke Zarathustra: *Before Sunrise*, ed. J. Luchte, 9–28. London: Continuum Publishing.
Parr, Jamie (2022). "'What Do I Matter!': Nietzsche on Pascal, Self-Obsession, and Good Cheer." In *Joy and Laughter in Nietzsche's Philosophy: Alternative Liberatory Politics*, eds. P.E. Kirkland and M. J. McNeal, 105–122. London: Bloomsbury.
Pickard-Cambridge, Sir Arthur (1962). *Dithyramb Tragedy and Comedy*. Second Edition, rev. T. L. Webster. Oxford: Clarendon Press.
Pippin, Robert B. (1988). "Irony and Affirmation in Nietzsche's *Thus Spoke Zarathustra*." In *Nietzsche's New Seas: Explorations in Philosophy, Aesthetics, and Politics*, eds. M. A. Gillespie and T. B. Strong, 45–71. Chicago: The University of Chicago Press.
——— (2006). "Introduction." In *Thus Spoke Zarathustra* by Friedrich Nietzsche, eds. A. Del Caro and R. Pippin, viii-xxxv. Cambridge: Cambridge University Press.
Plato (1997). *Plato: Complete Works*, ed. by J. M. Cooper. Indianapolis, IN: Hackett Publishing Company.
Platt, Michael (1988). "What Does Zarathustra Whisper in Life's Ear?" *Nietzsche-Studien* 17:179–194.
Poellner, Peter (1995). *Nietzsche and Metaphysics*. Oxford: Oxford University Press.
Pütz, Babette (2003). *The Symposium and Komos in Aristophanes*. Stuttgart: Verlag J.B. Metzler.
Reginster, Bernard (2006). *The Affirmation of Life: Nietzsche on the Overcoming of Nihilism*. Cambridge, MA: Harvard University Press.
Remhof, Justin (2022). *Nietzsche as Metaphysician*. New York: Routledge.
Riccardi, Mattia (2017). "Friedrich Nietzsche." In *The Routledge Companion to Free Will*, eds. K. Timpe, M. Griffith, N. Levy, 364–372. London: Routledge.'
——— (2021). *Nietzsche's Philosophical Psychology*. Oxford: Oxford University Press.
Richardson, John (2009). "Nietzsche's Freedoms." In *Nietzsche on Freedom and Autonomy*, eds. K. Gemes and S. May, 127–149. Oxford: Oxford University Press.
——— (2020). *Nietzsche's Values*. Oxford: Oxford University Press.
Ridley, Aaron (1997). "Nietzsche's Greatest Weight." *Journal of Nietzsche Studies* 14:19–25.

Riedel, Manfred (1988). "Nietzsches Gedicht 'Sils Maria'. Entstehungsgeschichte und Deutung." *Nietzsche-Studien* 27:268–282.

Risse, Mathias (2003). "Nietzsche's 'Joyous and Trusting Fatalism'." *International Studies in Philosophy* 35(3):147–162.

Röllin, Beat (2012). *Nietzsches Wekpläne vom Sommer 1885. Eine Nachlass-Lektüre. Philologischchronologische Erschließung der Manuskripte*. Munich: Wilhelm Fink

Rosen, Ralph (2000). "Cratinus' *Pytine* and the Construction of the Comic Self." In *The Rivals of Aristophanes*, eds. D. Harvey and J. Wilkins, 23–39. Swansea: Duckworth and the Classical Press of Wales.

Rosen, Stanley (1995). *The Mask of Enlightenment: Nietzsche's Zarathustra*. Cambridge: Cambridge University Press.

Ruin, Hans (2019). "Saying *Amen* to the Light of Dawn: Nietzsche on Praise, Prayer, and Affirmation." *Nietzsche-Studien* 48:99–116.

Rutherford, Donald (2011). "Freedom as a Philosophical Ideal: Nietzsche and His Antecedents." *Inquiry* 54(5):512–540.

Salaquarda, Jörg (1989). "Der ungeheure Augenblick." *Nietzsche-Studien* 18:91–136.

——— (1997). "Die fröhliche Wissenschaft: Zwischen Freigeisterei und neuer 'Lehre'." *Nietzsche-Studien* 26:165–183.

——— (2012). "Die Grundconception des *Zarathustra*." In *Also sprach Zarathustra*, ed. V. Gerhardt, 51–68. Berlin: Akademie Verlag.

Santaniello, Weaver (2005). *Zarathustra's Last Supper: Nietzsche's Eight Higher Men*. Burlington, VT: Ashgate.

Schaberg, William H. (1995). *The Nietzsche Canon*. Chicago: Chicago University Press.

Schacht, Richard (1983). *Nietzsche*. New York: Routledge & Kegan Paul.

——— (2023). *Nietzsche's Kind of Philosophy: Finding His Way*. Chicago: The University of Chicago Press.

Schutte, Ofelia (1999). "Willing Backwards: Nietzsche on Time, Pain, Joy, and Memory." In *Nietzsche and Depth Psychology*, eds. J. Golomb, W. Santaniello, and R. L. Lehrer, 45–71. Chicago: Chicago University Press.

Seung, T. K. (2005). *Nietzsche's Epic of the Soul:* Thus Spoke Zarathustra. New York, NY: Lexington Books.

Shapiro, Gary (1989). *Nietzschean Narratives*. Bloomington, IN: Indiana University Press.

——— (2017). "Nietzsche and Anaximander: The Innocence of Becoming, of Life without a Mortgage." In *Nietzsche and the Philosophers*, ed. M. T. Conard, 86–103. London: Routledge.

Shepherd, Melanie (2011). "Affirmation and Mortal Life: Nietzsche's Eternal Return and the Death of Zarathustra." *Philosophy Today* 55(1):22–36.

——— (2018). "On the Difficult Case of Loving Life: Plato's *Symposium* and Nietzsche's Eternal Recurrence." *British Journal for the History of Philosophy* 26(3):519–539.

——— (2022). "Nietzsche's *Übermensch*: From Shared Suffering to Shared Joy." In *Joy and Laughter in Nietzsche's Philosophy: Alternative Liberatory Politics*, eds. P. Kirkland and M. McNeal, 47–64. Bloomsbury.

Simmel, Georg (1991). *Nietzsche and Schopenhauer*, trans. H. Loiskandl, D. Weinstein, M. Weinstein. Urbana, IL: University of Illinois Press.

Sinhababu, Neil (2015). "Zarathustra's Metaethics." *Canadian Journal of Philosophy* 45(3):278–299.

——— (2022). "Zarathustra's Moral Psychology." In *Nietzsche's Thus Spoke Zarathustra: A Critical Guide*, eds. K. Ansell-Pearson and P. Loeb, 148–167. Cambridge: Cambridge University Press.

——— (forthcoming). *Nietzsche on the Eternal Recurrence*. Cambridge: Cambridge University Press.

Sinhababu, Neil and Kuong Un Teng (2019). "Loving the Eternal Recurrence." *The Journal of Nietzsche Studies* 50(1):106–124.

Skowron, Michael (2004). "Zarathustra-Lehren *Übermensch*, Wille zur Macht, Ewige Wiederkunft." *Nietzsche-Studien* 33:68–89.

——— (2016). "Das Gewissen des Tänzers, Selle, Leben, Weisheit, Wahrheit, Ewigkeit, Liebe und Tod in und um Zarathustras anderes Tanzlied." *Nietzsche-Studien* 45:189–219.

Small, Robin (1983). "Three Interpretations of the Eternal Recurrence." *Dialogue* 22:91–112.

——— (1998). "Zarathustra's Gateway." *History of Philosophy Quarterly* 15:79–85.

——— (2001). "Zarathustra's Four Ways: Structures of Becoming in Nietzsche's Thought." *British Journal for the History of Philosophy* 9(1):83–107.

——— (2010). *Time and Becoming in Nietzsche's Thought*. London: Continuum.

Soll, Ivan (1973). "Reflections on Recurrence: A Re-Examination of Nietzsche's Doctrine, Die ewige Wiederkehr des Gleichen." In *Nietzsche: A Collection of Critical Essays*, ed. R. C. Solomon, 322–342. Anchor Books: Doubleday.

——— (1988). "Pessimism and the Tragic View of Life: Reconsiderations of Nietzsche's *Birth of Tragedy*." In *Reading Nietzsche*, eds. R. Solomon and K. Higgins, 104–131. Oxford: Oxford University Press.

Solomon, Robert (2002). "Nietzsche on Fatalism and 'Free Will'." *The Journal of Nietzsche Studies* 23:63–87.

——— (2003). *Living with Nietzsche*. Oxford: Oxford University Press.

Sommer, Andreas Urs (2012). "Nietzsche's Readings on Spinoza: A Contextualist Study, Particularly on the Reception of Kuno Fischer." *The Journal of Nietzsche Studies* 43(2):156–184.

Sorgner, Stefan (2017). "Nietzsche, the Overhuman, and Transhumanism." In *Nietzsche and Transhumanism: Precursor or Enemy?*, ed. Y. Tuncel, 14–26. Cambridge: Cambridge Scholars Publishing.

Söring, Jürgen (1990). "Nietzsches Empedokles-Plan." *Nietzsche-Studien* 176–211.

Stambaugh, Joan (1972). *Nietzsche's Thought of Eternal Return*. Baltimore, MD: Johns Hopkins University Press.

Stegmaier, Werner (2013). "Oh Mensch! Gieb Acht! Kontextuelle Interpretation des Mitternachts-Lieds aus *Also sprach Zarathustra*." *Nietzsche-Studien* 42:85–115.

——— (2016). "Zarathustra philosophische Auslegung des Mitternachts-Lieds." In *Nietzsche zwischen Philosophie und Literatur. Von der* Fröhlichen Wissenschaft *zu* Also Sprach Zarathustra, eds. K. Grätz and S. Kaufmann, 425–442. Heidelberg: Universitätsverlag Winter

Stellino, Paulo (2013). "Nietzsche on Suicide." *Nietzsche-Studien* 42:151–177.

Stern, Tom (2008). "Nietzsche on Context and the Individual." *Nietzscheforschung* 15:299–315.

——— (2011). "Back to the Future: Eternal Recurrence and the Death of Socrates." *The Journal of Nietzsche Studies* 43:73–82.

——— (2013). "Nietzsche, Amor Fati and the Gay Science." *Proceedings of the Aristotelian Society* 113:145–162.

Strawson, P.F. (2020). "Freedom and Resentment." In *Freedom, Resentment, and the Metaphysics of Morals*, ed. P. Hieronymi, 107–134. Princeton, NJ: Princeton University Press.

Sutton, Dana F. (1980). *The Greek Satyr Play*. Meinsenheim am Glan: Anton Hain.

——— (1984). "Aeschylus' *Proteus*." *Philologus* 128(1):127–130.

Tevenar, Gudrun von (2013). "Zarathustra: 'That Malicious Dionysian'." *The Oxford Handbook of Nietzsche*, ed., J. Ricahrdson and K. Gemes, 272–297. Oxford: Oxford University Press.

Usher, M. D. (2002). "Satyr Play in Plato's *Symposium*." *The American Journal of Philology* 123(2):205–228.

Velkley, Richard L. (ed.) (2017): *Leo Strauss on Nietzsche's* Thus Spoke Zarathustra. Chicago: The University of Chicago Press.

Vivarelli, Vivetta (1989). "Empedokles und Zarathustra: Verschwendeter Reichtum und Wollust am Untergang." *Nietzsche-Studien* 18:509–536.

——— (1992). "Metaphern des Dionysischen bei Nietzsche." In *Nietzsche und die antike Philosophie*, eds. D. W. Conway and R. Rehn, 153–171. Trier: Wissenschaftlicher Verlag.

——— (2012). "Umkehr und Wiederkehr: Zarathustra in seinen Bildern." In *Friedrich Nietzsche: Also sprach Zarathustra*, ed. V. Gerhardt, second edition, 243–263. Berlin: Akademie-Verlag.

——— (2017). "Das Mitternachtslied im 'Zarathustra' und die Nacht des 'Tristan': Reime und Schlüsselworte." In *Nietzsche und die Lyrik: Ein* Kompendium, eds. C. Benne and C. Zittel, 310–314. Stuttgart: J. B. Metzler Verlag.

——— (2018). "Der Bildner des *Übermenschen* und der dithyrambische Künstler: Michelangelo und Wagner in *Also sprach Zarathustra*." *Nietzsche-Studien* 47:326–339.

Waller, Bruce N. (2011). *Against Moral Responsibility*. Cambridge, MA: The MIT Press.

Westerdale, Joel (2006). "Zarathustra's Preposterous History." *Nietzsche-Studien* 35:47–69.

Whitlock, Greg (1990). *Returning to Sils-Maria: A Commentary to Nietzsche's "Also sprach Zarathustra."* New York: Peter Lang Publishing.

Williams, Bernard (2006). "Nietzsche's Minimalist Moral Psychology." In *The Sense of the Past: Essays in the History of Philosophy*, ed. M. Burnyeat, 299–310. Princeton, NJ: Princeton University Press.

Wohlfart, Günter (1997). "Wer ist Nietzsches Zarathustra?" *Nietzsche-Studien* 26:319–330.

Young, Julian (1992). *Nietzsche's Philosophy of Art*. Cambridge: Cambridge University Press.

——— (2010). *Friedrich Nietzsche: A Philosophical Biography*. Cambridge: Cambridge University Press.
Zamosc, Gabriel (2015). "Life, Death, and Eternal Recurrence in Nietzsche's Zarathustra." *The Agonist* 8(1–2).
——— (2015b). "What Zarathustra Whispers." *Nietzsche-Studien* 44:231–266.
——— (2022). "Joyful Transhumanism: Love and Eternal Recurrence." In *Nietzsche's* Thus Spoke Zarathustra: *A Critical Guide*, eds. K. Ansell-Pearson and P. Loeb, 205–224. Cambridge: Cambridge University Press.
Zavatta, Benedetta (2022). "Laughter as a Weapon: Parody and Satire in *Thus Spoke Zarathustra*." In *Nietzsche's* Thus Spoke Zarathustra: *A Critical Guide*, eds. K. Ansell-Pearson and P. Loeb, 15–40. Cambridge: Cambridge University Press.
Zittel, Claus (2000). *Das ästhetische Kalkül von Friedrich Nietzsches "Also sprach Zarathustra"*. Würzburg: Königshausen and Neumann.

INDEX

Note: Page numbers followed by "n" denote endnotes.

Aeschylus 50, 64–65, 68, 261
aestheticism 6–7
affirmation of life 5, 8, 10, 72, 84–86, 169
agape 141, 149, 170–173, 220, 262
agon 28, 31, 141, 327–328
amor fati 53, 70, 75, 90, 96, 105, 107, 111, 113, 130, 197, 206, 213, 237, 242, 250–251, 324, 330
Anaximander 23, 74, 172–173, 194
Apollo 165, 183; the Apollonian 48, 65–67, 92, 98–100, 110–112, 165, 177, 183–184, 189; Apollonian *Übermensch see Übermensch*
Ariadne 39, 49, 110, 112, 184, 244–247
Aristophanes 31, 148, 302, 327–283; *see also* comedy
Aristotle 60, 63–64, 108, 131, 167, 321
art 6–7, 10–11, 22, 52, 54–55, 61–62, 65–69, 72, 169, 273–274, 291–292; *see also* comedy; dithyramb; music; poetry; tragedy
ascetic ideal 31, 38, 54, 186

asceticism 54, 144, 215, 272–273, 289–291, 312–315, 318
autonomy 98, 151–152, 323, 326; *see also* freedom

backward willing (*Zurückwollen*) 90–91, 105–106, 195–196, 204n25, 216, 255
Baubo 30, 284
Bayreuth Festival 9–10, 19, 24–25, 68–69, 121; *see also* Wagner, R.
becoming 6, 23–24, 71–77, 106, 168, 182, 237, 282; dive into 95, 101, 113, 231, 235, 246; innocence of 8, 16, 29, 61, 75, 77, 86, 108, 113, 172–173, 214, 261, 316; who one is 25, 28, 114, 170, 264, 323, 326; *see also* Heraclitus
being 6, 23, 33n9, 71–77, 106, 168, 181, 237, 282, 316; *see also* Parmenides; Plato
Bildungsroman 12, 38
Brobjer, T. 28, 34n30, 234
Brusotti, M. 91, 105, 137, 151, 174, 178, 193

camel 21, 128–129, 150, 156, 177, 279
chance 101, 214–216, 231–232, 255
child 21–24, 44, 67, 74, 86, 93, 100–101, 104, 112–113, 121, 128–131, 150, 152–156, 162, 165–166, 170, 173, 201–202, 214, 232, 245, 261, 329; *see also* Heraclitus; Zarathustra's children
chorus 44, 66–67, 242, 257
Clark, M. 15, 248
comedy 16, 28–32, 35n41, 40–41, 55, 59, 113–114, 148, 248, 292, 302–303, 309, 312, 321–322, 326–328; *see also* Dionysus
courage 141, 208, 215–217, 292

dance 65, 69, 112, 123, 139, 178–181, 214, 217, 221–223, 226, 247, 255–257, 269, 289; *see also* Dionysus
Danto, A. 14, 17–18
death 45, 67, 70, 100–101, 122, 132, 140–141, 152, 155–159, 162, 180–181, 192, 201, 208, 228, 235, 244–245, 251–253, 258n2, 261–262, 274, 280, 296, 299, 309–311; of Socrates *see* Socrates; of Zarathustra 26, 40, 45–46, 157, 159, 235, 243, 246, 253; *see also* God, death of
despair 24, 75, 283–284
determinism 7, 33n10, 80, 107, 118n59, 210–211, 318–320; *see also amor fati;* fatalism; fate
Dionysus 5, 29, 31, 39, 49–51, 53, 64, 66–67, 76, 96, 101–102, 110–112, 139, 148, 178, 183–184, 228, 230, 244–247, 254, 256–257, 273, 280–281, 295, 299, 321, 325–326, 328; the Dionysian 24, 48, 61, 65–67, 92, 177, 185, 199, 233; Dionysian art *see* art; Dionysian mysteries *see* mysteries; Dionysian *Übermensch see Übermensch;* Nietzsche's discipleship to 31, 101–102, 325–326, 328
disciples 110, 120, 157, 159–161, 186–187, 191–192, 229, 303–304; *see also* Zarathustra's children

dissonance 23, 65–66, 252, 256, 300
dithyramb 29, 37, 60, 69, 112, 158, 177, 213, 254, 273, 290
Dühring, E. 79, 116n29, 174, 317

Empedocles 10, 68; *see also* tragedy
equality 89, 102, 143–144, 153–154, 173–175, 287
eros 88, 106, 147–150, 160, 181, 200, 220–221, 223, 251, 311; Platonic 167, 181, 311, 315; poetic 148, 251; *see also Selbstsucht;* will to power; will to truth
eternal recurrence 2, 7, 15–16, 19, 22, 27–29, 32n2, 41–44, 49–53, 56–57, 70, 76–87, 89–92, 98–113, 119–123, 161–162, 164–165, 198–202, 205–206, 208–210, 212–214, 232–238, 240–244, 248–253, 280, 282, 296, 309, 316–317, 320–321, 325
eternity 28, 49–50, 161, 206, 208, 213, 249–257, 280–282, 299–303

fatalism 7–8, 33n10, 53, 96, 100, 102, 107–108, 309, 322–325
fate 8, 46, 53, 70, 90, 108, 191, 201, 234–237, 321–326, 329; *see also amor fati;* fatalism
Förester-Nietzsche, Elisabeth 9, 13, 49
freedom 140, 150–151, 171, 189, 226, 257, 291, 309, 317–329, 330n1; *see also* free spirit; free will
free spirit 10–12, 124, 279, 291; works of the 10–12, 21, 133–134, 137, 151, 176–177, 272
free will 85, 175, 314–323
friendship 144, 150, 153, 165–167, 172–173

gift-giving virtue *see* self-love (*Selbstsucht*)
God 84, 108, 113, 129, 142, 167–168, 175, 225, 302–303, 317–318; death of 20, 28, 54–55, 88, 109, 114, 124–125, 129–130, 133–134, 137, 145, 162, 171, 177, 255–257,

272, 274–276, 283, 287, 290, 294; shadows of 20, 129, 272
gods 53, 65, 92, 98–99, 129, 132–133, 147, 168, 175, 187–189, 217–218, 226; *see also* Apollo; Dionysus; God
Goethe, J.-W. 40, 96–97, 169, 324–325, 329
going under (*untergehen*) 43–44, 67, 70, 74, 100–101, 112, 122, 125, 127–128, 152, 162, 192, 225–226, 228, 235, 243–244, 252–253, 304
Grätz, K. 16, 127, 141, 144, 151, 159, 166, 173, 174, 190–192, 218, 220, 246, 272, 281, 290, 292–293, 303
guilt 94, 96, 104, 108, 136–137, 150, 154, 316–318

Hanswurst 42, 59, 114, 261, 263, 284, 328
Heraclitus 23–24, 71–76, 79–80, 86, 100–101, 138, 141, 173, 195, 214, 256, 311–312; *see also* becoming; child
Higgins, K. 14–16, 38, 42, 286
higher human 261–263, 267–271, 279, 283–305
highest soul 95, 232–233
Hollinrake, R. 70–71
Homer 6, 65–66, 99
Huddleston, A. 2, 8, 69

incipit parodia 30, 38–39
incipit tragoedia 11, 19, 30, 38–39, 52, 60, 120, 122, 236
innocence of becoming *see* becoming

jester (*Possenreisser*) 127, 162n6, 227–228

Kant, I. 19, 22–23, 61–62, 68, 135, 151, 175, 317–318
Kaufmann, W. 13, 30, 96, 219
Köselitz, H. (Peter Gast) 13, 47, 58, 218, 273, 303

Lampert, L. 15, 39–42, 91–92, 206, 229, 236, 247–250, 254
last human 87–89, 125–126, 128, 140, 155, 268, 301
laughter 28–31, 71, 113–114, 138–139, 166, 190, 192, 211–212, 217–218, 257, 261–262, 266, 283–285, 288–294, 302–304, 327; *see also* lion
Leiter, B. 6–7, 33n10, 77, 322–324
life *see* affirmation of life
lion 21–22, 128–130, 137, 201–202, 302–304; laughing 43, 114, 129–130, 192, 212–213, 226, 262, 265, 285, 290, 297–298, 302–304
Loeb, P. 26–27, 38–35, 58, 89–91, 94, 98–99, 107, 157–158, 187–188, 229–230, 240–241, 248, 252–253, 267–270, 309
love 69, 87–88, 95, 123–126, 147–150, 152–157, 160–161, 170–173, 178, 197, 223–224, 232–233, 248–253, 274–276, 287–288; *see also* agape; amor fati; eros; neighbor love; self-love

marriage 154–155, 233
melancholy 111, 138, 156, 178, 191, 193, 236, 246–247, 266, 277–278, 281, 290, 292–293; *see also* spirit of gravity
metaphysics 6–7, 23, 33n9, 60, 71–77, 81–86, 116n29, 132–135, 174–175, 282–283, 294, 311–313, 315–318; comfort of 29, 113–114, 294; crackpot 2, 7, 77; need for 75, 81–83
missrathen (ill-constituted) 106, 116n44, 156, 262, 265, 267–268, 276, 279, 284, 287–290, 301; *see also Wohlgerathenheit*
morality 20, 30, 55, 85–86. 122, 126–128, 214, 225, 318–319; of truth 54–55
music 37, 47–48, 65–68, 109, 210; *see also* dissonance; Socrates
mysteries 39, 44–45, 51, 101, 178, 228, 242–244, 249, 251, 254, 260–261, 295, 310, 312–313, 316, 320, 325; *see also* Dionysus

naturalism 6–8, 77–86, 308–309;
   system of 29, 36, 83, 238, 282, 309
nausea 173, 181, 211–212, 240–241,
   268–270, 273–274, 277–278, 287,
   290, 296
necessity 41, 53, 70, 74, 98, 101, 113,
   201, 206, 226, 234–235, 245–246,
   250, 315–316, 321, 323–326; *see
   also amor fati;* determinism; fate;
   fatalism
Nehamas, A. 6–7, 37, 323
neighbor love 141, 143, 149–150, 222,
   224, 227, 262, 287–288; *see also
   agape;* love; pity
nihilism 4, 32n5, 195, 235, 267, 314,
   318
nobility 97, 101, 114, 227, 230–231; *see
   also* noble soul
noble soul 101–102, 228, 230, 268; *see
   also* nobility
noon 24, 28, 49, 58, 68, 86, 161–162,
   222, 226, 254, 279–282, 287, 300,
   312

Oedipus 8, 104, 108, 184, 200, 314,
   321–322

parabasis 28, 31, 326, 328–329
Parmenides 23, 168, 312
passion 132, 134–136, 140, 220–221;
   for knowledge 134, 200
pessimism 3, 32n4, 32–33n5, 85, 169;
   evaluative and factual 4, 9, 22, 24,
   61–64, 141, 195, 221–223
pity 71, 141, 170–172, 208, 211,
   215–216, 261–262, 266–269,
   274–276, 304; and fear 60, 63,
   67, 108, 245, 321; *see also agape;*
   neighbor love; tragedy
Plato 5–7, 33n7, 117n53, 134–135,
   146, 148, 160, 167, 220–221, 286,
   301–302, 309–316
play 23, 45–46, 74, 100, 113, 130, 153,
   156, 173, 254–256, 261; *see also*
   child

poetry 37, 54, 63, 65–69, 91–92, 98–99,
   110–111, 148, 165–168, 186–188,
   290; quarrel with philosophy
   6–7, 38, 63; *see also* art; comedy;
   dithyramb; tragedy

Randich, A. 162n4
redemption 93–94, 165, 176, 184–185,
   192–196
Reginster, B. 3–5
renunciation of life 140–141
ressentiment 96, 102, 154, 174, 193,
   293, 317–320, 330
revaluation of values 27–28, 42, 46,
   59, 61, 114, 149, 190, 218–225, 234,
   262, 305
revenge 93–98, 102–103, 106, 137–138,
   143, 154, 164–166, 171–172, 174–178,
   193–195, 236–239, 241–242, 247,
   275–276, 315–317, 320, 330
rulers (lords) of the earth 130, 203n15,
   264, 287, 297–298, 307n13
Rutherford, D. 321–322, 324

Salomé, L. 48–49
satyr play 5, 16, 26–32, 41–46, 56,
   59, 113, 114n2, 261, 283, 286, 290,
   294, 302, 305, 327; analeptic 26–27,
   41–45, 129, 229, 253, 296, 302
Schacht, R. 14–15, 33n19, 114n3
Schopenhauer, A. 4–5, 7, 9, 19, 22–23,
   60–64, 77–86, 134, 140–141, 144,
   148–149, 159, 169, 181, 190, 220,
   244, 251, 264, 267, 272, 314–315; *see
   also* pessimism
science 290–291; natural 75, 82, 84, 109
Selbstsucht see self-love
self 7–8, 74, 134–135, 158–159,
   163n11, 206, 235, 243–244, 330n8;
   old and new 46, 54, 113, 325, 329;
   transfigured 66, 228
self-creation 322–327
self-love (*Selbstsucht*) 50, 99, 106, 111,
   116n44, 120, 122, 148, 159–160, 185,
   219–222; as gift-giving virtue 96,

122, 148, 159–160, 221, 223, 236; *see also* eros; love
self-overcoming 89, 94, 125; of humanity 89, 94, 267; of the will to truth 22, 54, 86, 109, 272
Seung, T. K. 39–41, 91–93, 98, 101, 111, 152, 194, 200, 234–235, 277
shame 123, 165, 170, 199, 202, 275–276; *see also* child
Shapiro, G. 42, 194
Silenus 60–65, 78–79, 99, 190; Papa 113, 261, 263
Socrates 9, 61, 62, 250, 286, 302, 327–328; dying 51, 107, 159, 309–316; music-playing 22, 25
solitude 44, 121, 142–144, 150, 218, 261–263, 304
Spinoza, B. 50, 309, 321, 325, 330n6; *see also Übermensch*
spirit of gravity 45, 51, 111–112, 123, 127, 130, 138–139, 163n14, 166, 178–180, 205–208, 217, 223–226, 236, 247–248, 254, 257, 266, 283, 292–295
Stern, T. 91–92, 116n44
Stoics 79, 131, 200, 297, 309, 321, 325
Strawson, P. F. 319–320
suffering 3–5, 22, 24, 48, 62, 64–66, 132–133, 135–136, 141, 169–170, 194, 208, 251–252, 300, 316–317; *see also* pessimism; pity

tragedy 4–6, 9–11, 16–26, 28–32, 36–40, 44–48, 51–56, 59–68, 71–76, 108–110, 113, 120, 201, 207, 228, 244, 252, 257, 302, 310–315; Aristotle on 60, 63–64, 108, 321; Empedocles 10, 68; effect of 108, 113, 300, 321–322, 326–327; rebirth of 9, 11, 16, 19, 22, 25, 61–62, 67–68; *see also incipit tragoedia*
tragic worldview 23–24, 71–77, 79, 82–83, 109, 310–312
transience *see Vergänglichkeit*
Tristan chord 65, 252

Übermensch 2, 15, 32n1, 41, 86–101, 110–111, 116n36, 116n43, 119–120, 124–127, 130–131, 140–142, 147, 149–157, 160–162, 164–165, 170–171, 175–177, 187–191, 198–199, 212–214, 223, 226–227, 232–233, 287–288, 297–298, 304–305, 306n5; Apollonian and Dionysian 98–102, 110–112, 117n48, 131, 152, 165, 183–184, 187, 189, 305; Faustian and Spinozan 92, 98, 101, 152, 194, 321, 323; as species 26, 89, 97–99, 116n39, 152, 163n26, 187–188, 240, 306n5

Vergangenheit (the past) 102–105, 165, 180, 192–195, 236, 251, 282, 298, 316
Vergänglichkeit (transience) 70, 102–103, 117n53, 165, 180, 190–195, 236–237, 251, 280, 282
Vivarelli, V. 252–253

Wagner, R. 4–5, 9–11, 22, 24–25, 33n12, 39, 47, 61–62, 65, 67–71, 252, 272–273, 327–328; *see also* Bayreuth festival; Tristan chord
will to power 2, 7, 15–16, 32n3, 76–78, 80–85, 106, 109–110, 120, 142, 145–148, 165–167, 171–186, 220–224, 267, 315; *see also* eros
will to truth 30, 109, 167, 176–182, 220, 292, 311, 315; *see also* eros
Wohlgerathenheit (well-turned-outness) 96, 101, 106, 116–117n44, 156, 158, 262, 265, 287–288, 292, 298, 305, 306n5; *see also missrathen*

Zarathustra's children 212–213, 231, 253–257, 285, 298–299, 303–304, 306n4; *see also* disciples
Zoroaster 86, 120, 162n2, 172, 225
Zurückwollen see backward willing

For Product Safety Concerns and Information please contact our EU representative GPSR@taylorandfrancis.com
Taylor & Francis Verlag GmbH, Kaufingerstraße 24, 80331 München, Germany

www.ingramcontent.com/pod-product-compliance
Lightning Source LLC
Chambersburg PA
CBHW070259240426
43661CB00057B/2588